THE COMPANION GUIDE TO

LONDON

THE COMPANION GUIDES

GENERAL EDITOR: VINCENT CRONIN

*It is the aim of the Guides to provide a Companion,
in the person of the author, who knows intimately
the places and people of whom he writes, and is able to
communicate this knowledge and affection to his readers.
It is hoped that the text and pictures will aid them
in their preparations and in their travels, and will
help them to remember on their return.*

OUTER LONDON · EAST ANGLIA · NORTHUMBRIA
WEST HIGHLANDS OF SCOTLAND · IRELAND
ROME · FLORENCE · VENICE
PARIS · THE LOIRE · NORMANDY · THE SOUTH OF FRANCE
MADRID AND CENTRAL SPAIN
MAINLAND GREECE · THE GREEK ISLANDS
JUGOSLAVIA · TURKEY · NEW YORK

In preparation
OXFORD AND CAMBRIDGE · THE SOVIET UNION

THE COMPANION GUIDE TO

LONDON

DAVID PIPER

COLLINS
8 Grafton Street, London W1

William Collins Sons and Co Ltd
London · Glasgow · Sydney · Auckland
Toronto · Johannesburg

First edition 1964
Reprinted 1965
Second edition 1968
Third edition (Fontana Books) 1970
Fourth edition (Fontana Books) 1972
Fifth edition 1974
Sixth edition 1977
Reprinted 1981, 1985

Piper, David
The companion guide to London. — 6th ed. —
(The Companion guides)
1. London (England) — Description — 1951-1980
— Guide-books
I. Title
914.21'04857   DA679

ISBN 0 00 211478 X

Made and Printed in Great Britain by
William Collins Sons and Co Ltd, Glasgow

Contents

❧

Illustrations

꙳

Maps

All the maps are by Charles Green except where otherwise indicated

Introduction

❧

'LONDON is the most interesting, beautiful, and wonderful city in the world to me, delicate in her incidental and multitudinous littleness, and stupendous in her pregnant totality. . . .'

Though H. G. Wells wrote that (in *The New Machiavelli*, 1911), before the onslaught of two world wars, and when London was the hub of the world in her imperial might, it is still some sixty years later as true—and even though she is no longer the largest of cities, third now to Tokyo and New York, and on some counts (depending where you fix her limits), tenth or eleventh in the world. Greater London is usually accepted as holding somewhat over eight million Londoners. Enough anyway, and the size of their corporate home strikes dumb many a traveller whether stooping in over the great web towards London Airport through the shifting cloud, or driving in from the Airport to a London air terminal (a journey which is likely to take him longer than the transit from London Airport to Paris), or coming in by train or car through mile upon mile of brick villas and terraces. The impression of stupendous totality will remain with the traveller even when well orientated within London, but in contrast with it the investigation of the city's incidental and multitudinous littlenesses is all the more astonishing and rewarding. To know London, who is liable to conceal her delights, the only way is by close scrutiny.

Yet London is also the classic example of the scattered city, as against the concentrated city such as Paris; her observers still often analyse her as a network of villages about the two twin cities of London and Westminster, and this also is still true. To deal with the whole system of these 'villages' would involve many more years' work and a length of text beyond the scope of a single volume, so this book has, in the interests of practicability, to be confined to the heart of the matter, virtually the City and the West End. I have made attempts, in

Chapter 28, to indicate the nature of the interest of areas and individual attractions outside the centre, but they can be little more than mere signals. The chapter (18) on the Thames also glimpses areas to east and west beyond the main concern of this book. So reluctantly I have only glanced at whole districts that most (and certainly their inhabitants) would consider as integral, central even, to London—Kensington west and north of Hyde Park; Bayswater, Paddington, Islington, Clapham, Hampstead and Highgate. The East End—this in particular worried me greatly, but I could find no compromise between a pointer in a few paragraphs, and a largish book on its own. For reasons of space I have also had to renounce detailed accounts of the major museums, though I have lingered longer on some smaller, relatively less well-known ones. But those who fall in love with London will extend their own knowledge by their exploration far beyond the confines of this book. If one does fall in love with London—I rather doubt if many do. One is affected, then infected, by London as by some insidious drug that can act now as stimulant now as sedative, but ruthlessly becomes addiction. As addict, I have happily written this book, in the modest hope that it may infect one or two others.

The system I have used is to take an area, and walk through it. These routes are merely those that have seemed to me most rewarding, but there is a considerable degree of personal choice in them. I hope they may serve for those with limited time, and act for those with more time as mere routes for reconnaissance —but they are certainly not Ariadne's threads. No tourist worthy of the name has ever stuck to anyone else's footsteps. The chapters need not be followed in any particular order, though I have started with the Tower because it images such a depth of London's history. But as arranged thereafter, the chapters start, like most visitors, in the West End, and progress gradually east.

The best base for the visitor is conditioned naturally by individual interests and individual pockets. All things being equal there is no substitute for one of the luxury hotels, with the whole of the western area covered here within comfortable walking distance. As for the eastern area, the City, people just don't stay there—though if you wish to, there is always the Great Eastern at Liverpool Street. But the west is for hotels, for shopping, for most museums, for life that flowers re-

newed at dusk in theatres and restaurants. Even to Londoners
—those who live beyond the area of this book—I would
suggest that an ideal holiday in the approaching age of
leisure, is the mid-week (as distinct from the week-end) in a
good hotel in Town. The range is large: the latest in contemporary American-styling (London Hilton, on Park Lane,
with iced water piped to all rooms; Westbury on Bond Street;
Carlton Tower in Sloane Street over Belgravia). The Dorchester on Park Lane. The famous old ones, with long-
established individual felicities of service: the Connaught,
Claridge's (still specialising in crowned heads); cosy, delectable
Brown's—all in Mayfair. In Piccadilly, by Green Park, of
course, the inimitable Ritz; in St. James's itself, tucked quietly
away against Green Park as if in sanctuaries, the little Stafford
and the Old St. James's (both usually booked up well in advance, so needing forethought). And then, away over between
Strand and river, with its wonderful Thames views, the Savoy.
These are all world-famous, and also expensive. But desirable.
Less expensive, but convenient and still central bases are
offered by big establishments like the Cumberland at Marble
Arch, the Regent Palace, right on Piccadilly Circus, the
Strand Palace in the Strand. Museum addicts are well catered
for in hotels ranging from the good to the modest to the
boarding house, in Bloomsbury for the British Museum, in
South Kensington for the Victoria and Albert and the others.
All the railway termini are set in clusters again of hotels (for
those like myself who wish on a first visit to a city to have their
escape lines clear), and the establishment of the West London
Air Terminal has multiplied the hotels about it along the
Cromwell Road. A select list of hotels is given in the Appendix,
and for overseas visitors with a hotel booking problem the
London Hotels Information Service (88 Brook Street, W.1;
telephone 629 5414/6) is a most helpful institution.

Best time of year to come to London? there is none, and the
weather abides by no rules. Bring a light mackintosh, but one
that breathes; do not despise the umbrella. My own favourite
months are April to June and September to October, and yet
having written that I am immediately struck with a sense of
betrayal. London under snow, for example, is enchanted—as
long as the snow is falling at least, even if purgatory when it has
fallen and slurs to black slush. And mist is of her essence; you
get it all the year round, and even a pellucid summer day,

which to the Londoner seems of crystal, will strike people from a drier climate as hazy.

The problem of getting where you want to go from your chosen base involves transport, and London, like all capital cities, is currently in difficulty with her transport—hence the advisability of settling as near as possible to centre, and using your feet. But transport is an essential aspect of the London townscape, and to it as such I have devoted, I think justifiably and necessarily, a longer meditation in the Appendix. The taxi is the real answer, but bus and underground are integral to experience of London. Buses run fairly late, but if dependent on one for return at night you need to find out when the last one goes—usually somewhere between eleven and midnight, on Sundays earlier. The Underground begins at 5.20 a.m. and goes to rest around midnight. Most cinemas and theatres are over by eleven (though a few cinemas now hold late shows starting about eleven); the night after that in London is continued, but indoors—in restaurants, night-clubs, jazz-clubs.

The sight-seer in his perambulation needs to stop fairly often for refreshment or simply to take the weight off his feet. For this need, London does not offer the large extrovert welcome of continental cafés spread over the pavements. The natural answer is the pub, but the pub is conditioned by the licensing laws of the realm; most are open from 11.30 to 3 and from 5.30 to 11 (Sundays, 12 till 2 and 7 to 10.30 or 11). This leaves an awkward gap in the afternoon, which can be filled by the tea-room or by the institution that has swept London over the last ten years, the coffee bar, which you will find through this area in full motley of their variety.

The viable day begins relatively late, certainly not before 9 a.m. except for markets. The big museums open at ten and close at either five or six (Sundays 2–6); most shops in our area close at 5.30 p.m., but some of the departmental stores stay open until 7 p.m. on one night a week, generally Thursday; many close on Saturdays at 1 p.m. To find out what is on where, the two evening papers, *Standard* and *News*, are invaluable, *What's On*, and the British Travel and Holidays Association (64 St. James's Street, S.W.1; 629 9191) publish a good guide *This Month in London*. When lost, ask a policeman; if there is no policeman, ask the first passer-by. Even though the chances seem always to be unnaturally high that he will be a foreigner passing through, he will, if a native and he understands your query, be as helpful as he can. London is one of the few world capitals where this is so—and I think it still is so, even if not so much as it once was. I do not for a moment suggest that your informant will give you the right answer, but he will at least, unless you are exceptionally unlucky, instil a little hope.

Behold then what Blake called the 'human awful wonder of God', in the delicacy of her littleness among her huge totality, but behold her with open curiosity and be ready to follow your nose whither it may take you. Above all, do not treat her as a monument; she is stuffed with monuments, but still quick and live about them. H. G. Wells was right when he said, following the passage I quoted at the beginning of this introduction: 'I cannot bring myself to use her as a museum or an old bookshop. . . .'

P.S.

The decade since this guide was first compiled has seen London change a good deal, though her essence, it seems to me, has remained undisturbed. Some of this change is not peculiar to London but is national. Thus decimalisation of the coinage preluded Britain's entry into the Common Market in 1973—and the effects of that on Britain, as on London, are unpredictable. But the shilling is no more, nor the half-crown, the florin, and soon the Cockney's beloved 'tanner'—the sixpenny piece. Some ephemeral fashions have swept across London's fabric, and vanished though perhaps not entirely without trace. Such was the phenomenon dubbed 'swinging London': the focus of that, Carnaby Street, has passed into the language yet is already itself museum-piece, a picturesque tourist-trap as antiquely fetching (and expensive) as Burlington Arcade. The hippies, who were in the late sixties briefly dense as rusty iron-filings about the magnet of Eros in Piccadilly Circus, have thinned out, perhaps in favour of Kabul. The backlash against the permissive society begins, and the porn shops of Soho stand irresolute whether to follow the hard line set by Copenhagen or not.

More substantially, the fabric itself, in the sixties, went high-rise with a vengeance; especially in the City and to the east, the upper air is stabbed and studded with angular novelties, each accompanied at ground-level by its own private hurricane of down-draught blasting scornfully and impartially all passers-by. By 1970, 'high-rise' had become almost a dirty word among architects, yet still proves to be, for the developers, often the only answer in viably financial terms, to the fantastic land-values in the centre, though it is virtually out, one hopes, for residential buildings from now on. But even so, the developers move inevitably in terms of larger and larger slices of land. So the visitor to London in the seventies will find massive areas in the chaos of massive development, and these include some of the most famous, most historic, sites of England, let alone London. Plans, ranging from firm to vague to shelved to vague to firm, indicate re-shapings at both ends of Whitehall, including extensions to Parliament itself. Victoria Street, having been virtually rebuilt from one end to the other, may perhaps rest unlovely a while, but Scotland Yard's building has been saved. Following the virtual closure of the whole vast dock area between Tower Bridge (and even the wondrous mechanism of *that* is threatened) and Greenwich, the developments of the banks and basins downstream will be staggering, and will further inevitably be conditioned to a degree by the proposed Thames barrage, far to the east, which is now under active consideration to prevent the ever-growing threat of the flooding of Central London. Then London Thames will be virtually tideless. Even west of Tower Bridge, along the banks of the Pool of London, the old spectacular wilderness of gaunt and spooky warehousing is to yield to complete redevelopment.

Elsewhere Covent Garden has now yielded up the market, and argument rages about what shall take its place. Piccadilly, after a quarter of a century's planning and counter-planning, seems to be going to be allowed to retain its Circus much as it is today. For the cultural visitor, institutional extensions are promised almost ubiquitously; one hopes only that a reasonable proportion will remain visible during expansion; all over the world now it is so often impossible to see exhibits because the facilities for seeing them the better seem so constantly in progress that one can't see anything except notices saying: 'Galleries Closed for Improvement'. But the National Gallery has extended northwards while the Portrait Gallery's once envisaged new home immediately west of the National recedes from possibility.

The Tate Gallery is to demolish an entire military hospital and expand on its site, while plans for the British Museum's take-over of southern Bloomsbury have been scrapped in favour of a new site for the Library north of St. Pancras. In 1972, the National Army Museum at Chelsea, and the Royal Air Force Museum at Hendon, were opened. And the period has seen one signal triumph—the cancellation, after a month or so in action in 1974, of the wicked Act of Parliament that imposed on mainly stoutly-protesting museums the duty of charging an entrance fee. Most museums and galleries are still free: long may they remain so.

This edition is, at the time of going to press, I hope up to date, but a degree of error is inevitable in guides such as this, and I would be grateful if interested readers, who do discover inaccuracies, could let me know.

D.P.
1976

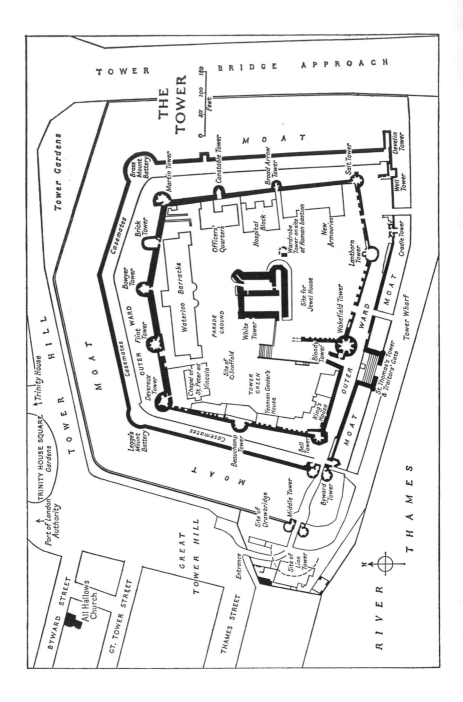

CHAPTER ONE

The Tower and Tower Hill

✣

Tower Hill proved a harsh end to many, but it can equally provide an excellent if challengingly stringent welcome to anyone who offers himself as willing victim to London. It is not even particularly easy to reach; it is bus-less and best arrived at by Underground Railway (District or Circle Lines). The old Tower Hill Station in Byward Street has been replaced. The new station nearby, of undistinguished modern design, pushes you up a short stairway and abandons you on the threshold of an unenclosed square. Towards the south, you will see Tower Hill with the Tower of London directly below you opposite. The Tower makes the eye a bit dizzy; the prospect of a grey uneven maze, harsh in the texture of its stone, rugged with crenellation, bastions and the turrets of the White Tower (which is in fact a paler grey) rising from its midst. But even seen from above, it is most of all vast, and heavy below you as if it had sunk the depression in which it is built, too massive for the hill to hold. But in fact it is built on the fall of the hill to the river Thames, and beyond the Tower, as if an extension of it, rise the twin turrets of Tower Bridge, and a haze of tree tops, prickly in winter but in summer softening too much grey with green, along the river bank. From here you cannot see the water itself, and even the angular beaks of the cranes on the docks, once seen through tree tops, are gone or going.

Tower Hill is old, and in its stony soil lie some of the oldest bits of London. Inhabitation of the banks of the Thames in this area goes back perhaps, but sporadically and thinly, through the Bronze Age, to the Stone Ages, but London was surely never a major settlement of the Celts. London was a creation of the Romans: Londinium—almost an overnight job. The legions of Claudius, the first to invade with distinct and successful intentions of annexation (as distinct from Caesar's invasions of 55 and 54 BC), began the occupation of England in AD 43; by the year 60, when the famous revolt of the first and toughest of English patriot heroines, Boudicca, better known as Boadicea, took place, London was already according to Tacitus 'a celebrated centre of commerce'. Boudicca's sack of this new town seems to have been appalling in its thoroughness; the inhabitants were massacred and the buildings burned to the ground. The subsequent suppression of Boudicca's revolt was carried out with a matching cruelty, and her people, the Iceni, were liquidated and their name is not found again. Which done, briskly the Romans rebuilt London, and it became a city of the north bank of the Thames, built about two hills, Corn Hill and Ludhill. It was a natural port, the most convenient gateway to the Continent; from it a firm grasp could be kept on the southern half of England—the Roman roads soon spoked out from London and straddled the country. Perhaps as early as AD 100 the engineering of the great Roman wall of London began; a wooden bridge was flung across the Thames and at its southern end on the south bank a suburb began to build at Southwark. For hundreds of years (till 1750), London possessed only one bridge, rebuilt from time to time but always approximately upon the site of the Roman one. London became the biggest city in the Roman Empire of the West, covering almost 330 acres and girt by the massive two-mile-long defence of the Wall; it held public buildings of some pretensions, a Forum, and a Basilica almost as long as present-day St. Paul's. The Romans left Britain in 410—that is to say, England was a Roman dependency for a period almost as long as the post-Renaissance period of modern history, from the reign of Elizabeth I to the close of the Victorian era. Yet almost all of London now visible was made in these last four hundred years; the shards and few surviving monuments earlier than that have to be sought out. But you can still find them—the relics of Roman London: a dusty streak of the Wall itself, laid bare by twentieth-century high-explosive, or preserved by chance in the foundations of cellars in the City; glints and fragments of bronze, gold and glass in the Guildhall Museum or the British Museum, and ragged pieces of patterned tessellated floors. You can still find, though perhaps even rarer, witness of the dark ages, that cloud the history of London for centuries after the Romans' departure, when the city decayed, holding barely against the Saxon invaders, then sacked by the Danes in the ninth century, restored by the legendary king who turned back the Danes, the great Alfred, in the 880s, only to be sacked again by Danes a hundred years later. In the eleventh century, even before the Norman conquest of 1066, Edward the Confessor began building Westminster Abbey in the Norman manner; then came William the Conqueror, and one of his first actions after his crowning was to begin the White Tower that still confronts you after nine hundred years as you look down from Tower Hill.

But the shrine of pre-Tower London is closer still: the church that is the first thing you see on Tower Hill: **All Hallows Barking**. Come into All Hallows, ignore for the moment the bright brick spareness of its nave and ask to be shown the crypts, the undercroft. At the bottom of the stairs that lead down from the west end of the church you will find a rough and battered patch of tessellated paving—part of the floor of what was once a Roman house laid bare; below All Hallows, in excavations, have been found a layer of ashes—the mark of Boudicca, the cinders of the first Roman London that she burned in the year 61. There are also some other Roman masonry fragments, and the tombstone of one Demetrius. But look at the wall, of rough-hewn blocks of grey stone, that rises by the pavement and you are six centuries on, for this is part of the original Saxon church built somewhere around 700; later, but among the most important of their very rare kind in London, are two squarish carved stones, pieces of Saxon crosses of the early eleventh century. If you come back up now into the main body of the church you will find, behind the screen at the west end, what is claimed to be the oldest arch in the City of London, of *c.* 680, a plain round arch without keystone, and incorporating Roman tiles in the arch.

The original Saxon church was aisle-less, but aisles were added in the Norman period; the aisle walls that you see now are mainly fourteenth and fifteenth century. The handsome brick tower was added in 1659, and from the top of it in September 1666 Samuel Pepys watched the Great Fire of London at its height until 'I became afeared to stay there long and down again as fast I could'; the fire was halted literally at the porch of the church, and it survived until December 1940, when it was gutted in the Blitz, only the shell of the walls and of the tower being left over the crypt. What you now see within is therefore of the 1950s, and though some of the detailing I find uncomfortably reminiscent of cinema-styling of the 1930s, this is one of my favourite London churches—so airy, bright with an almost marine light that floods the interior through the huge plain east window. The side windows are starred with heraldic glass, and little elegant ship-models ride buoyantly in mid-air, for the church has always been associated with men of the sea. Most of the furnishings were destroyed in the war, but there have survived some very pretty eighteenth-century sword rests in iron, and what is perhaps the most delicately exquisite of Grinling Gibbons-type font covers in London—a richly lyrical little fretted pyramid in limewood of cherubs, fruits, wheat and foliage, topped by a bird with wings uneasy for flight.

All Hallows (the Barking part of its name comes from an abbey in Essex to which it was once related) is now widely known as the church of Toc H, that Christian fellowship founded in the First World War by the famous Tubby Clayton near Ypres. The ever-burning Toc H lamp is in a little casket that stands at the east end on a good fifteenth-century tomb; close by (you have to get the carpet lifted that normally protects them), in front of the altar, are some of the best memorial brasses in London; brass, too, are the unusual and most elegant communion rails, replicas mostly of those destroyed in the bombing.

Outside, the graveyard is tidied and swept of ghosts; it was the most macabre of London transit camps in its time, the temporary resting places of many headless bodies, harboured here after execution on Tower Hill before being moved to their permanent graves. Here a Catholic martyr paused, Bishop Fisher, and here an Anglican and Royalist martyr, Archbishop Laud; here stopped off briefly the poet Earl of Surrey. And before leaving All Hallows go round to the west end and enjoy the odd marriage of brick tower, with its sophisticated tapering black steeple angled winningly askew, to the grey walls of the church.

The natural sequel to All Hallows is now, still not the Tower, but **Trinity Square** over the road. This is dominated, positively sat on, by the gigantic firmly blowsy headquarters (1912–20) of the Port of London Authority. From its topmost tier the hoary figure of Father Thames gestures with vehemence to the open sea, and from its vast recess are governed the even vaster reaches of the Port of London, from Teddington in the west, to the Nore lightship, far down the estuary to the east, including the 4,000 odd acres of the great dock systems that are cut into Thames side beginning at St. Katharine's Docks, which you can see, beyond the Tower, from Trinity Square: once the greatest port in the world. On the north side of the square, austere and controlled as a cool rose-bud by the monstrous wedding-cake of the P.L.A., is Trinity House: a point of elegance and good manners. A grave and lovely façade, with its scrolled columns and crisp shallow shadowing of sculptured decoration; it is a splendid example of the poise and self-confident restraint of the late eighteenth century (it was built by S. Wyatt in 1792–4, and though bombed, has been excellently restored), still unfancified by the taste of the Adams. The Corporation that inhabits it, the Brethren of the Trinity, are far longer established than the P.L.A., though likewise concerned with the marine; its charter dates from 1514, and it controls all sea-marks, lighthouses and lightships, and also the pilotage.

The garden of Trinity Square has a memorial to the war-dead of the Mercantile Marine. In winter it is bleak, and the gravel shows through the earth of the flower-beds, and the smallest monument of all (which you can easily miss) seems more prominent. A little rectangle of bricked paving, with chains about: the site of the old scaffold of Tower Hill, where those attainted of treason were beheaded between 1388 and 1747. It is a horrid place, black and tidy and bleak. I always avoid it because it literally makes me ache; the only story connected with it I like to remember is that of the last execution there, of the Jacobite Lord Lovat, in 1747. The usual auxiliary scaffolding about the spot had been built for the spectators, but this time collapsed under the weight of about 1,000 curious bodies; twelve died, and Lovat (whom Hogarth drew like a sinister but jovially twisted human toad), was apparently pleasantly diverted by the downfall of so many of his enemy Whigs, even though his own life was chopped all the same a few minutes later. The men and women who died here had little in common except the way of their death. They included criminals and wastrels, like the Duke of Monmouth; most of them perhaps were guilty of arrogance in ambition and of simple failure, but among them too were some of the greatest and noblest men in our history: Sir Thomas More died here in the most superb refusal of apology ever made, 'protesting that he died the King's good servant but God's first'

But the trail from All Hallows and its antiquities leads over Trinity Square to its east side. Here you come abruptly on a stretch of the **Roman Wall** of London, a great rough slab 20 feet high and 50 long. It always arouses disbelief in me, and I have to touch it. But there it is, showing now mostly the medieval facing, with the Roman red bricks re-used among it. Close to it in a little garden is set a curious and moving evocation of Roman civilisation. It is a modern facsimile of a monument commemorating a great administrator. The original is in the British Museum, having been salvaged in bits. Its subject is Gaius Julius Alpinus Classicianus, the Procurator sent by Rome after Boudicca's rebellion, and a man of remarkable humanity in his time, responsible for controlling the revengeful Roman general from devastating the whole country.

Another bit of wall that may be accessible is in the cellars at No. 42 Trinity Square. This was till recently the headquarters of the famous TOC H Club, the warder of which was always accommodating in allowing enquirers in, and it is to be hoped that the new occupants will be equally so. In this section, you can see the exterior facing, formidably tailored of hewn stone, ragstone, and brick.

The appalling devastation of the blitz on the Tower Hill is now almost completely restored, and the redevelopment has opened up a great deal as open space and gardens. The post-war mingling of twentieth-century ruins and Roman and medieval fragments is no longer so confusing for the unwary visitors, though the old pre-war scale has deen disrupted by the emergence of modern mammoths. But below, one of the great set-pieces of London history stands inviolate.

If you have the luck it's best to come upon **the Tower** around midnight, and floodlit. A daylight approach is always conditioned by the context of docks, nineteenth-century office buildings, twentieth-century traffic and tourism; even in winter when its walls are unsoftened by the leaves on the trees. Its setting has, inevitably, been municipalised into the setting for an Ancient Monument; neat shrubberies slope down to what was once the moat, drained in 1843 and now grassed, with a hard tennis-court and, in winter, goal-posts; but still the size and the very stoniness of the outer walls refuse entirely to be tamed. You can see the plan of the outer wall clear, and less clear the line of the inner wall with its round towers, and from Tower Hill it looks as though built solid up to its core, the squarish bulk of the White Tower lifting its four capped turrets high above the rest. Ochrous grey, crusted in parts with London black. Fortress first, but prison too almost at once (Ranulph Flambard, Bishop of Durham, who seems to have been responsible for the completion of the White Tower for Henry I, became also, in 1101, the first of a long line of distinguished prisoners in it); it was also, and still is, a garrison and an armoury; and until Cromwell pulled down the royal quarters, a royal palace and the starting-point for the coronation processions.

But for a long period its most popular associations were more curious, and you are reminded of them as you come down the hill, though the original Tiger Inn on your right (Queen Elizabeth, they say, stopped off there) to the entrance by the river was demolished in 1963; here is the ticket office (the Tower is open, 9.30 to 6.0 on weekdays, 2.0 to 6.0 on Sundays, and no admissions are permitted in the hour before closing time. In winter, the Tower closes an hour earlier). The restaurant (the best institutional one in London known to me, and licensed—avoid coffee and custard) is built on the site of the Lion Tower, where the royal zoo was installed from the fourteenth century until 1834, when it transferred to Regent's Park. But not a whiff of lion lingers now, and you go over the causeways that now replace the second and third drawbridges of the defences, through the Middle Tower, where in spring birds nest in the royal arms, and Edward I's Byward Tower, and into the deep echoing channel between the outer and inner walls. The centuries merge into one another. The Bell Tower (where once lay Fisher and More; Princess Elizabeth and Monmouth) of 1200 merges into the Queen's House of the sixteenth century; there is the new but massive masonry of the postcard store and the lavatories. Over Traitors' Gate the Tudor black-and-white half timbering of the Private Residence of the Keeper of the Jewel House, with flowers in the window; here and there the figures of the Yeoman Warders in dark blue, with capes and squashed puff-hats, and sometimes in wet weather, oddly, an umbrella; the lanterns of the lamps, agreeable Victorian whims, blue with gilt turrets. The Tower tends to run with children; squads of tourists straggle and re-form about the guides, and all the languages of the world flow through the stentorian voices of the guides that retail a toll of deaths. A raven croaks, as though some instrument of torture, rusty with disuse but still with carnivorous longings, had found voice; until the early 1960s the Tower was still also loud with the military, but the barking of the Royal Fusiliers (City of London Regiment) is no longer heard, even though a great roaring and stamping of boots signals at appointed times the changing of the guard.

Stop by **Traitors' Gate**: a vast depressive arch sunk in the outer walls with its portcullis. Dry now, a stone den below you fit for Daniels, but once the entry by water to the Tower when the Thames was the main highway of London; through it passed out of hope and the sky-lit expanses of the river countless prisoners, to their last stop before death. It is quiet now, but the moat-waters, at low tide, used to flood out through it in cataract, making 'so terrible a noise that it's enough to fright a prisoner that lodges within the hearing on't out of the world before his time of execution'.

Opposite is the main entrance (in the Middle Ages the only one) into the Inner Ward, through the inner wall between the great buttress of the Wakefield Tower and the Bloody Tower (not a new name, it was known thus in the sixteenth century, as the site of the murder of the little princes, Edward V and the Duke of York); past the queue for the Crown Jewels, and climbing you see how the inner precinct is built up the hill, and how it opens out now round the central massif of the White Tower with an illusory sense of freedom; the sky is suddenly available, there are trees, even a blackbird, and English lawns, but Please Keep Off. On the left indeed is a marvellous piece of grass, **Tower Green**, between the pretty late perpendicular flank of the Chapel of St. Peter ad Vincula at the north end and the inner façade of the Queen's House at the south; it looks at first most restfully picturesque, timber-framing giving way to seventeenth-century prime brick, like an extract from a cathedral precinct, with a dapple of light and translucent green. But part of this is the old burial ground; under it still lie perhaps the chopped bodies, and Macaulay said of it that there 'was no sadder spot on earth'. In the middle, thoughtfully squared out with granite at the behest of Queen Victoria, is the site of the scaffold where the more illustrious victims—including Anne Boleyn, Jane Grey, Catherine Howard and Essex—were granted the mercy of execution somewhat more private than on Tower Hill. It attracts like a magnet; you float there, wondering and helpless as though

there ought to be something that you were doing about it.
A couple of ravens crank up, their metallic feathers bloated,
hopping with ghastly elasticity, their clipped wings making
lurching gestures as they flap sideways like crabs. They are
shockingly big to eyes used to crows or rooks, the low villainy
of the brows emphasised by their vast and obscene beaks. They
have always been there, and the legend is that if they disappear
the Tower will fall. Six are formally on the establishment, with
a weekly allowance of 12½p for horseflesh, of which I grudge
them every penny.

The various towers that form the strong points of the
Inner Wall were also, and perhaps for the most part of the
Tower's history, primarily prisons: a heavy binding for an
anthology of famous captives. More like a shaping of solid
stone than architecture, they have mostly small and dark rooms
breathless under the pressure of masonry; the stone is chill
and always seems a little damp, the stairways burrowed out of
darkness. Everywhere in them you come upon the pathetic
protests of prisoners, the assertions of identity carved into
the stone: names, prayers, monograms, coats of arms and
devices. The two biggest concentrations of them are in the
Beauchamp Tower and the Salt Tower. In the former, most
notably, is the compact but complex device of the five Dudley
brothers; one of them, Guildford, consort of the ten-days
Queen of England, Lady Jane Grey, was beheaded in 1554;
another was killed on active service, and the most famous,
Robert, lived to become the dominant favourite of Elizabeth,
and Earl of Leicester. One of them perhaps carved also into
the stone the name IANE, for the seventeen-year-old girl
who, from a window of the Queen's House close by, saw
her husband go out to execution on Tower Hill and return,
headless, while below her the scaffold on the green was being
prepared for her own execution later that day.

But most of the towers hold in their history a weird con-
cordance of great names. **The Bloody Tower** is not only said
to be the site of the murder of the little princes in 1483 but
housed also Cranmer, and nearly a century later, Archbishop
Laud, who from a window here blessed Strafford as he passed
below to execution; here Sir Walter Raleigh spent thirteen
years. The Bell Tower housed in its time Fisher, More,
Princess Elizabeth and Monmouth; the Bowyer Tower is
supposed to be the site of the famous butt of Malmsey in which

Clarence was drowned in 1478; Essex lay in the Devereux Tower. The Queen's (or King's) House, the peaceful, half-timbered house that fronts the green and is now the Governor's residence, together with the adjoining Yeoman Gaoler's House, knew Anne Boleyn, Guy Fawkes and the Jacobite rebels of the '15—and much later, in 1941, the bewildered Rudolf Hess after his sensational landing in Scotland; it holds too a happier memory of Lord Nithsdale, the gayest of escapers from the Tower, who in 1716 whisked out disguised as a girl the night before he was billed for execution.

With others the preciser associations of lodging are lost. Two kings of Scotland, unwilling, stayed here, and one of France. The poet, Charles of Orleans, started the long decades of his imprisonment here after Agincourt. Henry VIII married his first Queen in the Tower, and executed in it his second and fifth (Anne Boleyn and Catherine Howard); under Elizabeth a crowd of Catholics suffered; each attempt at revolution stranded its human wreck here: the regicides after the Restoration; not only Monmouth but the bloody judge of his supporters, Jeffreys; the Jacobites. The Rye House Plot in the latter days of Charles brought Lord William Russell and Algernon Sidney; the Popish Plot, unexpectedly, Samuel Pepys. Later, in 1780, the No Popery riots brought Lord George Gordon. The last attempt to besiege the Tower, by Sir Thomas Wyatt the younger in 1554, led almost only to his execution. Nor is this roll-call necessarily closed and academic: somewhere in this complex of brick and stone, in both the recent wars, spies have been shot down by firing squads.

One Tower, the Wakefield, holds more peaceful memories, in spite of the fact that it is associated with the murder of that sad king, Henry VI, in 1471. It held for about four centuries the Public Records, and then caged **the Crown Jewels** until 1967, when they were rehoused in a super-secure cavern under Waterloo Barracks (see plan), where you now find them.

The theory, as it were, of the Crown Jewels is fascinating; with the insignia of coronation before your eyes you can reconstruct the tradition and practice of English majesty: the symbolism of the various crowns, the anointing spoon, the eagle of the Ampulla, orbs and sceptres, swords, rings, bracelets and spurs. In fact, your reaction to all this will depend as to whether you are fascinated by sheer accumulation of gold and precious stones or whether you are depressed by it. I confess to depression; gold, in wrought and laboured bulk, always strikes me as a soft, vulgar and ostentatious substitute for honest brass; nor do I go for diamonds—the famous Koh-i-noor (108 carats) or the large Star of India (530 carats and the biggest cut diamond ever) rouse me only to thoughts of the life I could lead if they were mine to sell. Gold is a barbaric, brutal matter, and tells best when used blatantly as it was before the Renaissance. The trouble with the Crown Jewels is that, although certain stones can be traced back into the Middle Ages, the plate itself is almost entirely of after 1660; for to the victorious Parliament, after the Civil Wars, the dream came true, and they melted down all the old regalia, and cashed in; everything had to be recreated for Charles II's coronation. But whether you care for them or not, they should be seen at least once in a lifetime, piled up behind their doubtless bullet-proof glass.

But the core of the Tower, the hard heart of the matter, we have not yet considered: **the White Tower** itself. This is the essential strong-point, 90 feet high from ground to battlements; the rest has grown, almost organically it seems now in its variegation, about it through some eight and a half centuries, as the Norman keep was modulated first into a fortress with curtain walls and bastion towers, and then the inner wall was doubled by the outer. The White Tower was once white, white-washed, as you can see it, startling against the grey of the other buildings, in a famous illumination in a manuscript of the poems of its one-time captive, Charles of Orleans, in the British Museum (MS. Roy. 16 F.ii); its façade, too, was originally tougher and more sheer, before the original Norman windows were enlarged by Christopher Wren in the second half of the seventeenth century; the present ogee-shaped caps to the turrets, which can seem a little too fancy for the tower in certain moods of weather, were originally more primly conical. When it was first built the White Tower stood within London, and the wall of London ran north from the river a few yards to its East (you can still see an outcrop of the wall, looking geological rather than archaeological, in the remains of the Wardrobe Tower).

From the outside then, in spite of a certain softening by later modulations of its original severity, the White Tower is still a fortress, a rough square between its corner turrets, and apart from Colchester, the biggest of its kind in England. And truly Norman—built of Caen stone transported from Normandy. Inside, it is again of vast and massive simplicity, each of its four floors divided into three by great supporting walls; its strength is indicated by the window recesses that cut through 12–15 feet of stone. But its simplicity is not immediately obvious, because, within, the White Tower is a museum: the national hoard of armour and weapons. Among its steel, note perhaps the armour of the Kings of England in series; this includes what I always think to be the best portrait, in some ways, of Henry VIII. Not the elegant, almost mincing suit of Milanese armour made for him about 1510, Milanese with its tutu-like tonlet or skirt in steel, but the tremendous bulk of the Greenwich suit made for him about 1535 to fit his grossness, with a 52-inch girth, and curved gauntlets hanging gorilla-like; an image that fits Henry better even than the brutal and detailed candour of Holbein. As Raleigh wrote, in the walls of the Tower—'for King Henry the Eighth, if all the Pictures and Patterns of a mercilles Prince were lost in the World, they might all again be painted to the Life, out of the Story of this King'. (And in a wall-case Henry's armoured codpiece, which in the seventeenth century was a totem in which barren women stuck pins to ensure conception.)

From the top (second floor of the Tower), as you can't get on to the roof or into the turret where Flamsteed, the great rival of Newton, had his observatory, you descend, spiralling endlessly (and on a right-hand spiral, like most in the Tower, so that your sword-arm is free for action) to the cellars, laid out like some gargantuan wine repository with gun-barrels and frog-throated mortars. This according to tradition is where most of the torturing went on.

But the true splendour of the White Tower is not in the Armoury but in the **Chapel of St. John** on the first floor. Although its crypt, on the ground floor, is occupied by the most unpleasant objects—the instruments of torture, a choice of fetters, Lord Lovat's block—the Chapel itself, even if like everywhere else in the Tower unpleasant things have happened there, is an oasis of calm and ordered dignity: the finest and purest Norman ecclesiastical architecture, to my mind, surviving. Even when you know it, it comes as a shock, unannounced where the stair ceases: it has immense strength in its naked majesty. Simply, a barrel vaulted nave, closed by the round apse at the end; the nave flanked by the two-storied arches of the aisles that continue round the apse. The capitals of the lower arches, severe and clean-cut, bear only a Tau-shaped cross as decoration. It seems in almost pristine condition—the windows have been enlarged, but for most except the purists this may be gain rather than loss—and it is miraculously of a piece, with a rare finality. The eye moves about it, as once the monks in the ambulatories of aisles and gallery, and calmed, rests in satisfaction. It's a fine and refreshing place to rest, while the feet and the voices come stumbling up the steps behind and fall silent suddenly, when over the threshold, and pass on. You can leave the chapel with a sense of a shape to the mind, and a roof to it.

It has accumulated about itself, in its long history, the usual weird associations—the usual, that is, in the case of The Tower. Two senior priests were seized here by Wat Tyler's rebels, and removed from prayers to ultimate execution; it was burnt out, restored; Jane Grey worshipped here, and Mary Tudor got married (by proxy to Philip of Spain) in it; it served as repository for state Papers, for the purposes of the Ordnance and (nearly) as warehouse for Army clothing. Under threat of death, men recanted their religion before the altar; the murdered Henry VI lay in state, and also the White Rose of York, Elizabeth, whose union in marriage with the Lancastrian, the first Tudor, Henry VII, sealed the century-old breach of the War of the Roses. For two days she lay under this vaulted roof, at the heart of eight hundred candle flames. But the Chapel's closest link is with the second-oldest Order of Knighthood in England: the Order of the Bath. After ritual ablutions in tubs in the room next door, aspirants to the order dined with the King, and then set up their vigil in the Chapel all through the night before their armour laid before the altar. A serious and moving memory of chivalry, and a ceremonial most apt for the majestic composure of this building.

Best leave the Tower as you entered it, rather than through the modern breach by St. Thomas' Tower. Out through the Byward Tower, over the causeway over the moat and through the Middle Tower. There on your left is the river, relief and freedom. Behind you, the gates will be closed, and locked. Each night, withdrawing into the Inner Ward by the Bloody Tower, the party with the keys are challenged by the sentry:

'Halt! Who comes there?'
'The Keys.'
'Whose Keys?'
'Queen Elizabeth's Keys.'

At which the guard presents arms, and the Chief Warder removes his bonnet, and says: 'God Preserve Queen Elizabeth,' and the guard answers: 'Amen!' Thence the Keys proceed in state to safety for the night in the Queen's House.

But on the Wharf, at midday on a fine day, people relax. On the far bank freighters are unloading; beyond Tower Bridge to the East the river opens up between the gaunt fringe of docks under an immense sky; tethered flocks of barges ride the water. Past the railed-off paddocks, empty now, waiting for the guns of the Honourable Artillery Company to fire royal salutes on royal occasions, to another long display of guns laid out along the edge of the river. 'The Public must not manhandle these Guns', but they sit on them and small boys hurdle them. About the boles of the plane trees in early spring time the crocuses are garish as splinters of coloured glass, then blown and bird-battered like dishevelled party candles; and in summer imported sand gleams startling yellow in two or three bays of the wharf, and the children come from miles to play there.

NORMAN LONDON
The massive privacy of the
Chapel of St John, within the
walls of the Tower
Right, a great monastic church,
St Bartholomew-the-Great; the
delicate sixteenth century oriel
window was added by Prior
Bolton as a private oratory

MILITARY LONDON. The Tower of London — fortress, palace, prison and barracks for 900 years. Guardsmen at Wellington Barracks

CHAPTER TWO

Piccadilly, Green Park and the Haymarket

۶

FOR the average Londoner, who lives and works in London, Piccadilly may mean no more than a change on the Underground, a daily battle in subterranean corridors or a tiresome obstacle in traffic to be overcome. But to a Londoner in exile the name may set off an unreasonable but almost unbearable nostalgia, crisping the skin with a slightly electric randiness that is both of the senses and of the mind. An appetite for stimulation, for competition, for metropolitan danger and the vital variety of London's jungle; for friendship, and even for the huge, ballooning loneliness that is most sharply defined in a crowd—in the emporia for eating, watching the jaws move; or, on emerging at dusk from the steps from the Underground, to be confronted, outside Swan and Edgar's, by the necessity of choice.

Piccadilly then is a street a mile long, the first long stretch if you are fleeing London—after the complexities of Trafalgar Square—of the escape to the Bath and Bristol Road; going west, it begins historically at the top of Haymarket, though in most people's minds it begins more practically at the recent insert of Piccadilly Circus. If you are entering London, Piccadilly begins at Hyde Park Corner; at Apsley House, sometimes known as No. 1 London. It is as new as the West End generally, and has followed the usual pattern, from grand residential to commercial. After the Restoration of Charles II in 1660 its south side, as far west as Green Park, became the northern edge of the elegant, planned urban development of St. James's (see p. 59), while its north side, from Hyde Park Corner to what is still called Burlington House, developed in a number of large, very select estates bearing virtual palaces in gardens like parks.

Through the eighteenth century the houses closed up, the gardens vanished; trade infiltrated (from then both Fortnum and Mason and Hatchards survive still); at the west end the

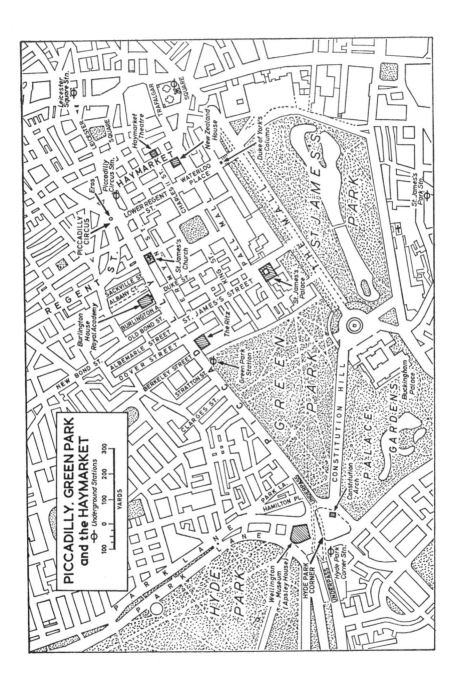

PICCADILLY, GREEN PARK and the HAYMARKET

⊖– Underground Stations

YARDS

100 0 100 200 300

clubs began to bloom, while Piccadilly Circus was carved into
the east end; then in the late nineteenth century big business
swamped and remade much of the street. The monster
Piccadilly Hotel set a new scale, and the sumptuous stone
façades laboured onwards; now there remains little of the
residential about Piccadilly; from the west end, so promis-
ingly giving on to the Park, even the clubs have all but
yielded.

I will start just a little way up (east) from Hyde Park Corner,
looking up Piccadilly. Before you the wide roadway dips, and
lifts again, half a mile away to the Parisian roof of the Ritz;
the road is streaked with cars and above them the air is
cluttered with lamp brackets like derelict railway sleepers. On
the left runs the irregular, greyish cliff of the Piccadilly
façades, but on the right, clear up to the Ritz, is a stretch of
green, swelling and subsiding like a great feather bed under its
eiderdown of trees: **Green Park**. The Park is defined sharply
along a diagonal away from your right—by the wall of
Buckingham Palace gardens, armoured with spikes—but
beyond to your right front it dissolves into distance. In winter
the trees make spidery patterns of a delicacy that rebukes the
gross architecture of the Piccadilly frontages; in a November
dusk they drip, and all is haunted with a grey melancholy in
mist, most abruptly rural. On an early summer morning the
grass is bright with pearls and diamonds, and dogs run wild.
Green Park has no such sophistications of water and orni-
thology as has St. James's; blackbirds there are, naïve, but
the enamelled ducks do not cross the Mall. Here is, quite
simply, grass and trees and paths; no formal flower-beds, but
a sweetly contrived undulation of ground, and in spring a wild
and gaudy flare of daffodil yellow on the fringes of the Park as
the trees begin to haze with green.

Of course it was not always thus; it has taken three centuries
to distil it down to its present artful naturalness since Charles
II added it on to St. James's Park in the 1660s. It held, after
the Restoration, one of the earliest of refrigerators—'a snow-
house and an ice-house, as the mode is in some parts of France
and Italy, and other hot countries, for to cool wine and drinks
for the summer season'. It witnessed a number of duels, but
then every open space in London has done that; about the
time of the 1715 and 1745 rebellions it became very military,
and George II held one famously macabre parade of Dragoons

there in 1747, at which full strength was insisted on: the turn-out was complete, those absent sick being represented by their boots in their riderless horses' stirrups; these pointed toe forwards, but those absent dead were represented similarly but with their boots pointing tailwards. About 1780 this Park suddenly became the fashionable parade for social display as distinct from military, instead of St. James's Park. Flower-beds pushed up; there were grandiose but often ultimately inefficient (though dangerous) firework displays. There were abductions; there were flights of balloons, like that of Mr. Green in 1820, who launched thence at a venture and arrived at Potters Bar. There were odd suicides (in a small reservoir); there was a Temple of Concord; there was a very great number of robberies. Now, in spite of the increased roar of Piccadilly alongside, there is a calm in the Park almost as though a cur-tain had been drawn between it and the roadway. And we must revert to Piccadilly; Green Park, you can take or leave it. It is always there, an essential part of that wonderful system of holes that aerate the whole of the West End, offering oasis: parks, squares, the river, all with their empti-nesses, the envy of all capital cities.

The springboard of Piccadilly, **Hyde Park Corner**; a rough triangle that has strenuously resisted for the last two centuries the attempts of pageant-architects to bring it into shapely order as the grand, ceremonial entry into London from the west. Robert Adam, Jeffry Wyatt, Soane, all produced plans, all abortive; then in 1825 Decimus Burton designed that pretty tripartite screen at the entry to Hyde Park; Constitution Arch went up at the end of Constitution Hill, that oddly void, most gently sloping way that drives down along the wall of the Palace garden to the Palace itself, and which saw in the 1840s no less than three assassination attempts on the life of the young Queen Victoria. In 1845 a colossal equestrian statue of the Duke of Wellington was set on top of the arch; in 1883 the whole arch was moved slightly, to the top of the hill, more or less, and the statue was sent to Aldershot; in 1912 the arch was recrowned by, unprophetically, the present group of Peace in a Quadriga, the fame of the Duke having been earlier placated by the erection of a slightly less large equestrian statue by Boehm opposite the entrance of Apsley House (the horse is the famous Copenhagen, 1808–36, buried at Stratfield Saye with full military honours). After the

First World War memorials, to the Royal Artillery, to the Machine Gun Corps (with a rather good, if very archaic, Rupert Brookeian, statue of David as symbol of the machine gun slaying its ten thousands against Saul's thousands), were set about. Very soon they were inaccessible, as more than a hundred cars a minute throughout each day's twenty-four hours snarled through the busiest traffic centre in London. Between 1960 and 1963 the planners were busy under-passing the Gordian knot, and the entrance to London from the west is now by a tunnel from Knightsbridge to Piccadilly. In making the tunnel a secondary warren of pedestrian subways has also been created, in which, every time I have been there, I have found some lost soul on the verge of tears—but you can at least now get close to the memorials if you persevere. They live alone in their patch of green, hedged by traffic, and the Arch which had before no function now has one: through it are funnelled up into the skies the lethal exhaust gases from the underpass beneath.

On the north side, washed and restored, Burton's screen remains: a charming folly now, dwarfed by buses and too narrow, like a needle's eye, for Rolls-Royces—it was scaled for a carriage or a man on a horse. And next to it on the east, **Apsley House**, too, remains, isolated in its turn, chopped on its eastern flank by the new road where once Rothschilds resided. For all the hazards of subways involved, Apsley House must be visited; part now of the Victoria and Albert Museum holdings, it is touching, absurd and has major beauties. The house itself, basically an Adam design of 1777–8, was the home of the victor of Waterloo until his death at the age of eighty-three in 1852, and the warm Bath stone that now clothes the building, and the giant portico with the giant elevated pillars in front that seem to demand more house behind than they've got, these aré Wellington's improvements. As also were the (long-vanished) iron shutters that he installed in his windows after the mob broke all his glass in 1831. His conception of duty did not provoke popularity at all times; you can see from that gaunt profile, mirrored so often within the house like some antique but still potently intransigent weapon displayed in ritual, that its owner did not greatly care.

Inside the house (weekdays, 10–6; Sundays, 2.30–6) disposed about the ground floor are mainly those honours that were heaped upon him and from under which he has long since slipped out and away. Medals, decorations, swords, batons, orders, shields, flags, even snuff-boxes, even suites of Berlin porcelain, gorgeous and hollow as glory. Then, in the well of the staircase, ridiculous, superb, suddenly Napoleon, all but stark naked and eleven feet high in white marble, captive in the embrace of the white and gold winding stair. It is one of Canova's largest works, rejected (according to the story) by its subject in imperial pique because the little gilt figure of Victory is poised on his palm *away* from him, as if about to quit: subsequently it was bought by the Prince Regent for Wellington, with whom in fact Victory in 1815 had lodged.

Upstairs the display of Wellingtoniana continues: the painted effigies of five kings and two emperors congregate in homage to him (note especially, two remarkable whole-lengths by Wilkie, the successor to Lawrence, of George IV (kilted) and a splendid bravura painting of William IV, perhaps the last flash of grandeur in the tradition of English state-portraiture). The pageant of the Duke's immense, sumptuous funeral unrolls on a coloured strip engraving. In the deep red Waterloo Gallery, where he held reunion banquets of his veterans, a mahogany table as big as a cricket pitch on a playing field of Eton, between two giant candelabra in mauve Siberian porphyry; disporting about its arena is the Waterloo service like a display of eurythmics in silver and gilt, made for the Duke in Portugal. But some rooms on this floor are smaller, and retain a flavour of domesticity (if that word can be used of the Duke); they retain also above all pictures. More portraits, a whole suite of studies by Piene-mann of Waterloo heroes; the Duke's own collection, evidence of the contemporary taste, much fostered by George IV, for small Dutch seventeenth-century paintings: some boisterous Jan Steens, a very beautiful romantic Pieter de Hooch—that master of the escape route: music from the little group in the foreground of the room echoes back through a soft glowing of reflected and refracted light, to the open window behind and the cool evening in dark trees. There are many others, and also the famous Wilkie genre scene of the Chelsea Pensioners (for whom, see p. 211) reading the news of Waterloo. But the *clou* of the collection is loot: the paintings which Napoleon's brother Joseph, King of Spain, had 'won' from the Spaniards, only to lose them with his baggage train to Wellington after the Battle of Vitoria in 1813. The Duke, correct as ever, was stopped from returning the pictures to Spain by a message from the restored King Ferdinand; the latter expressed himself touched by the Duke's delicacy, but unwilling to deprive him of 'that which had come into his possession by means as just as they are honourable'. So it is that the house of the soldier holds one of the noblest collections in England; Spain is better represented here than anywhere but in the National Gallery; Ribera, Murillo (especially the extraordinary and Rembrandtesque 'Isaac Blessing Jacob') and above all Velasquez. There are, too, a row of Teniers; some fine Italian pictures, a Sassoferrato and a magnificent little Correggio of Christ, luminous in agony, on the dark mountain—a picture to which the Duke is said to have been especially attached, unlocking its glass from time to time, and dusting it with a silk handkerchief. But the three Velasquez will be for most people the great reward of the house, and among them perhaps most of all, the early 'Watercarrier of Seville', in its monumental and lucent stillness.

Then there is *passim*, the Duke himself: the Lawrence of 1814, in which he seems, hanging so politely over the fireplace, already rejuvenated for posterity, glossy, the flesh well-fitting and sleek as his red coat (compare the musculous thrust of his jaw in Chantrey's bust of him); the big Goya Equestrian, disappointing now, as in time the horse has 'sunk' into the canvas and the Duke has a macabre clownish air of Carnival (it was painted too fast, inside a month in 1812, as a topicality for exhibition, and Goya's real *ad vivum* impression is the head-and-shoulders (whose temporary abduction held the headlines for years) in the National Gallery, or perhaps the drawing in the British Museum). But all the portraits of the Duke do not summon up his ghost (he would not have consented to anything so incorrect as a ghost), though they do, as it were, posit his absence. We miss him still, that figure of straight rectitude so firmly upright in honour even when wrong, and God knows he was a formidable reactionary.

From Apsley House, then, swinging round into Piccadilly, down the slope and up, past the loaded façades of the clubs or former clubs (note the 'In-and-Out', the Naval and Military Club, where once Lord Palmerston lived, a sudden cool of restraint in the architectural sequence of Piccadilly). Half-way up, set oddly in the rather meanly practical concrete-cum-wire netting on the Park side of the road, a florescence of blue and gilt iron, best English iron work in its ornate manner; triumphal gates, they used to belong to Devonshire House on the other side of the road; now they never open, but the eye can ride through them, on through trees to a glimpse of the angel over Queen Victoria outside Buckingham Palace. Devonshire House itself has gone, demolished, flattened even now from memory, and where the smile of that most famous of Duchesses (that Whig toast, she who kissed a butcher for the advancement of the Party) Georgiana—mysterious, with a charm that still lives in the paintings of her by Reynolds and Gainsborough and Downman—where her smile once kindled is office masonry and the chromium fangs of motor-cars exposed for sale behind plate-glass. So to Green Park Station, to **the Ritz** on the right: a French urban château for all that it is one of the earliest (1906) London buildings with an iron frame, formidably closed with pink Norwegian granite. Solid on the far corner of Green Park, it may seem to claim the latter as its own demesne; among the great hotels of London, it preserves—providence willing—a wonderful old-fashioned luxury of withdrawal in privacy and discretion. Its plain front is defended by its shadowy arcades, and its only advertisement is the magic of its name: RITZ, spelled out in light bulbs.

From the Ritz onwards to the east Piccadilly is channelled deep between hulking masonry on each side, cleft by the narrow entrances to Mayfair on the left—Dover, Albemarle, Bond Streets; Burlington Arcade; Sackville Street (see Chapter 5); on the right the broad drop of St. James's Street that was once closed at the bottom by the tower of St. James's Palace, but now is overridden by the tall point block of the new Vickers building, dwarfing the Palace tower from a mile away on Millbank. On the right then, the great shops begin, the opening of the Piccadilly Arcade, bijou boutiques; Duke Street; and then neo-cheery-redbrick Queen Anne style, ah **Fortnum and Mason!**—mecca for the moneyed shopper, its windows fascinating as a tropical aquarium with all varieties of rare food in all variety of rare packaging; a glass jar at Fortnum always seems to be handmade from crystal. The shop goes back to 1707, to William Fortnum, a footman to Queen Anne, and its court connections and traditions of luxury, its position as grocers to St. James's and to Mayfair, have remained fairly constant ever since. It is quite free to go in; the shop-walkers wear frock coats and there is a slight risk of becoming mesmerised, deep in the pile carpet under the chandeliers, by so much of so much and all costing so much. Watch the new clock chime at the quarters.

Then there are shops like Swaine, Adeney and Brigg, specialists in umbrellas and all sorts of reminders, among the automobiles, that the horse still exists, noble if captive (all kinds of whips). Or Hatchards, last survivor of a colony of distinguished eighteenth-century bookshops. There is the opening to the little specialist shops of Prince's Arcade, and then a big plain block, ornamented with medallions of famous British water-colour painters and long the headquarters of various typically English art societies, though its original purpose may well be lost to sight through the ground-level seductions of the lush offices of Pan-American Airways. There is a bank, a branch of the Midland, which is well worth two looks, a most delicate and delightful conceit by Lutyens; and then the open place, with its catalpa leaning meditatively on the elbow of an iron prop, of St. James's Church, the church itself (which we discuss as the Parish church of St. James's elsewhere, p. 71) set back squat towards Jermyn Street. Simpson's, one of the first (1935–6) good modern, functional, shops in London, is notable for off-the-peg gents' clothing.

Before we engage with the Circus itself, a look at the north side of Piccadilly, down to the brash entrance to the very refined tourist-trap of Burlington Arcade (see p. 82) brings you to the dominant feature of **Burlington House**. This is the last survivor of the great eighteenth-century palaces of Piccadilly, though sadly altered, with a huge Victorian neo-Renaissance façade (enlivened with flags when exhibitions are on); a big archway leads through into a courtyard, where to left and to right, apparently in deep slumber behind deep-set windows, are contained the premises of the Geological Society, the Chemical Society, the society of Antiquaries, the Linaean Society, the British Association for the Advancement of Society and the Royal Astronomical (in the latter premises I observed, 10 February 1961 at 2.30 p.m. on a calm afternoon, two middle-aged gentlemen of staid and learned silveriness at a second-floor window, observing objectively the progress of a clockwork tic or bug up the window-pane). Actually all these establishments, if not audibly humming, are very much alive, although the most famous of them, the Royal Society, removed to Carlton House Gardens in 1968. The Antiquaries, open only by introduction, is a thriving body and the originator of much important antiquarian and archaeological research; it has a formidable library, a curious and important collection of early English portraits and a reputation for some of the most spirited blackballing in London.

But the best-known part of this complex, opposite the archway and behind the rather archly a-tiptoe figure of its first President, Sir Joshua Reynolds, is the **Royal Academy of Fine Arts**. The building goes back to the 1600s, though (architecturally) its most important phase came after its remodelling in 1715–16 by Colen Campbell for the great Earl of Burlington, the patron of that most Englishly Italianate precocious swing of neo-classic taste; it became the model Palladian town house for the aristocracy, with a celebrated curved arcade embracing what is now the squared-off courtyard. This was all swamped by the gargantuan improvements when it was turned into the home of the various Academic bodies in 1867.

In 1769 the founding of the Academy marked as it were the coming of age of British art, establishing it as a recognised profession; bestowing on it a social stature, a constitution under the equivalent of a royal charter, and, in its annual exhibitions, a most effective market-place. Also, most important, its own permanent and continuing training school— one of the best in the country. From the very beginning there were outsiders. Romney never exhibited there, and Gainsborough in his later years more or less withdrew. For Blake, Academy and the name of Reynolds were anathema; Rossetti never belonged, nor of course did Whistler; and from the 1890s on, the solid rejection by the Academy of the successive revolutions against the Renaissance tradition—the triumphs of the -isms: Post-Impressionism, Expressionism, Abstractionism, etc.—brought its reputation very low. Since the 1930s, the Anti-Establishment (the art-patronage extended on the one hand by the Bond Street dealers and on the other by the Arts Council) has nourished *outside* the Academy almost all the talents known *outside* England as the pioneers of a new English achievement of international stature. One hopes that this situation, still idiotically fraught with the hangover of now dead personal animosities, may not endure much longer. The Academy itself is now a very liberal institution, with many advantages to offer any artist, and the split does nobody any good. Meanwhile the annual exhibitions continue between June and mid-August, dismissed by the critics generally as a social rather than artistic occasion. But for those interested in art, the major contribution of the Academy, especially since the war, has been its promotion (sometimes at a loss) of great loan exhibitions during the winter months of the year.

The interior of the building itself, following the Academy's re-couping of its financial position by selling to the nation the Leonardo cartoon now in the National Gallery (for £800,000) has been lavishly restored to a fresh brilliance. The hall on the ground floor has ceiling paintings, by Angelica Kaufmann (left and right) and B. West, which were once in the Academy's first permanent home at Somerset House (see p. 296). There are some good busts here, and towards the right end of the hall a lift (one of the largest and I suspect the slowest in London) which goes up to the Diploma Galleries on the top floor; this suite of galleries nominally houses the Academy's collection of works by its own past members (every Academician, upon election, has to deposit a work, known as his Diploma piece); this collection includes splendid paintings by Reynolds, Gainsborough, Constable, Turner, Wilkie (to name but a few to offset the roll of anti-academicians I have previously called) but is visible perhaps too rarely—the Galleries are also used for smaller loan exhibitions. The main Galleries for exhibition lie up the grand stairway that leads steeply from the centre hall, with excellent decorative paintings by the Venetian Ricci; the staircase doubles back on itself to the old private apartments, now happily open to the public during the summer months; they include some fine rooms with good eighteenth-century plasterwork, ceilings by Kent and others, some pictures and most notably, now that the Leonardo has gone, one of the greatest works by Michelangelo visible in England, the early (c. 1505) 'Madonna Taddei', an unfinished marble tondo with an exquisite tenderness. The most marked feature of the exhibition galleries is perhaps simply that they are very big, and in the summer exhibitions too full (usually over a thousand exhibits are shown), but though the spirit may flag perhaps with an impression that too many people have been confronted with canvases that somehow they must cover, there are always (despite the critics) individual items that reward attention.

In Piccadilly again, going eastwards, there is the almost secret little courtyard of the **Albany**, very reticent and discreet, almost a collegiate building for literary eminence (you can glimpse its nature perhaps better from the back entrance in Burlington Gardens, p. 82); then Sackville Street, a long strip of mainly Georgian houses with some good shops; and so to Piccadilly Hotel with those extraordinary pillars in a sky-high screen, as if sheltering a lofty patio for angelic tea-drinkers, and on to Swan and Edgar's, and **Piccadilly Circus** itself.

Only underground does the Circus have the virtues of a circus; dive down one of the entrances to Piccadilly station, with its great circular foyer deployed about the rumbling cascade-head of the many-banked escalators; this is one of the great rendezvous of London, here there are always people waiting and people meeting in an air of expectancy and incipient drama. Above ground we have the hub, they say, of the Empire, once upon a time of the world even, and anyway still of sightseers' London. And yet the most striking thing about Piccadilly Circus to the naked eye is that it is almost utterly ignoble; the most curious thing, at least to the biased mind such as mine, is that it is also utterly irresistible. Maybe it should never be seen by day, for by night, though it may not flower in classic beauty, it does reveal itself in vitality, in the garish lights of its advertisements. It is not even a Circus but roughly triangular, the confluence of Regent Street, Haymarket and Coventry Street; of Shaftesbury Avenue, Piccadilly, Lower Regent Street, all pouring in or out of it between huge bluffs of masonry. It owns Eros, that winged statue in the central island, apparently inaccessible through the grinding circling vehicles, yet most often thickly inhabited by the idle. The statue has nothing to do with Eros: it is the Angel of Christian Charity wrought by Sir Alfred Gilbert in 1892-3 in Art-Nouveau aluminium in memory of one of the most truly noble of Victorian philanthropists, the 7th Earl of Shaftesbury. It is the centre on nights of national emotion for rejoicing and whoopee, but above all a magnetic centre for people to drift about eddying in and out of the mass feeding shops, the pubs, the underground bars, the snack counters, the cinemas. Recently the Circus has been the centre of a violent controversy in which public opinion fought and held—for the moment anyway—a major and hideous project of commercial exploitation on one of the major sites of London. From this emerged Sir William Holford's overall plan for Piccadilly Circus, and two subsequent schemes, the latest published in 1972 in which it seems destined to become a kind of piazza. Perhaps the only thing yet certain, for the development will take decades no doubt, is that Piccadilly will change—but that Eros will remain.

Piccadilly Circus was once a pivot in the greatest single gesture of town-planning that London has known; the way of state, of order, cut out by John Nash in the early nineteenth century between the Prince Regent's mansion at Carlton House and his new park, Regent's Park, to the north. This was not merely a suitably princely avenue, but an act of definition, demarcating the relatively planned areas of St. James's and Mayfair, with their great squares, from the older confusion to the east.

Lower Regent Street was the first stage, proceeding from south to north; typically, years before the whole was completed, its very springboard had been demolished—Carlton House itself, where now, looking down Lower Regent Street from the Circus, you can see the Duke of York's column. The triumphal way paused at the end of the first stage at the Circus, side-stepping into the sweep of the Quadrant of Regent Street; between the Circus and Carlton House was the shimmering line of plain and elegant stucco. Where now is mostly tedium; not an original house remains, and Lower Regent Street is a curiously dead deep channel for the one-way traffic attacking Piccadilly Circus. It has indeed Lillywhite's if you require correct accoutrements for any form of sport; it has vast travel offices and the Tea Centre for an excellent cup of; it has banks and the tiring new building of Atomic Energy Authority, but its real virtue consists in two good views—one down to the Column from the Circus, and the other from the junction with Charles II Street near the bottom, looking left to the façade of the Haymarket Theatre and right to William III prancing between his drooping trees in St. James's Square (see p. 72).

But our way lies rather into the Haymarket, going east

from the Circus, the Criterion Theatre on your right; if on the wrong side of the road, crossing may be difficult, as pedestrians are railed in as if criminal sheep, but aim to swoop down to the right into the **Haymarket** proper. This, unlike Lower Regent Street, is basically old; it was what it is still called, besides being the main route out of London to the west. In 1720, 'a spacious Street of great Resort, full of Inns and Houses of Entertainment'; the market for hay and straw was held here three days a week, and where Her Majesty's Theatre still stands was once the theatre built by Vanbrugh in 1704, the Haymarket Opera House, to be associated with Handel and with Haydn, with Vanbrugh again in his capacity as dramatist, with Congreve and Sheridan. The only old survivals of fabric in the street are the late eighteenth-century shop window, near the top, of Fribourg and Treyer, tobacconists, small and pretty as a toy or a snuff-box (which indeed it also is), and, with the stucco of the American Express beyond, towards the bottom of the street, the façade of the Haymarket Theatre, pillared and painted. This was founded in 1720, but rebuilt by Nash in 1820. In the nineteenth century (1830), the Hay Market itself was cleared, but another market continued and apparently increased—according to no less a witness than Dostoievsky in 1882: 'the district where in certain streets at night the prostitutes gather in their thousands'. This too has now vanished from the street, and at night it is usually quiet apart from its two theatres. But by day its vitality is still there. It has the Design Centre, a successful innovation, didactic about standards of quality and taste in an almost Prince Consortian manner; this has a changing exhibition of the best of goods available from British manufacturers, and though you cannot buy here, you can see, from the exhibition or from an extensive card-index, what is available in the line you are looking for, and where. The Haymarket has also other and famous establishments, like Burberry's, and on the corner of Orange Street you can see behind banks of flowers through into the sumptuous cavern of the headquarters of Dewar's, the whisky-distillers, where glows supernaturally the original of Raeburn's 'Macnab'. And on the corner at the bottom on the right, New Zealand has contributed an admirable addition to London's contemporary architecture, **New Zealand House** (opened in 1963). On a frustrating site, worried by traffic about its base, and victim to some extent of planning (which chopped several stories off its original tower plan, impairing the proportions), it is nevertheless of solid and direct honesty, and positively noble in the massive simplicity of its planning (which has incidentally injected a new spark of life into the Victorian fuss of Her Majesty's Theatre alongside, in happy contrast). From the top there is a fine view.

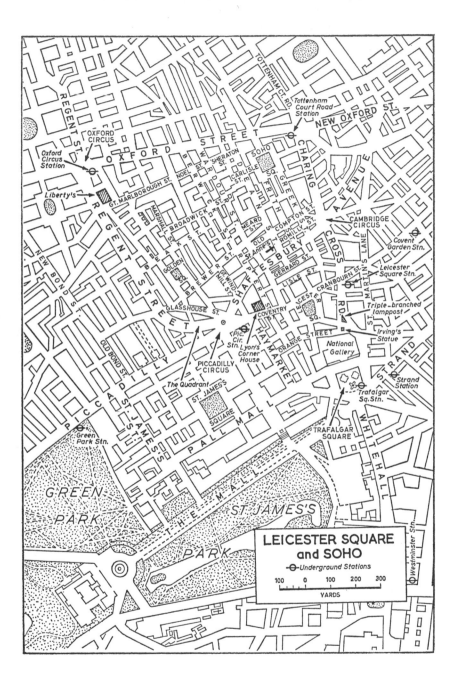

CHAPTER THREE

LEICESTER SQUARE
and SOHO

-O- Underground Stations

100   0   100   200   300

YARDS

Leicester Square and Soho

❧

ONCE, on a fine May morning about nine o'clock, I heard a cornet playing in **Leicester Square**, at the north-eastern corner, and it played that it dreamt it dwelt in marble halls as though its heart was going to burst. That I thought was the noise of Leicester Square for me, though it was looking, as it can do early in the morning, swept and slightly prim, with the tulips just so and the clean new foliage of the plane trees sprigging the upper air. In the golden morning haze, even its attendant buildings hinted at charm which is not the characteristic of Leicester Square, for its true heart is of brass among its lumping flanks of near marble all festooned with neon. Mostly, Leicester Square is large. With Piccadilly Circus it is one of the main London axes on which the crowds sway making up their mind what to do next, and for them are the mass entertainment palaces, the mass eating and drinking places, and correspondingly the voluminous underground lavatories. Along the north and east sides of the square, chickens twirl on grills, pubs dive into the ground, and the draughty air is slowed by the smell of frying and barbecuing, and revived again by the hot-house bouquet, of thick-pile carpet and definitely *parfum*, given off from the cinema entrances. Leicester Square is for food and films.

The 'Leicester' of the Square comes from Sir Philip Sidney's family; his collateral descendants, the Earls of Leicester, had their London house on the north side of what was then Leicester Fields. The 'Fields' had been enclosed and laid out as a Dutch garden in 1720; in 1748 Fred Prince of Wales, by way of indicating contempt for his father, erected a gilt equestrian statue of his grandfather (George I) in the middle. Popularly known as the 'Golden Man and Horse', this was the centre of public admiration during the period of the Square's high fashion, but as the area decayed so too the statue decayed; in 1851, somewhat battered already by vandals, it was banished for some eleven years; then, resurrected (though minus a leg), it survived unsteadily, by degrees losing its rider until its final indignity when in a night of revelry it was whitewashed and covered with large dapple spots like a rocking-horse. By then the area, besides being a hunting-ground for hooligans, had already for years been a centre of popular entertainment.

The garden of the Square is still much as it was after being salvaged from dereliction and presented in 1874 to the people of London by the picturesquely fraudulent tycoon 'Baron' Grant (*né* Albert Gottheimer), described by Sir Osbert Sitwell as 'almost the first "Englishman" to realise the possible personal benefits to be derived from the practice of public benevolence coupled with a high patriotism'; his career burst two years later in the 'Emma Mines Scandal'. To him are due also the splendour of the plane trees, now clear past their centenary, and in which, for two haunted years in the 1950s, there used to sing a thrush—it has since left. To Baron Grant also we owe four coarsely indifferent busts set at the corners of the garden, which are almost all that is left to evoke the memory of the fashionable hey-day of Leicester Square, and a copy of Scheemakers' statue of 1741 (in Westminster Abbey) of Shakespeare, here enhanced by a water basin and stone dolphins, but looking, it seems to me, faintly apprehensive in his pensiveness, with the Dental Hospital behind him and the old Empire in front.

Between the south side of the Square and the back of the National Gallery the southernmost extremity of Soho has almost gone: narrow streets, small shops, a publisher, a butcher, drinking clubs and the odd tart, all now overshadowed by an overweening development where was Macmillans the publishers. Still, **Orange Street** is worth a glance: at the Haymarket end the municipal garage, you may note, is of a long odd shape, for it still reflects its original function which was that of Charles II's tennis court; farther east is the re-built Orange Street Chapel—formerly a centre of worship for the Huguenots who so thickly populated the area; the entrance to the National Gallery extension of 1975; and at the far end, past the academically-gowned bronze statue of the actor Irving, on an island in Charing Cross Road is a truly magnificent triple-branched lamp-post, perhaps the finest of its kind left in London. Hence you may look up the bleak vista of **Charing Cross Road**, the eastern perimeter of our area in this chapter, and if you wish, easily devote a whole morning to it. Hewn through a swarming complex of slums in the 1880s, it is architecturally depressive, and in all weathers feels slightly fly-blown, but its shops are famous—for books, musical (especially jazz) instruments, snuff and left-of-centre clothes for young men. For the book-browser the opportunities are wide, including the facilities of Zwemmer's, with a remarkable stock of art books, and the great Leviathan, Foyles.

However, I must leave those who wish to graze the pastures of the Charing Cross Road to their own devices, for the sake of the interior, the jungle itself, of the area it fringes—**Soho**. To confront the challenge of the name squarely—no one really seems to be able to prove its derivation, but certainly the most emotionally satisfying is that it comes from the rallying cry—*So-hoe*—used by the adherents of one of its more notorious inhabitants, that Duke of Monmouth, bastard of Charles II, who rebelled against his uncle James II in 1685 only to die ignominiously on the scaffold. *Soho*, anyway: a slightly raffish yet gay cry: a definitely raffish place, both gay and sinister. It lies between Leicester Square on the south and Oxford Street on the north: Regent Street on the west and Charing Cross Road on the east, though it spills over to the north beyond its original confines (see p. 235). Though it could be nowhere but in England, the foreign flavour in its garish blend is quite definitely foreign—and has been almost since the area was built up. The first great influx was of French Protestants after the Revocation of the Edict of Nantes in 1685, and since then the foreigners, speaking their own languages, have always been there.

So go north from Leicester Square—up Wardour Street perhaps, where one of the staples of Soho already predominates, the small restaurants of all nationalities, including one or two of long-established character with a devoted clientèle like Chez Victor. In Gerrard Street to the right, a few old houses linger from the early eighteenth century, though mostly much altered (John Dryden died at No. 43 in 1700). But this seg-

ment of Soho was sliced, as you will find if you proceed
north, from its parent body by the cutting of **Shaftesbury
Avenue** about 1880. There is not much to detain anyone in
Shaftesbury Avenue, unless you are going there by night, in
fact, theatre-going. There are four theatres at this end of the
Avenue (Lyric, Apollo, Globe, Queen's) plus the former home
of traditional strip-tease, the Windmill (now a cinema), just
off the Avenue, and, at Cambridge Circus, the huge amphi-
theatre for musical spectacle, the Palace. The West End
theatres are south to the Haymarket and the Strand, and east
from Piccadilly Circus as far as Drury Lane, but for some
reason Shaftesbury Avenue is the label applied to West End
theatre as Broadway is to New York theatre. Through the
centuries the London theatres have moved, like so many
other things, gradually west; starting almost opposite the
Tower in Shakespeare's time, on Bankside, then in the
eighteenth century, at the two major centres of Drury Lane
and Covent Garden, though the Haymarket, too, was the
home of early Italian opera; now they are dotted along the
Haymarket, Shaftesbury Avenue, Charing Cross Road and
its parallel, St. Martin's Lane, and eastward down the Strand
to the Aldwych and Drury Lane, with ballet and Grand
Opera still queening it central in Covent Garden.

Even for many Londoners Soho has only two connotations:
a place where one eats out at a continental or at least conti-
nental-styled restaurant after the theatre; or, involved in a
head-line, a signal of a news story in which crime of a generally sleazy or vicious nature is featured. It is in fact a weird,
anomalous and archaic area, and can be, for those involved in
its inner jungle life, a dangerous one. It is the centre of the
drinking club and the strip-tease business; junkies and drunks
lie about it, heroin is consumed; girls at a price (driven indoors by strict vice laws) still signal with a flash of teeth
from upper windows, and from time to time guns go off,
even, occasionally, striking innocent passers-by at a venture.
But be not alarmed, the chances of being shot by mistake in
Soho are a million to one against, and although Soho is the
nearest thing in central London to a red-light district, it is
also the area where countless addicts of garlic and wine
cookery do their daily harmless household shopping, and
where the most respectable people eat deliciously. Strike
therefore without fear north from Shaftesbury Avenue into

Soho's heart, which is sited to the east, though some might argue about that, for Soho in texture, while extraordinarily dense, can change in quality almost from house to house. Take any of the three famous culinary streets that run parallel northwards, Dean, Frith or Greek, and you are at once in another country. Most noticeable first is perhaps the scale, for Soho's unit is still that of the two or three bay, three or four storey, dwelling house, very astonishing to find at the centre of a great capital city, and still reflecting the original lay-out of the area mostly in the 1680s, though the fabric is predominantly eighteenth century or early nineteenth. At the first crossing (**Romilly Street**) pause and look left; do this preferably (perhaps before or after eating at Kettner's) in a warm hazy London dusk when the sky is green, and against it the weird tower of St. Anne's Soho makes its hauntingly exotic silhouette, almost Russian, bulbous under its dark lead spire. Little of the church remains from the blitz except the tower, which is very eccentric early nineteenth century (1802–6, by S. P. Cockerell), added to the original Wren church. Somewhere here Hazlitt is buried, and a memorial to him is on the wall of the tower; he died a few hundred yards away, at No. 6 Frith Street, in 1830. On the west side of the church, on Wardour Street, is a garden with seats excellent for sunning in. The second crossing going northwards is **Old Compton Street**, a main axis for restaurants, delicatessen and wine shops: here you can at times almost float on the aroma of coffee and garlic, and here are famous long-established restaurants from Wheeler's (fish specialists) to Chez Auguste, and a French butcher and an Algerian coffee shop, mixed into the espresso bars and displays of sausages and cheese from all over the world, and the odd nudist cinema, with Cinerama bulking huge at the eastern end. Northwards again **Dean, Frith** and **Greek** continue in the same vein, with a flowering of neon and photographs of glossy nudes at the strip clubs. Every house seems to carry a minimum of three establishments; thus some of the moderately priced but good restaurants tend to be on the first floor or in the basement. Drinking clubs (for which a nominal introduction by a member is needed) are legion, and in them the afternoons flower beyond the English licensing laws into strange oddly submarine alcoholic dusks; time slows and through it move brilliantly vivid creatures like neurotic angel fishes: a surrealist world charted with precise accuracy in the works of the late Mr. Anthony Carson.

Restaurants, in a survey as broad as this, are perilous to particularise; they change character almost overnight with the passing of a chef, and expert up-to-date minute advice should be taken before indulging if your time is too limited to allow of an empirical exploration. But in Soho you can eat as well as anywhere in the world (and just about as expensively), but the traditional accent is on the small and intimate. The pubs are equally legion and equally famous: the best known perhaps the York Minster (Dean Street, Shaftesbury Avenue end), known as French's or Frenchies owing to its long-established French *patron*, always packed, thick with beards and Gauloises that flood out into the street in summer, a rendezvous of artists and writers especially; poets again at the Helvetia or Swiss House in Old Compton Street; artists, and film people strayed from Wardour Street, at the delectable Dog and Duck in Bateman Street, and so on. Off Dean Street is Meard Street, chaste houses of 1732, and at No. 88 Dean Street miraculously still there is a unique survival, a rococo shop front that dates from about 1760. Dean Street runs through to Oxford Street at the north, but Greek (not perhaps from the local Greek inhabitants but from the name of Gregory or 'Grig' King who developed this area in the early 1680s) and Frith end in **Soho Square**. This, on the site of the Duke of Monmouth's house, is nearly all built-up offices; the square of green remains, however, Soho's village green, distinguished by a ghostly weathered statue barely recognisable as Charles II (the remnant of a pompous monument featuring the king set among the figures of the rivers of England; the latter have migrated to Grims Dyke, Harrow Weald). On the corner of the Square and Greek Street, behind a bleak if civilised exterior, there is an interior from the grand days of Soho (visitable on Mondays, 10.30–12, and Thursdays, 2.30–4.30), the House of St. Barnabas, built originally as town house for the Beckfords by Joseph Pearce in 1746, but from 1861 a charitable home for 'distressed people in London' (a curious and elaborately textured chapel dates from then).

Leaving Soho Square, proceed westwards through Carlisle Street and Sheraton Street which brings you into **Wardour Street**, once the stronghold of glámour. The name is to the British cinema what Shaftesbury Avenue is to the theatre, and

here in the 1920s and 1930s the giants of cinema established
their headquarters.

Moving west again, Noel Street leads through to Great
Marlborough Street, at the far end of which, on Regent Street,
are the contrasted splendours of the medieval elevation of
Liberty's (as compared with its Renaissance-Baroque façade
on Regent Street) with its timbering made out of real ships'
timbers, no expense spared, and all, in proportions, stagger-
ingly wrong. But before that, the first crossing of Noel Street
is at **Berwick Street**, with a crowded street market at its end
that is prolonged south through Rupert Street to Shaftesbury
Avenue, good for fruit and vegetables. As busy as Old
Compton Street, or busier, but here the tone seems always
to me to have changed: this is predominantly Cockney and
Cockney-Jewish as distinct from the mainly Latin cosmopoly
of Old Compton Street. It is worth lingering if only for the
smell of vegetable greenery and the hoarse and acrid banter
of the stall-keepers, but also, if it be only to linger a little
sadly, for the visible forerunner of the shape of things to come
in Soho. For in Berwick Street the first stages of a proposed
redevelopment of Soho have gone up, in a high block of
municipal flats flanking the market. But the pullulating
vitality of Soho may well depend on the closeness with which
its workers and its 4,000-odd residents are forced to live; if
its warren quality, if all its narrownesses, alley-ness, its
animation in decay, are taken from it, what will be left?

At the bottom of Berwick Street you can slip through such a
characteristic Soho footpath—past a do-it-yourself shop for
lampshades, past the glamorous Jewish eating house, Isow's—
into Brewer Street, but I recommend instead a detour through
west Soho via **Broadwick Street** and **Beak Street**. In Beak
Street a blue plaque, on the wall of No. 41, announces the
one-time presence of the Venetian Canaletto, who stayed
there in 1749–51. One may wonder if indeed anyone but
Canaletto ever saw London as he did, whether he did not
import, built into his eye, a Venetian azure sky; certainly his
London views now seem a dream, brilliantly precise in their
perspectives though they be. In them, Wren's spires pierce the
sky white as the day they were made and over all rides the
dome of St. Paul's, and in the foreground figures, drawn in
Canaletto's fluent and idiosyncratic calligraphy, gesture with
an elegant rococo grace in a flash of scarlet or royal blue

cloak. But Beak Street was then called Silver Street, and when I last passed that way Canaletto's old lodging house was to let; past me went a man in shirt sleeves, carrying a dozen half-finished jackets of sober charcoal grey on one arm, and in the other hand a raised umbrella of mourning black, for it was raining.

Cloth is still a main staple of business in this part of Soho, as it has been for century and more; here are not only the big wholesale establishments, but still also the little men, the Jewish small tailors and the specialists in sartorial detail; finishing work still comes hither from Savile Row over the other side of Regent Street, and in places you can still glimpse the sewing girls bent over their machines or even over archaic needle and thread, and the tailor in shirt sleeves cross-legged on his table. Yet, running north from Beak Street, there is Carnaby Street, which almost overnight in the 1960s usurped the glamour of Savile Row as swinging centre for high fashion—at any rate for the very young. But Carnaby Street already verges on the museum piece itself, a myth, a nostalgic tourist trap, as the action shifted to the King's Road, Chelsea —for the time being anyway.

A little south, you come into the first (1681) of Soho's squares, named **Golden Square**—according to legend, a refinement by its superior inhabitants of an original Gelding. Only a couple of early houses remain among the massive modern homes of cinema, television, cloth-merchants and hospital, and the square garden has been municipalised in an oddly suburban way, with Cotswold stone and seats with striped canvas awnings for the summer about the statue of George II (by J. van Nost, 1753). Grand in Roman tunic and kilt, but democratically low on no plinth, he stands with one hand untiringly extended as if greeting guests at a reception. Still farther south, the way is crossed by Brewer Street, the southern east–west axis of the area, usually humming with shoppers at its excellent and exotic food specialists, its admirable ironmongers, or at the corner of the street market, on Rupert Street; and at No. 42 Brewer Street behind a modest front, *the* shop for buttons. At its western extremity Brewer Street runs into Glasshouse Street, sunk deep in the high backsides of the Quadrant (in the Quadrant Arcade, if so minded, you can buy saris) of Regent Street, and into a fresh density of restaurants, cafés and bars, and so to Piccadilly Circus.

But if you leave now, you should return later, when the street markets have closed, leaving only a straggle of debris and a fruity greenery aroma pendant in the dusk; as the lights thicken and flash, and the rumble of drums and the keening of horns begins to seep from the opening and shutting doors in basements; the taxis bearing diners fight their way through, and always, standing about till deep in the night, the little groups of men who have time, it seems, as has no one else in London.

ST.JAMES'S

Underground Stations

100   0   100   200   300

YARDS

CHAPTER FOUR

St. James's

❦

ST. JAMES'S is a fairly sharply defined area—defined on the
south and west by two Parks, St. James's and Green, on the
north by the main thoroughfare of Piccadilly and on the east,
less sharply, by the twin routes of Lower Regent Street and
the Haymarket. Its origins are equally clear; St. James's
began as a court purlieu, almost precinct, materialising in the
magnetic field of force set up first by Charles II's dominant
affection for Whitehall Palace as a residence after the Restoration of 1660, lapsing perhaps a little as William III preferred
the suburban amenities of Kensington, then reviving, re-
developing as the Hanoverians in the eighteenth century
settled for St. James's Palace itself. In Victoria's reign, as
the main town house of the Crown became Buckingham
Palace, Belgravia (see p. 157) became the new focus for the
aristocratic residences of the high servants of the Crown, and
the big establishments in St. James's began the slow process
of yielding to clubs and commerce.

I have chosen to approach from Trafalgar Square; either of
the two exits westwards from the Square, Cockspur Street and
Pall Mall East, will serve, for they converge. **Cockspur Street**
is the home of some of the great shipping companies, now
strangely old-fashioned. It is adorned though by the only
modest equestrian statue I know—George III (by Wyatt,
1836); he was born up the road, in St. James's Square. It is a
touchingly affectionate image, offering neither support for the
animosity of long-memoried republicans nor any indication
of the terrible madness that benighted the king's later years.
There he goes, sitting his safe bronze horse most comfortably,
his cocked hat held low at his side as though he has just given
one discreet, almost bourgeois, cheer for constitutional
monarchy; admirable object, it gets less attention than it
deserves. South of Cockspur Street, on Warwick House Street,
a bland repetitious new development; here you may shed a

tear. It was till 1969, when barbarously torn down, the echoing Carlton Mews full of ghosts of horses.

Westward from the bottom of the Haymarket stretches the vista of **Pall Mall** between its massy masonry; immediately on your right, behind the New Zealand House, another charming left-over, the Opera Arcade: a passage-way roofed with a sequence of elegant lanterns, and a miscellany of little shops. It used to be full only of the noise of your own footsteps, but its re-smartening, as almost an extension of New Zealand House, may bring it back to fashion; though it lose its secrecy, this will be good, for it is the most purely handsome of all London arcades (by Nash and Repton). Then comes **Waterloo Place** (bottom of Lower Regent Street); north, Edwardian banks open about the Crimean War Memorial, which is moulded from real Russian cannon, slightly absurd, touching, with a female Honour poised above bear-skinned guardsmen whom she appears to have just won by skilful quoiting of the wreaths in her hands. In front, unreasonably (and unhistorically) sweet and mild, the tender figures of Florence Nightingale (with lamp) and that admirable statesman, Sidney Herbert, whom Florence ruled with a rod of iron. And another of those tremendous Trafalgar-Square-type lamp-posts. South of Waterloo Place, the splendid, for once ample enough, flight of steps leads down to St. James's Park behind the round, pink granite, column built for the Duke of York in 1831–4 (much more satisfactory in design than Nelson's Column, Tuscan as against Corinthian). The Duke, 124 feet above you (so high, they said, to get him out of reach of his creditors), has a crisp and satisfactory silhouette; he is approachable by steps inside the column, but these have been closed to visitors for years owing to the suicidal invitation of the open top. He was a good Royal Duke, as George III's sons went; an able administrator as Commander-in-Chief, but his reputation condemned irrevocably by a nursery rhyme, as he who led his troops up the hill and down again. To left and to right of him **Carlton House Gardens**, the back of Carlton House Terrace, the Nash-planned complex still maintained, calm and dignified, although Carlton House itself, built by Nash for the Prince Regent and the closing point of the great Regent Street axis, lasted very few years before it was demolished. In the centre is Edward VII, his plinth scarred by blast from the last war, but himself undiminished, in meaty and joggy bronze on his charger. But the gardens here, between Carlton Terrace and the backs of the Pall Mall clubs, form another oasis on, say, a moody July day at lunch time, with the sun coming suddenly hot on the shoulders between showers; the stucco shines and from the noise of the traffic there is peace. The heavy plane trees, the dark sleeping backsides of the clubs. Bureaucracy, various forms of which, some with resonant or even glamorous titles (Royal Fine Art Commission, or Standing Commission for Museums and Galleries), occupy these stately houses, does not exactly seem to hum. Yet at No. 4, as you may note from a plaque, de Gaulle had his headquarters in the war, on a site where Palmerston lived for nearly twenty years (their ghosts must, to put it mildly, clash); and, behind a most staid façade at No. 16 is the most famous of London gambling clubs: Crockford's. Founded in 1827, by William Crockford (said to have died of a broken heart after his horse lost the Derby to a ringer), the club boomed after the new Betting and Gaming Act of 1960. Carlton House Gardens have been enlivened in 1968 by two immigrants: the Royal Society, and, in ambitiously adapted new quarters, the Institute of Contemporary Arts (entrance, down Waterloo Steps and to the left, in the Mall). The Royal Society, founded in 1660 and deriving from a shadow group meeting in young Christopher Wren's rooms, is still a focus of the most eminent scientists in Britain (it has a remarkable collection of portraits of past Fellows, including Wren, Newton, Sir Humphry Davy).

At the west end of the Gardens, by way of contrast, is the memorial statue to George VI, looking out over St. James's Park, with a spruce terrace and a flight of steps down to the Mall, rather meanly managed in austerity days. Under the trees in the Gardens, the statues: Lord Curzon, aristocratic, regal almost, if rather small in big robes, and (flanking Waterloo Place, some with their heads in the trees) Empire builders and explorers peering ferociously out from the prison of their effigies.

Here pause for reflection, with the Athenaeum Club on your west and the former United Service Club to your east, for you are on the brink of St. James's proper. An American once told me that two of the main reasons he liked London were its quiet and its exotic quality. Neither, for Londoners, seem notable traits of their city; yet, relatively in terms of the great metropolises of the world, London has both, and both are still to be found—for a few years yet perhaps—especially in St. James's. Quiet has withdrawn only very recently, with the routing of buses, from Pall Mall and even St. James's Street, but it still can hang, almost tangible, in the by-ways and back-waters, and at evening and early morning in its heart. At nights and at week-ends there is a divinely urban hush in which individual footsteps take on again their magic and human resonance. This is still essentially a male district, laid out for the service, well-being and pleasure of the English gentleman. Here, if nowhere else, you must realise that the embodiment, if not the spirit, of the English upper-class male still persists. Here he can buy, bespoke, his hats, his shirts, his riding-boots; his cigars, wine and spirits, his English eighteenth-century old masters; snuff-boxes, silver, even, still, his swords. The taste catered for is that of the connoisseur, the bon-vivant, of traditional background and with a house in the country. Modern art is only beginning to infiltrate into the St. James's dealers from Bond Street and Mayfair. Though Turkish baths yield to saunas, here, at Floris, he can buy hair lotions of the most antique and expensive distinction; his flavour in St. James's, though gradually becoming diluted, persists. Here he is still to be seen, dusted, darkly tailored, wearing the delicate, almost imperceptible shadow of his perfect shave as a plum wears its bloom; pinkish in the face, with the purpling of club lunches beginning (if he's still young) to mantle the little veins on the cheekbones; a crisp zest in his tie, his cuffs showing a half to an inch of virgin linen; the clean fall of his trousers postulates clean limbs beneath. And on his arm, on his head, the insignia: the black umbrella furled tight as a bud; the matt black carapace of the bowler hat. Perfect specimens are rare, but they still exist, with a tailored discipline of presentation that is unique in the world. And they have, of course, outstayed their *raison d'être*; the discipline they perpetuate is that first laid down over a hundred and fifty years ago by Beau Brummell, and its aim was a quintessence of then current fashion, so perfect that it was not even noticeable. Now it is against all contemporary way of life and is most noticeable.

This archaic costume is to be found elsewhere, of course— massed in the City, dotted through the higher echelons of Whitehall. But St. James's is its true habitat, the clubs of St. James's. The clubs began as coffee-houses in the mid-seventeenth century. In the beginning different groups of people began to meet by custom in different coffee-houses; some of them soon became almost political centres or propaganda seminaries, though it is easy to over-estimate their political significance. Still, in 1675, Charles II tried, and failed, to suppress them. At the time of the Dutch wars, Pepys was asked to float atrocity stories in the houses 'where they would spread like leprosy'. Most, then, were in the City. Dryden held sway at Will's in Covent Garden; in St. James's, White's Chocolate House flourished from 1693—by 1755 it had become exclusive, no longer as it were an open café, but a closed shop for members only (this is far from a trades union invention), and the club as we still know it—and White's itself is still on its original site—was in being: a sodality, a solidarity of people with certain common interests. Some of the interests were frivolous—in the eighteenth and nineteenth centuries gambling, in some of them, was the major frivolity, on occasions on a life-destroying scale, more generally as a mild zip in an already deep-seated metropolitan *ennui*: 'Mr. Cavendish bets Mr. H. Brownrigg 2*s*. that he does not kill the blue-bottle fly before he goes to bed.' More essentially, the clubs were clearing-houses of information; here inside information was released and filtered out to the world; climates of opinion brewed. For probably the vast majority of their members today they are no more than luncheon clubs, and status symbols, and of course, hives of agreeable gossip. Yet at several of them it may well be that decisions with national repercussions are confirmed, perhaps even arrived at, almost daily by two or three gathered together in the great dining-rooms, the bars or over the minute cups of (generally indifferent though always scalding) coffee in the saloons.

In the public mind the clubs are faintly absurd, persistently glamorous and perhaps (as all closed shops must be) rather sinister (bastions of privilege and snobbery; hotbeds of black-balling). Be that as it may, to the public eye at least the club façades in St. James's are a pleasure.

Starting from our vantage point at Waterloo Place, let us survey briefly the clubs in their setting. At Waterloo Place, on the east side, the **United Service Club**, founded in 1815 for the great fraternity of veteran officers from the Napoleonic wars, and cased in a massive building that is basically by Nash (1827) but more obviously of Decimus Burton's alterations of 1842: Doric columns, Corinthian portico, an interior of vastness with a most ample staircase, and portraits about that seem to be mainly of uniforms, plumes and face-hair. But where now the portraits, and where their living heirs—generals, admirals, air-marshals? In late 1975 the unthinkable occurred: the Senior fell victim to the wasting disease of London clubs, and died. Its stately physical shell remains, but, at the time of this revision, void.

Opposite, the **Athenaeum**, in paler stucco with a Wedgwood-like panathenaic frieze over the main windows—a pronouncedly neo-grecian flavour with its gilt statue of Athene. It was built by Decimus Burton (1829–30), for an artistic, literary and scientific clientèle, and its initial committee included Sir Thomas Lawrence, Sir Humphry Davy (of the lamp) and Sir Walter Scott. The Athenaeum's popular reputation nowadays, perhaps not without all reason, is that of *the* centre of back-stage but top-level administrative manoeuvre, diplomacy and intrigue. The leading civil servants belong; so do distinguished scientists, politicians, eminent lawyers and of course the admirably picturesque bishops. The walls closely resemble those of the nineteenth-century rooms of the National Portrait Gallery—Darwin looms over you in the entrance hall, but the Drawing Room on the first floor is, quite simply and beyond argument, one of the grandest rooms in all London.

Westwards down Pall Mall the main concentration is on the left (south) side. Next to the Athenaeum, the **Travellers'** (1829–32) and then the **Reform** (1841) announce a departure in the architecture of clubs; both by Sir Charles Barry, supreme master of Parliamentary Gothic, they are on the contrary, and as distinct from the Hellene echoes of the Athenaeum, pure reflections of the High Renaissance, of Italian *palazzi*. The Travellers', modest in its small elegance but immensely smart, founded for gentlemen who had made the Grand Tour and still with a mileage qualification necessary for membership, is fairly expensive, but both easy in manner and very sophisticated. The Reform is a much more massive symmetrical statement on the same theme; founded in 1832, and the premier Liberal club, as its name implies. Then bleakly intrudes a slab of newness with dead window sockets and cretinously low forehead, offices that replace the blitzed Carlton Club. Next comes the Royal Automobile Club,

Leicester Square in spring. St James's Park in winter

ROYAL LONDON. The gates to Green Park, and through them the sober façade of Buckingham Palace. *Below*, the Queen, returning from the Trooping of the Colour, rides back behind the tide of her massed music

elephantine in Edwardian francophile opulence: in the pediment high on its façade you can see a naked Italianate cherub or putto at the wheel of what looks like the original T-model Ford. Immediately after, a ghost of the late seventeenth century—the façade of Schomberg House, a sobriety, among so much stucco and masonry, of red-brown brick of domestic proportions, and porches with caryatids; much restored, and its inside gutted and re-filled with modern offices—but Gainsborough lived here after he moved from Bath in 1774. Farther down the last of the clubs, this side of the road, is the cumbersomely named *United Oxford and Cambridge University Club* which is what its name implies (rather pretty little panels inset high on the façade include Shakespeare and Orpheus, more liberally, for they do not strictly belong). On the north side of the road, the only remaining club in full possession of its site was the **Junior Carlton,** with tremendous pillars and cast-iron torches that could flare with gas-jets; it began in 1864 simply to cope with the waiting list of the Carlton proper, and so is Tory; it has now been redeveloped into a vast mixed-purpose pile.

Otherwise, on the north side and some of the south, insurance reigns supreme, though some trade establishments devoted to individual service of high quality still remain. At its west end, tucked rather obscurely into the corner of Marlborough Gate, Pall Mall has the entrance to **Marlborough House**, designed (1710) by Wren though bloated by subsequent alterations. Edward VII lived here for years as Prince of Wales, but it is most sharply associated perhaps with two famous women: its termagant creator, Sarah, Duchess of Marlborough, and the late Queen Mary; its best features are a very sumptuous hall and staircase, tumescent with horses' rumps, in huge frescoes of Marlborough's victories (by Laguerre), good iron work and a beautiful allegorical ceiling of classic monumentality, painted originally for the Queen's House at Greenwich by one of Charles I's imports from Italy, Gentileschi. The house has been restored and adapted as a sort of warren of *pieds-à-terre* for Commonwealth Prime Ministers on their visits to London, but it is opened to the public when circumstances permit. Alongside, in Marlborough Gate that leads through into the Park, stands the **Queen's Chapel**, genuinely by Inigo Jones (*c.* 1626–7); it is still used for services and is otherwise occasionally visitable on Marlborough House tours, and should be seen: the first classical church built in England, small, but of a massive proportion and severe simplicity that is ultimately sumptuous. And outside, in strong contrast, a complex, fluent memorial in art nouveau bronze to Queen Alexandra (by Gilbert).

And then, over the road, the original *raison d'être* of the whole quarter, at the junction of Pall Mall and St. James's Street: the blue-diapered red brick, with its pale stone edgings, of **St. James's Palace** itself. Built by Henry VIII, the handsome gate-tower that closes the vista from St. James's with its ornate clock is about the only visible remnant of its original fabric. The rest has been much altered and remodelled, but was never very grand in scale. Inside, an original and magnificent painted ceiling (doubtfully ascribed to Holbein, 1540) survives in the Chapel Royal, where, at Epiphany each year, amidst song, gold, frankincense and myrrh are still regally offered; there are grand staterooms, from the period after the fire at Whitehall when for a century and more St. James's was the main royal residence in London—by Wren, by Kent—and even (decorations) by William Morris. These are only visitable on very rare occasions, but the rambling courts and precincts of the Palace are for the curious pedestrian fascinating enough. The Monarch no longer lives here, though the Court is still officially the Court of St. James, to which visiting ambassadors are accredited. But Mary I died here, and the Hanoverians lived here until Victoria moved to Buckingham Palace; commodious, it could house also the Royal mistresses like George I's—the Schulenburg, Duchess of Kendal (German) and Miss Brett (English). The Old Pretender was born here, but so was George IV; more movingly, it was here that Charles I spent the last days of his life before walking, one cold winter morning, across the Park to his death on the scaffold at Whitehall in 1649. Now it is a lowish ramble of brick courtyards, where the stamp of the bear-skinned guards echoes, and tourist cameras click; its windows and doors are firmly closed, private, and bear fabulously polished brass plates that can announce, improbably but as a matter of fact, statements such as: Yeomen of the Guard. The complex involves Ambassadors' Court, York House, Friary Court (where the guard gets changed at 10.30 when the sovereign is not at Buckingham Palace, and whence, from the balcony, new Kings and Queens are proclaimed). Here are the headquarters of the Gentlemen at Arms and the Yeomen of the Guard, better known as beef-eaters (?'*buffetiers du roy*'), each body with its picturesque and antique uniform. Here is the Lord Chamberlain, controlling the public aspects of royal hospitality, though he has now ceased, after centuries, his practice of rather oddly, stubbornly —and without thanks—blue-pencilling the more advanced plays before they were allowed to reach the public stage. The whole Palace area is weird, tantalisingly accessible yet inaccessible, as if a stage set on which the characters never appear.

The Palace does not cease, but seems to evolve westwards until halted by the trees of Green Park. At Stable Yard Gate, Clarence House, built in 1825 for the Duke of Clarence (later William IV), is now the home of the Queen Mother. All very withdrawn, at this point; all traffic seems chauffeur driven, and a horse and hansom would not surprise; a backwater in the corner where two parks meet. Cleveland Row: **Lancaster House.** A mad place, madly splendid; conceived for another royal brother (Duke of York, he of the column), basically by Smirke, after 1841. Severe externally, with giant capacious porticoes, solid, squarely free-standing; but inside a famously ample staircase under a formidable central lantern, doubling back on itself among panelled marbles and shiny copies of Veronese, and a long gallery on the first floor. A ripe sumptuousness of the early Victorian, it was a focal point of high Victorian social and cultural life when it belonged to the Dukes of Sutherland; it now houses government receptions and congresses. It is often open to the public at week-ends, and is well worth a stare. In Cleveland Place, hard by, another of Sir Charles Barry's *palazzi*, Bridgewater House (1849), extremely rich and massive, yet with an austerity and crisp detailing still unchallenged by the taste that prompted the Baroque flowerings of the Lancaster House interior; now given over to commerce, but once it was the home of the extraordinary Ellesmere (or Bridgewater) collection of Old Masters. Beyond is Green Park.

Coming back to **St. James's Street**, one can consider it fragmentarily, hotch-potch that it now is, studded with individual felicities. The sense of scale, the relation of window apertures and height of houses to width of roadway and to one another—that still persists in Pall Mall—has long been lost to St. James's Street as it mounts to Piccadilly. A street to dive off from, into the narrow creeks that lead to Green Park, or into the shops and clubs. It is also changing fast; the handsome Norman Shaw building, bold red brick banded with stone, on the Pall Mall corner is mortally threatened, though the equally fine Shaw Post Office on the opposite corner still holds; **Boodle's** is now almost surrounded by the new Economist buildings by A. and P. Smithson in a fascinating contrast of old and the very good new. On the left going up, three clubs: the **Union**, in floral High Victorian, then chaste Palladian (once the **Bath**), and then the **Carlton**. But over the road, hanging on among the slabby masonry, some rare survivals of late eighteenth-century trade: wine at Berry Bros & Rudd, and hats of course at Lock & Co.—with a famous interior, and all the charm of a miniature, with its mere three and a half stories; note the lettering on the board. Close by, but concealed through an easily overlookable arch, an odd little enclave, charmingly informal compared with the pomp of St. James's Street outside—**Pickering Place**, just four little eighteenth-century houses in brick; placid, but here the last duel in London is said to have been fought. In Byron House (No. 8 St. James's Street) nothing is left of Byron's residence except a singularly brutal plaque of the poet's head in the hall, but in a house on this site, in 1811, he awoke one morning to find himself famous. Over the road, where the Union Club now is, Gibbon died in 1794. About here, even if clubless, you can eat, in style, though fish-famous Pruniers closed in 1976. At Chubb's you can buy a safe. And then, you can dive off left into **St. James's Place**, a narrow, well-painted, well-groomed alley of escape towards the Park. Note No. 14. Almost all offices of course now, but in houses of chaste domestic proportions, and at the end on the left a brilliant aristocratic London palace (by Vardy, 1765), **Spencer House.** Of this the façade is the real magic, bearing white statues that hover in the air when seen through the green of trees from Green Park. St. James's Place is select—next to Spencer House is one of the best blocks of luxury flats (by D. Lasdun) built in London since the war, a massively severe luxury (around £70,000 each, the flats) to prove, hard alongside the lighter elegance of Spencer House, that the twentieth century can when it tries, match and marry in quality the eighteenth.

Back in St. James's, clubs again, the famous trio that

announce themselves to the eye by a distinction that is almost one of tailoring rather than of architecture. **Brooks's**, on the left (by Holland, 1788), originally the great Whig club where the bristling black personage of its co-founder, Charles James Fox, was to be found, a little gross perhaps in contrast with its palest beige brick walls and excellently mannered pilasters (he's still there, but subdued into white marble, in a bust by Nollekens). More or less opposite on the other side of the road, **Boodle's**, once a great betting club, where Brummell gambled, now fairly sedate and full of gentlemen up from the country (observe them, as they observe you, through the famous bow window on the ground floor). Then, near the top, **White's**, with still a very hard-drinking and conservative tradition, perhaps the most arrogant of all London clubs (it was on the steps of White's that, in 1950, a drunken member kicked Aneurin Bevan, that Socialist).

Near the top of the street on the left, Bennet Street takes you into Arlington Street and out into Piccadilly by the Ritz. Arlington Street includes still some eighteenth-century interiors of grandeur, including one at No. 22, by William Kent, built for the expert Whig financial manipulator, Henry Pelham (and now, not inaptly, housing the Eagle Star Insurance). The main pillar of the Whig hierarchy, Sir Robert Walpole, lived at No. 5 for the last three years of his life, 1742–5, and his equally famous son, Horace, was born where now is No. 22.

Now, east of St. James's Street, we aim for the kernel of St. James's proper. Deep and narrow between its houses, Jermyn Street runs clear through to the far limit at Lower Regent Street (but vice versa if you are in a car, for it is one way west-bound); south of Jermyn Street is St. James's Square. The germ indeed of fashionable West London is hidden here; this was agricultural land in 1640, but almost fully built over by 1680. Its promoter was a stout aristocrat, Henry Jermyn, Earl of St. Albans, who, having supported Charles I's widow, Henrietta Maria, through miserable years of exile in France (and according to some, actually married her), returned in 1660 and forthwith acquired rights over St. James's; the success of his speculation was secured by the gravitation westwards of moneyed householders after the Great Fire of 1666, and St. James's became the fashionable address for many of Charles II's courtiers, including his mistresses. Though it has its half-concealed crevices and inconsequential yards, the plan of St. James's is still much as laid out, and it *is* a plan, about the symmetry of the Square itself. Only Inigo Jones's venture in Covent Garden precedes it in date. And the plan was of course residential (the shopping services were supplied by St. James's Market, which vanished when Nash resolved its labyrinthine complexities into the thoroughfare of Regent Street); and grandly residential— 'palaces fit for the dwellings of noblemen and persons of quality'. So it remained through the eighteenth century, its lesser streets holding lesser houses that were still commodious enough to hold gentlemen such as Boswell up for the Season. Thence it came to be famous and notorious, as an area where bachelor gentlemen could find chambers, and there still clings an aura of moneyed, fairly discreet, loose-living about Jermyn Street.

In the nineteenth century the 'palaces' in the Square itself began to give way to clubs which in the twentieth century moved out again as the financial pressure of the real estate speculators grew and business moved in. The area is now in a precarious state of transition; the high quality shops, smallish, with traditional standards of individual service and expense, still continue, but most of the residents have fled. Before ten and after six the area is empty; officially its unique character is recognised, but too often the recognition is mere lip-service and development continues often irresponsibly.

Jermyn Street is no pleasure as architectural progress, but at ground level its shops—still almost all small—will magisterially enlarge covetousness. The street is in part the backside of Piccadilly, to which it is joined, notably, by two arcades, Piccadilly and Prince's. The former is very pretty doll's-house taste: black and white marble floor, and a ripple of bow-fronted, shining-glass, shop windows down which the eye runs with the pleasure of running a stick down iron railings, and a top floor apparently for dwarfs tucked under the roof. Only a few favourite establishments in Jermyn Street can here be mentioned. Floris (No. 89) which has dispensed celebrated unguents and lotions for men since the Regency; hand-made boot and shoe shops, the pipe specialists Dunhill; sweater specialists, tie specialists, noble wine-sellers; Paxton and Whitfield for cheese and ham—the queue that tends to form there before the week-end must be one of the most distinguished in England. The Savoy Turkish baths at No. 91 have faded into myth; the legendary Cavendish Hotel (corner of Duke Street) has been demolished and built again, with the same name but in lush anonymous international style. Other famous restaurants, such as the Ecu de France, still survive. And religion, like a phoenix, has been resurrected from the blitz in the parish church of **St. James**, the Jermyn Street entrance to which is just east of the opening to Prince's Arcade. Although the blitzed spire on its squat tower was at last restored in 1968, with its hard, new-pointed red brick the church is not comely from the outside, but the restored interior goes far to justify the opinion of its architect, Sir Christopher Wren, that in it he best realised his ideal conceptions of a parish church (here, for once and unlike almost all his City churches, his plan was not pre-conditioned by the quirks of a confined site). Built in 1682–4, it served this then new but at once and enduringly highly fashionable area, and it is a rich church. Although the plain exterior reflects a fairly tight budget in building, inside it is large, airy and of most handsome spaciousness; its galleries, its barrel-vaulted roof on the Corinthian pillars, its paint and gilt, encompass a rather worldly piety with sumptuousness. Many of those who were baptized or buried here have names that still echo beyond their parish, but in a way the two most typical are James Gillray, marked by a stone renewed there recently (Piccadilly side), the greatest and one of the most outspoken of visual satirists after Hogarth: and actually under the altar, that reprobate, profligate, gambling aristocrat of Piccadilly, the Duke of Queensberry, better known as 'Old Q'. Yet this church can on occasions— baptisms, the weddings for which it is famous, memorial services—conduct its ceremony with such perfect style that the ritual of music, flowered hats, morning coats and top hats, can transcend its social surface gloss, and seem a true performance to a higher glory. A memorial service I once attended there, on a brightly merciless spring day, seemed to me, in its exquisitely restrained and modulated expression of a genuine emotion, to be as fine a valedictory as any mortal man could wish. And, salvaged from the blitz, there is still the copious fluent harvest exuberance of carved flowers and fruit on the reredos; in the organ (by Renatus Harris and once in Whitehall Palace) was found buried during repairs in 1897, in its own minute and particular coffin, the skeleton of a bird.

At the east end of Jermyn Street, past the back entrance of Simpsons, Piccadilly, small shops again, an aroma of cigars and leather and of gentlemen having their hair cut, apparently being censed the while. To the north, a simply stunning vista from Eagle Place across Piccadilly to the columned bridges of Regent Street melodramatic in the sky; to the south an odd opening called Babmaes Street, which immortalises Charles II's most trusted pimp, Baptist May. But to reach the heart of the district, descend south through Duke of York Street; on your right, the Red Lion has one of the best and ripest of late Victorian pub interiors—such deep glossy mahogany, such glitter of carved glass. Duke of York Street opens then upon **St. James's Square**, on the central rounded garden edged with its flowering trees, through which spring washes almond, cherry, lilac, laburnum, before the great planes in the middle set into their full summer foliage that rains elegiac about the statue, dark, high and tossing on its plinth, of the equestrian William III—a very belated rococo-tinged statue (by Bacon, 1807), but a most successful one. The garden is private, its lawn reserved for pigeons and for those who work in the offices in the Square. Its walls, the houses of the Square, are set back at a handsome distance, and though the skyline is lumpish to the south, and jagged with intrusion to the east, north and west still present a comely old order and elegance in the main. It is the oldest of London squares, and though nothing survives from its origins in the 1660s, there is enough from the eighteenth century. On a summer morning or evening, when the offices are empty, you can still walk the Square at ease, and even catch in the echo of your footsteps perhaps a rumour of its most famous anecdote—of Dr. Johnson and the poet Richard Savage, both young, poor and still unknown to London and to fame, walking about the Square for hours in the night with nowhere to sleep: 'not at all depressed by their situation, but in high spirits, and brimful of patriotism . . . as they traversed the solitary square, inveighed against the prime minister, and resolved they would stand by their country . . .' There is no record of the response of the distinguished aristocracy trying to get to sleep in the houses about, but that they were anyway distinguished is reasonably certain: in 1721 the Square housed, among others, six British dukes and seven earls; some years later (1738) a king, George III, was born there (in

Norfolk House, now demolished). At the close of the nine-teenth century a number of private residents were still left, of aristocratic blood and doubtless whim as well (like Lady Strafford, who in 1899 was causing concern as she 'continually used the Square for cycling'); but now the Square is business, though the London Library, the biggest private lending library in the country and an inestimable boon, at No. 14, and No. 4 (formerly Arts Council), are notable exceptions.

Another exception—to look now at some individual houses is the plain but elegant dark brick of Nos. 9 and 10, on the corner of Duke of York Street as you come into the Square; now called Chatham House (an institution for the study of International affairs), it was built about 1736 and since has housed three prime ministers: Pitt the Elder, Earl of Chatham; Derby; and for a brief year, 1890, the Grand Old Man himself, Gladstone. On the west side, a magnificently assured façade by James ('Athenian') Stuart, once the town house of the Earls of Lichfield, is now an Assurance Company, but has its interior well-preserved; a very pure, very classical, gentle-man's town house of 1763. Then there is the opening west into King Street, with still a distinctly St. James's atmosphere, though the St. James's Theatre has fallen to the speculator and the south side is largely re-developed, but there are antique shops, and on the north (No. 1c) lived Louis Napoleon, awaiting his coup d'état between 1846 and 1848. The street leads through to St. James's Street, with two tributaries to the north, Duke and Bury Streets, both rich in art dealers and bootmakers. There is Leggatt's, old-established specialists in English masters, in St. James's Street itself, and Hazlitt, Gooden and Fox in Bury Street and L. Koetser in Duke Street (he who bid over a quarter of a million pounds for the Duke of Westminster's Rubens 'Adoration' at Sotheby's), and others, clustered about the central St. James's art hive, the premises of **Christie's**, the auctioneers, in King Street, now moved back on their original site after the blitz. From Reynolds and Gainsborough (who painted the first Christie) onwards, the luminaries of the art world have dropped in at Christie's, and it's still a fascinating haunt—and free, unless you lose your head and start to wave a catalogue (London sales are generally in the morning, so the best time to view is the afternoon). At the west end of King Street, cutting south to Pall Mall, is one of those cheerful, unexpected and busy

London alleyways, with cheap cafés; the local shopping centre for ordinaries.

Back in the Square, towards Pall Mall, No. 20, an original Adam façade (1775–89), repeated in 1938 on to No. 21; the south and east of the Square is mainly rebuilt, but in the north-east corner, at No. 4, are elegant unspoiled premises, built probably by Shepherd (of Shepherd's Market in Mayfair) in 1725, with a beautiful plaster staircase hall, and a fine drawing-room where chamber concerts and poetry recitals were held. The house was familiar from the frequent exhibitions organised there by the Arts Council till it departed in 1968. And so, from St. James's, eastwards down Charles II Street, down that most urbanely handsome of London vistas to the Haymarket Theatre, exit whistling:

> She shall have all that's fine and fair,
> And ride in a coach to take the air,
> And have a house in St. James's Square . . .

Alas, she will not, even if she be a duchess, though if she's a typist they will welcome her anywhere here in working hours.

CHAPTER FIVE

Mayfair and Perimeter—Park Lane, Oxford Street, Regent Street

꙳

MAYFAIR itself has no official definition in terms of being a postal district or a borough. It is of course postally and positively part of W.1, the most aristocratic part of aristocratic W.1, in fashion at least if no longer so conclusively so in pintage of blue blood. Mayfair is glamour, its name synonymous all over the world with high life, and much of it is still residential though the residences are mostly flats or hotels now, and the individual mansions shrink to the fabulously priced minute mews houses. Mayfair is still certainly expensive, the most smart in London. The source of its name, however, is not so; the May Fair was an annual event which took place in an open space between Berkeley Street and Park Lane until its goings-on became intolerable and it was suppressed in George III's time as a public nuisance. Shepherd Market (to which we shall come in due course) marks the spot more or less, but it is discreeter now than when Ned Ward described it about 1700—'I never in my life saw such a number of lazy-look'd rascals, and so hateful a throng of beggarly, sluttish strumpets, who were a scandal to the Creation, mere antidotes against lechery, and enemies to cleanliness.' But that was before the aristocracy moved in on West Mayfair. The plan that settled on the fields of Mayfair between 1700 and 1750 is still there. Old Bond Street had started north from Piccadilly, to be continued about 1721 by New Bond Street up to Oxford Street, the axis of asymmetrical Mayfair. About it were plotted the focal points: between 1715 and 1750, Hanover Square grew up in the north-east, Berkeley Square to the west with Grosvenor north of it; in the extreme west the busy little hive of shops at Shepherd Market. Among them, in their gardens, the great free-standing houses of the great aristocrats—Devonshire House between Piccadilly and south Berkeley Square, with Lansdowne House; Chesterfield House away over to the west; on the fringe of Hyde Park the

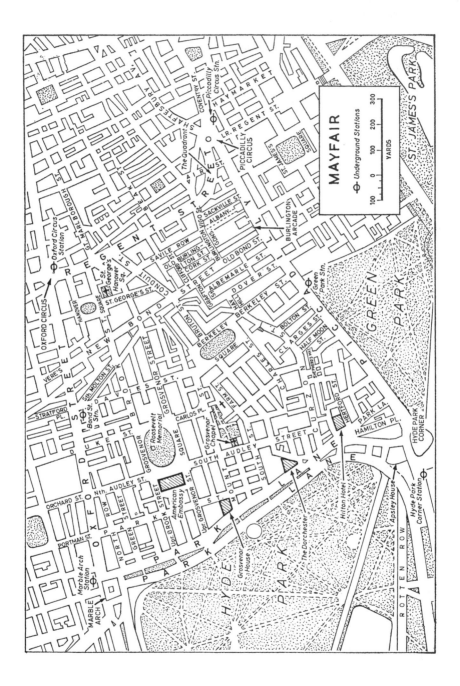

pompous and ornate nineteenth-century giants, often in the
elaborate Italian style, like Grosvenor House with its colonnade, containing the Duke of Westminster and a great art
collection, or Dorchester House that housed the world-
famous Holford collection. But by 1800, the character of
Mayfair had settled for a greater density, terrace-like frontages
of four-storey houses with neat roof lines lining streets and
squares echoing with horses' hoofs; often narrow but grand
houses, the town abodes of aristocracy and high gentry.
Order was well-established, footpads and highwaymen on the
way out, though not so long before Dr. Johnson, venturing
farther west than his usual beat and in one of his brusque
moods, grappled with 'a sturdy thief who had stolen his handkerchief in Grosvenor Square', seized him by the collar, shook
him violently, 'then letting him loose, gave him such a smack
in the face and sent him reeling off the pavement'. Since then,
though constantly building and re-building on itself, Mayfair
has not looked back.

Now Mayfair is like a chocolate stuffing of the most various,
rare and expensive ingredients, and if not officially defined,
in fact it is clearly contained by the more commonly grained,
and sometimes positively gross, casing of Piccadilly (south),
Park Lane (west), Oxford Street (north) and Regent Street
(east). But these great thoroughfares offer an excellent foil in
contrast to the delicacies which they wrap about in Mayfair
itself, and I propose to examine them first (except Piccadilly,
for which see Chapter 2), while the appetite is still robust.
If you are content with simply looking, both outer and inner
parts of the area can be covered comfortably in a morning or
afternoon, but should you succumb to the lure of shops and
start diving in, it will take very much longer and you will be
much poorer. For the delicate, the first part may be omitted,
and the interior broached from p. 81 onwards.

Start up **Park Lane** from its Hyde Park Corner (south) end.
For the corner itself, and Apsley House, see p. 36; Park Lane
itself is no lane, and the park has been pushed back from it
like a receding tide by the recent Hyde Park Corner/Marble
Arch traffic 'improvement', which has turned the lane itself
and the outer road of the Park's edge into a hurtling double
carriage-way. The south end of the lane is preoccupied with the
contortions of this double road and is dominated by newish
(finished 1963) 328 feet high, 30 storeyed and 512 guest-

roomed London **Hilton** hotel—not large by American standards but very American by London standards, and yet to be
assimilated entirely into the townscape, as if a lone rather
fancy trial tooth awaiting the insertion of the rest of the den-
ture. But this is the logical development of what has been
happening in Park Lane. From the eighteenth century on,
great private palaces went up on the edge of the Park, and the
lane was select. In this century, they sold out (one should not
perhaps grieve too much for their owners; the Grosvenor
estates in 1962 were still reckoned to hold some £20,000,000
worth of property in Mayfair and Belgravia); and in their place
and in their names the palace luxury hotels went up—
Dorchester, a little north of the Hilton; Grosvenor House, a
little north of that. About the last of the private houses,
Londonderry, with its grand and famous ballroom on its
first floor, was sold at auction in 1962; the sale lasted only
five minutes but the price was half a million. Park Lane is
now a centre for dances, charity balls and commemoration
banquets; conventions. Premises that are not hotels are mostly
offices. Yet here and there a Mayfair flavour seeps through;
particularly at the north end there survive still some of those
rather weird bow-fronted houses of Brighton-like elegance,
and suddenly Park Lane is a promenade beneath their bright
windows and canopied balconies, a strand beyond which,
and beyond the stream of cars in the road, the green of the
Park has an almost marine sparkle. At night on a warm
summer evening, near dinner time, glamour is manifest as
men in black and white, with sleek hair and shining shoes,
and women in the butterfly brilliance of evening dress shine
briefly between taxi and hotel portico, or emerge on foot from
the narrow streets of Mayfair.

At its northern extremity Park Lane again convulses for the
traffic climax of Marble Arch (see p. 171), but we swing right
into **Oxford Street**. The change of mood is violent, and as you
stare down the dip of the road between its brutal, sometimes
brutish banked emporia and up again towards Oxford Circus,
your spirits may flag. Oxford Street is not an easy road for the
fastidious; it is sometimes cited as the symbol of anonymous
hideousness and soullessness alleged to be overtaking London,
and it is true at least that to attempt one's own pace through
the drifts of people is to court apoplexy by frustration, even
though it is now in part pedestrianised. This is bazaar;

people seem to float, slow and turgid with the swaying drift of jelly-fish in the doldrums, along and in and out of the maws of the bazaar. Here the principles of window dressing are quantity and glitter—hypnotise your customer. It seems to work; the crowds eddy into voracious grottoes of chromium, neon and glass scooped into the façades, where thousands of shoes gape for each pair of feet. Here there is more of everything, and the newest of mass-produced everything a fortnight perhaps before it reaches the suburbs. Here are department stores as big as towns: C. & A.; the great cliff of columns of mighty Selfridge's; Marshall and Snelgrove, D. H. Evans (first in London to install escalators to all floors); John Lewis resurgent in sleek contemporary from its blitzed ruins.

Selfridge's, on your left near the west end, is perhaps still the key, an imperial palace of trade set up by the American, Gordon Selfridge, in 1909, when the west end of Oxford Street was still of little importance. Whether or not it is still the biggest and the mostest, it set the original standard of exuberance, politeness and of quantity; it was perhaps the first to encourage shoppers to drift without being importuned to buy—a market but also a spectacle. 'This,' said an enraptured French boy recently, 'is the best museum we've visited yet.' Thus Bleriot's aeroplane was on view there the day after it flew the Channel; it was in Selfridge's that Baird gave the first public demonstration of television. It established perhaps even the characteristic basic smell of the great London stores, basically canned, yet plushy, except where the soap and cosmetics counters drench the air. If it be true that Selfridge's and its rivals along the road tend to lack subtlety, it is also true that neither they nor their street can, once you have happened on them, be ignored; at their busiest times, as on a pre-Christmas shopping day, they are as compulsive as a segment of Dante's inferno. It was not originally Oxford Street by name; its true and appalling title is Tyburn Road. 'This street has its Name,' says a 1708 guide, 'as being the next street to Tyburn, the place for Execution of all such Malefactors (generally speaking) as have committed Facts worthy of Death.'

In your course east towards Oxford Circus, you should take your eyes off the shop windows for a little enclave, just beyond Selfridge's, called Stratford Place, a cul-de-sac in the shadow of that great treasure house of shoes, Lilley and Skinner's;

across its end, unreal almost as a stage drop, is the façade of
Derby House, Adam-ish, with quiet Ionic pilasters and a
pediment, a model of discretion that may linger at the back of
your eyes as you push on down past the commercial business
in Oxford Street, each shop striving to out-do its neighbour,
past the traffic lights that seem to come every fifty yards, past
the street-hawkers, the people and again and again the shoes
(one can come to think Oxford Street is a fetishist's temple of
shoes)—past all this to Oxford Circus where you turn right,
down **Regent Street**, the tempo again shifts; the crowd,
though it may well be thick, is less solid and one can make out
individual human beings darting to and fro in their egocentric
way. And although this too is the home of many vast and
famous emporia, the tone is generally almost genteel in comparison with the bazaar-wonderland of Oxford Street. It is
also much more solid-seeming, with a more or less uniform roofline, and a certain coherence of line and style.
This clarity reflects in faint degree the nature of its original
creation, for Regent Street was the middle phase in John
Nash's triumphal way for the Prince Regent from St. James's
Park to Regent's Park (see p. 247); it was drawn starting with a
clean, scimitar-like curve from Piccadilly Circus—the Quadrant, lined with colonnades—and then running straight to the
conical spire of All Souls in Langham Place well north of
Oxford Circus. This was the defining eastern boundary of
Mayfair, ordered and new, separating it from the old, un-
disciplined and teeming jungle of Soho to the east, and as such
Regent Street remains. Its architecture, though, is no longer the
bright variegation of stucco, but the massive stone facings
that we saw fit to substitute for it earlier this century.

In Regent Street, as in Oxford Street, you can buy almost
anything: motor cars, clothes, silver trophies, fridges, whole
kitchens, cameras, jewels, china, toys, corsets—everything,
until your only want is to get away from it all. In which
Regent Street also specialises; any one of a number of tourist
agents and tourist offices of divers nationalities scattered up
and down it will be delighted to tell you how to get to heaven
out of London. Though it be more and more the home of
great emporia, survivors of small shops of specialist quality
still linger, like Negretti & Zambra with their name like an
incantation and their windows broody with owl-faced baro-
meters. But mostly they are bigger even if specialising, and

many of them are household names throughout England, like Hamley's for toys (a magnificent inferno when Christmas is near, full of children and middle-aged men making sure that the toys they are buying for children really work); Lawley's for china; Wartski's for fabergé. For men's clothes off-the-peg, Austin Reed's, Aquascutum (and nearer Piccadilly on the left), the shop that deals only in trousers. And then the great stores, from Dickins and Jones at the northern end to Swan and Edgar's on Piccadilly corner. My personal favourite is Liberty's, about half-way down—an architectural extravaganza of mad folly; Imperial Roman almost with grand columns worn high on its breast, and on top the refreshing if not entirely original fancy of statuary leaning over the balustrade, contemplating with studied calm the rat race below. (A bridge links this bit on to the Tudor bit behind—see p. 55.) Inside is a series of labyrinthine Aladdin caves, enclosed courtyards with balconies strewn with luxury, swathes of silk, sheen of glass and metal.

All these and many more you will see as you wander from Oxford Circus to Piccadilly Circus. But pause at the Quadrant, that broad sweep at the end that takes you round to Piccadilly; while one cannot but regret its former Regency colonnades, their replacement has its virtues, especially in its earliest part (by the Circus) which is by Norman Shaw in a mood of bold drama, romantically and splendidly picturesque. Look up, in a gusty winter dusk, at the columns bridged mightily over Air Street, with the cloud racing beyond. Walk up from the rounded prow of Swan and Edgar's; by its bright windows, newspapers placard disaster, but confidently the vast sweep of the B.O.A.C. plate-glass window advertises escape; then down a narrow slot, Man in Moon Alley. And over the road, restored somewhat to its 1890s brilliance, is the Café Royal, where George Moore, Beerbohm, Augustus John, Orpen and many other littérateurs and artists used to talk and drink, and occasionally eat.

But it is time to engage with Mayfair proper. So from Regent Street, at the north end of the Quadrant by Austin Reed's, enter in by the narrow slot of Vigo Street. At once on your left the straight run of Sackville Street, with its plain and modest Georgian frontages (these remained almost unbroached till 1962) all on a domestic scale, though almost all are offices and shops, sets a key of proportion that still survives in many parts of Mayfair. Then as Vigo Street bottlenecks into Burlington Gardens, Savile Row itself is on your right, and on your left between two lodges, almost invisible in their small modesty, the entrance to **Albany** (which we glimpse also from Piccadilly, p. 44); a closed and sternly private vista down the somehow rather sea-sidey central gangway of that monastic-seeming community. If you wish to visit, you have, I'm afraid, to get yourself invited. It is really no more than a lot of flats, but of unusual and exclusive glamour; built in 1770 by Sir William Chambers and converted in 1812 into 'residential chambers for bachelor gentlemen', on a rather collegiate lay-out. Byron is the most romantic of its inmates, but they have also included Macaulay, Gladstone and many famous men of letters—a tradition that has continued till the present day in the persons of writers like J. B. Priestley, and Graham Greene.

Savile Row can need no explanation; as an adjective applied to men's suits it is world famous. It holds (besides the West Central Police Station, the Forestry Commission and, alas, an intruded multi-storey car park) the survivors of gentlemen's tailors of the highest quality. Savile Row in fact rather unfairly hogs the credit, for the great tailors are scattered elsewhere in the area as well. Moreover at least one establishment in Savile Row now sells clothes off-the-peg; in fact, it boasts of so doing. And the women are in there too— one of the top ten London couturiers is in Sheridan's house, Hardy Amies, striped blinds and all. This corner of Mayfair was once the masculine province of the area but is yielding and its glamour has been somewhat diminished, at least for the young, originally by the efflorescence of Carnaby Street over the other side of Regent Street, in the 1960s.

Farther along Burlington Gardens, the ornate Italian of the former first headquarters of London University (1869: studded with statues of international genius from Plato to Goethe, whitish ghosts stained with London black as if by the trail of dark tears), is now an extension of the British Museum, in which the magnificent treasures of its ethnographical collections, from Africa to Polynesia, are at last worthily shown. Then another enclave more feminine perhaps than masculine: the opening into **Burlington Arcade**, that runs through into Piccadilly. A prettiness of duck-egg paint and glass within, and some admirable shop-lettering in gold on black glass surviving to set off gifts to take home, at a price: silver, toys (there's a specialist in toy soldiers), jewels, glass, coloured waistcoats. The Arcade was the brain-child of Lord George Cavendish, supposedly to prevent the rabble throwing rubbish into his garden from that side, though avowedly 'for the gratification of the publick and to give employment to industrious females'. Now two beadles in fancy bowler hats patrol the Arcade for its well-being.

Off the north side of Burlington Gardens go Old Burlington Street and Cork Street, in parallel with Savile Row and similar in atmosphere. At the far end of Burlington Street, Buck's Club, looking almost cosily rural but full of beautifully dressed young men with faces keen as hatchets. In Cork Street the dealers begin, with the speculative succulence of mostly modern art: Roland Browse and Delbanco; the Redfern; the Piccadilly (often rewarding for young and little known painters); Waddington's, sponsors of some of the best British abstract painters like Hilton, and sculptors like Frink. But, moving west along Burlington Gardens, you are brought to a stop at the T-junction at its end: **Bond Street**. Here Old Bond Street joins hands (in a very complicated clasp—the numbering is crazy) with New Bond Street; together they cleave Mayfair north and south in two between Piccadilly and Oxford Street.

Pause. And survey; survey at least your bank balance if not the architecture. Bond Street has never been remarkable architecturally; a critic in 1736 found 'in the whole prodigious length of the two Bond Streets' nothing worthy of attention—'several little attempts there are at foppery in building, but too inconsiderable even for censure'; and it is still mostly so. Bond Street is as it were above architecture, mostly narrow frontages with over-wrought masonry and a jumble of signs and letterings; even the window-dressing is sometimes throw-away, archaic and often in quality incredibly low in relation to Bond Street's stature in world luxury. (Pause again and remember poor Lawrence Sterne, writer of *Tristram Shandy*, who died neglected in this street in February 1768; 'his attendants robbed him even of his gold sleeve-buttons while he was expiring'.) But luxury is really here, and if you are not blasé but still sensitive to it, the Bond Street atmosphere will set your senses twitching, drunk as a water-divining rod exposed to the Pacific. Stand here at this corner on a crisp October morning and watch the moted autumn sun settle on the pavements like gold dust; stand on a fine May morning perhaps a little farther north, at the junction of Bruton Street and Conduit Street (where in *Sense and Sensibility* there was so much setting down and taking up of visitors), and close your eyes: feel that early London sun bland yet zestful on the forehead, inhale the petrol and all the scents of Paris (for Bond Street is not narrowly national), and hear clip-clopping on the pavement, not horses, but the smart trot, toe and high heel together, of a woman in her morning splendour, though perhaps no more, no less, than a shop-girl.

The Bond Street area is the display ground of *parure*, the gilt upon life's lily, in all forms. Jewels, dress, hats, hand-made chocolates. Antique furniture shops (Partridge's, Mallett's); the most expensive of modern (Hille in Albermarle Street); shops like Asprey's that cater still for the wildest whims, even an apparently inexhaustible demand for complex dressing-cases in pig-skin, for swizzle sticks in gold and platinum. The boutiques of the international beauty trade. Gold, diamonds, sapphires; the latest in anti-snatch-and-grab security chains. Money. Books—not ordinary books, Mayfair is not strong on those, but rare books in world famous shops—Sotheran (Sackville Street), Quaritch and Sawyer, Maggs in Berkeley Square. Autographs. Art; millionaires in dinner jackets on hard gilt chairs, sweating, flicking away thousands beneath the flickering closed circuit television at an evening auction sale; the dealers with velvet-hoarse polyglot voices breathing cigar smoke. The smell of paint, artist's paint, marries with the smell of rich people and deep pile carpet, and very heady a concoction it is too.

These establishments that deal in these commodities are, in comparison with the huge stores that fringe Mayfair along Regent Street and Oxford Street, relatively small-premised, select and specialist, though some, like the car shops in Berkeley Square or the dress shops of Fenwick or Wetherall, in size threaten at any moment to bloom into emporia. In Oxford Street you may at times feel that you are merely a permutation of a range of standard measurements; if your particular permutation cannot be matched—be fitted—this will not be due to any failure in the supply offered by the shops—it will be your fault; in fact, you may feel, you are a freak, abnormal. But Mayfair still generally admits each customer as a new, different and unique proposition; it allows for the individual whim, and the personal obstinacies of taste; it deals with the hand-made, the individual order, and is not always to be rushed. Its three best-known long-established hotels are characteristic. Claridge's (Brook Street), comfortable in red-brick and gables, discreetly flush with commissionaires and bell-boys, sumptuous and generally flying, quite negligently, a flag or so of some monarch or ex-monarch or president in residence. The Connaught, in Carlos Place by Grosvenor Square, charmingly late Victorian, unintimidating and personal; and Brown's—that stretch of Dover Street, almost invisible in its discretion, solid and un-hurrying, with world enough and time to read a Henry James novel in, even to *be* a Henry James novel in. In contrast the newer, more American type hotels, the Hilton, the Westbury, even the Dorchester, with their rather mechanical articulation of architecture, seem still to have to settle in.

It is time to walk up Bond Street, the axis of Mayfair. The choice as you start from Piccadilly is bewildering—almost at once in Old Bond Street two formidable specialists, Sac Frères (No. 45) said to be the only specialists in amber in the world (and they include flies, if desired), and Barrett & Son (No. 9) for ivory; and then a sequence of famous names in art-dealing, jewellery and female beauty culture. The Mayfair art-dealers offer through the year (though they tend to be weakest in August and September), shows often of very high quality and often free; pictures are there to be looked at, so do not be dismayed by an aura of grandeur but walk right in and look. At Agnews (No. 43), Old Masters in general and in special (they are one of those firms who are prepared to pay out £100,000 for a few square inches of old paint and cloth apparently without blinking); also for English water-colours and oils, with a most agreeable top gallery, in plushy red with sofas. Marlborough, who have become since the war perhaps the dominant London firm in great international contemporary names; they have under contract many of the leading British artists (non-academic) of the middle generation—Henry Moore, Francis Bacon, Armitage, Pasmore—and they are built into a glossy façade apparently indissolubly with Lloyd's Bank. Enter their public galleries by Albemarle Street. On the other side of the street, Colnaghi's for Old Masters, paintings, drawings and engravings, with a formidable and well-earned reputation for scrupulous scholarship and for quality—their annual shows startle not only the connoisseurs but their rivals in the trade; the New London, a chaste basement de luxe, where the Marlborough displays exhibitions of graphics from all over the world. Then the velvety windows, starred with wealth condensed into the minute brilliance of diamonds, into wrought gold, of Boucheron and of Cartier's; the elegant doors of Elizabeth Arden, Yardley, Max Factor opening to the fountain of eternal youth, and, at the corner of Burlington Gardens, the magnificent folly of Atkinson's with Gothic gable and gilt of 1926, and a flèche with a carillon of twenty-three bells that on rare occasions go off like a musical box, sparkling the air up and down Bond Street.

Beyond Burlington Gardens going north, a bottle-neck, the pavements so medievally narrow that two can barely walk abreast, past ties, shirts, past the broad windows of Asprey's holding their display as if in aspic; past Grafton Street and Clifford Street (some good old houses, and a shop for kilts); Churchill's the night-club, and so down to the Time/Life building on the corner of Bruton Street gazing grimly across at the twin grim Westbury Hotel on the corner of Conduit Street. High on Time/Life is the well-known Henry Moore frieze, difficult to see and lost as sited, but the interior of the building is well worth a look, already almost a period piece of (1952–3) Royal College of Art taste excited by a sudden affluence of American money in the midst of post-war austerity: a big Ben Nicholson painting, a fine Henry Moore reclining figure on the terrace, creating its own characteristic and massive solitude here as the frieze cannot. And so Bond Street continues up to the bleak bright contemporary façade that closes its vista the other side of Oxford Street. On the left, Wildenstein's, Partridge's, and a deliciously slender-stemmed shop window salvaged from an old chemist's shop and inserted into the new (No. 13); the Fine Art Society behind a façade designed by E. W. Godwin; Wallace Heaton for cameras; and so on. On the right, hiding its millions of pounds' annual turn-over behind quaint, antiquated round arches, the auction-rooms of **Sotheby's**.

Sotheby's were originally specialists in rare book auction sales, but particularly since the war they have become the leading art auctioneers in the world. In the reception offices downstairs a constant flow of hopeful owners bring, wrapped in brown paper, old blankets, shopping baskets, what they trust may prove to be the long missing Rembrandt or a unique piece of Chelsea porcelain, equalling x thousand pounds. Upstairs, in the suite of top-lit galleries, throughout the year except August and September, you can see the next sales exposed for viewing and what is equally fascinating (as Rowlandson and Daumier long ago sharply observed), you can see the viewers viewing, the dealers and the connoisseurs in action; stooping, craning, investigating with the aid of a little spit an alleged signature or working at two inches' range through a lens. If you are buying at Sotheby's or in any London auction room, some knowledge is indeed advisable, if only of the accepted shorthand for description. It is not always realised, for example, that in picture sales a painting listed as 'Reynolds' will be what the auctioneers believe to be a genuine picture of Reynolds's period and influenced by his style, but certainly not by him. If it is listed as by 'Sir J. Reynolds', it may be as much as a studio piece, but if it is allowed the full sonority of 'Sir Joshua Reynolds, P.R.A.', then you may, you *may*, be in the presence of paint distributed by the hand of the master himself. It is worth looking in at a sale, but do not get carried away or mesmerised; the speed with which money is bid can be breath-taking, and you can, if you have it, dispose of up to a couple of hundred thousand on one object inside a minute and a half (average speed of a sale is about two lots a minute).

Outside, Bond Street continues undiminished towards Oxford Street; there is Harmer's, the leading stamp auctioneers, there are the finest shoes and linens and clothes for top tots. There is much more, but in limited space I can no longer dwell there but must glance at the north-east corner of Mayfair, Hanover Square. To reach this most profitably, turn up Conduit Street by the Westbury Hotel (Conduit Street has some houses remaining of modest plain elegance; the most elegant and far from modest one (No. 9), by James Wyatt, 1779, and said to be the first stuccoed house in London, has been snapped up and painted up by Dior); almost at once turn left up St. George's Street which funnels the view direct to Hanover Square and its presiding statue of

Pitt, a huge bronze by Chantrey set up in 1831 (and very nearly pulled down forthwith by radicals with ropes). On the right a famous church projects its pillared portico assertively beyond the pavement on to the street; **St. George's Hanover Square**; built by John James, 1713–24, it is somewhat Wrenish but seems to be the first London church to wear a huge-pillared portico, a fashion that had an immense success. In the portico are two agreeable cast iron dogs (ascribed to Landseer), as though awaiting their masters from Matins, and inside is fairly rich and painted under the barrel vault, although not quite big enough for the exterior; but inside are above all the weddings of the splendid. Here in 1791 Emma plighted rather unsteadily her troth not with Nelson but with Sir William Hamilton; down this aisle with the organ fluting came Shelley (with Harriet Westbrook, 1814, consolidating their Scottish marriage); came Disraeli; came Mary Ann Evans better known as George Eliot; Theodore Roosevelt; the Asquiths, and the roll in the registers continues unabated. The interest of Hanover Square is mainly historic in a planning sense, as the original focus of this corner of Mayfair; in the four-storeyed red and grey brick of No. 24 you can still gauge something of its original scale as it was built from 1715 on, and in viewing sales at Knight, Frank and Rutley at No. 20, something of the ampleness of the old interiors, but mainly the planes and grass of the Square are shadowed by the twentieth-century invasion of Regent Street-scaled buildings and by the looming towers of Oxford Street.

From Hanover Square, **Brook Street** runs west, crossing Bond Street, to Grosvenor Square, Hanover's greater counterpart for the north-west sector of Mayfair. At No. 25 Brook Street, behind a plain front Handel lived for nearly forty years, and there the *Messiah* was written; in South Molton Street that goes off at an angle to Oxford Street, there are excellent shopping possibilities, and among the dealers Mayor, with cafés, boutiques, a post office, all set in a now prettily pedestrianised enclave. Then Claridge's (see p. 85) at the crossing of Davies Street (which has more dealers of quality). And so on to **Grosvenor Square**, which was building in 1725, 'and will', commented the *Daily Journal* in that year, 'for its largeness and beauty exceed any yet made in and about London'. Developed by Sir Richard Grosvenor, its garden (then circular) was designed originally by Kent, with a statue of George I, whose mistress, the Duchess of Kendall—a tall girl known as the Maypole—almost at once moved into No. 43; the house next door, No. 44 (south side), seems to be the only house in the whole square now left in private hands. Large the Square still is, six acres, with a broad opulence of grass under its trees, but its beauty is less generally admitted. It has now for years, together with its purlieus, been known as 'Little America', and from 1785 when John Adams, later President, but then the first American minister to Britain, moved into No. 9, American associations have been close, though it was only during the war and since, that the Square has really been taken over almost in its entirety. Shining white across the north side of the grass is the monument to F. D. Roosevelt, including a statue by Reid Dick (1948); this is a sincere tribute from the English even though it may stagger some Republican visitors from the States. But the real presence of America is now in its **Embassy** that since 1960 has brooded massively under its brooding eagle over the Square, occupying the entire west side. By Eero Saarinen, it has roused considerable controversy, but it seems to me an admirable expression of almost Roman power. Even if the articulation of its upper stories, with its complex, massive and very ingenious detailing (though not its gilt), pay deference to an original Georgian character of the Square which was no longer there even when the Embassy started building, it seems to me not fussy but grandly alive, and, seen from the east end through the flickering branches of winter trees, very successful.

Grosvenor Square has indeed become fairly formidably official in character. But this, the western flank of Mayfair, has much still of the residential about it; in Park Street, Green Street, South Audley Street, a lot of living goes on behind the whitest of white flimsy curtains and glossy black railings. If you leave the Square at the south-west corner down **South Audley Street** you come to the Grosvenor Chapel, rather American Colonial in feeling with a neat bluish spire (built 1730); here lie buried a miscellany of exalted characters from Lady Mary Wortley Montague to John Wilkes ('The remains of John Wilkes, a Friend to Liberty'); during the war the church was adopted by the United States Armed Forces. Behind it is a rather unexpected garden, deep in trees and towering brick walls, with at the far end, the neo-Gothic of the very smart Jesuits' Mayfair establishment, the Church of the Immaculate Conception. As you go south down towards Piccadilly, the texture becomes denser, more residential, with new but small blocks of flats going up and always among them here and there the little mews houses and the survivors from the eighteenth century with their blessings of elegant and finite, humane, proportion and calm. No. 71 South Audley Street is one of the best (*c.* 1736, with a charmingly pretty doorway); this was and is a smart street—two French kings lodged there (Louis XVIII and Charles X), and so did Queen Caroline while awaiting her divorce by George IV. In 1763 the autocratic Lord Bute had two women sent to Bridewell for singing political ballads outside his door. The road ends at **Curzon Street** that runs east again, usually very busy, hairdressers, offices again, restaurants including the very glamorous Mirabelle which even has a garden restaurant, and set back off the road behind a superb lawn one very grand white town palace (Crewe House, about 1730 but later altered) as reminder of a former spacious scale of living. Off the right hand side of Curzon Street, you can engage into a still tighter mesh, the little maze of **Shepherd Market**, of small houses and shops jammed together about footways and the tiny market-place; now very smart, full of cafés, souvenir shops, with a famous pub (Shepherd's), and painted up to the nines. Back in Curzon Street the way leads east past Half Moon Street (where lived, most famously, Bertie Wooster helped by Jeeves)—here and in Clarges and Bolton Street, as in Curzon Street, quite a proportion of eighteenth-century terrace houses preserve a decorum of scale. Curzon itself, however, finds its doom in a drab channel which slips by at the flank of an embattlemented Ministry building and takes you past the doors of the Lansdowne Club into the south end of **Berkeley Square.**

Perhaps, and if so rightly, your attention in Berkeley Square will first be claimed by the gigantic planes with their smoothly mottled limbs, their cascades of black branches or green, filling the gentle rise of the green grass to the north. They are just about the most venerable things left in the Square (and how long, how much longer can they last) for they were planted around 1790. The planes alone, and perhaps the idiotic little Pump House central in their midst with its chinoiserie roof, make talk, memory even, of nightingales bearable. Beauty otherwise has to be imposed mainly by the historic imagination—on the south side the delicate restrained grandeur of Robert Adam's Lansdowne House; on the east side the smaller houses in one of which Horace Walpole lived the last few years of his life—these have been obliterated by mammoth monsters in brick, even reaching out into Bruton Street on the east side to engulf the site (No. 17 Bruton Street) where in 1926, Queen Elizabeth II was born. But on the west side there are still survivors, though not from the earliest buildings of the Square, which seems to have been complete by about 1740; Nos. 46 to 44 are the most interesting, the first two stone faced with massive rustications on the ground floors (about 1745). In No. 45, the founder of British India, Clive, committed suicide in 1774. No. 44, warmer in its brick, built by Kent in 1744, has an interior of the most grandly lavish ingenuity with a famous staircase (not open to the public, but it has recently been richly restored as the premises of one of the grandest of gaming clubs).

Off the south-east end of the Square, Berkeley Street leads to Piccadilly past a singularly capacious Thomas Cook's, and Hay Hill mounts very brusquely east against a downward torrent of taxicabs up to **Dover Street**, and here we are back in the full Bond Street aura. No. 37 Dover Street is an important architectural essay in Palladianism (by Sir Robert Taylor, 1772; once the West End *pied-à-terre* of the Bishops of Ely). That most lively institution, the Institute of Contemporary Arts, a sort of forcing-house, laboratory even, of avant-garde art, moved from No. 17 to Carlton House Terrace (p. 61) in 1968. Parallel with Dover Street, **Albemarle Street** has a famous print shop, Parker's, at the Piccadilly end, and entrances to Agnew's and the Marlborough. Then, right at the Grafton Street end, the giant Corinthian columns strung along the front of the Royal Institution; this was founded in 1799 for the 'promotion, diffusion and extension of scientific knowledge'; here Humphry Davy lectured, and later that great, good and most modest of geniuses, Michael Faraday, demonstrated the dangerous wonder of electricity; here still lectures are held in gallant competition with television, but it is particularly perhaps for the children's lectures at Christmas time (when the speakers generally include a Nobel prize-winner or so) that the Institution is now known. Also in Albemarle Street, No. 50, still, is Byron's publisher John Murray, the firm still headed by a John Murray, his sanctum hung with portraits of great writers. No. 7, a nice eighteenth-century house, is the National Book League.

Only one street east again now, and we arc back in Bond Street, and I've a feeling somehow I've missed Mayfair. For Mayfair, even more than most of London, is its people, and if you go there by day you cannot help but see admirable examples of the London Look. And what, an American fashion expert was asked, is the London Look? It is, she said, herself unabashedly and warmingly understating, 'elegant and understated; it has quiet distinction, with a definite touch of fashion'. Maybe she spoke before the phenomenon of swinging mid-sixties mini-skirted London and subsequent eccentricities and dishevelments, but she can still be shown to be right.

CHAPTER SIX

Trafalgar Square

Ꭷ

TRAFALGAR SQUARE[1] is easily approached by bus, for buses seem to swarm there, or by Underground to Trafalgar Square Station or Strand Station. Both of these are at the south-eastern corner of the Square, and the Strand Station puts you out into the courtyard of **Charing Cross** main line railway station by a replica of 1865 of the original Charing Cross—the last of the stone crosses that Edward I set up in 1291 to mark the resting places of the slow funeral cortège of his Queen Eleanor as it passed from Nottinghamshire to West-minster Abbey. But Charing Cross was originally on a spot a hundred yards to the west, at the top of Whitehall and in what is now Trafalgar Square; demolished in 1647, it was replaced in 1675 by Le Sueur's bronze statue of **Charles I.**

When Dr. Johnson remarked that 'Fleet Street has a very animated appearance, but I think the full ride of human existence is at Charing Cross', Charles was the hub of West London. From his plinth, already then weathered to its sepulchral Portland white with its sooty shadowings, he looked south down Whitehall, while from the north-west the main road from Piccadilly and the Haymarket came in, and from the north-east the great highway that linked the City of London to the Parliament at Westminster, the Strand. This vital Strand–Whitehall axis, linking also the then only two bridges across the Thames (London and Westminster), followed the river line; and at Charing Cross, with the river, lost its westwards drive, to plunge due south. There was then no great open space here, just the natural widening where the three main arteries of West London traffic met, and in its middle, Charles on his bronze horse. The Square as we know it was conceived, though not executed, by John Nash early in the nineteenth century, and named Trafalgar as early as 1820. To make it, almost as if in fore-knowledge of the motor car,

1. See map on page 102.

acres of stabling were cleared: Great Mews, Green Mews and, forthrightly, Dunghill Mews. All the King's horses moved out of their stabling that had been palatially designed by William Kent, and the National Gallery went up in their place.

As the Square was levelled out of the slope, and the column rose, so the emphasis withdrew from Charles to Nelson, and eventually Charles—although remaining, as you can see from a little bronze plaque in the pavement beside him, the centre for all signposts, the point from which distances to and from London are measured—became a rather precarious islet, dwarfed, even when seen from his mortal Whitehall, by the column. About him swirls, or perhaps more often stands with panting exhausts, no longer the full tide of human existence but still a considerable density of automobiles, waiting the green light to leap forth down Whitehall, into the Mall or up Cockspur Street. The statue is difficult to see from a distance because of the cars and buses in between, and hazardous for the same reason to approach nearly. It is, if not a great statue formally, still a fine one, and redolent of melancholy as the martyr King rides for ever down into Whitehall, where three hundred yards away, on a scaffold outside his Banqueting House, he died with such dignity and courage in 1649. Yet in fact—although even as object the statue has had its vicissitudes: sold by Parliament to be melted down, but instead furtively buried, and resurrected after the Restoration of Charles II—the melancholy is imparted to it by association; if you look at it with an honest eye, you must admit the king looks singularly well-dined, almost debonair. Incidentally, together with the loftier figure of Nelson (in person adding 17 feet 4½ inches to the 167 feet 6½ inches of his column), it is a splendid vindication of the big man that tries to get out of every small man. Charles was about 5 feet 4 inches tall, but the contract for his statue specifies 'the figure of his Maj. King Charles proportionate full six foot'; Nelson was no bigger.

It took time to get **Nelson** up; he died with a courage and dignity equal to Charles's, and with surely far more warranted glory on the deck of H.M.S. *Victory* at Trafalgar in 1805. His devotees, spurred on perhaps by the success of the rival column to the Duke of York, on Carlton House Steps, which went up in 1834, managed at last to push Nelson up (his column a clear forty feet higher than the Duke's, and his person three feet larger) by 1842. About his base, in bas-reliefs cast from gun-metal captured at his victories, they set spirited representations of his sea-fights, and completed the composition by 1867 with the famous quadruplet lions, twenty feet long, all cast from a single original modelled by Landseer.

The emphasis of Trafalgar Square was on naval power and glory, and on the Empire which that power secured. Not only on Nelson, but on admirals as recent as Jellicoe and Beatty, whose busts are set against the wall on the north flank of the Square, while on the south-west the vista up the Mall to Buckingham Palace is obstructed by the massive triple archway of the Admiralty Arch, part of the national memorial to Queen Victoria and a ponderous overstatement of triumph in an Edwardian neo-Roman imperial style. On the west side is Canada House (incorporating now the old College of Physicians building) confronted across the Square on the east by South Africa House, which begins to rise with some dignity only to flower in its upper stories into fiddle-de-dee. Memories of India are evoked by the statues of Generals Havelock and Napier. The roll of statues actually in the Square is completed by a very chill equestrian of George IV, improbably bareback and barefoot in a toga, and by—outside the National Gallery —one of the best bronzes in London, James II. Although affected in costume again, in Roman kilt and laurel wreath, this has an easy, charming, elegance; Grinling Gibbons was paid for it, but the Flemish sculptor Quellin may have had a considerable hand in it.

Sir Osbert Sitwell long ago pointed out that all the statues of famous Englishmen in the Square had their backs resolutely turned on the National Gallery; true enough, but unfair on the royal statues, for Charles I, James II and George IV were, of all English monarchs, those most actively and fruitfully interested in the arts. The National itself, as architectural composition, is inadequate for its site; raised above the Square, and the longest uninterrupted façade of the Square, it should both anchor and set the scale by a majestic presence. Horizontally, it has elegance, symmetrically controlled about its famous portico (the columns of which are actually surplus stock from the demolition of Carlton House, thrust upon the architect, Wilkins, as an economy measure); but, above, the little dome and its flanking pepper-pots are utterly and meanly inadequate for the exclamation they should provide. Indeed, all the buildings of the Square as such are flawed—not only the massive and miscellaneous congregation at the south side, that look like an overspill from the Victorian excesses of the City, but even **St. Martin's-in-the-Fields** itself.

St. Martin's is a bewitching church, but even in his original designs, its architect, James Gibbs, never succeeded in marrying the steeple and the body of the building into a whole. After years of watching, and loving, this church in all lights and weathers, I still have the feeling that if only one could catch it at the right moment, spire and church would click in heavenly harmony, but circumambulate it though I will, they never quite do, and obstinately the spire still insists and projects through the building like a misplaced eye-tooth, though a beautifully designed and turned one. Inside it is grand, with pilasters and plaster and gilt, much as Gibbs built it in 1722–6, with a handsome pulpit (which you can see in its original state in Hogarth's second plate for the 'Industry and Idleness' series). It is a roomy and airy church; if it lacks a climax, it is nevertheless admirable for well-furnished and well-dressed weddings, and indeed sees a great many of them. The monuments from the early church (it goes back to the twelfth century, and the parish is said to have been created by Henry VIII, so that pestilential bodies for burial could be buried there rather than carried unwholesomely past his new-built palace of St. James on their way to St. Margaret's Westminster) are, some of them, re-erected in the crypt of the present building, together with an old whipping post dated 1752, and Gibbs's model for the church. It has long been a fashionable, indeed, a royal church. Charles II was christened in it; George I gave the organ. And in its now extinguished graveyard were buried a remarkable medley of famous bodies: Francis Bacon, John Hampden, Nell Gwynn, the highwayman Jack Sheppard. But the creation of Trafalgar Square was really responsible for its position of spectacular prominence, for only then did its handsome façade emerge from a close cluster of mean buildings to ride so dream-like in the eye.

I see, looking back, that I have been tending to denigrate Trafalgar Square, as though one would be unwise to visit it. I certainly would not advise a first visit on a day of uniform greyness, or of wet greyness; then Trafalgar Square is dour, and depressive, a vast roundabout for cars. But go on a fine

ST JAMES'S. The palace —
Henry VIII's gate-tower (about
1532). *Below*, Lock's, 6 St
James's Street, the birthplace of
the bowler hat

Trafalgar Square — with Nelson, Charles I, Landseer's lions, and the usual congregation of pigeons

day, or a day of broken lights in a wind that flings the fountain spray. Come to it best from Pall Mall, and thence you catch one of the prettiest views in London: looking along the columns of the old College of Physicians entrance on your right, and those of the National Gallery on your left farther on, up to the façade of St. Martin; a rippling yet serene passage for the eye to that spire that lifts its pearly white out of the grey London haze. Catch the Square after spring rain, in a hiss and slither of car tyres; the pavements flash steel and then in patches pure azure as the clouds part, and the column of Nelson, the granite of which can seem, while undoubtedly confident, somewhat coarse, will stand against a pure sky edged razor-sharp. Or come at Christmas dusk, when the giant fir tree that Norway has given London every year since the war is all lit up; come at noon, when the pigeons on the Square are sucking up to the tourists and pretending that they are nice, decent birds, tame to sit on your hand or your head (but go after to, say, the front of Whitehall Court, and see the full squalor of buildings befouled by the action-decoration of their droppings). Clap your hands or backfire your car, and see the pigeons explode like shot in flight. Come—and perhaps this is best of all—at five to ten in the morning of a fine May day that promises heat later, and sit on the edge of the basin of one of the two big fountains. Though the morning traffic will be going round and round, there won't be many people on the Square itself yet; the morning mist is lifting, tinged with the sun as if with gold-dust and the young leaves of the plane trees, still tender, can be nearer gold than green. The air is cool and fresh, with a zest of petrol; above the traffic's hum, the pigeons croon their uvular platitudes, and then, up Whitehall, throbs the long boom of Big Ben striking ten: faint, yet full-bodied in a ghostly way, like a foghorn. And you'll have to move, because the fountains, that have been quiet, begin now to swell, to fill, to overflow; to spray, and then—the main jets—to heave themselves in jerking stages to their full height. It's a splendid ceremony, and opens the day. Fountains there are in London, but relatively few, and very few of calibre, jets, plumes of dazzling clarity, water-works better than fireworks in dark London for catching rainbows.

But Trafalgar Square is more than roundabout or a stage for fountains, in the presence of the cock-hatted figure with its empty sleeve so far above. Trafalgar Square is a rallying point and a rallying cry, the great London theatre of the open-air meeting. Revivalists of all kinds—Religious, Trades Union, Political, Communist, Labour and Neo-Fascist; hot air blasts upwards but fails to rock Nelson. Such meetings on a Sunday afternoon, when wet as it usually seems to be, can look like a rite of some nomadic sect tented in black umbrellas.

Meetings in Trafalgar Square generally happen however only on Saturday or Sunday afternoons, and the main draw in Trafalgar Square is of course **the National Gallery**—over the road to the north, past the assiduous display of the pavement artists or 'screevers' (whose work probably has a bigger audience than any living artists' in the world), up the steps past the sublimely indifferent gaze of the art students generally to be found taking the air on the porch and into the big entrance hall.

The National began, as such national collections go, very late—1824, and unlike some it had no expropriated royal collection to serve as foundation. It had however, instead, as possible sources of enrichment, a remarkable number of private collections within the country, brought together by English aristocrats shopping on the Continent during and after the grand tour. These indeed, supplemented by some inspired buying abroad, particularly by a great director of the mid-nineteenth century, Sir Charles Eastlake, proved rich enough to permit the formation of a collection of a quality which has few rivals in the world, and in some respects, none. The Italian paintings of the fifteenth and sixteenth centuries are of a quality and representativeness unparalleled outside Italy; its holdings of early Netherlandish, of seventeenth-century Dutch and Flemish, of seventeenth-century French, are especially rich. The English school is left mainly to the Tate Gallery, but the cream of the English eighteenth century, and of Constable and Turner is shown here. It is relatively weak on the German school (though the Spanish are magnificent) and on certain schools and painters, such as Georges de la Tour and the French Impressionists, which came into their own after the awakening of the great American millionaires with bottomless purses in the late nineteenth century. Its scope is from the thirteenth century to the early twentieth; from Giotto to Cézanne—twentieth-century painting, British and foreign, is the province of the Tate Gallery (p. 153).

The paintings are exhibited in a more or less chronological sequence, into which you can engage by turning left up the stairs from the entrance hall. There seems to be no alternative between describing the Gallery at length, involving a brief outline of European art and at least a chapter, and simply giving the visitor a push into the Gallery in a paragraph—and space forbids the former alternative. For Londoners, the National Gallery—even though as L. P. Smith remarked, while we may go there constantly in the spirit, how rarely do we go in the flesh—is an oasis of refreshment, a haven for contemplation, in the business of the City. It is also one of the classic traditional trysting points for lovers, perhaps partly because, in front of such painters as Piero della Francesca, Raphael, Vermeer or Seurat, there may seem a real possibility of stopping time in the enchanted moment. But the overall quality of the paintings is such as to inhibit suggesting what can be no more than a personal choice—you must make your own, any time between 10 and 6 on weekdays, 2 and 6 on Sundays (the National is also experimenting with evening opening but it is uncertain whether this will continue).

A big extension on the north of the National (that can be entered also from Orange Street) opened in 1975. Plans for taking over the present National Portrait Gallery site and re-housing the latter immediately west of the National on a long-vacant plot, seem fairly cloudy and unlikely of resolution for some years; and meanwhile you can find the **National Portrait Gallery** just off Trafalgar Square at the bottom of Charing Cross Road, a rather thin building in an Italian Renaissance late Victorian vernacular, wrapped round the back of the National, and open 10–5 weekdays, 10–6 Saturdays and 2–6 Sundays. Again, I cannot attempt a guide, but a brief note on its character is necessary, as the word 'Gallery' can be misleading. The National Portrait Gallery has in fact to do with history rather than with art, and that it possesses some absolutely stunning pictures is almost incidental to its purposes; it has equally gladly some absolutely appalling ones, as far as artistic quality is concerned. Seek out for example the water-colour of Jane Austen by her sister Cassandra, a daub, but the only authentic portrait of Jane from the life and one of the Gallery's dearest treasures. But contrast on the other hand Holbein's tremendous cartoon of Henry VIII, wherein art and history fuse in inextricable magic. The primary interest however is always in the subject of the picture: this is history seen through the people who made history—a shrine of national piety peculiar to Anglo-Saxons (you hardly find institutions of this kind on the Continent). If you are touring London in earnest, you will find here contemporary portraits of most of the great Londoners of the past mentioned in these pages— Pepys, Wren; Hogarth, Newton, Nell Gwynn; Nelson and Wellington; Lamb and Hazlitt, Lamb painted *by* Hazlitt. You will find, to choose just one example, Johnson set in the midst of the members of The Club, Boswell alongside, and most of them painted by Reynolds.

CHAPTER SEVEN

Whitehall and the
Houses of Parliament

✤

WHITEHALL is two things; a concept, and a physical site in which that concept is said to live, though what one has to do with the other isn't always clear. As concept, it is not of course a popular one. For the average citizen, including me, Whitehall only too easily becomes synonymous with any and almost every kind of public control of individual enterprise and individual taste, whenever that control affects one personally. Whitehall is the amorphous, impersonal 'They' who refuse to let you do something that is obviously to your great advantage and really not at all to anyone else's disadvantage.

Before inspecting Whitehall in some detail, I must indicate how it came about. From 1245, this was York Place, the London residence of the Archbishops of York, but it did not get really grand until Cardinal Wolsey's time; Wolsey elaborated the buildings, and set a scale of living of which one example must serve as symptom—'a most sumptuous supper, the like of which was never given either by Cleopatra or Caligula'. Of his works, now only part of the wine-cellar survives. But at Wolsey's fall in 1530, York Place passed into the hands of the Crown, those most capacious hands of its then tenant, Henry VIII, who in a few years managed to obliterate all memories of the name of York or of Wolsey, in favour of Whitehall. But more than that, when Henry turned it into his main London palace, with splendid apartments of state, the seat of the government's administration of England moved there too, a few hundred yards north up the road from Westminster (though the legislature remained there). English monarchy slipped a little apart from both church and parliament, as if to emphasise its control over them. (It was in the last years of Henry's life, 1530–46, that the Reformed Religion was established and the King of England, head of the State, became also head of the Church.) Though the

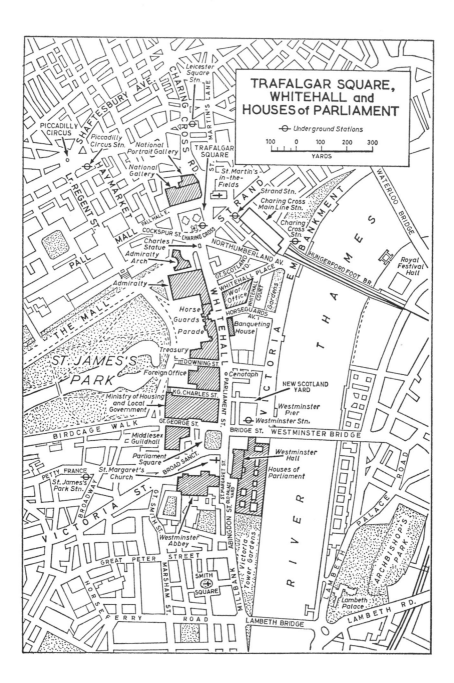

TRAFALGAR SQUARE,
WHITEHALL and
HOUSES of PARLIAMENT

⊖ Underground Stations

100 0 100 200 300
YARDS

LEICESTER SQUARE
Leicester
Square
Stn.

SHAFTESBURY AVE.

CHARING CROSS RD.

ST. MARTIN'S LANE

PICCADILLY
CIRCUS

Piccadilly
Circus Stn.

National
Portrait Gallery

TRAFALGAR
SQUARE

St. Martin's
in-the-Fields

HAYMARKET

LT. REGENT ST.

National
Gallery

ST. STRAND

Strand Stn.

Charing Cross
Main Line Stn.

Charing
Cross
Stn.

WATERLOO BRIDGE

PALL MALL E.

COCKSPUR ST. CHARING CROSS

Charles I
Statue
Admiralty
Arch

NORTHUMBERLAND AV.

HUNGERFORD FOOT BR.

THAMES

Royal
Festival
Hall

PALL MALL

Admiralty

GT. SCOTLAND YD.

WHITEHALL PLACE

War
Office

WHITEHALL COURT

Gardens

Horse
Guards
Parade

WHITEHALL

HORSEGUARDS AV.

Banqueting
House

VICTORIA EMBANKMENT

THAMES

THE MALL

ST. JAMES'S
PARK

Treasury

DOWNING ST.

Foreign Office

Ministry of Housing
and Local
Government

KG. CHARLES ST.

Cenotaph

NEW SCOTLAND
YARD

Westminster
Pier

Westminster Stn.

PARLIAMENT ST.

BIRDCAGE WALK

Middlesex
Guildhall

GT. GEORGE ST.

Parliament
Square

BRIDGE ST.

WESTMINSTER BRIDGE

ROAD

PETTY FRANCE

St. James's
Park Stn.

BROADWAY

BROAD SANCT.

St. Margaret's
Church

ST. MARGARET ST.

OLD PALACE YARD

Westminster
Hall

Houses of
Parliament

VICTORIA ST.

GT. SMITH ST.

Westminster
Abbey

ABINGDON ST.

MILLBANK

Victoria
Tower Gardens

RIVER

PALACE ROAD

ARCHBISHOP'S
PARK

GREAT PETER STREET

MARSHAM ST.

SMITH
SQUARE

LAMBETH

Lambeth
Palace

HORSEFERRY ROAD

ROAD

LAMBETH BRIDGE

LAMBETH RD.

Court did not really settle in one home till the Stuarts, before Henry VIII the primary palace had been Westminster for nearly five hundred years—since it moved from Winchester. After the Stuarts royalty moved from Whitehall, but the country's administration was to stay, and has now been there almost as long as it was at Westminster.

A White Hall was a term in use in the early sixteenth century for any grand hall designed for festivities, and, curiously, the major building in Whitehall is still the Banqueting House (see p. 108), though it is many years since that saw a banquet. Henry built fairly lavishly, besides installing one long gallery torn lock, stock and barrel out of another of Wolsey's palaces at Esher. His building, judging by plans of it, was probably not architecturally very striking as a whole, but included some parts of which the loss is still sensible. The two gates, for example, that controlled the roadway where it passed through the palace grounds; one of them, famous (wrongly) as 'Holbein's Gate', survived till 1759. But the major loss is certainly of that suite of rooms which probably contained both the Matted Gallery with a ceiling said to be by Holbein, and the Privy Chamber, which certainly did contain Holbein's great wall-painting of the Tudor dynasty, wherein that colossal straddling whole-length stance of Henry VIII was first portrayed. Early, there was a strong and English emphasis at Whitehall on health-giving sport. In the sixteenth century there were three tennis courts, a cock-pit, a tilt-yard, even a 'ball-house, where they play at featherballs' (? badminton) and a bowling alley.

But already in Henry VIII's time, the associations of Whitehall with the more serious matters of government and its administration began. Government and its administration were still of course very much the king's affair, with Parliament still well under royal control. Elizabeth did not love Whitehall as much as her father, and spent as much time elsewhere especially at Greenwich, but when, with her, there died the Tudor dynasty, the Stuarts moved in thoroughly upon Whitehall and made it their main seat and centre of government; a government which, if not essentially more absolutist than Elizabeth's at heart had been, lacked tact (to say the least) in expressing itself and acting as such. In 1642, the doctrine of Divine Right was tested by the sword and found wanting, and seven years later absolute monarchy was beheaded on the

threshold of its own palace in Whitehall, in the person of
Charles I. And although Charles II returned to Whitehall
after the Restoration and apparently loved it, the royal grasp
on Whitehall was failing; James II, the Stuart who never
learned, was thrown out of it, and William III took against
it, and built Kensington Palace instead, where he found a
purer and keener air more suited to his asthma.

His decision against Whitehall was confirmed with drastic
and dramatic thoroughness on 4 of January, 1698: on
the 5th the aged John Evelyn noted starkly in his diary:
'Whitehall utterly burnt to the ground, nothing but the walls
& ruines left.' The fire started about 4 p.m. (owing to a
Dutchwoman [in moments of disaster, always blame a
foreigner] 'having a sudden occasion to dry some linen in an
upper room, for expedition's sake lighted a good quality of
charcoal and carelessly left the linen hanging round about it')
and burnt till next morning; the main palace of the Kings of
England, apart from the Banqueting House and Whitehall
Gate, was then extinct, and though there were plans for rebuilding, the monarch never returned to Whitehall to live.
There had been plans for consolidating Whitehall into a grand
baroque palace, a showcase of royalty fit to rival the Louvre
but they had never materialised. The Banqueting House was
the index of what might have been, as a foreign visitor noted
in 1665; it looked, he said, 'very stately, because the rest of
the Palace is ill Built, and nothing but a heap of Houses,
erected at divers times, and of different Models'. But by the
time of the fire the real source of power was no longer in the
royal palace, but in Parliament at Westminster, and Whitehall
was still the obvious site for the offices of the administration
of government, and soon the beginnings of that huge expansion of government buildings that has wrought out the
present Whitehall became visible. After the fire the various
government departments were scattered in make-shift way
about buildings in Whitehall, but in 1732 William Kent's
plans for a Treasury building were accepted, and in the same
year a famous house in a street then still known as the Cockpit
was assigned to Sir Robert Walpole in his capacity of the
First Lord of the Treasury, better known nowadays as the
Prime Minister: No. 10 Downing Street.

From then on, much is still visible, and it is time to take a
look at it. Although the individual Civil Servant and the

Service as a whole may lack glamour, its main habitat certainly possesses it, even though much of the glamour in Whitehall is provided by the sister services, the senior branches of the Armed Forces of the Crown, the Army and the Navy. From the Parliament Square end of Whitehall the entry into it is satisfactory: a wide vista with plane trees closed by the curve half-way up. From **Trafalgar Square**, the vista is muddled, and there is a collapse of perspective caused mainly by the abrupt narrowing at Charing Cross and the sudden lurch up towards the Square that the roadway takes there through an ill-assortment of odd buildings. But Whitehall proper—for its two ends are technically Charing Cross and Parliament Street respectively—is a broad, serene and majestic entity, in spite of some weak elements and only perhaps one truly major building, the Banqueting Hall. But first, standing by the pale plinth of **Charles I**, as beautifully decayed and shadowed as a great actress in her evening, glance to right and to left before leaving Trafalgar Square. On the right the arched and triple-arched massif of Admiralty Arch, the entrance to the Mall; it was built in heaviest Edwardian Roman, part of Queen Victoria's National Monument (1910). And on the left, the entrance to Northumberland Avenue; here, till 1874, stood the town house of the Percys, Dukes of Northumberland, a tremendous Jacobean creation that forms the background to many topographical eighteenth-century views of Charing Cross. The avenue made in its place is an oddity in London; it looks almost Etoile, evenly tall over depressed plane trees, with copious but somehow disguised windowings. It never shows much sign of life, because it goes nowhere except to the Embankment; its vista is closed, on the far side of the river, by a slab of the new Shell building, like a four-letter word with the consonants asterisked instead of the vowels. It houses, notably, what was the Royal Empire Society and is now, as a carved stone on its front announces with recent and un-ashamed whiteness, the Royal Commonwealth Society.

Some suave banks on the right, and the rather sepulchral front of the Whitehall Theatre, and miscellany of pubs, etc., on the left (among them the entry to Craig's Court, where there is a very handsome façade of 1702 incorporated unconvincingly into a telephone exchange). The headquarters of the Anti-Vivisection Society heralds the War Office later on. But then Whitehall begins, opening out to ceremonial width; in the best English way, it has no claims to composition, but marches more as a set of variations on a theme. On the right, the old **Admiralty** of 1722-6, well and rather drably-bred about its deep forecourt, but shielded by a light and elegant screen (very early Adam of 1759-61) of columns shadowed against a wall and lifting, at the opening, a pair of rain-washed and fabulous sea-horses; behind, the dark brick Admiralty buildings carry on down Whitehall in a reserved fashion topped by old-fashioned radio masts like maypoles. On the other side of the road, Great Scotland Yard, where once the kings of Scotland stayed, and then, for a longer period, the police, is down a side street and now transmogrified to a recruiting centre for the Army. Then a façade with the first murmur of brass, the Crown Estate Office with the Ministry of Agriculture and Fisheries (universally known as 'Ag and Fish'), preluding the sonorous, almost Wagnerian, full statement of the **War Office**. Tuba, euphonium and big bass drum perhaps, rather than mysterious deep-banked horns. Ponderous among its four cupolas, the stone heavily rusticated and then formidably wealthy with Corinthian columns high up; it is late Victorian baroque of 1898-1907. In full harmony with it, the bronze of the royal Duke of Cambridge, a curious inventory of uniform, plumes, boots, cape and whiskers, rides down to Westminster on a strong bronze horse: permanence was anyway perhaps his strongest characteristic for he was Commander-in-Chief of the British Army for forty years (1856-95).

On the right again, the **Horse Guards**, built to William Kent's design in 1750-60, and a whiff of real horse among the petrol vapour. The Whitehall façade particularly is immediately lovable, almost miniature in comparison with the War Office, receding back in rhythmical steps to the archway under the pale clock tower with the neatness of a chess-knight's moves. In the twin sentry boxes, the two troopers of the Household Cavalry, impassive on their fine horses, bright as the coloured postcards of them, in the red tunics and white plumes of the Life Guards or the blue tunics and red plumes of the Royal Horse Guards. Pure ceremonial, of course, and perennially successful. It is most difficult to find out what they are guarding; even their uniforms are a concoction, the breastplates almost part of the Gothic Revival and introduced by the glamour king George IV. It's a shock to find real young men inside the impassive uniform, live eyes lurking between the lid of the helmet and curb of chin-chain. It may seem almost an unjustifiable indignity, but the toughest of British shock-troops bear it with equanimity, and have never been known to lean forward in the saddle to chop with the ready bared sword the head of a simpering tourist posing for the camera; besides, they never know, the tourist may be one of those who slip banknotes into the top of the boots to see if the sentry will move. Unmounted, the men in uniform are tremendously deprived of horse, in their flapping thigh boots, as out of element as sea-lions out of water. Between ten and four, while the sentries are posted, there is always a cluster of tourists here, but the draw of course is when the guards change, with great noise and clatter and wordless roaring and music, in the mornings at eleven o'clock.

The Horse Guards are succeeded, still on the same side towards Westminster, by the purer, discreeter elegance of Dover House with its domed entrance hall of 1787; it houses the Scottish Office, with Walter Scott visible from the entrance. Then the restrained early Victorian frontage of the Treasury, more columns along a straight façade. This, with much of **Downing Street** adjoining, has recently been gutted, and entirely and at vast expense been rebuilt within. In Downing Street itself, No. 10 (also rebuilt internally) is of course the draw, normally watched by a constant knot of sightseers, eyes and cameras tense as sharp-shooters' for a sight of the most powerful man in the land as he emerges from the characteristically nondescript front of the Prime Minister's official residence (it is misleading though, as behind it extends considerably). The Cabinet Room is on the ground floor, where toppest of top-level decisions are, perhaps not made always, but first debated by the Cabinet before the wider debate in the Commons. No. 11 is the Chancellor of the Exchequer.

There follows down Whitehall the **Foreign Office**, mid-Victorian pile, and the outcome of a long architectural saga: designed by Gilbert Scott as Gothic, vetoed by Palmerston who wanted Italian; the architect countered by a face-saving compromise, involving Byzantine elements, which Palmerston threw out as 'a regular mongrel-affair', and Gilbert Scott after much expense on source books and homework produced reluctantly the present building in North Italian, an elaborately fronted palazzo lavishly inset with portrait medallions (it was recently threatened with demolition but now seems secure). And then the colossal block built round two court-yards and finished in 1920, home of the Ministry of Housing and Local Government, the major part of the Treasury and other offices, and with its southern flank bordering Parliament Square. Both these buildings are of a complexly sombre surface texture, pointed happily by governmental window-boxes, admirable backdrops to the highly-coloured ceremonial of Whitehall on great occasions.

On the other (river) side of the road, reverting back to the War Office, is the **Banqueting House**, one of the most import-ant buildings in the history of English architecture. It bears its importance, however, with a discretion that is almost self-effacing—thousands of people must have passed down White-hall without seeing it. Built by Inigo Jones, starting in 1619, it was the first building within London to be conceived and carried out in the classic Italian tradition; before it, English architecture had slapped classical motifs happily about its structures, but not integrated them. It does not look particu-larly big now, small even alongside its neighbours, two main stories only, but in the seventeenth and even eighteenth century prints it looms high above Whitehall and seems to rival Westminster Abbey. It has never quite been integrated into its surroundings, but rather remained through three and a half centuries almost a sample of style. It is in fact essentially a hall, compact and self-contained and self-sufficient, its exterior composed in two storeys of seven windows divided up by Ionic demi-columns below and Corinthian pilasters above. It has symmetry, and a cool dignity of restraint, and a lovely delicacy across the slight advance and withdrawal of its façade, its expression. It was also one of the first, if not the first, big buildings in London in Portland stone; it is Portland stone that is a major ingredient in many of the more magic effects of the London townscape, for it darkens in London dirt from the ground upwards, and then, where the rain catches it, for ever washes itself. The shadowy modulation of Portland stone, touched in its deepest shadows with a sooty richness, ranging on its surfaces from purplish to ochre tones, lifts gradually in the spires and pinnacles and domes into a pallor that in certain lights, in certain hazes, becomes all but insub-stantial as though the architecture were still floating in the first glimpse of the artist's imagination. However, the Banqueting House itself has now been cleaned.

Inside, the Banqueting House has been used and abused through the centuries; for masques and feasts; as passage for Charles I in the last moments of his life on his way to the window in a now demolished annex that gave on to the scaffold outside (was it too from the Banqueting House that later, after the Restoration, the funeral effigy of Cromwell was hanged by the neck?). In 1890 it was granted to the Royal United Service Institution as museum. Which it still was till 1963, though once again it serves for state occasions—but also dress shows; perhaps no other nation than the English would have employed their grandest room so incongruously and so consistently. The great glory is the ceiling, commissioned by Charles I from Rubens in 1630, and featuring the apotheosis of the Stuart Dynasty in the person of James I; it is a complex allegorical demonstration proceeding through the nine large panels set in a richly coffered framework, and it is 'read' from the far end of the room, whence the perspective falls into place. It is now open again to the public.

Linked on to the Banqueting House, going towards Westminster, a sober late eighteenth-century mansion, Gwydyr House, and then, mercifully set back from the road behind a green lawn, a huge barracks-weight of bureaucracy, one of the by-me best-hated buildings in London: now the **Ministry of Defence** and nicknamed the Quadragon. It provides, says one guide, 'accommodation for 5,360 Civil Servants, an increase of 4,175 in the number previously occupying this site'; and you can well believe it does. It looks like an invention for the fabrication of processed Civil Servants, irrespective of any rights they may have as human beings. Underneath it is the last of Wolsey's palace of York Place: a 70-foot-long brick-vaulted cellar which was ordered into the new building by being moved bodily 40 feet to one side, being sunk 20 feet lower and then being moved back to where it was before on a lower level. Also underneath this new mammoth (already extinct before born) are the memories of the former Whitehall Palace and of the eighteenth-century mansions which succeeded that—Richmond House; Whitehall Gardens (where lived Disraeli and Sir Robert Peel), and the Victorian splendours of Montagu House. In front a recent statue of Raleigh seems too small.

But in spite of this latest sadness, Whitehall is splendid as a whole, lining the broad processional of the road behind the plane trees. Down the centre of the road go the monuments: the Duke of Cambridge already mentioned, the Haig equestrian statue, a little vapid, but not meriting the hail of abuse that greeted it from horse-lovers all over the Empire (owing to an alleged discrepancy between the intentions of the fore and rear legs) in 1937; and then the austere gesture of the **Cenotaph**, set like a stele, with the colour and soft wind-stirred movement of the flags fixed on its sides only, but enough to startle the mind open over the loss and courage and vanity of two world wars. All men used to raise their hats when passing the Cenotaph; not so many do now, even when they have hats to raise.

Whitehall is an arena for state ceremonial, and a good one in its oddly a-formal way. It comes to life well when the state coaches and landaus ride down it towards Parliament Square amidst the clatter and bone-shaking jog of the Household Cavalry. But it has also at all times a steady magnetism, not of spectacle, but of the sense of the exercise of power in administration. The Prime Minister and his colleagues come and go in chauffeured limousines; the policeman stands outside No. 10; in and out of the doorways of Whitehall go the drab-suited anonymous officials. Down miles of corridors behind the august façades, tea-trolleys, files and minutes are on the move, discharging at surface levels compact briefs for Ministers and Parliamentary Secretaries. Here are by no means all the headquarters of all Ministries (which have long been scattered out from Whitehall from pressure of space), but here most certainly is the distributor-head of the vital essence that keeps the State moving—money—the Treasury.

To east and west of Whitehall, leading to the river and to St. James's Park respectively, flow the minor tributaries. Flow is perhaps the wrong word; they are more like canals, placid beneath the high walls of the Ministries, with cars tethered thick down their sides. Between the back of Whitehall and the river, a garden, of municipal flavour; squads of tulips in May, broad asphalt and close, razored grass with park-type benches, some of them rather splendidly Edwardianly monumental to look at though in practice they reject the body; at fairly regular intervals the huge, Trafalgar Square-scale bronzes of benefactors in the usual mood of benign severity;

it hurts me as much as it hurts you. Farther up river, the completion of the Ministry of Defence cliff has left a wide stretch of clear grass; at the foot of the cliff, let in even, into the tedious prose of the masonry like a lost quotation from a classical poet, there is a sunken ruin, from which an elegant curve of stairway climbs to expire on the blank new wall. And here you realise that you are standing in what was once the river itself. These are steps where the boats landed you from the water, and all the land between here and the parapet of the Embankment is no more than a hundred years old, the great swag of embankment consolidated by Sir Joseph Bazalgette (subject of a rather agreeable bust let into the Embankment wall opposite the opening of Northumberland Avenue) in the 1860s.

At the west end of Whitehall, down by the river, where the traffic piles up at the T-junction at Westminster Bridge, is Westminster Pier for the river boats, and opposite it the baronial keep started by Norman Shaw in 1891 for the Police Headquarters, **New Scotland Yard**. It is a strong, self-confident building, large but somehow rather crouching among its horizontal layers of brick and stone; it was also of course very strategically sited between the Gothic pinnacles and towers of the legislative at Westminster and the more Italian order of the administration in Whitehall. Parliament proposes, Whitehall disposes and Scotland Yard is there to enforce if necessary and to keep the peace. The building became very well known, thanks to detective films, which generally show it in action with a police car and motor-bicycle roaring out with a continental scream of tyres. In practice such action was rarely seen, and now is not seen at all, for in 1967 the police moved out—lock, stock, criminal records, their own sinister private museum and all—into a hygienic new building at the top of Victoria Street, the other side of Parliament Square and their old home has only been saved by a vigorous campaign.

But as everyone knows, our policemen (besides getting stupendously younger every day) are wonderful. And so indeed, barring all policemen who have caught you on some parking sin, or gonged you for speeding, or beaten you up, or otherwise abused their discretion, they are, for they have good manners to a degree undreamed of in any other police force I have met. They may not always know the way, but getting out their little directories they will always look it up

for you; their characteristic reproof is more in terms of
sorrow than of anger, and their characteristic admonition is
to move along there please. In fact, in the minds of the great
majority of the population they are associated with a positive
and helpful function (in spite of the ever increasing range of
petty restrictions, spawned by ever increasing urban complexity and forced on them by the legislature), rather than with
an oppressive one. The most important factor in this confidence is probably, paradoxically, the lack of a revolver
holster at their hip. Their tradition is the more remarkable in
that it is not, relatively, very old; Peel's Police Act was only
passed in 1829, creating for the first time a centralised uni-
formed force (long known but no more as Peelers in honour
of their creator, Sir Robert Peel). And their headquarters had
only been at New Scotland Yard since the 1890s—and indeed
had no right to be there at all. Scotland Yard hides in its
basements one of the great lost causes of art in England, a
National Opera House. The foundation stone was laid by the
(then) Duke of Edinburgh in 1875; all was set to go except the
money. Through a series of delaying operations, the project
languished and never rose above its foundations, which, in
due course, the police adapted as far as practicable into
their own building. Some years later the same drill was
observed in the case of the National Theatre on the South
Bank, though that, surprisingly, actually got built by 1976.

   To the west, Whitehall itself resolves into the hub of
Parliament Square—blank, green with good grass. Recently
redisposed, it is a desert island with rhododendrons and a
fringe of bronze colossal statesmen under colossal planes.
Cross to it if you can; it is likely to be difficult, for Parliament
Square is where the roundabout system was initiated (in 1926)
for the benefit of London motor traffic and the detriment of
pedestrians. Ringed by the booming traffic, you may then
brood on formal benches among the brooding statesmen:
Derby, Peel and Beaconsfield. Behind them, on the other
side of the road, Canning (in an exotic cross between early
nineteenth-century English dress and Roman toga) and
Lincoln. The latter is a replica of the strange and rather
charming statue at Chicago by St. Gaudens—an unusual
formula for public statuary incorporating an empty (and
Greek-ish) chair behind the standing figure; although, after
one has seen the statue a few times, one begins to long that it

might be allowed to rest awhile, just to sit down, in that vacant chair that now seems to mock it. A recent addition to this assembly is Epstein's Smuts, a vigorous and brave attempt to inject life into the public memorial. For me, however, it fails. Most recent of all, still awaiting a consensus of approval or disapproval, is Roberts-John's eloquently stubborn Winston Churchill, unveiled late in 1973.

From Parliament Square, looking south, you have the north flank of Westminster Abbey, looming high over the tower of St. Margaret's, the little parish church that sits cosily on the lawns like a lamb beside its mother. And you have the long patterned western flank of Parliament receding from you along the river bank, anchored securely at Westminster Bridge by the 320-foot vertical of the Clock Tower that houses the famous bell (not clock) known as Big Ben, and hundreds of yards away to the south by the complementary and even bigger Victoria Tower: this is in fact the biggest square tower built, 336 feet high.

They are so solid, these two great buildings, and so vested with memory, that it is hard to discount them even in the imagination and look back to their beginnings. The Abbey we shall survey in the next chapter, and our present concern is with the **Palace of Westminster**, which is what the Houses of Parliament are still sometimes called, and which it was from some time in the early eleventh century when the seat of government shifted there from Winchester: the palace where the monarch lived, in close harmony with the nearby Abbey, in which as like as not he would be buried. But it was to begin with more than residence; it had not only its own religious foundation (independent both of King and of Abbot of Westminster) the college of St. Stephen, but contained also in its precincts the early Parliaments. In 1265 the first shire representatives, summoned by Simon de Montfort, met here, and a hundred years later, when the Commons had separated off, they sat generally in the Chapter House of the Abbey itself across the way.

Then, from 1530, as we have seen, the Crown moved out into Wolsey's Whitehall, but both Parliament, the legislature, and the administration of the law remained in Westminster. After the Reformation, the Church, too, moved out, but the upper chapel of the foundation of St. Stephens' was assigned in 1547 for the House of Parliament, and it was in a chapel that the English Parliament debated its business for most of the next three hundred years. About it through the years there was of course a great deal of rebuilding, but all vanished on the night of 16 October 1834 when Westminster burned. It burned through the night with considerable spectacle and magnificence, and most of London turned out to watch (including Turner, with his notebook, and Constable). Next morning the English nation was confronted in the ashes with the necessity of rebuilding its seat of government. Authority decided, among other stipulations, that the architectural style suitable for modern British government was 'either Gothic or Elizabethan', and held a competition; this was won by Sir Charles Barry (known before especially for such admirable exercises in the Renaissance vernacular as the Travellers' Club and the Reform). The plan and overall design of the building we now know was Barry's, and was built between 1840 and 1852 (the clock tower finished only in 1858, the Victoria Tower in 1860), but the detail—the expression of a copious, learned, passionate, seemingly inexhaustible invention—is mainly due to that furious genius of English Gothic, Augustus Pugin, who died insane at the early age of forty in 1852. The story of their collaboration and their rows is one of the sagas of British architectural history, but of the success of its outcome as an asset to the architectural texture of London there is no doubt—that long fretted and pinnacled façade in the grey limestone that warms so gently in the sun and seems, in the river fogs, to be but an enchanted precipitation of the mist along the water-line between the tall buttresses of its great towers. Even though it shrinks yearly, as do all the senior majesties of London, in the context of the new skyscrapers (the Shell building away on the south bank, the Vickers looming almost over Parliament from Millbank), its romanticism is only the more enhanced in contrast with their severity.

Cross to it via **St. Margaret's**, the little church slewed alongside the Abbey. The Abbey more than fills its own chapter, and anyway St. Margaret's belongs as much to Parliament, for it has become (since 1614) the parish church of the House of Commons. It was built in its present basic shape (1504–23) at much the same time as Henry VII's chapel in the Abbey, but the apse of the latter, beyond St. Margaret's, looks positively jazzy in contrast with the traditional late perpendicular of the little church, with its elegant square tower (re-gothicked in Portland stone in the early eighteenth century). Inside there is a famous, much travelled window made about 1501 upon the betrothal of Catherine of Aragon to Prince Arthur (who died, whereupon Henry VIII, Arthur's younger brother, took Catherine as the first of his wives). The glass is Flemish, of good colour with admirable blues and stylistically a fascinating point of balance in the transition from Gothic to Renaissance. There are some good monuments too (my own favourite that to Mrs. Brocas (d. 1654), prim in a curtained oval). Here too as so often in London east or west, one encounters the pleasant memory of Samuel Pepys; here he was married in 1655; and here Milton, next year, was married and Winston Churchill in 1908. With any luck you will sight now at St. Margaret's a marriage with acres of tulle, queues of Rolls-Royces, squads of pages and bridesmaids, top-hats, morning coats—for the church is still, though it has rivals, perhaps *the* church for marriages of high fashion.

Now we can cross to the Houses of Parliament. To your left on the corner of the approach to Westminster Bridge, with Big Ben high above (topped, if the House is in session, by the light that only goes off at night when the House rises), is New Palace Yard, the fine severity of which a monster car park has wrecked; right of that, a relatively low and plain bulk, almost barnlike, with plain steeply pitched dark roof, is Westminster Hall (see p. 120), the oldest surviving part (it escaped the fire) begun in 1097, but remodelled between 1394 and 1402 by the greatest of English Gothic architects, Henry Yevele, who built the nave of the Abbey. In front of Westminster Hall, a burly nineteenth-century evocation (1899, by Thornycroft) of the most formidable Parliamentarian who ever dominated the Commons, Oliver Cromwell (in dark bronze, but great thigh boots and buff coat and sword; he might well appear in the House not much differently dressed 'his linen plain and not very clean . . . a speck or two of blood upon his linen band . . . his countenance swollen and reddish, his voice sharp and untunable and his eloquence full of fervour'). Next to this is a porch, St. Stephen's Entrance. Here you may see people queuing or milling around; they may be waiting to lobby their member (i.e. are constituents waiting to catch the member who represents them in order to convey to him the urgency of their feeling on some political issue) or they may be waiting for a seat in the Public Gallery of the Commons. You too can enter by this porch to the Public Gallery, but to do so you need a ticket, attainable either through your M.P. by writing, or on application to the Admission Order Office in the hall through the porch (the latter method is, however, fallible, especially when controversial debates are in progress, for those introduced by M.P.s have priority and you may never get a seat). Admission to a tour of Parliament is easier, on days when the Houses are not sitting (i.e. on Saturdays, some Bank Holidays and on Mondays and Tuesdays in August; 10–5, free); then the public entrance is at Victoria Tower at the south end of the building. Entrance to the Strangers' Gallery of the House of Lords is also from St. Stephen's Porch, but the Lords sit less diligently (Tuesday to Thursday only; admission from 2.40—Thursdays, 4.10). Westminster Hall, which is not normally involved with Parliamentary business, is generally open on weekdays from 10 until an hour before the Commons sit, or till 4 (Saturdays till 5) when they are not sitting.

I will assume it is a Saturday, or other open day, and that you mean to tour the building. South of St. Stephen's Porch, a courtyard, also full of parliamentary cars (the portcullis badge is of the House of Lords motoring club), opens back from the road. Above, Richard I, Coeur-de-Lion (by Marochetti, 1860) rears up on his horse, his sword flung heavenward. But it is the unseen that claims attention here, for this is Old Palace Yard, where died on the scaffold Guy Fawkes and some of his colleagues in the Great Gunpowder Plot, in memory of which the night skies of London flare with rockets and fireworks every 5 November—but also where died a far more extraordinary Englishman, in some ways the most various, most fascinating, of all the great Elizabethans: Sir Walter Raleigh. From a scaffold in Old Palace Yard, at eight o'clock on the morning of 29 October 1618, clad in black velvet, he addressed the crowd. Then he tested the axe—'a sharp and fair medicine to cure all my diseases'. Without fear, he refused to be blindfold; without fear, he rebuked the fearful headsman—'What dost thou fear? Strike, man, strike!' And so, went. (He is buried, probably if not entirely certainly, in St. Margaret's across the road, but the memorials to him there are modern.)

So you come along the flickering stone panelling of the façade to the **Victoria Tower**; the tower itself is stately, showing no traces of a recent undignified operation in the course of which it was gutted, its stories doubled up and its air conditioned. It is the home of some million and a half Parliamentary documents, including the original copy of every Act of Parliament since 1497—a very rich archive for historians, its range not merely Parliamentary but including curiosities such as a couple of forged tombstones sent from Ireland about 1850 in support of a claim for a title.

The entry is up the Royal Staircase to the Norman Porch; it is the entry to some eight acres submerged under stone and over a thousand rooms, a hundred staircases, eleven courtyards and miles of corridors. However this conglomeration, of which one sees only a section, is planned according to a fairly strict ceremonial and functional logic, into a coherent body politic. The part of the body which we traverse is its spine, the nerve channel of the whole organism. It is disposed according to the chain of command—Crown, Lords, Commons, though in practice the reality of the sequence is the other way round. But when Parliament is opened, the Queen enters under Victoria Tower, climbs the staircase and enters the **Robing Room**. This is no cosy chamber for a quick change, but a huge state room 54 feet long, and every inch of its surface elaborately decorated (it is in fact perhaps the most tellingly characteristic of the Palace's interiors for Pugin's style—note the fireplace with its mosaic and gilt statuettes). The paintings, of the legend of King Arthur, are by Dyce, and here it should be mentioned that, as will be borne in on all visitors, the occasion of rebuilding in the 1840s was accepted as a deliberate challenge to promote the fine arts of England. Dyce was one of the most successful of the artists employed, much influenced by the German Nazarenes and with a clearer grasp of the problems of composing on a large scale than his rivals. But the frescoes are dimmed by time, and here already the sombre if rich characteristic colour range of the Houses of Parliament is established—deep browns, reds, greens, with the lustre of encrusted gold, were agreeable to Pugin. In this room, the House of Lords sat in 1941–51, when the bombed-out Commons moved into their abode. The next room is the **Royal Gallery**, a hall 110 feet long, with various large painted royal portraits and a full set of monarchs in gilt statues, from Alfred to Queen Anne. The two enormous paintings, by Maclise, are the most interesting in the building—the *Death of Nelson*, and *Wellington Meeting with Blücher*. The floor is intricately patterned in buff, red and blue in another of Pugin's favourites, Minton's encaustic tiles. Beyond this, as ante-room to the actual House of Lords, the Prince's Chamber, dark with panelling, and with an overweening but very competent marble group of Victoria between Justice and Mercy (by John Gibson, 1854), and much brilliant detailing of lively quality—the fireplace, the lamp brackets.

This admirable detailing is again triumphant in the **House of Lords**, reinforced by a splendid dominance of rich red in the dimpled benches where the peers sit. At the south end, the formidable carved and gilt canopy over the Queen's throne, with a second throne a little lower to the right for the Consort. In front of that, a stuffed object is the famous Woolsack, whereon the Lord Chancellor presides over the house, with the mace behind him—a tradition that goes back to the days when the wealth of England rested more literally on wool than it does now. A session is worth attending; the Lords tend to get rather a poor press, being quoted frequently as an outstanding example of the English institution in need of either radical reform or abolition, or dismissed with epithets such as 'the last infirmary of noble minds'. Their debates are indeed sonorous with copious lardings of lordships, but also often very cogent, very acutely informed, and at times less inhibited by considerations of party than those in the Commons. The institution of life peerages has quickened proceedings considerably. And it is in the Lords that Parliament retains its last vestige of judicial power (other judicial functions having all shifted east, see Chapter 21). The Lords are the final Court of Appeal for all other courts.

The way thence is through the Peers' Lobby, the Peers' Corridor (with some rather spirited historical scenes painted by Cope, especially perhaps the famous one of Charles I's coffin in the snow), into the Central Lobby, a formidably decorated octagon under a vaulted mosaic-glinting ceiling seventy-five feet up (it supports the middle lantern tower of the Houses of Parliament). This Lobby is the common ground between Lords and Commons, and also the rallying point of those with business with their members. We shall return to it, but in the meantime pass on into the Commons' Corridor and through to the Commons' Lobby (with statues of modern statesmen). Thence through the Churchill Arch—made from stones damaged in the fire of 1941—into the **House of Commons**, and, alas, visually, anti-climax. The chamber wherein the voices of Macaulay and Lord John Russell, of Bright, Gladstone and Disraeli, of Randolph Churchill, of Lloyd George, had sounded was bombed out in 1941, and the replacement gives the impression, after the wealth of the old parts, of being done on the cheap, although furnished with loyal wood from the Commonwealth. However, the traditions remain; the two parties still are ranged opposite each other, with the two red lines in front of the front benches still set two swords' length apart to avoid unseemly fracas between members. When in session, the daily business is still announced by the procession of the Speaker still in black knee-breeches, gown and wig, with the Sergeant-at-Arms with Mace, train-bearer, chaplain, secretary. And passion and tempers still rise, invective still stabs against sweet reason or adept ministerial side-stepping, and though suspicion grows that Britain is really governed from the Cabinet Room at No. 10 Downing Street, it is in the Commons that the fate of individual freedom still lies.

Back in the Central Lobby, worked into Minton's encaustic tiles, you will find the Latin text from the Vulgate, meaning—'Except the Lord keep the house, they labour in vain that build it.' The lower reaches of the space are frigid with marble Victorian statesmen, and more of them (supplemented by the most recent, rather pastelly, history paintings, unveiled only in 1927) are in the long hall leading off to the west. This is St. Stephen's Hall, and replaces the old upper chapel of St. Stephen's, which was for so many years the House of Commons (which is still sometimes referred to as St. Stephen's). Four brass rosettes in the floor mark the spot where once the Speaker's chair stood—whence Speaker Lenthall denied Charles I when he came to arrest the five members: 'May it please your Majesty, I have neither eyes to see nor tongue to speak in this place, but as this House doth direct me whose servant I am . . .' Since that encounter, three and a quarter centuries ago, the Sovereign has never been admitted to the

House of Commons. Hence steps lead down to St. Stephen's Porch, and thence to Westminster Hall. First perhaps go on down (a staircase from the south-cast angle of the hall) to the so-called crypt of St. Stephen's (which was originally, like the Sainte Chapelle in Paris, in two stories, of which this was the lower, rather than the crypt). It was begun in 1292, and still has what are perhaps the earliest of lierne vaults, but is now emblazoned with the copious decoration of nineteenth-century restoration. Here M.P.s may marry, and have their children baptised.

Westminster Hall is simply tremendous and its roof in particular is tremendous, perhaps the best in Europe of its kind and date, a massive oak hammer-beam, much as it was (though the wood has been restored against the death-watch beetle) when finished in 1402. It has some good late-fourteenth-century statues of kings, and the angels at the end of the beams have a quite cheerful grace, but apart from its tremendousness, Westminster Hall has, most acutely in winter, a chill that is almost an ache. It echoes; a fog can almost dissolve it; it is above all empty, as if exhausted of occasion that has seen so much occasion. For here from the thirteenth century till the nineteenth were the chief courts of law of England. Edward II abdicated in this great room, Richard II was deposed, and the air should be keening with death sentences—on Sir Thomas More, Bishop Fisher; on Protector Somerset and on the Earl of Essex, and many more. But most resonantly on Charles I in 1649 . . . 'for all which Treasons and Crimes this Court doth adjudge, that he, the said Charles Stuart, as a Tyrant, Traitor, Murderer, and public Enemy to the good people of this Nation shall be put to Death by severing of his Head from his Body'.

Over the road from St. Stephen's Porch is the memorial, smoothly severe, to George V, the statue by Reid Dick; and then, set back from the road, in a little moat (where there are trout and goldfish though the trout tend to eat the goldfish), is the last surviving relic of the old domestic Palace of Westminster: the **Jewel Tower**. Of antique, battered fabric (built probably by Yevele originally) it was once Edward III's personal treasury, but became later the record house for the House of Lords. Now restored, it is open to visitors on week-days (10.30–6.30; October to February to 4), and is a little museum of relics and documents relating to the Palace of

Westminster. Farther west from this is a big late bronze by Henry Moore, and, along the river side of the road the pleasant strip of green of **Victoria Tower Gardens**, with huge plane trees, an excellent command of the river, and statues to the militant Mrs. Pankhurst (d. 1928), who led the suffragettes to victory, and to the Burghers of Calais who surrendered to Edward III in 1347 to prevent the destruction of their city—a cast of that great group by Rodin. Inland, there is a complex of little roads with little houses, very pretty in parts, about the southern skirts of Westminster Abbey, once very slummy but now very smart (desirable residences for M.P.s). In **Smith Square**, besides some old houses on the west side, and the contrasting habitats of party machines of Left and Right (the Labour Transport House, the Conservative and Unionist Central Office), is the astonishing presence, emphatically and sonorously Baroque after so much Gothic, of St. John. Built by Thomas Archer between 1713–28, it was known to Londoners, puritanically scornful of its flamboyance, as the footstool church—from a story that Queen Anne gave the architect its principles of design by kicking a footstool upside down. And it has indeed, over the gigantic porches with gigantic columns and spectacularly interrupted pediments, four highly unrestrained towers with pinnacles. Bombed, it used to be the most resonantly forlorn of London ruins, a gorgeous hulk behind barbed wire, boarded windows, with two glorious plane trees loaded and weeping at its blocked entrance—but now, after much campaigning, has been restored to include a successful small concert hall.

A little farther south brings you to **Lambeth Bridge**, whence you can take a last look at the Houses of Parliament, at the river front—in a clear light so symmetrical ('All Grecian' said the contemptuous Pugin, 'Tudor details on a classic body') and yet so mysterious above with towers and pinnacles. And on a misty day, hauntingly romantic, melting and merging in haze along the river.

I have here attempted to describe the Palace of Westminster in its *status quo*, but in the decade 1960–70 there shimmered through the actuality mammoth planners' dreams in concrete of extensions between Big Ben and the Ministry of Defence. Parliament Square might even become a pedestrian precinct— an unlikely but happy thought.

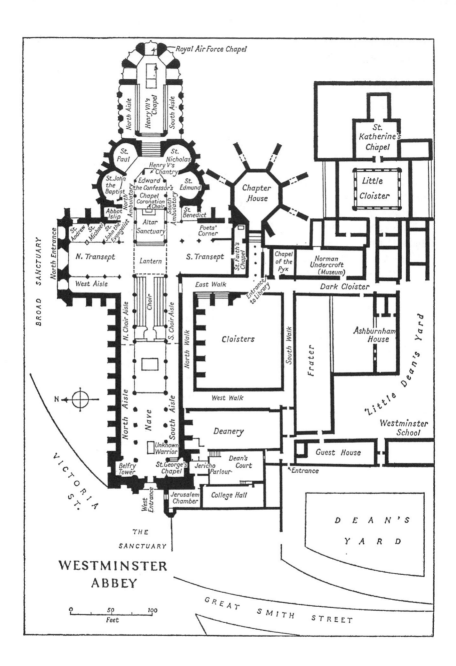

Royal Air Force Chapel

North Aisle

Henry VII's Chapel

South Aisle

St. Paul

St. Nicholas

Henry V's Chantry

St. John the Baptist

Edward the Confessor's Chapel

Coronation Chair

St. Edmund

North Ambulatory

South Ambulatory

Abbot Islip

St. Benedict

St. Andrew

St. Michael

St. John the Evangelist

Altar

Sanctuary

Poets' Corner

St. Katherine's Chapel

Little Cloister

Chapter House

BROAD SANCTUARY

North Entrance

N. Transept

West Aisle

Lantern

S. Transept

St. Faith's Chapel

Chapel of the Pyx

Norman Undercroft (Museum)

East Walk

Entrance to Library

Dark Cloister

N. Choir Aisle

Choir

S. Choir Aisle

North Walk

Cloisters

South Walk

Frater

Ashburnham House

Little Dean's Yard

N

North Aisle

Nave

South Aisle

West Walk

Deanery

Westminster School

Unknown Warrior

Belfry Tower

St. George's Chapel

Jericho Parlour

Dean's Court

Guest House

Entrance

West Entrance

Jerusalem Chamber

College Hall

VICTORIA ST.

THE SANCTUARY

DEAN'S YARD

WESTMINSTER ABBEY

0   50   100
Feet

GREAT SMITH STREET

CHAPTER EIGHT

Westminster Abbey

COME now, as did James Boswell near two hundred years ago, when he 'amongst the tombs was solemn and happy'. The site of Westminster Abbey is Thorney Isle, a firm strip of gravel in what was riverside swamp, as was all this bend of the river almost as far as Chelsea; the Romans were here, but the Christian connections only begin perhaps in the eighth century, and the true founder of the church was Edward the Confessor, who began to rebuild it and its attendant monastic buildings about 1050. The actual fabric that we now know dates in essentials only from 1245 onwards, inspired initially by Henry III, who had as patron saint his predecessor the Confessor. In 1269, the body of the Confessor was translated into the still uncompleted church of the Abbey of St. Peter's, and a certain amount of building went on until the addition of its most perfect magnificence, Henry VII's chapel, begun in 1503. A quarter of a century later we might well have lost Westminster Abbey, when the Reformed Religion carried out the ruthless dissolution of monasteries. But the church of Westminster survived, although not a cathedral, because of its already intimate bonds with crown and government, already sanctified by centuries of coronations, already the mausoleum of generations of English royalty, and with the embryonic Parliament meeting in its Chapter House and the Royal Treasury firmly established in the Chapel of the Pyx. So it survived. Thereafter the history of its stones is already one of restoration as much as of addition. Restoration was necessary in the early seventeenth century, and has continued ever since, so that the exterior we see now is (relatively) modern; the last major addition came in the early eighteenth century, the towers on the west front built to the designs of Wren and Hawksmoor.

These twin towers are confusing. They are best seen, I

think, distinct from the body of the church, that is from St. James's Park through the trees, and preferably on a summer evening incandescent against the lowering sun. Then they are exactly right, a water-colourist's dream beyond the water and the foliage; not truly Gothic, but eighteenth or early nineteenth-century Gothic picturesque. And they are in Portland stone, with that luminous but hazy insubstantiality that is the quality of a much later London skyline than that of the Abbey proper. Seen from Parliament Square or from Victoria Street even, they appear to be grafted on to the Abbey from some much smaller stock; they neither anchor it nor resolve its composition. Indeed, the mass of the Abbey is a great cross-shaped, blackish hulk, of immense power and weight. Before it had its towers, before the surrounding buildings, pushing ever upwards, began to hide it, it used to emerge from West London among its buttress bones like some divine railway shed, rather brutal, functional and even unfinished (in fact the central accent that should exist over the crossing of transepts and nave and chancel was never completed, and the skyline of the roof is bleak).

Best, even if you start from Parliament Square, to enter not by the door of the north transept immediately opposite you by St. Margaret's, but to go round to the west door and enter under the towers. Thus you come in at the foot of the cross-shaped plan, and can scan the building according to its logic. (I do not propose to attempt a precise and detailed account of architecture or of the furnishings of the Abbey; as Daniel Defoe remarked—about 1725, well before many of the most massive tombs had been installed—'the particulars are too long to enter into here, and are so many times described by several authors, that it would be a vain repetition to enter upon it here; besides, we have by no means any room for it'. The best brief guide is Professor Pevsner's, in his Pelican *London*, volume I, but even that most succinct of cataloguers takes ninety pages over it. For more detail, see the famous books by W. R. Lethaby.)

Any visitor coming to the Abbey for the first time should be forewarned that, if he wishes to get the most out of it, he must be prepared to perform a mental and visual splits of great dexterity; for the Abbey is two things. It is a beautiful and remarkably coherent church in the idiom of the thirteenth century; an English restatement, though still with an unusually

French accent, of the themes of Reims and Amiens—lofty, exalted, exulting to its vaulted roof. From where you enter, your eyes rise with it all the length of the great nave: from the dark purplish-greenish-greyish piers in the suffused tinted light from the coloured glass of aisle windows, lifting with the clean spring of the white arches to the fretted gallery and up into the clear light of the clerestory windows, into the roof. As now cleaned, and defined by slim gold lines, the vault looks like a linen-drape canopy, pinned by gorgeously gilt bosses like brooches, and held by gold patterned transversal bars. Here is a serene statement of the confidence, the harmony of the immortal spirit of man with God; a prophecy of heavenly mansions. But it is unlikely that your mortal eye will allow you to linger within this vision for long, because all about you, at ground level, in utter confusion, riot the memorials to the great English dead, in all sizes, styles and shapes, fitted together, or rather wedged together like a solution imposed by force upon a mixed bag of jigsaw puzzles. And the dead are not serene, not reconciled. For all that—as their epitaphs proclaim—they were of great distinction, and are all now indubitably dead to the world; yet, in the sheer size and material wealth of their memorials, they deny the epitaph's admission and renunciation of human vanity, and stake a last material claim for continuation on earth in the eyes of the curious sightseers of the centuries. Simultaneously, they have frozen themselves in their own time; in the dateable cadences of the epitaphs even; in their costume and in their gesture; in their style. Along the walls of the nave they are at least mainly co-ordinated tolerably flush with the walls, but elsewhere, in the transepts and in the chapels of the apse, they are cluttered like the discarded furniture in an attic, sometimes even emerging forlorn from piles of stacked chairs or cleaning instruments. There can be no argument but that they clash with the architecture; they do not (unless you are of extreme delicacy of sensibility) quite wreck it, for you can always look up, but they clog the take-off of this aerial building maddeningly. It is as though the clean floor of a northern beech forest had been infested with tropical undergrowth.

But take courage and embark. Best perhaps to tour the whole building first, swiftly to establish its geography, if you have the strength of mind to resist the distractions that

beckon to you every inch of the way. Up the nave then to the
central obstruction of the choir-screen with the organ, a
crash of gaudy ninetecnth-century red and gold and blue
containing, pale as if drowned, the marble figures of Sir Isaac
Newton and of Lord Stanhope; right round it and up the
south aisle to the crossing of the transepts, with the high
altar central beneath it and a huge lift of space left and right
to the rose windows that close each transept. On—but here a
fee payable unless it's Friday—into the chancel with its apsed
end, and off the curve of the apse the radial chapels bulging
with the haphazard lumber of the dead. At the end of the
apse, bear hard round to your left and up a strange bridge,
squeezing past a headless effigy stranded mid-passage on a
table-tomb (can *this* be Henry V?),[1] and so into a barbaric
and hushed plateau hollow among a defence of tombs: the
shrine of Edward the Confessor. Back then over the bridge,
and straight on up a wide stretch of serene steps into another
world: the appendix to the Abbey, linked on to its eastern
extremity. Unseen, unsuspected from the main body of the
Abbey, this appendix, this Lady Chapel, affects not like an
afterthought, but like a triumphant coda in a startling change
of key. If you're in luck, and its upper air is shot with sunlight, it can stop you in your tracks as if a volley of silver
trumpets had sounded in your face. This is Henry VII's
Chapel (see p. 134), built in 1503–12, at once the swan-song
of English Gothic architecture and the prelude, though already in superb confidence of achievement and of continuation of a new royal dynasty: the Tudors.

Then, if you can get away from this, one of the loveliest
things in all England, you come back into the northern curve
of the Abbey apse, with radial chapels again on your right
and the wall of Plantagenet tombs on your left, chill and
sombre after the radiance of the chapel, down to the crossing
and so back down the nave towards the west door with a
marble Pitt gesturing for ever onwards above it.

Just by the door is the tomb of the Unknown Warrior, that
inspired expression of mourning for a whole generation laid
waste, for a whole world lost: the fern-fringed slab in the
Abbey floor containing earth of France and clay of a nameless
English soldier killed in France in the First World War. The
only dust in the Abbey floor on which you do not walk. From

[1] Indeed: he was supplied with a new head in 1970.

here I can only drift, stopping here and there, but leaving out most, for the Abbey is not for a few hours but for days and weeks before you begin to know it.

An essential part of getting to know the Abbey is to attend a service there. I wonder how many of the thousands who go think of the church as still active. The great ceremonies of state, of course, are now known to the nation via television even if few are privileged to go in person; but the church is also daily alive with prayer and song. Its status is odd; it has neither parish nor bishop but is, like St. George's at Windsor, a 'royal peculiar', its Dean responsible only to (after God) the Crown. But to hear, at evensong, from somewhere in the Abbey's depth a prayer intoned by a single voice, to hear it rise, lonely, almost as if groping against the immensity of the building; then to hear the lift and surge of the choir, music flooding to the vault—this is to have the building's fabric as if lit, re-defined by some other sunshine. When services are in progress, movement of visitors is restricted, so that if you are intent on study of the building the best times are between about 11 a.m. and 4 p.m. Admission to an ever-increasing amount of the eastern end becomes chargeable, but I hope the perambulation suggested here may still be practicable, though even Poets' Corner be no longer free.

My personal way from the **West Door** starts a little way up in the north (left) aisle with the monument to Charles James Fox, shown in the collapse of his flesh, togaed, expiring on his couch, a female Liberty supporting him, Peace at his feet and a Negro mourning for Fox's part in the abolition of slavery—though rhetorical, it is more moving than that monument to his great rival Pitt over the west door (they died in the same year, 1806, and are buried not far apart in the north transept). Thence you pass the monuments, serried against the medieval wall arcading, but this is perhaps the least interesting aisle of the Abbey, and is not enlivened much by the windows (the windows throughout the Abbey are mostly late). Yet, having said that, I will no doubt be immediately rebuked by some visitor who is precisely most interested in the north aisle of the nave. Indeed, as everywhere in the Abbey, there are here the surprises, sometimes almost hidden. Thus, still in the north aisle, but right up by the screen just before the opening of the north transept, I knew that monument, singularly large, to a son of 'Sir Edward Carteret,

Knight, Gentleman Usher of the Black Rod and First Gentleman Usher Daily Waiter in Ordinary to the King, etc., etc.'—his titles absorbing far more room than the notice allowed to his son who caused the monument by dying in 1677 'Aged Seaven Yeares and Nine Months' but I had missed, just above and right of this on the wall, a delightful little medieval boss of a plump, leering man's face (the best place whence to see this is to stand on either Darwin or Herschel).

The **north transept**, with one of the main entrances to the Abbey (Solomon's Porch) at its end, is formidably crowded, and divided into three, as it were a west aisle, a 'nave', and an east aisle. The west aisle has some good busts, with a high proportion of Empire builders and a couple of philanthropists: Jonas Hanway (d. 1786; Londoners owe a debt to Hanway, not mentioned on the epitaph, for he popularised the umbrella); and Elizabeth Warren, who died in 1816 at the age of 83. She is immortalised by a very distinguished statue of a beggar girl with a baby at her breast, signifying charity (by Westmacott). The bosses in the roof also reward attention. The centre or nave of the north transept has a number of nineteenth-century statesmen standing rather larger than life in white marble on circular tuns of the same material, rather macabre, like a surrealist dream of Speakers' Corner; they include Canning, Castlereagh, Peel, Palmerston, Disraeli, Gladstone, pale and still, the torrents of words that poured from them in Parliament over the other side of the road all drained away. Of earlier monuments the most remarkable (west side) is the huge allegorical extravaganza to the elder Pitt, Earl of Chatham (by Bacon; cost £6,000—a fortune then). In an inset niche, you can see him in his eloquence, as on his last appearance in 1778 when he came, mortally ill, to the Lords to deliver an impassioned appeal against the dismemberment of the Empire (against the severance of the American colonies); it was his swan-song—having spoken, he collapsed with his final stroke. On the east side, a good complex double monument for the Cavalier Duke of Newcastle and his eccentric blue-stocking Duchess ('a wise wittie and learned lady which her many Bookes do well testifie . . .'): the Duke holds a baton, though he was far from an effective soldier, his wife has an open book, probably by herself.

The entrance to the eastern aisle of the north transept is

Rain at Westminster, on bus, taxi and umbrella

Snow in Trafalgar Square, on lions, George IV and St Martin's

Westminster Abbey, the west front. The towers are the latest (1735–40) major addition to the Abbey: the lower parts go back to fourteenth century work of Henry Yevele, the great architect of the nave beyond the iron gates which divides off the east end of the church and to get through which you must (except on Fridays) pay, so I will for the time being leave it, and cross instead through to the south transept. But pause a moment in front of the central altar, whence you can see the sheer and lofty splendour of the transept rising to the great rose windows (both restored) and above you the lantern. Here binoculars are needed, to focus what are perhaps the most magical sculpture in the Abbey, the censing angels in the corners under each rose window in the transepts, relations in their radiant and smiling spirituality to the figures of Reims. Behind you the choir, with its banked stalls, is open.

The **south transept**, which repeats the plan of the north, is held in affection as **Poets' Corner**, centred on the monument to the father of English poetry, Geoffrey Chaucer, who lived in a house where now is Henry VII's chapel, and was buried in the Abbey; his monument (he died in 1400) was only set up in 1555, but the burial of Spenser close by began the congregation of poets in this spot which has continued ever since, and they now occupy much of the south transept. In the early eighteenth century their ranks were swelled by the erection of retrospective monuments, to some degree in reflection of a patriotic awareness of the achievements of the British muse and also perhaps of a not disinterested exaltation of the literary profession. Dryden's bust (by Scheemakers, 1731); Ben Johnson's and Milton's (both by Rysbrack in 1737)— these and others were joined in 1741 by the Bard himself; if belatedly, then given the pre-eminence of a full-length standing statue (by Scheemakers). This cross-legged figure, pensive, is properly elegiac, but this is also very much Shakespeare as recreated by the Augustan imagination—both Pope and Lord Burlington were on the committee responsible for it. In front of him, under the flagstones lies his greatest idolater, the actor David Garrick, who is celebrated on the opposite wall by an effective monument showing him parting the curtains as if making his final bow. Just to the left of Garrick is a charming conceit: one John Grabius seated comfy on a sarcophagus, with his feet dangling almost as if picnicking. Here also you will find (a very incomplete selection, this) Wordsworth, Coleridge and Southey; Dr. Johnson (a splendid bust by Nollekens); Addison and Burns; Goldsmith, Thackeray, Scott, Camden, Ruskin, and a hypnotic interpretation of

Blake's life-mask by Epstein. But the two sculpturally most remarkable monuments are not literary: the Handel monument (1761), and that to John Duke of Argyll (1748–9), both by Roubiliac; the latter in its delicate virtuosity combined with a magnificent baroque sweep of composition is probably Roubiliac's greatest work. Two early poets' monuments have been removed to the gallery above the transept, those of Rowe and of John Gay, the latter with its famous quote from himself—'Life is a jest, and all things shew it: I thought so once, and now I know it.' This gallery (accessible only from the Library), with a big fourteenth-century painting of Richard II's White Hart, was perhaps originally the Royal Pew. At the end of the south transept are two recently recovered murals of the late thirteenth century, attenuated, battered but moving ghosts, St. Thomas and St. Christopher, and also the door into St. Faith's Chapel, which is reserved for private prayer but has excellent grotesque corbel heads at the springing of the arches which should be seen by the discreet visitor.

The way back towards the west door goes via the **south choir aisle**, in which is most remarkable the monument to Thomas Thynne, assassinated in the Haymarket in 1682 by hirelings of Count Konigsmarck, who wanted Thynne's bride, the richest heiress in England; it includes a spirited relief of the scene of the murder. Here are also memorials to Admiral Blake, Clive and an extraordinarily pompous celebration of the drowned Admiral Cloudesley Shovell, and, skied high, that to Sir Godfrey Kneller, who is curiously the only painter with a monument in the Abbey (his epitaph is, according to its composer, Pope, the worst thing he ever wrote; his body is elsewhere, for Kneller himself said: 'By God, I will not be buried in Westminster . . . They do bury fools there').

Continuing back down the south aisle of the nave, two monuments connected with American wars: to Major André, hanged in 1780 as a spy, and to Roger Townshend, who was killed in America in 1759 and is shown dying in strict classical dress, upheld by two Red Indians. Then another spectacular Roubiliac monument, to General Hargrave (1757), the warrior starting from his grave, and an illusionistic rendering of a collapsing obelisk above. Mrs. Bovey (d. 1727) has a charming medallic portrait and a simply endless eulogy as to how a rich lady *can* pass through the eye of a needle. Then there is Dean Wilcox, with a pretty little relief of the towers of the Abbey, erected in his tenure of office; and Congreve, with dramatic masks, in a memorial put up by the Duchess of Marlborough (Sarah's daughter) who doted on him, and is said, after his death, to have had a small ivory facsimile of him which moved by clockwork and with which she had conversations. Under the South Tower by the door (St. George's Chapel; dedicated to the dead of 1914–18), a figure of most elegant pathos leaning on an urn, James Craggs by Guelfi, with an epitaph by Pope; this was, formally, a most influential statue, its cross-legged melancholy repeated not only by Shakespeare in Poets' Corner, but by Hudson, Devis, Reynolds and Gainsborough. On the pillar by the West Door hangs usually the colossal contemporary painting of Richard II; a formidable rendering of enthroned majesty.

Thus far the perambulation has been almost peripheral, and it is time to approach the crux—the **High Altar** under the crossing, where the great symbolic rites of the nation are observed, weddings, coronations and funerals. Here is the Sanctuary, set among its gabled tombs that date from the early fourteenth century (the effigies worn to anonymity but with names like bells—Edmund Crouchback, Aveline Countess of Lancaster, Aymer de Valence); its pavement is one of the most exotic things in the Abbey, mosaic by Roman craftsmen, the Cosmati, brought to London by Abbot Ware in the 1260s. This tends to be invisible under a carpet, but you can catch a strange echo of it in the National Gallery, for Holbein copied part of it in the pavement of his portrait of *The Ambassadors*—over four and a quarter centuries ago, yet the pavement was a good 250 years old when Holbein knew it. And in the sedilia, three eight-foot high painted figures, sinuously and elegantly stylised in dark but wine-clear colour; the most important English wall-paintings surviving from the fourteenth century. Choir and sanctuary form part of a building within the building; an enclosure, roofless between its screens, free-standing under the great Abbey vaulting above, and studded with old and new. This inner building proceeds upwards in stages from west to east, and the heart of its matter, and indeed the heart of the whole Abbey for me, is the highest and most easterly stage, beyond the high altar: the Feretory, the Shrine of Edward the Confessor.

To reach this you have to engage into the south ambulatory,

the curved way round the apse, through the painted iron toll gate. And before we reach it, we must first glance at the chapels off the ambulatory on its south side. The first (St. Benedict's) is dominated by a huge monument with pyramiding obelisks to the Countess of Hertford. In the next (St. Edmund) is the tomb of John of Eltham (1337), with fascinating weepers, with a curious almost affected swagger of posture; the cross-legged alabaster effigy itself is potent (he was a son of Edward II), but still more so is the battered, engraved and enamelled figure, in copper of William de Valence (d. 1296—half-brother of Henry III); this is probably Limoges work. Outside, in the ambulatory, on the flank of Edward III's tomb, splendidly visible sculpture of high quality from the late fourteenth century—weepers again, touchingly awkward, frail-limbed as gilt wooden dolls (the third from the left represents the Black Prince). Further on, on the left a battered predella painting needs a close look to discover the quality of its stylised elegance—it has been called the most important surviving painting in north European art of the late thirteenth century. Back to the chapels on the other side of the ambulatory, and the brilliance of recent restoration now comes clamouring through the screens that half veil their mouths. This brilliance—of scarlets, crimsons, blues, of silver and gold —has disturbed some critics, yet it probably reflects fairly closely the original effect: particularly of course for Elizabethan and Jacobean tombs of whose 'barbarity' even a contemporary sophisticate like Sir Henry Wotton complained. A particularly operatic note is struck by the flashing colour of the wall-monument to Lady Fare, the figures almost as if in a box, with billowing curtains, at the theatre. But perhaps most notable are early representatives of one of the enduring dynasties of England's aristocracy, the Cecils (marquesses of Salisbury), especially in the complex tomb to Mildred, wife of Elizabeth's first Lord Burghley, the founder of the breed, with their daughter behind. Burghley himself can be seen kneeling in the superstructure, and at the near end their son Robert, later Lord High Treasurer and the builder of Hatfield. A tomb in the middle bears a perhaps even more remarkable sire, Sir George Villiers (1605); though in other faculties undistinguished, to him the pedigrees of an astonishing number of subsequent outstanding figures in English history go back— even that of Sir Winston Churchill. And now, at the top of the apse, if you bear hard round to your left, you will find yourself in the Shrine of Edward the Confessor.

The shrine is a magic place, sombre, cut off; once in it you are enclosed, walled in by tombs of kings. Its texture is barbaric, bruised and pitted by time, and it contains a regality of decay matched nowhere in England—

> Here are sands, ignoble things,
> Drop't from the ruin'd sides of Kings . . .

And here people whisper (mostly, in the Abbey, there is a cheery coming and going of feet and voices; for all its regiment of tombs, its fabric does not abash but encourages). Central in this strange place, and too bulking big for it, is the great blind two-storied catafalque of the Confessor. Edward, who consecrated the original church here in 1065, still lies where he was transferred in 1163. The base of his tomb is (like the pavement here and in the Sanctuary) Roman work by the Cosmati of 1270, chipped and damaged and of the most forlorn majesty.

Opposite, behind the High Altar, stands normally the **Coronation Chair**, knocked uncomfortably together by Master Walter about 1300 to encase the Stone of Scone that Edward I brought back from Scotland. It is signed copiously by eighteenth-century visitors. This was the traditional seat for crowning of the Kings of Scotland, and its incorporation with the English seat signifies also the union of the two countries— a union still militantly resisted by some Scots from time to time, as when recently the Stone was abducted and withdrawn briefly back to Scotland. The whole area is as if embattlemented around by the ponderous royal tombs, that bear their effigies shoulder-high. Edward I, un-effigied, secret in massive black marble. Edward's Queen, Eleanor, and Henry III both have effigies by the same sculptor (Torel) in 1291, both figures of unexpectedly gentle sensitivity, in sweet and flowing folds of bronze-gilt, almost Burne-Jonesian in feeling. Between them, a small chest of dark marble, placed almost as casually as a trunk for leaving, holds a daughter of Henry VII, Elizabeth Tudor. Philippa of Hainault, on a blue marble tomb; marble herself, too, and once brilliant with gold glass and beads—now long despoiled, and her face pitifully punched about. Edward III, placid and utterly venerable, his face flowing calmly into his long beard; and side by side on a bronze-gold plate, Richard II and his Queen, Anne of Bohemia, laid out in tender and sophisticated resignation. These last were made during the King's lifetime and doubtless to his pleasure (in 1394–5, by Yevele, Lot, Broker and Prest), and the portrait of the King himself is the first portrait of an Englishman that is demonstrably a likeness, as you can check if you look at the monumental painting of him crowned in majesty that hangs by the west door of the Abbey, or at his portrait in the Wilton Diptych in the National Gallery.

The way-out, the escape from this haunted and over-charged arena is through the chantry of another king, under a heavily carved screen over which ride the helm, shield and saddle of Henry V and past his freshly headed effigy; his original head was silver, and irresistible as loot. Beyond this, we are again in **Henry VII's Chapel,** perhaps for hours. The floor is discreetly civilised in black and white marble diamonds, and is eighteenth century; beneath are Hano-verians. It strikes an oddly lay note after the great stone grey flags of the Abbey, but matches the sophistication of the sixteenth century chapel perfectly, an admirable foil for the consummate virtuosity, the aerial acrobatics in stone that go on overhead. The fan-vaulting is in fact not fan-vaulting, but an illusion of fan-vaulting conceived in sheer exuberance of invention, as if in mischief to contradict the proposition that a groin-vault is not a fan-vault. If you look hard, or if you help yourself with binoculars, you can see the prim functional shape of the groin vault driving skywards, you can see it actually through the apparent ceiling of the fan, which is no more than a canopy of (brilliantly balanced) solid carved stone that the ribs of the vault, the transverse arches, as it were extrude. Like a lovely rich-textured fan of foam on the edge of the tide, it is the last fling of the Gothic, for the sheer heaven of it. It is also peculiar to England, and to be found nowhere else. And below, in another medium, Gothic makes a severer, almost final blow in iron—the rich grille behind the altar; and through the grille, through the intricacies and angles of the Gothic you see, harmoniously contained by it, the first full flowering of the Renaissance in England; the bronze tomb of Henry VII and Elizabeth of York made by the Italian Torrigiani between 1512 and 1518. The effigies them-selves are of radiant dignity, but almost impossible to see; but the little stout boys, so lightly portly, that adorn the ends of the tombs, speak in a new language of a paradise unknown to the Gothic church, of a resurrection not merely of body and soul but of all the senses into the bargain.

The texture of the whole chapel is for England incredibly rich; not only in ceiling and the intricacies of the stalls, in the floating banners, the blazoned stall-plates of the Knights of the Bath, and the vivid enamelled helms and crests of the knights, but in the wealth of sculpture, beautifully preserved, the figures of saints that line the nave. With a pair of glasses, a manual of saint recognition and the Golden Legend, you could pass hours working them out, and they are remarkably individualised, unparalleled in England for their vividness and vitality at this period, though their makers are still unknown. Then swoop floorwards, literally under the seats of the stalls, not to miss the crisp plebeian fantasies going on in the misericords.

There is no tomb other than that of Henry VII in the chancel of his chapel that is especially good, though the radial chapels are as usual very full, except the east one; this is dedicated to the Royal Air Force, with a new, fierce window (just in front of this, in the floor, an inscription for Oliver Cromwell, who rested here briefly between 1657 and the Restoration of 1660, when he and all other regicides were dragged forth and after indignities flung into a pit unnamed).

But do not miss the aisles on both sides of the chapel. In the south aisle, you can really see the nobility of Torrigiani's work, in the bronze effigy to Henry VII's mother, Lady Margaret Beaufort, perhaps the finest effigy in the whole Abbey; serene in dignity yet utterly human. Its apparently effortless finality and economy makes the much more elaborate four-poster Jacobean piece set up by James I for his mother Mary Queen of Scots seem all but redundant. In front of the altar Charles II, William and Mary, and Anne lie without memorial. (Without memorial, but thus was William's Mary buried: 'after the service of burial which is done with solemn and mournfull musick and singing, the sound of a drum unbraced, the breakeing of all the white staves of those that were officers of the Queen, and flinging in the keys of the rest of the offices devoted by that badge into the tomb; they seale it up and soe returne in the same order they went . . .'.) In the north aisle, James I, feeling obligations not only to his beheaded mother but to his predecessor on the English throne who was responsible for beheading her, erected also a (slightly less lavish) four-poster tomb to Queen Elizabeth I. Stiff she lies, Gloriana under her arch among her black columns, and her profile as fierce as a galley's. Her epitaph is unusually simple, matter-of-fact in glory, very apt—*Having restored religion to its original sincerity, established peace, restored money to its proper value, etc* . . . At the end of the aisle, two of the most popular monuments in the Abbey, irresistible conceits in memory of two infant daughters of James I, coloured to the life: Sophia who died in 1606 aged three days, and Mary who died next year aged two. Sophia especially, under her velvet coverlet, provokes mothers' tears; placid she sleeps in her hooded cot facing the end wall—you glimpse her reflected in a mirror. And above are the reinterred bones believed to be those of the little princes murdered in the Tower.

Emerging from Henry VII's chapel, bear right into the northern wing of the ambulatory, with the absidal chapels opening up on your right, and the royal tombs of Edward's Shrine high on your left. The first chapel (St. Paul) has various monuments of between 1580 and 1650; the next (St. John the Baptist) has the gaudy Hunsdon memorial of about 1600, with pillars and obelisks, coloured marbles, gilt and paint, presiding over some earlier tombs. Next is the Islip chapel, inset by the 'great builder', John Islip, Abbot (d. 1532); his punning device or rebus, an eye and a man slipping from the branch of a tree, is incorporated into the decoration; the story above is now a chapel for the Nurses of 1939–45. Lastly (under the crossing, and in fact the east aisle of the north transept) the grandiose pomp of Wilton's monument to General Wolfe, the hero of Quebec, veils a tremendous clutter behind it that include some of the most famous monuments in the Abbey. They tend to be knee-deep in actually impenetrable clutter of stacked chairs, but persist if you can—the monument to Sir Francis Vere (d. 1609) in black marble and alabaster, with four knights kneeling about the effigy and supporting above it a slab on which rest, empty as lobster shells, the warrior's discarded armour (an echo of the Nassau tomb at Breda). Farther in is the most famous of Roubiliac's tombs, the illusionistic skeletal Death emerging

from the wooden doors of the tomb to strike up at the
swooning figure above of Mrs. Nightingale, who died in 1731
following a miscarriage after being frightened by lightning.
At the far end a most ambitious homage to Lord Norris (d.
1601) and his wife, with their six sons in armour kneeling
about, and all around lesser monuments: to Mrs. Siddons
(very neo-Grecian, severely matronly); to the engineer,
Telford; Humphry Davy and many others. Among them,
in the epitaph from the Earl of Kerry to his wife Anastasia
(d. 1799), a curiously touching and rarely personal note
among so much rhetoric: '. . . Whom she rendered during
31 years the happiest of Mankind . . . And Hoping that his
Merciful God will consider the severe blow which it has
pleased his Divine Will to inflict upon him, in taking from
him the Dearest, the most Beloved, the most Charming, and
the most Faithful and Effectionate Companion that ever
blessed Man . . .'

You are now back under the crossing, and if you walk
across in front of the altar, and then bear right down the
south side of the church towards the West door, you will come
to a door on your left that gives on to the Cloisters.

These, arcaded about plain grass, are where much of the
ordinary business of the medieval monks was carried on; in
the South Walk the barber is said to have attended to the
monks' tonsures; in the East, on Thursday in Holy Week,
the Abbot began his Maundy ceremonies by washing the feet
of thirteen aged men. The oldest part is close to the north-east
entrance from the Abbey, thirteenth century, but like the
Abbey the cloisters are rich in graves and monuments—over
two hundred of them. One of the first on the wall of the east
walk is also one of the most famous in its sharp simplicity;
a tablet to *Jane Lister Dear childe Died Oct. 7th 1688.*

Off the east walk there are three important doorways. The
first leads into a low way clustered with an acutely complex
vault to a lift of roof and a lift of stairs, a most noble and
exhilarating progression that carries you as if on a tide into
the immense octagonal space of the **Chapter House**: an
exultant space flooded with light from its six great windows,
with a single slender exultant multiple column that jets like a
fountain shaft to the spring and spread of the vaults. This
was complete by about 1250, and though in its seven hundred
years it has undergone endless maintenance and restoration,

as you now see it, in its bare purity it offers one of the greatest architectural shocks in London. It has also seen more than the domestic conclave of the monks, for from 1257 until Henry VIII's reign this served as Parliament House for the Commons. The floor is an extraordinary survival, the original thirteenth-century tiles among which Henry III had placed, with good reason, the inscription *Ut rosa flos florum sic domus ista domorum*; vivid yet muted greens and yellows as of the sun filtering through to the floor of a beech forest in early summer; with lions and a stupendous type of gay centaur. Over this you swim with an also muted shuffle, for you are in felt over-shoes (issued at the door; a small fee to go in, but no better fee can be spent); yet if you speak, the vaults will resound your voice in acclamation. The walls are ringed with the stone plain seat level where the monks once sat; above that in the arcading are the traces of painting, but the carving of the capitals of the Purbeck shafts and the diapering is of a crisp and most pure precision and vitality— the easiest place in the Abbey to see English stiff-leaf carving at its best. The Christ over the entrance is nineteenth century, but the attendant figures are original. On the way out at the head of the stairs in the inner vestibule is the still older, a Roman sarcophagus (with a Saxon lid); and the newer, tablets for two American friends of Britain, both former Ambassadors, James Russell Lowell and Walter Hines Page.

The next door along the East Cloister is to the Library and Muniment Room (students only by appointment), and beyond that in the corner of the cloisters, the entrance to the low, massively vaulted **Chapel of the Pyx** (closed Sundays), which goes back in parts to the eleventh century, and in which was kept the Pyx, a box with the standard pieces of gold and silver currency against which, once a year, current coinage was tested for weight and metal.

Then comes a **museum** (another fee), with replicas of Coronation regalia, Nelson's cocked hat with its green eye-shield (and on loan from Lock's—see p. 68—their account book recording their dealings with Nelson in hats), but most famously, standing or lying about in their glass cases, the extraordinary array once known as the 'Ragged Regiment'. These are the effigies, used for lyings-in-state and funerals of great personages, from Edward III—a blotched and disturbing mask showing, it is alleged, the traces of his fatal stroke—to

Nelson, on which the hair is said to have been arranged by Lady Hamilton. The faces are generally wax, and the bodies of wood but clad in full costume; there is a curious rather macabre dichotomy—the clothes, though they are the originals, lend an air of charade—one can almost smell the dressing-up box from one's childhood—but the faces are often of the most disturbing actuality. Though Elizabeth I is mainly eighteenth-century restoration (the original of her head is probably the wooden one in the London Museum), Henry VII's mask is nakedly contemporary and alive. William III has to be raised on a little pedestal to bring him up to his consort's height; the face of Chatham has an unbalanced but vital glint as it rests at the feet of his robed torso (it is too fragile to be fixed on), and Charles II, with his awkward gesture and clown-like lift of the eyes under the monstrous hat of the Order of the Garter, appears to be evading some awkward question. The one that opens perhaps most mouths with astonishment, though, is Frances Duchess of Richmond (Charles II's 'la Belle Stuart', and the original of Britannia on the coins), dressed as if for a particularly important social occasion and accompanied by a withered parrot 'said to have lived with her Grace upward of forty years, and to have survived her only a few days'. Cromwell's is among those missing, for his was hung by the neck from a window in Whitehall after the Restoration (though what is probably a version of the head can be found, unexpectedly, in the Bargello at Florence). Nelson's is said to be a formidable likeness and not unworthily represents him in the Abbey (he is buried in St. Paul's), his right sleeve still achingly empty.

The east walk of the cloisters carries straight on at the corner into the **Dark Cloister**: a claustrophobic passage (eleventh century) between what once was the dormitory (over the Pyx) and the former refectory. Off it, to your left, plunges another passage, to the **Little** or Farmery (Infirmary) **Cloister**. This is small, and very warmly post-Renaissance (mainly seventeenth century, though largely restored after war damage) after the strenuous earlier architecture, snug even with its green flowery garden behind iron railings and the voice of a fountain in cadence upon its bowl. It is positively lived in, with shining brass on the doors, and I have even seen a dustbin; in a niche a plump Italianate putto, but also, to the east, the old and fine fourteenth-century doorway of the

Infirmary Chapel. Back in the Dark Cloister, the way south
opens upon **Little Dean's Yard**. Or at least it may do, for if it
is term time it may be barred and the yard full of young
gentlemen taking military or other exercise. For this is
Westminster School, whose buildings stray all about the
southern skirts of the Abbey; founded about 1560 by Elizabeth upon previous stock of a medieval monastic school, it is
one of the great 'public' schools of England, with a roll of
alumni the distinction of which can challenge any rivals—
Ben Jonson, George Herbert, Dryden, William Cowper;
Charles Wesley, Locke, Wren; Edward Gibbon; a pride of
bishops through the ages, great statesmen and great lawyers,
many of them buried in the abbey which is also the mother
church of the school (one of its cherished privileges is the right
of crying *vivat* immediately after the crowning of a new
sovereign in the Abbey). It is an irregular area, Little Dean's
Yard, aformal, with rough and ready and extremely antique
flooring; on the south side a long composite, slightly wobbly
façade of brick, which looks eighteenth century but is fairly
mixed up; on the east side (left as you come in) there is a
pretty view into a garden through an iron grille, but most
notably a formidable rusticated and pedimented gateway,
covered with the carved names of former scholars, built in
1734, and the entrance up an open stairway to the library
named after the school's most famous headmaster (famous
as master and as flogger), Richard Busby. On the north side,
behind a fairly modest exterior, Ashburnham House hides
(for it is not open) a very important seventeenth-century
interior ('the best example in London of a progressive and
stately mid-*c*. 17 house'—Pevsner), perhaps by John Webb.

To the west from Little Dean's Yard, a doorway leads into
Dean's Yard, but if you haven't succeeded in getting into the
Little Yard, the alternative exit from the cloisters is along the
south walk, which also lets you out into Dean's Yard—but
before you get there look into Dean's Court on your right, a
modest little cobbled place with a staircase going up from it.
Hereabouts once the Abbot lodged, and off it still is Jerusalem
Chamber (entry by arrangement only), where Henry IV died
and where are good tapestries and good thirteenth-century
glass.

Dean's Yard itself is a largish enclosed quadrangle of
mainly late building around a plot of green (where West-

minster boys on occasion kick a football about) and trees; it is dominated all along the far end by the large but rather ordinarily genteel face of Church House (built by Sir Herbert Baker, 1935–39), the headquarters of the National Assembly of the Church of England. The way out from Dean's Yard is at the other end, north side, through a gateway and back into Broad Sanctuary, noise, petrol fumes and the top of Victoria Street.

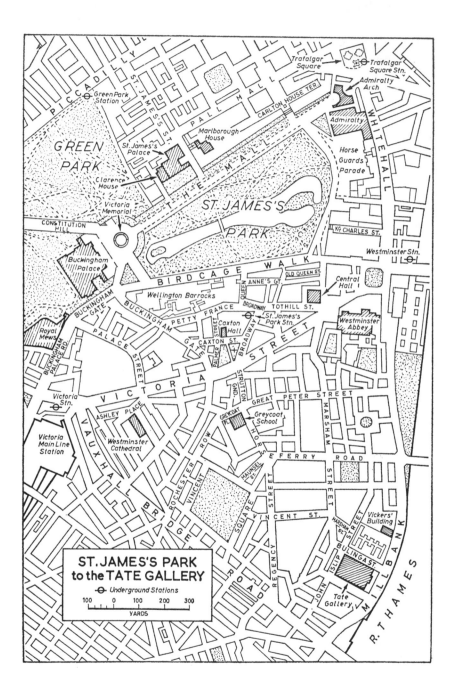

CHAPTER NINE

ST. JAMES'S PARK
to the TATE GALLERY

⊖ *Underground Stations*

100   0   100   200   300
YARDS

St. James's Park to
the Tate Gallery

❧

ST. JAMES'S PARK is approximately a long triangle with its base on the back of the Horse Guards side of Whitehall, with the Mall on the north and Birdcage Walk on the south, and Buckingham Palace at the apex. It is bisected, almost all its length, by the irregular sheen of its lake. It has so many aspects, St. James's Park, and is one of the best and happiest places in London. That it should be there at all to begin with is so astonishing, this green oasis of pure pleasure at the western hub of the great wen.

Its northern flank, **the Mall**, is a deliberate, composed (though incompletely) Processional Way, laid out by Sir Aston Webb as the National Memorial to Queen Victoria. It starts out of the Admiralty Arch from Trafalgar Square with most superior pomp, although almost immediately on the left a curiously brutal note is struck by the Citadel at the back of the Admiralty. Squared, functional, its forthright concrete takes little heed of its veiling of creepers; built as a bomb-proof unit in 1940, it is already almost as old-fashioned as the Horse Guards for military purposes and is far from hydrogen bomb-proof—it has already almost a period charm, enhanced when you know that it has over an acre of grass lawn on its roof, which it is one of the more unusual duties of the Superintendent of the Park to keep mown. Then on the right begins **Carlton House Terrace**, that twin range of giant pillars set back on its terrace which is fronted at Park level by more squat and sturdy pillars of cast iron; this is ceremonial pageant architecture of high order, excellent foil to the coloured processions that roll down to or up from Buckingham Palace on state occasions. It is cleft by the grand flight of steps that go up from the park to the Duke of York's column and to Waterloo Place. It is also extremely expensive to maintain, as like so much of Nash's building (for it is also the rich prelude to his great scheme of the Regent Street axis, and was built about 1830) it is shockingly shoddily built; but it is worth it and when gleaming with new paint, or floodlit with the shadow in the depths behind the façade of columns emphasised, it makes a magnificent theatrical drop-set. Then there is the memorial, high on the terrace at its end, to George VI, an austere statue with its approach by steps from the Mall, and then—as you begin to draw near to the climax of the way, to Buckingham Palace itself, the architecture on the right suddenly fades and becomes clearly the back gardens of Pall Mall—Marlborough House, the junction road with Pall Mall, St. James's Palace (looking from the Park, with its red brick topped by stone parapets, as though permanently touched with rather old snow), the wall of Clarence House, the Queen Mother's home, the opening of Green Park, and so to the formally composed semi-circle of the **Victoria Memorial**, with the plain but well groomed façade of Buckingham Palace behind.

The Victoria Memorial comes in for a lot of abuse: like a wedding cake, they say, set in the wide sweep of road; a chef's concoction in white marble. I would not for a moment suggest that this is great sculpture, but I do acknowledge gratefully its other virtues, civic, historical and sentimental. Set massive in her pyramidal cake, Victoria (13 feet high) looks down the broad avenue of the Mall to Admiralty Arch; she is attended on the other three sides by the figures of Truth, Motherhood (facing the Palace) and Justice. There are dark bronze groups around for Science and Art, Naval and Military Power, Peace and Progress, Industry and Agriculture, and at the top with a pale glint that seems gilt-winged, Victory attended by Courage and Constancy. It is the restatement in terms of Edwardian Beaux-Arts Baroque of the themes expressed in Gothic earlier in the Albert Memorial, and it is a very fair summary of the ideals of Victoria's sixty years' reign. Solid, rich, fashioned in genuine affection, elaborate in detail and virtuoso in handling (it contains some carving of a very remarkable technical skill), it is, like a wedding cake, perhaps a little tedious and indigestible, but it is also a proper centre-piece for ritual, when the Mall is bannered and the procession clatters round it and into the gates of the Palace. For me it has in its setting and in its function a fine sense of inevitability; also, without it, the inexpressive front of the Palace would be very void indeed.

Buckingham Palace itself, set back safely from the eyes of the curious behind its screen of pillars and ironwork and the deep yard, gives nothing much away. Automatically one looks up to see if They are in residence; if the standard is flying, one gives a little mental nod; if it isn't, one feels faintly injured. At least I—a middle-of-the-road monarchist—do. Through the iron grille cameras are thrust at the guards who have now withdrawn almost out of sight from their former patrol without the gates to the front of the building itself. There are, all through the day, a sprinkling of sightseers there, thickening to a rapt crowd when the guard changes. The cars swirl round the memorial, down to the Mall or up Constitution Hill along Green Park to Hyde Park Corner, or away to Victoria. As to what goes on inside, that I must leave to the gossip columnists. The real front, architecturally, of the Palace is the garden façade. At the summer garden parties, our Royal Family expose their persons with remarkable charm and devotion to a seemingly large (though in fact still highly select) proportion of their subjects. Over the lawns eddy the hats, floral female ones bobbing among the stately pure toppers; strawberries and cream are in the marquee; the Mall is choked with labelled cars. Then as the royal party appear, the army on the lawns congeals into compact swarms about their individual persons, the women well to the front, often I regret to say by virtue of some elbow work, and the men more cautiously behind guarding their hired top hats. It is a curious function, giving immense satisfaction to many.

The Palace is of course relatively new, bought by George III in 1762, but little used until after its remodelling by Nash, starting in 1824; only on Victoria's accession in 1837 did it become the primary London home of the Monarch, and almost all that you can see of it is Edwardian, the front added by Aston Webb from funds over from the Victoria Memorial project (and built in three months in 1912 while King George V and Queen Mary were out of town). But **St. James's Park** itself, over which it presides, is immemorially and inescapably royal, for all the civil servants who at lunch time throng its walks and eat sandwiches on its grass. On its north flank, the palaces of Clarence House, St. James, and Marlborough House; Carlton House Terrace. These are being expanded and restored in a sensitive scheme that preserves all the old. On the south, Whitehall itself, the former chief palace, and along Birdcage Walk the late Regency buildings of the barracks of the Brigade of Guards, the body-guard. The Park itself was near-marsh once, drained by Henry VIII for a deer-park. If you walk across it from St. James's Palace to the Horse Guards you will follow more or less exactly in Charles I's footsteps as he walked on the last morning of his life to the scaffold. His son, Charles II, was undeterred by any macabre memories, and used it as his favourite pleasaunce; it was then more formal in lay-out than now; what is now an irregular lake was a rather Dutch canal—but it was open to all, and on 15th July, 1666, Samuel Pepys—as so many of his successors in the Civil Service have done since—finding it mighty hot and himself weary, there 'lay down upon the grass by the canalle and slept awhile'. Charles himself, most approachable of English monarchs, walked there for exercise and conversation, to the dismay of his companions, for he was long and rangy and walked excessively fast, with dogs leaping about him. Charles too, swam in the canal, but to take to the waters in a London park now you have to go to the Serpentine in Hyde Park; the lake in St. James's is strictly for the birds. Charles considered at one point re-modelling the park, and consulted Le Notre with a notion no doubt of something to rival Versailles in mind; but the Frenchman, to his everlasting credit, 'was of the opinion that the natural simplicity of this Park, its rural and in some places wild character, had something more grand than he could impart to it, and persuaded the king not to touch it'. Actually the park was far from wild by our standards, and has been rehandled since, but beautifully under Nash's control; it lost a bit at the time of the Victoria Memorial, when the Mall itself was blown up into a triumphal way. The Mall was originally a grandish alley rather than avenue, of four lines of trees, and not intended as an approach to a palace (for that was not yet there) but as an arena where the king could play pall mall, which was a popular forerunner of croquet. The circus by the Palace knocked a bit off the lake too, and a famous amenity of London was lost soon after, perhaps the original milk bar, based on real cows—already in 1700 a Park cry was 'A Can of Milk, Ladies; a Can of Red Cow's Milk, Sir.'

'St. James's Park is the public walk of London and open to all, and it's a strange sight, in fine weather, to see the flower of the nobility and the first ladies of the Court mingling in confusion with the vilest populace. Such is the taste of the English; it is part of what they call their liberty . . .' So a French (pre-

Revolution) visitor reacted in 1731. And certainly the Park has always been a place for a promenade, for perambulation, and it still is. More everyday in tone than it used to be when Gainsborough painted those aerial dreams of femininity floating in the greenery of the old Mall, but loved and used between noon and three of weekdays by those who escape from their coops in Whitehall for refreshment. Out they come in twos and threes, through Admiralty Arch and past the citadel, through the Horse Guards and across the great, handsome desert of its arena; through the sunken depths of King Charles Street and down the steps past the statue of Clive; from the offices of all S.W.1. There one can sit in peace, while conversations float by in fragments on the tidal noise of the traffic like corks; the office workers, the officials with worried hair and mackintoshes and cardboard files; a drove of bishops with purple dickies under sail from the Athenaeum to Westminster, a debused tour of frauleins from Zurich, or fine, sunshine-haired and leggy goddesses from Scandinavia. An odd pram or so from the flats of Victoria, and bodies, in fine weather, strewing the grass like a battlefield. But it is astonishing how big St. James's is in its physical smallness (it is only half-a-mile long); it is extremely cunningly landscaped and undulated. In summer such a weight of leaf, voiced by pigeons, over the sweep and break of the close-shorn grass. And central to it, the jewel in the green setting, the lake, brilliant and loud with exotic ducks, and the pelicans lonely and aloof on the rocks at the Horse Guards end. Pelicans, though they supply one of the most exotic accents of the unexpected in the park, have been there for centuries; the first brace was a diplomatic gift from the Russian ambassador to Charles II—Pepys doesn't mention them but Evelyn saw them here in 1665. 'Visitors are requested not to feed the Pelicans,' but you will find it difficult, unless you're unusually lucky, to get near enough to them even to try—binoculars are advisable to study their preening habits and antique expression. Also at this end are what must be one of the most desirable residences in London: the guardian's cottage, all rustic, on the neck of the little peninsula; the teashop, and close by, the recognition pictures of the ducks and geese, which may be fed, and are, though the pigeons get most by sheer effrontery.

Half-way up, the new slim-line bridge which replaced, among salvoes of letters in *The Times*, the old suspension bridge in 1957. Clean-lined and elegant, it works well in winter, but is too scanty in weight to match the Park's summer full-dress of foliage, and seen from afar, the people on it seem somewhat improperly to be walking the water with no visible means of support. But from it the magic views east and south to the Whitehall skyline, a Whitehall now seen in apotheosis, bewitched into a fairy-story background of enchanted palaces that one can hardly believe are the white cupolas of the War Office dreaming against the black pyramids and spires of Whitehall Court, or the square, arcaded, turret of the prosaic Foreign Office. Not even the blunt weight of the new Shell Tower, heaved up on the far bank of the river, nor ·the triple regiment of the Ministry of Defence, can destroy this illusion floating on the sky. But if they pull down Whitehall Court, most valuable of black elephants, it will indeed dissolve, and a whole dimension will be lost to Westminster. At all times, in my experience, this famous view comes as a shock, but it is best of all towards the close of the day, when the smell of lazy water hangs over the lake, and perhaps a brief flight of duck in formation creaks swiftly over.

The southern flank of the Park is contained by the copious backsides of Whitehall, among which is inset the great parade ground behind the **Horse Guards**, walled by the Admiralty to the east, the Horse Guards in the centre, and the purlieus of the Treasury and Downing Street to the west; this expanse serves as car-park for select officials at most times, as a more general car-park at Christmas, but most notably, on a Saturday early in June, for the mysterious ceremony of **trooping the colour** in honour of the Queen's birthday. For a month before and after, the area is busy with erection and dismantling of tiered seats. On the day itself the seats are packed with a gay crowd, the area edged on three sides with herbaceous borders of new hats, with a sari here and a brilliant ceremonial robe from Africa there, for this is an affair of high fashion though liable nowadays to be accented by homely touches, such as a carry-cot parked under a cannon. Everyone waiting; the long lines of red, the guardsmen beneath their busbies; the massed bands over by the Foreign Office glinting with brass; the Household Cavalry and the mounted band, all gold and black, arrives jingling down the Park. And the Queen herself riding out alone in front, side-saddle in uniform. The bands breathe deeply into *God Save the Queen*, and the grooms indicate reverent attention by placing their top-hats against their bosoms. Then comes the inspection; the Colour is trooped past the men of the particular battalion of the Guards whose turn it is, and then the march and countermarch begins, the bands in slow tide of music pour across and across, folding in on themselves like some noble pastry as they turn about, and then as they break into quick march the plaids begin to swing on the bagpipers. Later, the Queen usually appears with her family on the balcony of Buckingham Palace, still in uniform. It is not a practical ceremony, but it certainly *is* a ceremony, and though televised should be seen in the flesh with its dazzling colour, with the full precise weight of controlled movement, to be really appreciated.

The most urbane exit from St. James's Park is across Birdcage Walk about half-way along, and through into **Queen Anne's Gate**. This road, which is almost a close, is a remarkably preserved remnant, the best in London, of early eighteenth-century domestic architecture; it is of long-mellowed dark brick, accented with clean paint and some civilly welcoming porches (some of them wooden) over the doors; with black iron railings, and torch extinguishers, and among the grotesque heads on the walls on the right, a weathered pale statue of Queen Anne that has been there since at least 1708; at the corner where it slews left, becoming Old Queen Street, the narrow half-concealed Cockpit Steps give on to St. James's Park again. But pressing on through to Broadway, you are confronted again by a mammoth surge of nineteenth and twentieth century: a controversial block by Sir Basil Spence has replaced Queen Anne's Mansions which was one of the oldest (1884) but also ugliest blocks of flats; in front of you, stepping heavenwards, is the headquarters of London Transport built over St. James's Park Station, for which the architect of London University, Charles Holden, was largely responsible (1929), its façade is adorned by sculpture by Epstein ('Night' and 'Day'), by Eric Gill, and (one of his very earliest public commissions) Henry Moore; these caused great scandal at the time, but now seem almost genteelly inoffensive. The west-east throughway here is Tothill Street— Petty France; the latter is very drear but has the Passport Office; the former ends at Westminster Abbey by the huge dome (third biggest in London) of Central Hall, which is the headquarters of the Methodist Church and widely used for mass meetings of all kinds. Both these streets were for centuries very fashionable for private residents: the most celebrated house lost however, is surely that, with its walled garden, where Milton began *Paradise Lost*, and where later both Jeremy Bentham and William Hazlitt lived. Queen Anne's Mansions swamped its site.

Hence Broadway leads straight to Victoria Street, but before that a meander about the streets on the south flank of St. James's Park can be rewarding in its variety. Turn right off Broadway into Caxton Street, where is first, on the right, Caxton Hall, where the registry office is famous for its turnover of fashionable out-of-church weddings, and where the photographers cluster and the flashes flicker on poised brides of all ages like freak storms of summer lightning; second on the left, in charming contrast with a very new building over the road, the antique survival (1709) of the old **Bluecoat School**, with a strong façade and doorway with the figure of a charity boy in a niche above; it is now preserved by the National Trust.

So to Buckingham Gate, and right through its tall red-brick façades towards the south flank of Buckingham Palace, discreet and apart behind railings on the other side where Buckingham Gate swings left. Cross to it, however, for here is the entrance to the public gallery, in what was a blitzed chapel, where a selection from the treasures of **the Royal Collection** are shown (fee for admission). The present policy is to change the selection, so no guide can be given, but a visit will always be worth while, for the Royal collection is perhaps the richest private collection in the world; some of it can be seen at Hampton Court, Kensington Palace and (when open) at Windsor, but in this gallery objects from other palaces also—Buckingham, Balmoral, Sandringham, and so on, which never open to the public—will come to light: not only pictures, but jewels, furniture and tapestries. Among pictures, there are not only the royal portraits to draw from, but the remnants of the matchless collection created by Charles I, a considerable proportion of which was recovered after Charles II's restoration; the Canalettos bought in mass from the painter's chief patron Consul Smith; seventeenth-century Dutch cabinet pictures added by the taste of George IV, and the primitives by that of the Prince Consort; there are drawings from Windsor Library—the Holbeins, the unparalleled holding of Leonardo drawings, and the brilliance of early English miniatures.

Outside, Buckingham Gate with rich stucco on the other side (and a rare medley of inhabitants, from the Central Chancery of the Orders of Knighthood to modern juggernauts like I.C.I.), and low, in massive grey stone on the right, the Queen's stables, with a pediment of a Herculean nude grappling with two horses; this will take you on into Buckingham Palace Road though the old-established department store, in its rebuilt modern premises, of Gorringes has closed for good. Otherwise, bear away from the Palace down Palace Street; here a rather lost isolated theatre, the Westminster, and then an immense modern development (finished 1963), including the huge tower block that dominates the Palace from the south-west as does the Hilton hotel from the north. The buildings stand clear of the ground on their pilotis, sprouting from a rich compost of parked cars, but there is a handsome blue-tiled pool with fountains and to the north-east, in contrast with the rigour of the modern, its modular repetitiousness (note the sculpted stag in the court of the new buildings, rearing, trapped, as it fossilises into a barren tree), the little eighteenth-century houses along Palace Street and its tributaries, in patinated tawny brick, have a most gaily civil individualism. Farther along, the Westminster City School, in front of a façade eloquent of narrow-gabled aspiring Victorian educational zeal in dark dirty brick, has a bronze statue of the philanthropist Waterlow including what is to the best of my knowledge the only bronze umbrella in London (a replica is in Waterlow Park, Highgate).

This brings you to **Victoria Street,** but before gazing with wild and helpless eyes on that, look from the corner of Palace Street to the opening of Ashley Place opposite: a most authoritative view of the tower of Westminster Cathedral (see p. 162) rising irresistible through its horizontal stripes to the climax of its finned, almost torpedo, nose (it has in the space-age assumed something of rocket character, as if the count-down were well under way—it is later than you think). Now a furtive glance at Victoria Street; it is now largely redeveloped in contemporary, fairly oppressive style, though no worse than what was there before. Built first in large monotonous blocks, it was like Shaftesbury Avenue or Charing Cross Road a resolute slash by Victorian reformers through the Gordian tangle of slums, that lapped about the flanks of Westminster Abbey—these were long notorious; the most famous highwayman, Dick Turpin, is said to have lodged near Petty France, and in 1775, Dr. Campbell could even note that the area around St. John's, Smith Square, seemed 'more wretched than the worst parts of Dublin'. Victoria Street certainly cleared a way from the Abbey to Victoria Station, if very glumly so, and its gayest days came surely when the first experimental tram service was laid on, from the Abbey to the Station. However, as you make your way in the direction of the Abbey now, you have on your right a famous department store, the Army and Navy, and on the left at No. 58, a blue plaque marks where Sir Arthur Sullivan, who wrote the music for the Gilbert and Sullivan operettas, once lived. Also here the opening on Palmer Street, a footway with little shops including a very precious flowershop, a left-over from some long-forgotten village life, and then a merciful green lawn under plane trees.

Now, crossing Victoria Street, you can engage via Strutton Ground into the very various texture of Westminster between Victoria Street and the river; much of it is a not uninteresting record of the efforts of charitable trusts, like the Peabody, and of the City Council, to create order from the slums, and reflects curiously the gradual advancement of ideas of authority on the minimum accommodation suitable for the poorer citizen. In Strutton Ground the scale is that of the old slums, three, even two-storied, and in its flourishing street-market it still preserves something of the warm, gossipy colour of the slums; it brings you to the **Grey Coat School,** an old charity school (1698), blitzed, but restored to a Queen Anne style primness, its white frontispiece set back in red-brick wings, with a pretty white lantern and over the door the old painted wooden figures of a Grey Coat boy and a Grey Coat girl (since 1873 it has been for girls only). To the left Horseferry Road is best avoided unless you are interested in Industrial Health and Safety, appliances for the promotion of which are exhibited in one of the odder of London museums there.

Otherwise into Rochester Row, past the early Victorian neo-Gothic of St. Stephen's and some almshouses with pale and bepigeoned busts of benefactors high in their brick, and then left into the unexpected tranquillity and openness of **Vincent Square.** This is the playing-fields of Westminster School, as demonstrated by cricket screens and the traditional half-timbered black and white pavilion; its southern flanks are dominated by hospitals; on the north side is the Royal Horticultural Society and some nice early houses (a good, very modest, now very smart, row of little terrace houses in Maunsel Street). Then through to Regency Street, not what its name implies, but a bitty near-slum street; in its midst though, like a manifesto of progress, Hide Tower (finished in 1961) lifts its near-square tower 23 stories high; so through the differing apartment-block styles of Vincent Street and Marsham Street till you sight, stalled like a hangar against the river, the brick back of **the Tate Gallery.**

The Tate's façade on Millbank rises from a massive rusticated basement story in green lawns to Portland pomp of pillars to Britannia among unicorns, queening it over the busy river. It is, like almost all the river frontage here, new: early in the nineteenth century, quail was still being shot in the marshy area by Millbank, and in 1812–21, 18 acres of it were covered by the brick fortress of the Penitentiary, an immense prison which was demolished in 1890. In its place, in 1897, bloomed the late Victorian peony of the Tate. The function of the Tate Gallery (open 10 a.m.–6 p.m., Sundays, 2–6) is threefold; it houses the main national collection of British painting from 1500 to the present day, but also painting of the modern continental schools (and now, formidably, the Americans) and modern (i.e. nineteenth and twentieth century) sculpture both British and foreign. Between 1965 and 1967 an almost complete re-hang of the galleries transformed the Tate. The decor throughout has lightened in key; the often rather aggressive and dominating character of the original modelling of the rooms has been played down, and an entirely new coherence of display and exposition has been achieved. Following the opening of the new extension (1976-77) on the north-west corner of the Tate's site, the arrangement of the collections will no doubt be modified. An earlier plan, involving the boxing-in of the Tate's florid familiar frontispiece in inexpressive boring 'modern', was abandoned after spirited public outcry in 1968-69, and revised, and richly ambitious, plans for further development involve the usurping of the site, on the other side of the road along the Gallery's north boundary, of the Military Hospital that at present occupies it. This may or may not materialize over the next decades.

Meanwhile—once you are through the entrance into the circular central hall, the routes are fairly logical and self-explanatory. Broadly, if you keep to your left, you are involved in the British School up to about 1930. If to your right, you go into dizzy orbit among the masters of 'contemporary art' (including the later British). At present the sixteenth and seventeenth century beginnings of British Art are somewhat victimised, expelled from their former home to hang around in circulation areas, Gallery I having been converted into the gaudy needs of commerce into a (very successful) Gallery shop. This one hopes will be rectified in the new hang, and the unique almost Byzantine nature of Elizabethan painting, and the voluptuous baroque of English seventeenth century (Lely, Dobson, Kneller) once again given their due. The better known beginnings of British painting are to be found in Room II, a small room but full of a large genius—William Hogarth (William Blake used to be here, but has been pushed out, to the annoyance of some of his devotees, down among the water colours on the Lower Floor). Thence there opens out the work of the great painters of the 'Golden Age' of British painting, with an often profound concern with man in his social setting in mundane and polite air of eighteenth-century civilisation—Reynolds, Gainsborough, Romney, Lawrence and that most classical and serene of English painters, George Stubbs, so long neglected as being a mere horse-painter. Representation of the painters of the picturesque, of the sublime, has recently been much strengthened (especially Fuseli); but the most famous splendour of the Tate, the un-rivalled collection of J. M. W. Turner, has been revealed afresh by careful re-arrangement, by extensive cleaning and often by reframing. You can see him in his youth, setting up in deliberate rivalry with the Old Masters, and thence developing his own unique style and vision, until late in his life he was sometimes painting in terms of pure colour, warm against cool, drifting on diaphanous veils of colour as fluently as if his medium were water and not oil. Light becomes the hero of his paintings, in glowing canvas after canvas—light, the creator and the destroyer. In certain of his pictures, he seems the earliest of all abstract painters.

Constable, his near contemporary, is also richly represented, if not so copiously as at the Victoria and Albert Museum, with his apparently direct apprehension of nature that makes the work of his predecessors—even that of Gainsborough—seem relatively artificial. Then, in sharp contrast, the minutely and factually detailed paintings of the Pre-Raphaelites, of the 1850s, generally small but jewelled with sharp colour like reliquaries. If sometimes rather affected, at their best of exquisite radiance—for the essence of English pastoral summer, look into F. M. Brown's tiny 'Carrying Corn'. Victorian and Edwardian Academicism, once again arousing interest, are here in quantity—painters such as Holl, Leighton, Watts, Frith, and Sargent, as too the counter-school headed by Whistler and practised so splendidly by Sickert. The British school (and water-colours, including, as noted, William Blake) continue on the Lower Floor, reached by stairs from Room VII or from off Room XIV, but many of the most famous living British artists are included, in their full European (and American) context, in the display of the Modern Collection on the other side of the museum.

The Modern Collection has improved beyond all knowledge, and is now impressively and revealingly displayed largely in terms of those 'Isms', which serve to categorise the main trends of twentieth-century art—Fauvism and Matisse (look out especially though for Matisse's quadrupal bronze studies of a monumental female back, and his large late collage, 'L'Escargot', hanging out like some divine washing its clear bright colours); Picasso who embraces and eludes so many 'Isms' in his multifarious exuberance; Cubism, Expressionism, Surrealism, Constructivism, Abstract Expressionism, and so on to Pop Art and Op Art, and the ping, whiz or whirr of kinetics. If some are not as strongly represented as others (the Germans, for example), the Tate's overall coverage is now very good; you can follow the history of art here dutifully if you wish, or you can drift as you will, mooring here and there as your sympathies arrest you. But however you go, you will probably find that one visit is nowhere near enough. In the meantime, however, there may be lunch, or tea—the Tate Restaurant (Lower Floor, from off the central round hall) was decorated by Rex Whistler in very pure English charm with the story of the 'Pursuit of Rare Meats'.

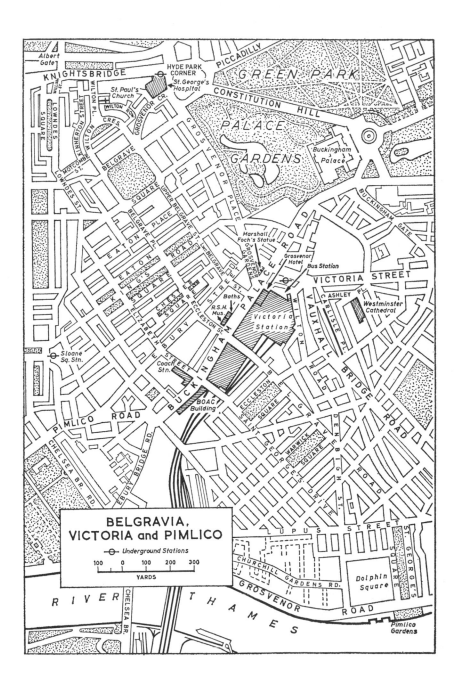

CHAPTER TEN

BELGRAVIA,
VICTORIA and PIMLICO

Underground Stations

100   0   100   200   300
YARDS

Belgravia, Victoria and Pimlico

❧

FOR years Westminster was contained on its western fringe, from Hyde Park Corner in a curve round eastwards down to where Vauxhall Bridge now is, by a broad strip, a green belt of marshy land and market garden and creeks from the Thames. Its desirability as building land for the westward expansion of the city had long been recognised, but what lifted it out of desirability into a prime urgency of fashion was the rebuilding of Buckingham House into Buckingham Palace in the 1820s: **Belgravia** was the natural extension of this, a provision of senior servants' quarters. It had been in large part a clayey swamp, notorious for highwaymen and footpads and violence at dusk, and for occasional eccentric displays such as de Moret's, who used it as a launching pad for balloons in 1784 (over towards Sloane Street, where it was built up already— but he caught fire before taking off, 'the unruly mob avenging their disappointment by destroying the adjoining property'). But in 1826, an Act of Parliament allowed the chief owner of the area (Lord Grosvenor, whose family names and titles still resound about Belgravia—the Dukes of Westminster are also Earls Grosvenor, and Viscounts Belgrave) to drain the site, raise the level, and exploit the building possibilities. The presiding genius of the plan was the great building speculator Thomas Cubitt; the clay was drained and much of it turned into bricks, and up on the firm base of the underlying gravel almost in a decade rose the stately homes of Belgravia, the finest flower of late Georgian.

The plan is ample: large squares and crescents set in a near-regular but relaxed grid (which is too mean a word for the scale); the roadways are broad and the pavements are expanses. But though in its ample solidity (and it is solid: Cubitt, unlike Nash, was no jerry-builder) it looks forward to Victoria, architecturally its stucco is still essentially Greco-Roman in flavour, and as such its aesthetic renown was swiftly eclipsed as the Victorians reacted with such fervour against monotony. Augustus Hare in the 1870s is typical—he found Belgravia 'wholly devoid of interest, which none would think of visiting unless drawn thither by the claims of society . . . wearily ugly'. But society at least has indeed been there since it was built. though the pattern of their residence has now shifted radically, In 1860, in Belgrave Square, there lived three dukes and thirteen other peers (excluding a small host of baronets) and thirteen M.P.s, each in his own vast separate establishment; the quality of this order is still to be found, but it has withdrawn from the Square which, the great handsome heart of the area, now lies organically extinct though activated artificially by the mechanics of the various embassies and institutions which alone can afford to occupy it. The sought-after private dwellings are now the smaller houses and the mews cottages where the forebears of the present owners housed their grooms, and the big houses are chopped into flats. It is in the mewses (if that be the plural) that the visitor may catch the most vivid impression of contemporary life in Belgravia; rows of irregular little garage-cottages, bright with paint and window boxes and the odd potted shrub, strung along sometimes cobbled ways between the looming backs of their former parent houses.

It is hard to believe that anyone can ever, even in the 1870's, have thought Belgravia ugly, even wearily so; but weariness—a nervous but contained restlessness of the imagination against the harness of street-plan and closed walls, an ennui—has become an integral part of the romance of any great city. Ennui in Belgravia is handsome, and even, though it is so profoundly English, exotic. If you scull through the wide streets in an open car, on a warm summer dusk under the still and heavy trees, you may catch a whiff still of some slower time, a whiff opulent as cigar smoke in the thinner familiar reek of cigarettes; and the bland and glossy stucco façades shimmer like ghosts of their staid solid daytime selves.

If you approach from Piccadilly, you can see Belgravia announced on the south west corner of Hyde Park Corner by the dignity of **St. George's Hospital**, once so far out of town that the 'surbuban' residence of Lord Lanesborough was here. The present building (by Wilkins of the National Gallery, 1827), is painted stucco, neo-Grecian, its serenity and calm disturbed only by the largest volume of traffic to pass probably any hospital in the world. If you turn left here (with the Hospital on your right and the high wall of Buckingham Palace gardens on your left), you can strike almost at once on your right down Grosvenor Crescent into the heart of Belgravia, Belgrave Square. But better perhaps for our purposes (to get a comprehensive walk through the district without too much redoubling on one's tracks) to follow along Knightsbridge to opposite Albert Gate, and there turn left down William Street into **Lowndes Square**; though lined with parked cars, the Square offers immediate hush after the Knightsbridge traffic. A long thin square contained by tall terrace houses of pale stucco and filled like a bath with tall, tall trees; the houses narrow in proportion to their height, which is emphasised by steep steps to the porticos. It is late-ish—1836–49—and indeed has evidence of the stirrings of Victorian discontent with the plain Georgian idiom: Jacobean motifs incorporated into the balustrades. The houses are almost all divided into flats, in which, although the bedroom is likely to have been chopped until it's twice as high as it is long, at least one room will be of its original admirably palatial dimensions.

Continuing straight down and out of Lowndes Square into Lowndes Street, turn left into **Motcomb Street,** where is Belgravia's most absurd charmer, the Pantechnicon; designed in 1830 by one Seth Smith, originally as a bazaar, it now hides, behind a giant screen of Doric pillars where a whole school of Greek peripatetic philosophers might have deliberated, an out-post of Sotheby's where they hold regular sales of Victorian art. Then left into Kinnerton Street which though recently bashed concentrates the full charm of Belgravian backwater as nowhere else. Trim little painted houses, shrubs and window boxes, two pubs of friendly smallness (Nag's Head and Wilton Arms), cobbler, dairy and a huge plane tree. Before turning off at the top on the right, look left through Studio Place at an awful vista of Knightsbridge backsides piled up against the sky. But having turned right, you are into **Wilton Place,** with a terrace of houses of the most fastidious neatness running up to Knightsbridge and down to Wilton Crescent. They are small for Belgravia (though 5-storeyed including basement) and in its context have a doll's-house false modesty; they are also brick: only the ground floors and the window reveals are painted, with handsome thin balconies with handsome thin iron work, and each one its flagged precinct in front with pots of shrubs—in fact, Pre-Cubitt. Opposite is St. Paul's Church, where they make lovely music in a prosaic building.

At the bottom of Wilton Place, Wilton Crescent will swing you round into the Square, and is already, on its inner curve, in full stucco fig of pomp pilaster, the essence of Belgravia. But if you want more mews culture, make a slight detour into Wilton Row with its almost concealed snug pub at the far end, The Grenadier (a very celebrated local among the cognoscenti). And then swim forth into **Belgrave Square**; this is for London, very big (almost ten acres), planned with severe and massive lushness. About its central green the four cream-painted flanking blocks (designed by Basevi, 1825), with heavy porticos, Corinthian pilasters of a giant order, and tall windows with a kind of brooding superciliousness, seem to demand a larger and ampler humanity than we can now provide. The Square is fed at each corner by two tributary roads, and across three of the corners magnificent free-standing mansions are slewed. Of these Seaford House on the east is by Hardwick—it looks as if it could house the Reform Club with comfort, though now full of high-ranking officers of the services on high-level strategical courses. The Square's inhabitants used to be 'heads of the highest titled nobility, and many foreigners of distinction'. Some foreigners remain. The big house on the south corner (built for Thomas Kemp, the founder of Kemp Town, Brighton) is the Spanish Embassy, and elsewhere in the Square you will find half a dozen more embassies mixed up with ambitiously-titled institutions like the Nature Conservancy and the Society of Chemical Industry.

Proceeding thence south-east, across Eaton Place (tranquillity itself resident behind its façade, but at No. 36, Field Marshal Sir Henry Wilson was shot dead on his doorstep by Sinn Feiners in 1922), into **Eaton Square**, even bigger than Belgrave but less of a Square than a park way: two long strips of tree-hung green inserted on each side of the King's Road, separating it from the tall terraces; fashionable when it was built, fashionable when certain of Henry James's characters lived there, and still—though much divided into flats— fashionable. All about here to left or right you can meander among mews and terraces, an agreeable background for meditation especially on a fine May morning, but if you want to see something of Pimlico on this excursion, you press

TRADITIONAL AND MODERN
Right, Thorn House and
Victorian pub, in St Martin's
Lane. *Below*, the Tate Gallery
and the new Vickers building

Battersea Reach at dusk. Lots Road Power Station was built after
Whistler's time, but he would have appreciated it

southwards, through Chester Square, quietest and most
secluded of the big Belgravia Squares, to **Ebury Street,** that
long, long street drawn out beyond its strength and of very
mixed constitution, now grand, now seedy; now with convincing echoes of Belgravia but more often both smaller and more
knobbly, heralding Pimlico. Here, among antique shops,
bootmakers, dressmakers, and houses that let off apartments,
at No. 121 there lived for years, before his death in 1933, the
'sage of Ebury Street', the Anglo-Irish man of letters George
Moore, whose portrait by Sickert is in the Tate. More
astonishingly, it was at No. 180 that Mozart composed his
first symphony in 1764; he was eight years old at the time.
Turn into Eccleston Street—but then you are stopped in your
southward course by the parallel traffic arteries running up
into London from the Thames: Buckingham Palace Road,
and the railway approach to Victoria Station.

In **Buckingham Palace Road,** the architecture has become
battered and transient—the whole road speaks of transiency
and of farewells amidst its flooding traffic. Away down on
your right lifts the stark tower of the BOAC building, whence
busloads of transcontinental passengers with eyes glazed by
distance come and go; closer (on the corner of Elizabeth
Street) is the big central station for long-distance motor
coaches; everywhere people waiting to go. In front of you, left
and right, runs the blank containing brick of the railway
tracks, so turn left and go north-east towards the Station,
Though the huge development plan for Victoria seems
shelved indefinitely, a sad victim to progress has been
claimed: gone from No. 90 the instructive, entertaining and
salubrious Museum of the Royal Society of Health. The
prow of Victoria Station is visible from this approach in
the shape of the heavy, heavily worked sooty stone of Grosvenor Hotel, vaguely French in its roof line, and proclaiming
the revolt of the 1860's against the unfeatured smooth planes
of the Georgian. Over the road on the left the accent is still
more French, emphasised by a drily pretty little triangular
garden with a bronze equestrian of Marshal Foch (by G.
Malissard, a cast of one at Cassel); this was given by French
generosity since the war.

And here indeed is the way to France—**Victoria Station,** at
rush hours teeming with commuters from the southern home
counties and from Brighton (served by an excellent hourly

service, and only an hour away), but also the traditional gateway to the Continent, to France and to Europe; all through
the summer still, in spite of the competition of the airlines,
claustrophobic islanders pile on to the boat-trains for Dover.
When you get to it, it is rather small but burdened with over-
large emphatic mermaids, and pigeons which the British
public, undeterred by a notice from British Railways pleading
for co-operation in not feeding the birds, resolutely feeds.
Inside, though the detail is undistinguished, the big twin glass-
roofed concourses are not without their drama, and there, with
its own private iron grille, used to be the Golden Arrow
express for Paris waiting to go. And how good to go, on a
sweltering August day—and yet how much better, for the
committed Londoner, to come back after a long transcontinental journey, to achieve a taxi and swirl through the
tree-heavy dusk of Belgravia homewards. Though the 24
acres of the station are at present under no immediate
threat of development, the cash potential of this and other
similar sites is so gigantic that it is hard to believe that plans
will not be revived some time in the future.

Before advancing on Pimlico, for variety and for an exclamation of more ambitious splendour, a short detour out of the
area may be refreshing. Cross Vauxhall Bridge Road, and
thread at Carlisle Place into the precincts of **Westminster
Cathedral**, the headquarters of the Roman Catholic faith in
England. To an eye soothed by sliding over the bland façades
of Belgravia, the Cathedral and its surroundings will come as
an almost ferocious shock. The long body of the church
crouches under its humped shallow domes in a confine of
high-faced blocks of flats in red brick striped horizontally
with cream paint; but any feeling that the Cathedral might be
as it were lurking is dispelled by the magnificent shaft, the soar
of its huge tower. Like the flats it too is brick, and nobly
striped, and it is in fact very new, still unfinished, though the
main fabric was completed, 1895–1903, to the design of J. F.
Bentley inspired by Santa Sophia and by Cardinal Vaughan.
London Byzantine, and even if allergic to revivalist styles in
ecclesiastical architecture, you should try it. The impact as,
inside, you come into full view of the 360 foot long church,
is more direct and dramatic than any comparable sight in
London; flanking your view, the lower walls and the chapels
in multifarious marbles, and above them the loft of the roof

in its rough brick, most satisfying in its change of texture and the purity of its line; the domes hold each one their defined yet mysterious shadow, the candles make little splashes in the darker aisles, and the still air is edged with incense, while to the east the church moves to its climax—stepping up through the Sanctuary under the great pendant rood to the altar, the ranged tall candles, up to the rounded close of the apse beyond. The proportion of this gradual lift has a grandeur that I find perennially and undiminishedly astonishing; it is obviously and unashamedly grand, but perfectly handled, lifting the spirit with it. Whether it will retain this quality when—if ever—it is finished seems doubtful, and most lovers of the Cathedral, I think, watch the gradual encroachment of marble and mosaic over the interior with regret, although this follows in principle the original design; in the end the whole church will be much as you can see it now in some of the completed parts—the Lady Chapel to the right of the Sanctuary for example, all a-glister. The furnishings are of course, mostly modern, the best of them the Stations of the Cross by Eric Gill (1913–18), some of his finest work in that characteristic shallow linear style, and contrasting splendidly with the sensuous colour that troubles the surfaces of the countless different marbles already used—blue Hymettian, white Penthelic; green from Connemara and red from Cork; they come from all over the world.

In the crypt are the monuments of Cardinal Wiseman and Cardinal Manning; Cardinal Vaughan, most closely concerned with the fabric of this building, lies in the chapel on the right of the transept porch. The music is famous throughout the world. And then there is the tower, the Campanile, a lift-ride up its 284 feet for 10p. Royalty-snoopers should be warned that the view over Buckingham Palace Garden is now closed by the new block at the bottom of Victoria Street on Watney's Brewery site, but for those with wider interests the view is still magnificent from the fretted brick galleries at the top. The walls there are carved copiously by the devout (some of them apparently of giant stature carving the brick at ten or eleven feet up) with names from all over the world, but with perhaps, understandably, the Irish predominating—one forthright inscription in large capitals, triumphant: GOD SAVE IRELAND.

The way south from Victoria Station, close round its

western flank into Wilton Road (avoiding the thundering ugliness of Vauxhall Bridge Road) leads into a typical transit area of small café-restaurants, barbers, rubber goods shops, cheap hotels. Here **Pimlico** has its own peculiar flavour and atmosphere: insecure and uneasily vibrant and lonely as telephone wires where migrant birds collect on autumn dusks. 'The name,' Pevsner notes, 'is said to mean a drink the composition of which is no longer known.' Apart from the mammoth frontage of flat-blocks along the river at its southern extremity, Pimlico is still remarkably of a piece and a period architecturally, in spite of war-damage—for it took, of course, the near-misses on Victoria Station. Built mainly in the 1850s, laid out by Cubitt like Belgravia, as almost a less grand annex to Belgravia, it survives in structure as it was, ranging from the tall and massive scale of Belgravia proper, as in the two deep, tree-filled northern squares of Eccleston and Warwick (these are indeed rather earlier than the bulk of Pimlico, 1830–40), through the average Pimlico, ranges of identical houses down wide straight roads, five stories plus basement, with stolid porticos and plain columns, and so through to a smaller module, two stories only even, like a small town development. All, at least almost all, is still stucco; it used frequently to be peeling in neglect, but now is mostly repainted, often with assertion of individuality remote from the uniform cream of Belgravian formality; from puce, purple, through to nigger brown, grey, yellow, pink even— painting done often by small firms or the householder doing-it-himself. Pimlico has an odd air of barely, even dangerously, prevented permanent decay in a nostalgic middle-age; certainly without 'sights' for the seer in the accepted sense, it is richly melancholic for the expert sniffer of metropolitan atmosphere.

Belgrave Road will bring you down into St. George's Square (of the 1850s), that heavily encompasses with its insistent porticos and weight of window pediments a long rectangle of green and trees; one side though is now replaced by an ambitious new G.L.C. comprehensive school. So down to the Embankment, here known as Grosvenor Road, for it is at this point not unpleasantly hedged from the Thames by wharves with old brick walls over which angle the tops of cranes. The inland edge of Grosvenor Road, going west, is flats: first, Dolphin Square—tedious to behold, but commanding mention as the biggest, once claimed indeed as the largest block of flats (over 1,200) in the world; popular for M.P.s and well-to-do bachelors. Farther along in very striking contrast, Churchill Gardens, thirty-odd blocks of flats, the first big municipal housing scheme to get under way after the war; the big glass tower holds the hot water for the whole estate, and is heated under the river from Battersea Power Station on the other bank. The riverscape here has, especially in lurid weathers, a weird and romantic starkness.

Just opposite St. George's Square, primly confined between Grosvenor Road and the river, is a strip of green called **Pimlico Gardens**. Here broods one of the oddest statues, pale marble in the greenery, a smoothly naked shoulder prominent from the marble drapery. It did not fail to catch Sir Osbert Sitwell's eye: 'A perfect type of its kind, this classic figure of Boredom rising from the bath, a speech ready in the left hand, could scarcely be improved upon.' But that such a modest man should be so unclothed seems hardly as it should be: its subject, William Huskisson, was at the time of his death, a Tory statesman of great eminence and respectability, and moreover he died a most modern if most shocking death—as one of the first victims of the Railway Age, being run over by the Rocket itself in 1830. The statue was carved by John Gibson, after a resolute stand on principle. Some seem to have thought that it would be more appropriate for the figure to be clad in modern dress. Gibson, however, was firm: 'The human figure concealed under a frock-coat and trousers is not a fit object for sculpture, and I would rather avoid contemplating such objects.' And perhaps Gibson was right; the incongruity of associations fades in time, but the pale stone endures: it is as though a male genius of a still-unravished Thames dreamed here of a golden age before industry polluted the river waters. He seems to have lurched very slightly to the right since this guide was first compiled, but is in good fettle and cared for, though the view beyond him has altered. On the far bank stretches now, marked by a high tower block, the acres of skylights of the new Nine Elms Market, where goes on all the business that was once Covent Garden's.

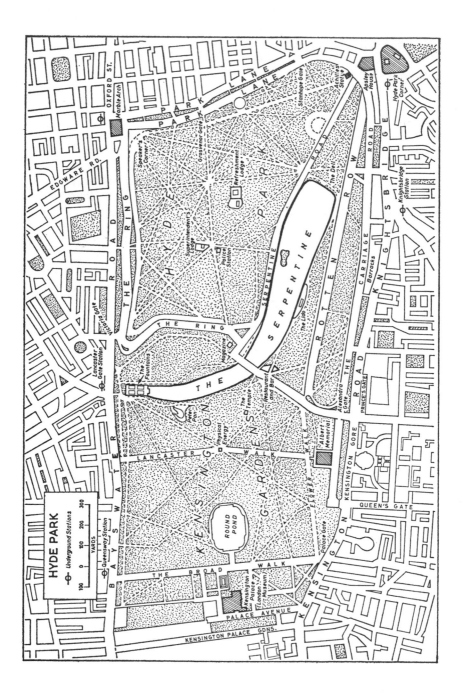

CHAPTER ELEVEN

Hyde Park

✤

AT times, in winter or in summer, as I have been walking up **Park Lane** on business, the sight of somebody launching himself from the other side of the double roadway on to the wide expanse of Hyde Park has filled me with envy, as though I were a prisoner watching a ship embark for freedom. Indeed, the promise of Hyde Park, even when you have got to know it well, can seem almost marine in its melting distances. The little human figures detach, cast off from the pathway and strike out across the green; suddenly, dwindling, they become heroic in courage and in loneliness even though one knows that their destination is doubtless as unromantic as Lancaster Gate or the Albert Memorial, or that it is only the dog's daily exercise or that, if together, young male and female, this is a straightforward quest for harbour in which to make love. It is also only an illusion that London, the London of business, the tyranny of nine-to-five, ends at the edge of Hyde Park, but it is a valuable and most sane illusion. Nor entirely without foundation, for Hyde Park, including Kensington Gardens into which it merges insensibly westwards, is an enormous area of parkland to find so centrally sited in a great capital city. From Speakers' Corner at the top of Park Lane on the east, to the westernmost edge where the gardens of Kensington Palace receive and subdue with shrubbery, Orangery, and dense flower beds the last tide of the Park, is two miles, and its northern fringe, the Bayswater Road, is in places near three-quarters of a mile from Knightsbridge and Kensington Gore on the south. The financial value of its immense acreage (over 630 acres) in terms of real estate for speculative buildings must be incalculable. That no tycoon has ever been able to take it over is partly due to luck, but more to the nature of the development of the British monarchy. Though nowhere near so big as Richmond Park, it is certainly the largest of the inner nucleus of London's Royal Parks—Hyde, St. James's, Green, and Regent's; they are all still the property of the sovereign, though since 1851 they have been administered by the Ministry of Works, and financed by public funds.

The Crown first won Hyde Park for itself in 1536, loot from the dissolution of the monasteries; Henry VIII preserved it, forest, for his private hunting, but James I opened it to the public.

In the Civil Wars, in the 1640's, it bristled with fortifications built by Parliament against the threat of the Cavaliers from their headquarters in the west; then, after Parliament had won, came the most serious threat to the Park in its history; it was sold to speculators. But Monarchy revived, the Parks too were restored; most of Hyde Park remained for long rural, not to say wild, but the Ring, throughout the second half of the seventeenth century, was a display ground for high fashion on horseback and in carriages. This was not quite where the present Ring is; it was altered when the Serpentine was formed. Even before the Restoration, the Puritans had cause to rebuke, in Hyde Park, 'most shameful powder'd-hair men, and painted and spotted women' (complaints about moral behaviour in the parks are as perennial as the salutes in *The Times* to the first cuckoo, though perhaps almost as often well grounded); Cromwell himself used to try out the paces of his carriage in the Ring, and there, on the 1st May, 1654, fell and was dragged by his horses, during which a pistol exploded in his pocket. Cromwell however, was tough; after a little blood-letting, he was reported well. A few years later Pepys, though less drastically, was also run away with, but his pride was mortified: he had dressed—'painted gloves, very pretty, and all the mode'—to show himself in the Park (leaving, it may be noted, Mrs. Pepys behind), but chose a horse which, while it matched his splendour in looks, also was beyond his powers of control. He had hoped to catch the eye of the King, and perhaps even more to impress that of Lady Castlemaine (it was in the Ring that the dramatist Wycherley did catch the Castlemaine's eye and so consolidated at least his social and amorous career). The original Ring was relatively small. 'A Circumference of two or three hundred Paces Diameter with a sorry Kind of Balustrade,' wrote an early specimen of those carping French commentators on English life, in the reign of Charles II; 'the Coaches drive round and round this. When they have turn'd for some Time round one Way, they face about and turn t'other: So rowls the World.' The tradition of Horses still continues in Hyde Park, though it is no longer a display-ground for human fashion and beauty at certain times of day, as it was for over two centuries. Another French visitor, Wey, in 1856 remarked that 'it was a unique experience, in the heart of a great city to wander about woods and meadows and embrace at a glance pompous equipages with powdered foot-men and rustic herds of cows, sheep and goats with elegant ladies trailing silks and laces among them. . . .

' "What has struck you most in London?" Miss B. asked me.

' "The coldness of your compatriots towards the fair sex and the warmth of their passion for horses," I replied.'

The circling habit of the Ring still persists, though one cannot any longer make a complete circuit by horse; on the perimeter, however, cars circle staidly, and now and again pull into the kerb, while their occupants read the newspapers behind closed windows under the greenery as boldly as though this were the most exposed of seaside promenades. Neverthe-less, the place is for exercise, and its presiding deity not really Rima or Peter Pan, but Watts's mystical view of Physical Energy. Military exercise is not so common as it has been in the Park since Elizabeth I reviewed her troops there; fortifi-cations in earnest the Park has seen twice: in the Civil Wars, and then in the 1939–45 conflict when it was scarred by anti-aircraft establishments.

Highwaymanship, vigorously practised especially in the eighteenth century when much moneyed traffic passed between the new palace at Kensington and the City, has almost entirely lapsed, and the coarse if fashionable habit of viewing hangings and floggings in the Marble Arch area (Tyburn) has given way to the more harmless pleasure of oratory at Speak-ers' Corner. Occasionally in the depths of winter even you may meet a mad runner. But the characteristic sight of Hyde Park remains that of a single figure setting off, keen in loneliness, to cleave the Park in two with long strides that seek nothing but exercise.

The essence of the Park is simply earth, and its grass and its trees, and a wide sky undefined by chimney pots or concrete sterile pergolas on top of office blocks. And water: **the Serpentine**. Hyde Park always had water in springs, and in the stream of the West Bourne; the consolidation of the latter into the Serpentine, in 1730, was due to that energetic queen of

George II, Caroline, with the connivance of Sir Robert Walpole. Caroline adored parks, and would, if she had had her way, have had all the London ones. But when asked by the Queen what this would cost, Walpole, according to a famous story, answered that the price would be three Crowns— England, Ireland and Scotland. Upon which, the Queen abandoned the project.

The Serpentine's virtues do not include that of living up to its name—it was built on one curve, not a sinous succession of them; it was also for many years extremely insalubrious, for as north London grew through the eighteenth century, the West Bourne became one of the area's principal sewers, and was also supplemented at the head of the Serpentine by the entry of others. In 1860, it was finally sweetened by diversion of the sewage channels, and the removal of a layer of mud or sewage fifteen foot thick from its bottom. Both before and after this operation, boating and swimming were popular; a hot Sunday in the 1850s would bring as many as twelve thousand people to bathe there. Skating too: hard winters seem now less frequent, but in 1825, for a wager, a Mr. Hunt drove a coach and four across the frozen Serpentine. In 1814, after the allied victories over Napoleon, there were terrific rejoicings on the Serpentine, including an engagement of frigates and a mock-up of the Battle of the Nile (the celebrations covered most of the Park with results that sound like the ending of a perfect Bank Holiday today—'The stench of liquors, *bad* tobacco, dirty people and provisions, conquers the air, and we are stifled and suffocated in Hyde Park,' Charles Lamb reported to Wordsworth).

Other activities in Hyde Park were more lethal (the Royal Humane Society was early on the site of the Serpentine, with a building well supplied 'with everything necessary to the resuscitation and comfort of those who may be suddenly immersed'), but suicides were frequent; Harriet, the sad first wife of Shelley, who drowned herself in the Serpentine in December, 1816, was only one of many. The water here retained its popularity for this ultimate pastime through all the swiftly-changing ups-and-downs of the Park as a fashionable parade; in 1820, Princess Lieven wrote that Kensington Gardens had been 'annexed as a middle-class rendezvous, and good society no longer goes there, except to drown itself'. By that date duelling at least was almost out of date, but in the eighteenth century Hyde Park was very handy for this. The most famous and perhaps the most brutal of Hyde Park duels was that in 1712, when both men concerned were killed, Lord Mohun and the Duke of Hamilton. The account of it reads like a butchery. Lord Mohun had previously survived two trials for murder, and his widow, when his body was brought back, made little comment other than that it should not have been put on her best bed as it spoiled the bed-clothes. The logic of duel etiquette was always elusive; in another famous combat, between the great John Wilkes and an M.P. called Martin, Wilkes was wounded; Martin ran to help him, but Wilkes courteously urged him away so that he should not be arrested. Subsequently it appeared that Martin, before uttering the insult that had provoked the duel, had been preparing for the day by constant practice in a shooting gallery for six months before; almost immediately after the duel he received political promotion.

But it is time to look more closely at the detail of Hyde Park. Best for the first time to set out, as suggested earlier, from the Park Lane end. At the top end by the **Marble Arch**, excavators have hewn out an underground car park for 1,000 cars, and painfully the tangled road junction has been sorted out and rearranged. The Marble Arch itself has survived the recent 'improvements', emerging at the end of them unscathed if even more isolated than before—the most grandiose of those supernumerary gates of grandiosity that are characteristic of Hyde Park; never opening, they survive as ornamental features. Marble Arch is supposed to open for royalty only. It has a worried history; designed in 1828 by John Nash as the main gateway to Buckingham Palace, it first failed to receive the equestrian statue destined for it (Chantrey's *George IV* now in Trafalgar Square); then it was removed bodily in 1851 to become the main gate at the north-east corner of Hyde Park, a function which it was too strait to cope with as early as 1908 in the thickening traffic; this was then re-routed round it, and it was left an island among the traffic, its gates firmly closed to all comers. It is not a very lovable object to look at, though held affectionately in regard as a landmark; for once Nash seems to have failed to revive pomp with a dash of gaiety: perhaps because here his design was realised not in the make-believe of painted plaster, but for once in the real thing, marble from Seravezza.

Inane the Marble Arch may be, but the site it adorns is hideous in memory, for this was **Tyburn**, where for centuries on a permanent multiple gallows, a triangle on three stout legs, public executions were carried out. From Newgate, in a tumbril, the condemned passed St. Sepulchre's and there traditionally received a nosegay, and at St. Giles a cup of beer; passed through Holborn and along Oxford Street, past the sites of the future Selfridge's, Marks & Spencer's, C. & A., to the gallows, where after prayers, the noose was attached and the cart driven from under the victim, leaving him or her hanging (this is the scene of Hogarth's 'Idle Apprentice Executed'). Here also ceremonial floggings and tortures were carried out. All these were performances with tremendous box-office appeal; public galleries were built to cope with the demand (not entirely without risk for the promoters, as when they were torn down by the disappointed mob when Dr. Henesey was reprieved in 1758). Really glamorous criminals drew tremendous crowds; the highwayman Jack Sheppard drew an estimated 200,000 on 16 November 1724, but this is claimed to have been improved on by his colleague Jonathan Wild (written up by Fielding) next year on 24th May. Wild gave good value, picking the chaplain's pocket of not a prayer-book but a corkscrew and dying with it in his hand. Traitors, rebels, forgers, sheep-stealers, murderers, pickpockets; saints and martyrs, and no doubt many in their outraged innocence, died here. The worst that the mob could do to the long-dead bodies of the three regicides, Cromwell, Ireton and Bradshaw, after Charles II's Restoration was to dig up their bodies and hang them at Tyburn. To watch executions was a fashionable diversion not only for the 'mob' but for men of high sensibility and intelligence, particularly in the eighteenth century, and also for women. The last peer to be hanged there was Earl Ferrers in 1760, wearing his wedding dress and insisting on the silken rope which was the privilege of nobility (his executioners fought for it), but the common show went on until 1783, when it shifted stage to Newgate, but still outside Newgate, in public. Still later, as public politeness or hypocrisy grew more refined, executions withdrew behind walls into secrecy.

Close by, at Marble Arch, there is ironically the now traditional arena for the Sunday demonstration of the English liberty of free speech—**Speakers' Corner**. Here, as on weekdays at Tower Hill, those with messages of salvation, political, social or religious, are free to deliver them provided only they keep without the bounds of obscénity and do not cause a breach of the peace; here is the display ground of the English non-conformist soul, old-fashioned but stubborn in its persistence. Without microphone, the harangues fade and merge with one another and the traffic din, and the audience shifts restlessly from one speaker to the next as at the side-shows in a fair; but there is always a proportion of the crowd bent on harrying the speakers, often for a laugh but often also in tortuous passion. Speakers' Corner, unlike the telly, still offers true audience participation, and keeps alive as much because of the hecklers as of the speakers.

A progress southwards down the Park Lane fringe takes you past a newish fountain with cavorting nudes (the Cavalry of the Empire Memorial has been moved to a site on Rotten Row). Then the revenge of convention on Byron in insipid bronze, just north of Apsley House, obviously in answer to his own ironic question as to the end of fame—*To have, when the original is dust, A name a wretched picture and worse bust . . .*—I could do without. Finally, the gigantic Achilles, twenty feet of him in dark naked bronze, higher still on his mound at the south-eastern prow of the Park, the archetype of that strange, characteristically English amalgam of the heroic, the portentous and the absurd in our public statuary. Its origins are inscribed firmly on its plinth: 'To Arthur Duke of Wellington and his brave companions in arms, this statue of Achilles, cast from cannon taken in the victories of Salamanca, Vittoria, Toulouse and Waterloo, is inscribed by their Country-women. Placed on this spot on the XVIII day of June MDCCCXXII by command of HIS MAJESTY GEORGE III.' Its formal connection with Achilles is not clear, as it is based closely on one of the famous statues of the Horsemen on the Monte Cavallo at Rome; as such, in the age of Canova, it might, one would have thought, have been acceptable, but in fact it aroused greater controversy than any piece of sculpture before Epstein's 'Rima' (see p. 176). Its largeness was admitted for admiration (a special breach in the walls then about the Park was necessary for its admission, as it was too large to pass through any of the existing gates), but it was found very wrong that the 'Ladies Trophy' as it was known, should be an 'undraped figure'; in short, Achilles was obscene (it is typical that when his figleaf is torn off by vandals from time to time, it is revealed that Achilles is far from being a normal man). The statue (made by Sir Richard Westmacott) is presumably not intended as a likeness of the Duke himself (who commanded a good view of it from his windows at Apsley House over the road, but whose views on it are not known) except in the most idealised, spiritual sense, but it seems to have been popularly interpreted as a portrait; in a party of tourists sight-seeing London about 1850 was a veteran of the Napoleonic armies, much depressed by the various evidences of the Wellington cult—but in front of Achilles his brow cleared. *Enfin*, he murmured, *on est vengé*!

The way is now clear for liberation into the Park itself. The northern area westwards is fairly open landscaping, a wide pattern of paths swinging over rolling grass and under great trees almost a mile till it is halted at the through-traffic road that bisects the Park from South to North, from Prince's Gate to Victoria Gate; more or less central in it are lavatories, a refreshment lodge, a police station and a superintendent's cottage. From Hyde Park Corner westwards the pattern is more complex. A roadway (but closed to cars) leads by the Band Stand to the northern flank of the Serpentine, while **Rotten Row** (said to be the *Route du Roi*, the royal way originally to William III's new palace at Kensington), leads straight until halted by the motor road at Prince's Gate. Here, in all weathers may be seen the happy horsemen or more usually the happy English horsewomen. Their numbers seem to dwindle steadily, but all the more magic their archaic elegance, a lilting trot on the soft, crumbling soil of the rise under the great trees' canopy, and like a song against the iron bass grind of traffic from Knightsbridge. More girls perhaps than others, but children too, and soldiers, even if not so often now, but including sometimes tremendous late Victorian sergeants, apparently on leave from the Boer War, moustaches waxed to kill.

Near Achilles there are some formal flower beds; there are bulbs in the spring, and later roses, but best perhaps in autumn when the autumn crocuses in their frailty star the grass under the trees, making the gaudy gros-point of the dahlia beds seem very loud indeed. At the beginning of Rotten Row on the north the ground sinks to the Dell, a most agreeable contrivance, a nook from some Arcadian landscape, ever green about its tumbling water. A large Stone looks faintly Druidical and is sometimes said to have been brought from Stonehenge by Charles I. It is in fact Cornish (a megalith?) and was erected as part of a short-lived drinking fountain in 1861; the stone, weighing seven tons, was not unnaturally left. Climbing out of the Dell, to the north you find where the waterfall comes from; it is the outflow from the Serpentine which ends here in melancholy under a white-balustraded bridge with enchanting furniture of black iron railings and the archaic slender lamp-posts of the park, with their gas-lights set in gibbous glass globes surmounted by fairy-story crowns. Westwards stretches the broad Serpentine, grey as steel in winter, green or sometimes even blue in summer; in summer the whole of the west basin can, in a heat wave, turn almost into sea-side holiday, with the white splash of crowding bathers over on the south bank by the marquees, boats idling, ducks clamouring for food, and the slopes lolling with deck-chairs. In autumn the marquees come down and the pretty brick box of the Bathing House stands lonely behind its colonnade; crowds are expected but do not come, and as winter strips the trees bare, the footsteps hurrying on the asphalt north of the Serpentine take on an iron ring, and the gulls, swarming in for easy food from the Thames estuary, echo screaming; in the afternoon children and dogs still come ('Please Prevent Dogs swimming to the Island and Disturbing the Birds'), but at times the Serpentine can be very desolate.

So to the bridge, fortunately the old one preserved (positively beautiful in its balance of elegance and massiveness, built by George Rennie in 1826), with a dreamy view to the south-east clear away to the towers of Westminster above the trees. To the south, across the bridge, you can see, and if necessary use, a new restaurant and bar, erected in 1964. The bridge carriage-way is part of the main north-south road that bisects the park. Beyond it is no longer Hyde Park but Kensington Gardens (though technically the Gardens extend west of the Serpentine north of the Bridge); the transition is almost imperceptible, but the pattern does become a little closer and gradually more formal. At the bridge the Serpentine curves to the north-west into a more classical, almost Claudeian landscape, with trees cunningly massed in variety, and the grass coming down to its banks; on the west side the path that undulates along it takes you past the statue of **Peter Pan**, which draws many children even in this ironic age that finds the whimsy of the Boy-who-never-grew-up either too whimsy or perhaps too Freudianly close to the bone; modelled by Frampton, it was put up in 1912, witness to the remarkable popularity of James Barrie's hero. Peter Pan with his pipes (his part played perhaps here, too, by a girl rather than a boy, as on the pantomime stage) stands on a tortuous art-nouveau spiral that oozes bronze fairies (winged, with rather Pre-Raphaelite expressions and in simple 1912-style party frocks), bunnies, mice and squirrels. Wendy is looking up rather puzzled to find out what's going on, and the rabbit's ears have a high gloss from the polish of countless children's loving hands. North along the water again, the path brings you to the head of the Serpentine, very formal, Italianate French with lots of marble, osprey-plumed fountains, medallions of Victoria and Albert and (why here?), seated on a bronze throne, by Calder Marshall, 1858, a post-humous statue of Dr. Jenner who discovered and fought for the use of cowpox vaccine. But one of the two springs that flowed here was medicinal, traditionally a cure for sore eyes; the other, St. Agnes Well, was for drinking. The Pavilion with loggia was once the Pumping Station and is alleged to have been designed by the Prince Consort himself, with the Petit Trianon of Versailles in mind. North of this is a truly enchant-ing object, **Queen Anne's Alcove**, in very delicate brick, shaped like a vast hooded porter's chair from a hall on Olympus. Nearby is the bird-sanctuary, memorial to the great naturalist W. H. Hudson, and incorporating the controversial but disappointing sculpture by Epstein, 'Rima', which was twice tarred and feathered after its erection in 1925.

West along the top of the park the north walk proceeds through grass and trees, to the Children's Playground (mark on your way the Dogs' Cemetery, founded by H.R.H. the Duke of Cambridge in 1880, for one of his wife's pets, recently deceased—it is incidentally often a source of mystifi-cation for tourists that whereas the Society for the Prevention of Cruelty to Animals is Royal, that for Children is merely National). In the playground here the swings were actually given by Barrie, but the stupendously pixielated object, the Elfin Oak, is more in the manner of Arthur Rackham than of Barrie.

In the centre of the garden are two main focal points; to the east where the paths converge under the great trees, Watts's statue of Physical Energy, a rider on a horse; it was put up in

1907, after Watts's death, the original being part of the Cecil
Rhodes Memorial on Table Mountain at Cape Town. Rather
mystifyingly asexual though it is (as indeed one would expect
from Watts), it has a pleasing silhouette from some distant
aspects, and close to, reveals a rather interesting even if not
entirely resolved use of simplified planes in its handling, as if
looking forward to the work of Mestrovic. The western focal
point, rather unexpected on the brow of the sharp rise from
the Kensington side of the Park here, is the huge **Round Pond.**
The Broad Walk splits the grass North and South, bleak now
as an East coast promenade since the huge elms that bordered
it had to be felled as unsafe; the bleakness is only temporary,
but its scale was expanded hideously and dramatically
throughout the Park and the Gardens by the ravages of the
Dutch Elm disease in the mid-seventies. The elms were said to
mirror the disposition of the Guards at the Battle of Blenheim;
the new trees are limes. On the southern slope of the Gardens
the trees are grouped fairly thickly, and diagonally through
them from the Palace Gate at the west to Mount Gate opposite
the end of Rotten Row, runs the very sheltered flower walk, a
highly gardened and lovingly calculated blend of flowers and
shrubs and trees with a rewarding answer to almost every week
of the year. Between it and Kensington Gore on the south is
the great gaudy jewel of the Gardens, the Albert Memorial.

The Albert Memorial, erected between 1864 and 1876, was
early held in its expected veneration (1882—'beyond question
the finest monumental structure in Europe'), but quite soon
became the standard example for demonstration of Victorian
ugliness, of barbarous eclecticism, of stodgy sentimentality.
In recent years, however, it has begun to awake different
echoes in the slowly re-orienting sensibilities of the mid-
twentieth century. It has surprisingly many moods for a thing
so uncompromisingly forthright; a bauble, almost painful in
its gilded harshness, when seen from the roadway in a brassy
noon. Seen, as dusk gathers deep violet almost palpable as
smoke in the winter tree-tops, with its fretty black pinnacle it
can be haunting as a painting by Caspar David Friedrich.
Inspected at close quarters, it reveals a lovingly intricate
storying of empire, industry, enterprise and benevolence;
in this, as in its unhesitating marriage of its classical base with
its Gothic canopy and pinnacle, of white Italian marble with
dark bronze, with the wrought iron of the canopy and the

inlay of 'agate, onyx, jasper, cornelian, crystal, marble, granite and other richly coloured hard substances' (by Skidmore of Coventry), with specimens of the new technique of electrotype casting—in all this a serene confidence of purpose may well now arouse a profound and nostalgic envy. On the first rising of the steps are the four marble groups of Asia, Europe, Africa and America; round the base of the plinth proper proceeds a triumphal frieze of the great artists of the world's history, a theme complemented by groups protruding at the angles and representing Agriculture, Manufactures, Commerce and Engineering. From the midst rise the four columns that bear the gabled canopy and its spire—'a kind of ciborium . . . on the principle of the ancient shrines', said its architect Sir George Gilbert Scott (no mean architect, and confident that here he had created his masterpiece); a shrine dedicated in blue mosaic letters on glittering gold about the canopy by 'Queen Victoria and Her People to the memory of Albert, Prince Consort, as a tribute of their gratitude for a life devoted to the public good.' And there indeed, sombre, in an attitude of massive yet relaxed platitude with a book on his knee, sits under his gothic umbrella that great, good, alarmingly unhumorous, devout and enterprising German princeling who worked himself to death in the interests of the spiritual and material prosperity of the British Empire. His monument here is an apt summary in its imagery of much that was best in the Victorian ethos, and he broods here too in sight, indeed almost as if controller or conductor, of that extraordinary, unparalleled, and still very vital concentration of institutions for the education of Englishmen in the arts and sciences, the South Kensington Museums (see Chap. 12), so largely inspired by his thought and by the profits of the project for which his persistence was largely responsible, the great Exhibition of 1851 in Hyde Park. To that vast and revolutionary show this monument is also a memorial, and the book the Prince holds on his knee is not a bible nor a manual of statecraft, but the catalogue of the Exhibition. The Exhibition, in the famous, now entirely vanished, Crystal Palace, was a little farther east.

At the west, central at the top of the rising ground, the Gardens are closed by the urbane and civilised brick of **Kensington Palace** among its trees. Its modesty is surprising, almost middle-class, though it is very much a royal palace;

William III acquired it, as more salubrious than the low-lying Whitehall or St. James's in 1689, the year after he arrived from Holland and triumphantly ousted the unwanted James II. It is so simple that it seems almost a deliberate renunciation from architectural competition with the Versailles of Louis XIV, or perhaps a puritanical rebuke to that overweening Catholic ostentation, the defeat of which William's plans, to be consummated after his death by Marlborough, were busy encompassing. It is part by Wren (Queen's Staircase and Gallery and the south front especially) and part, later in the 1720's by Kent, considerably more grandiose and considerably less well made. It has no grand entrance, and is set among a most domestic almost cosy lay-out of stables, yards, and, behind it to the west, a stretch remarkably like a village green. To the north, however there is one object of the most soothing elegance, the Orangery, a suntrap, excellently empty except of ordered space and light, quiet as after music, beautiful in its immaculate brick; it is ascribed to Hawksmoor. The Palace is fronted on the east by a hedge along the Broad Walk (against which is an odd, rejuvenated, limp, rather do-it-yourself, Queen Victoria in marble by her daughter Louise). The public entrance leads past that enduring delight of lovers of the bijou, the Sunken Garden with its herbaceous borders, formal basins and lead tanks, hidden yet displayed by its surrounding pleached lime tunnel, a most ingenious intimation of secrecy in public. Peeking on it, you may feel that it is very private and personal to you; in fact no one except gardeners ever walks there. Sometimes associated with William III's Queen Mary, it is really of this century, and not the whit less charming for that. The private inhabitants of Kensington Palace are royal relations or pensioners, most notably of course Princess Margaret and her two children, but on the first floor a long suite of state-rooms is open to the public; here in a twilight always stained a little green by the trees outside, the past inhabitants become a little more vivid. William III himself is elusive as he always was, and the statue of him outside the south front, given to Edward VII by Kaiser Wilhelm, looks in fact more like the Kaiser than William; but Anne, pathetic yet majestically stubborn, is here, and a portrait too of that delicate little boy the Duke of Gloucester, the short-lived but only survivor into boyhood of her numerous children. Here are the first two Georges and their concomitant architectural embellishment, most grandly the cupola room of 1717 with a coffered vault by Kent and gilt classic statues in niches, with in contrast a pale and most delicate relief by Rysbrack over the mantelpiece (note the central clock in the elaborate form of a Temple of the Four Monarchies). The palace ceased to be a main royal residence after about 1760, but its associations continue, the most cosy one of all being the reception there by Princess Victoria, in her night gown in the early hours of a chill day in 1837, of the Archbishop of Canterbury who had come to tell her she was Queen of England; the rooms about her bedroom are a delightful preservation and reconstruction of the bric-à-brac of Victorian childhood.

The last room in the main sequence (King's Gallery, by Wren) was designed originally for the finest pictures in the Royal Collection, and now once again has some of the most splendid seventeenth-century paintings: most notably one of Van Dyck's last masterpieces, the ravishing, silvery poetry of his *Cupid and Psyche*. Over the fireplace is the wind-dial made for William III by Robert Norden in 1694. The King's Grand Staircase (Wren) has fine ironwork by Tijou and lumpy illusionist wall-paintings by Kent, while the Presence Chamber is presided over by the not-so-elegant presences of Georges I and II, and of Frederick, Prince of Wales, under—in the ceiling—the earliest example of English Pompeian Revival painting.

When there are few people about, there may seem, in those shadowy rooms, an echo of ghosts, even if these, insisting, declare themselves as the tick-tick of security devices answering your every movement. If there are ghosts, they mourn perhaps, rather than long-gone royalty, the recent passing from the ground floor beneath of the **London Museum.** This closed in 1975, pending its merging with the **Guildhall Museum** and its re-emergence, phoenix-wise in the new building going up on the corner of London Wall in the City, scheduled for late 1976 or 1977, as the Museum of London. Meanwhile, I remember it as it was. Though only founded in 1911, it was the most intimately rewarding of all museums for the curious Londoner, making the mind clang with astonishment—consider the neolithic bowl from Heathrow: over its original site the jets now scream for their take-off. Here are the relics of the Romans, the Saxons, the Vikings, the fragments of their London existence; then the richer, more substantial evidence of the middle ages until in the dioramas sixteenth-century London itself emerges, remote and little in time now as a village. Then the best-known of the dioramas in which the London of 1666 forever burns in a flickering red glow. One of the things that lent the London Museum the special and slightly eerie stillness which it had for me was its very rich collection of costume; in many of the rooms, a long dead and gone figure presides in full dress and formidable actuality. The collection is ranged chronologically, but in memory and imagination they become inextricably confused; the Roman sandal, and the spindly boot with the brass supports that supported the rickety leg of the infant Charles I, both sounded on London pavements. A Georgian shop-front, salvaged bodily from old High Holborn, presents the proportion, manners and formal intimacy of a Jane Austen novel—how could High Holborn, overhung now by incompatible cliffs of buildings, have ever had this sort of proportion? and yet you can still find such shop-fronts, or something near them, as near High Holborn as the little passage, Cosmo Place, off Southampton Row. There is a hoard of jewellery found in Cheapside, probably a Jacobean jeweller's stock; there are broadsides, doll's houses, a splendid chess set that James II gave to Samuel Pepys; there are products of London, pottery, Battersea enamels, Chelsea porcelain. There are models of the carriages that have thronged London streets, and one of Piccadilly almost jammed with horse-drawn traffic about 1875. All this, and more, I hope you will be able to see in the new Museum of London.

Finally, westwards still from the Palace, the dense pattern of London housing covers the ground again, but is held at arm's length from the palace by the cushioning, opulent row of **Kensington Palace Gardens** (laid out from south to north in 1843, where once were the Palace's kitchen gardens); often called millionaires' row, it is a line of rich, mostly rather over-wrought mansions of high Victorian prosperity, each in its own gardens; it includes now the Soviet Embassy, and at the south end, which is called Palace Green, No. 2 is Thackeray's venture into house design (for himself) of about 1860. This, as Pevsner has pointed out, must be about the earliest neo-Georgian house in London. The road is still technically a private one: for residents, their visitors, their dogs, and—such is still the road's allure—their servants.

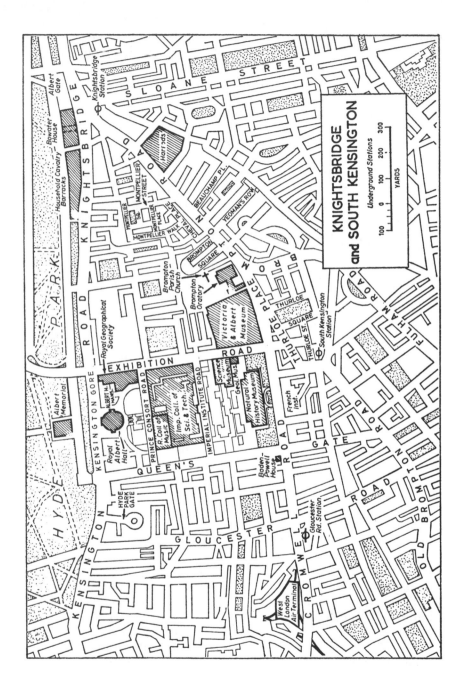

CHAPTER TWELVE

Knightsbridge and South Kensington

THE Knightsbridge was over the Tyburn river (that now, diverted, leaks out of the Serpentine into a pipe); the Knights seem to be lost in myth. Here on the western fringe of London, on the main road west, was a hamlet of doubtful inns and a church with some business in quick and doubtful marriages. In 1783 it was still 'quite out of London'; in 1850 people still remembered the days when pedestrians proceeding from London to Kensington via Knightsbridge did so only 'in bands sufficient to ensure mutual protection starting on their journey only at known intervals, of which a bell gave due warning'. All gone, the bridge, the pedestrians, the bell, the pubs (at one of which presumably Pepys ate a 'mess of cream', while another—The Fox and Bull—is said to have had a signboard by Sir Joshua Reynolds). Even the ghost of the ancient Mrs. Dowell, who kept a tobacconist shop and had a crush on the Duke of Wellington, laying always a place at her table for him who never came, that is gone. A later amenity, established only in 1885 on the west corner of Brompton Road and Knightsbridge, when it was pushed out of its original site in Belgravia, even that has gone—Tattersall's, the great horse mart that made Knightsbridge famous, is now only the name of a pub. And in the 1970s, according to a development plan, five acres on the Brompton Road/Sloane Street corner will dissolve and rise again in multi-level scheme including three high tower-blocks. Knightsbridge it is claimed, will then become the 'gateway to London'; it is to be hoped that it will also remain the gateway to itself and to South Kensington.

The great glittering burden of the area that is the subject of this chapter is of course the jewel-house of the complex of museums of South Kensington, the least of which, for adequate inspection, demands an afternoon, if not a day, a week, or months. But before we fall into their invitation, the area which encloses them should be at least glimpsed.

Knightsbridge itself is difficult of definition; on the map it is quite a brief strip of road along the south side of Hyde Park, running west from Hyde Park Corner; it has perhaps two focuses, however, considered as a district; one at the confluence of Knightsbridge proper with the Brompton Road and Sloane Street, where is the pompous splendour of Hyde Park Hotel and one exit of the Underground Railway. Here is the new Bowater House, herald of the new style of Knightsbridge in glass and steel, with a roadway and a busy, vigorous hunting group in bronze (not one of Epstein's successes) fleeing through underneath into the Park beyond. But here also are shop-windows, contrived and dressed with a sophistication that announce that this is a quarter of high fashion and expense; among them queen the sweetly odorous premises of big stores—Woollands, the most agreeable and informal of them all, has now gone, victim of the economic facts of life, but Harvey Nichols remains. The second focus, the deep heartbeat of the region, is some hundred yards to the south-west down the Brompton Road—Harrods. This twin focus is emphasised by the schizophrenia of the Tube exits, one of which lands you almost into Harrods. Flanking the big stores are smaller specialist shops of considerable class; Knightsbridge is far more than the gilded local village bazaar for Belgravia and East Kensington—it is a national, even an international, mart. For other Londoners, 'Knightsbridge', as an adjective, means an almost severe smartness of habit and an accent of almost theatrical poshness (many theatre people do live there).

Start at Knightsbridge Station at the Knightsbridge (not the Harrods) entrance. On the north side, a short strip of building fronts Hyde Park like a bastion, including the French Embassy (No. 58, at Albert Gate, and once the superior residence of a mighty Victorian speculator, who most spectacularly crashed, Hudson the Railway King), the contemporary glass of Bowater House (1959) and the Barracks of the Household Cavalry. These were of 1879 but are now a most modern barracks with a small skyscraper; they reflect barracks that have been there since the late eighteenth century; very early in the morning, the horses emerge to the Park for exercise, smoking like Boanerges; later in their day the khaki-clad riders re-emerge on ceremonial business in full fig of blue or scarlet, shine of black boots, white breeches, breastplates, the plumed helmets jittering, hoofs and harness jingling and clattering.

But the village street of Knightsbridge is the **Brompton Road**, in spite of its function as a main traffic artery. The trees, the stepped-up width of its pavements on the west side still (until such time as these too are liquidated for the benefit of motor-cars) raise fond memories of broad country-town main-streets, big enough to take market stalls, in spite of the gloss of much new building. Here shop windows are simply the thing, all the way down to Brompton Square; on the other side do not miss Beauchamp Place, as rare a series of exclusive boutiques for dress for the person and the parlour as is to be found anywhere in London. And of course, also on the east side, filling a whole block of it, the great senior (1901–5) dowager, in opulent terra-cotta, **Harrods** herself. Expensive, solid yet with a flair for the up-to-date, capacious and haughty, Harrods will provide you with almost everything smaller than motor-cars (though sometimes bigger—an estate perhaps in the Bahamas) provided your bank balance can cope with it; from rich and various foods to pets and library books. Her meat hall is a classic of London *art nouveau*. The archetypal figures of the neighbourhood come and go: the upper-class Knightsbridge madams, ageless in their smart black numbers and their hats, wearing faces of painted authority that cut with indifferent hauteur through the throng and somehow never crack, not even when greeting a friend, long-lost since yesterday, with a high strangled cry of stunned amazement. Ladies of indomitable courage of an older order, still almost capable of directing a bus where to go as if it were a taxi. In the streets they often are accompanied by dogs—it is in Knights-bridge perhaps that the inquirer first becomes aware of the infestation of West London by dogs, of the predominance of the poodle for whom especially the canine beauty salons thrive among those for humans; but other rare and pedigree breeds abound, and here too the chihuahua is worn.

On the Harrods side, the backwaters are banked by high, dark, red brick buildings, with some nice late-Georgian enclaves like Yeoman's Row. The proper doll's-house dwellings of Knightsbridge are, however, easily to be found by a detour off the west side at Montpellier Street, into trim low stucco and brick and trees—the Square, the Place, the Walk of the same name—beautifully kept-up small terrace houses, some with delicate balcony and ironwork, some little more than cottages, of around the 1830s; cunningly crafty antique shops for Victorian tat and lustre, and in Montpellier Street, by Cheval Place, an auction-room, Bonham's, for pictures and furniture and furs, often rewarding. Back via Cheval Place (with an oddly foreign vista of the dome of Brompton Oratory soaring over its south-west end) into Brompton Road.

Good antique shops this end, and all up the Brompton Road good chances of good eating. Just before the Brompton Road turns left for the Fulham Road (which it turns into) Brompton Square, tall and narrow, stucco of the late 1830s (?), is on the right, open to yet withdrawn from the road in the screen of its tall trees; it seems almost a precinct of the Brompton Oratory, which heaves, with some pomp of gesture, its dome up into the sky almost next door. The (London) **Oratory** (of St. Philip Neri), built in 1884 by H. Gribble, is a fervent and militantly aggressive architectural manifesto of the late nineteenth-century Catholic Revival in England, full-blooded Italian Baroque with trumpeting statuary against the skyline, and a splendour of marble and incense within (especially the giant marble Apostles, excellent emotional volutions by Mazzuoli of around 1680, and once in Siena Cathedral). Flamboyantly Roman, the Oratory makes the modest neo-Gothic of Holy Trinity, the Brompton parish church tucked away behind it, look very tight and buttoned up.

Hereabouts, at the junction of Brompton Road and Thurloe Place, Knightsbridge yields insensibly to **South Kensington.** The pavement widens, the roadway is positive estuary, on its south side the tree-filled brick and stucco retreat of Thurloe Square (rather Belgravian, by Basevi, 1843); on its north the high façade, crowned with its odd octagon with flying buttresses like some super wedding-cake decoration, of the Victoria and Albert Museum. It is no earthly good attempting to take the V. & A. or any of the other museums, in your stride; at this point you can only perambulate and return at your leisure to the interiors.

Continuing along the **Cromwell Road,** you have ample opportunity to contemplate the long long façade of the Natural History Museum, awesome, even if it cannot be said to relate very closely to the nature of its contents: like a château in oddly ecclesiastical Romanesque of 1873–81 (by Waterhouse), massive, and with a dour repetition of round-headed windows in tough mottled buff terra-cotta with chill blue-grey horizontal bands. It is set back from the roar of the Cromwell Road, and the plane trees, almost as if moated. On the other side of the Cromwell Road the French Institute in very sleek contemporary brick. This area teems with the young, especially with art students from the Royal College, often very picturesque, and is agreeably polyglot (the bridge-head for the Continent, the West London Air Terminal, is a few hundred yards farther down the Cromwell Road, amidst a swarm of hotels); French, however, sometimes seems pre-dominant and the platforms of South Ken station can at times almost be mistaken for those of the Metro.

Beyond the Museum, turn right and north up **Queen's Gate**; the new building on the opposite corner is an international residence for Scouts, with a chunky statue of their founder, Lord Baden-Powell. So to Kensington Gore with the spreading green of Hyde Park across the road. If you wish to salute the greatest Londoner of the twentieth century, a short detour here brings you to Hyde Park Gate opening off to the left; in this secluded cul-de-sac live the very grand–at No. 18 was Epstein's studio and No. 28 was the town house of Sir Winston Churchill.

But our main route is east along the edge of the Park, to pause between the Albert Memorial (see p. 177) and **the Albert Hall.** Under his canopy, Albert sits facing south, like a father-figure, brooding over the whole great complex of schools. museums, learned institutions, that are packed into the slope below him—there can hardly be a greater cultural density anywhere in the world. The whole complex is a magnificent expression of Victorian confidence in the education of mind and soul, in the propagation of knowledge, and Albert himself is not unjustly sited as its figurehead. The land that holds it was bought out of the proceeds of the 1851 Exhibition, which was one of the Prince Consort's dearest projects. After his death in 1861, his Memorial rose first, and then, on the other side of the road, the huge rotunda of the Albert Hall (1867–71). (It replaced a mansion, Gore House, famous earlier in the century as the home of Lady Blessington, where she entertained Dickens and Thackeray and many others.) The hall (oval in fact, rather than circular) is an admirably clear and functional design, basically a fine engineering job, a dark brick cylinder under a glass and iron dome, over seven hundred feet in circumference (by one Captain Fowke). Though girdled with a bold frieze of the Triumph of the Arts and Sciences, its simplicity makes a telling contrast with the canopied, fretted and wrought silhouette of the Memorial opposite. It is as it were the sounding board of the region, in which praise in music is offered up (the acoustics, once notoriously bad, have now been mysteriously improved by a crop of mushrooms growing from the roof); since the war most notably, and the blitzing of Queen's Hall in Portland Place, it has become the home in late summer of the packed series of the Promenade Concerts founded originally by Sir Henry Wood. But it is also one of the major London halls for all kinds of entertainment (it can take about 8,000 people); not only for concerts, but for boxing, wrestling, Russian dancers, and for all sorts of mass meetings.

West of the Hall on Kensington Gore, in a rather stark, almost industrial-looking, building of 1960, is the first instalment of the new premises of the Royal College of Art, with many departments ranging from Fashion to Painting and Sculpture; its reputation has rocketed since the war, and its students are in demand in an industry suddenly become design-conscious (its exhibitions are well worth watching for). East of the hall, on the corner of Exhibition Road, in lively and various brick by Norman Shaw (1873), the **Royal Geographical Society**, with statues of David Livingstone and Shackleton outside. It is generally not open to casual visitors, but has (besides a superb map collection) its own little museum with relics of great explorers from Livingstone to Scott, and later—Sir John Hunt's Everest Diary is here. The huge block of flats (also by Norman Shaw) by it, Albert Hall Mansions, cliffs of arches, dormers, gables, oriels, was among the earliest (1879) of such blocks in London, if not the earliest, and had enormous influence that you can see reflected through Kensington to Earl's Court and in many other districts. Round at the back of the Albert Hall is Albert again, standing now in dark bronze (by Durham, 1858), with, behind him on his right, the highly decorated façade of the Royal College of Organists, and in front of him a sweep of steps. This brings you on to Prince Consort Road; opposite you, the **Royal College of Music**, looking rather darkly dull—but as you approach, it may seem to bulge and quiver as if in a Disney cartoon with the pressure of noise within. In the porch is a very fetching marble statue (by Gleichen) of Queen Alexandra in mortar board and gown, clutching a scroll and inside (visitable by appointment) an important collection, the Donaldson Museum, of old musical instruments including Handel's spinet and Haydn's clavichord. The portraits, too, are interesting. The concerts by students are (like the Royal College of Art exhibitions) well worth looking out for: in movements of considerable brio, one may have an impression that orchestra and conductor are competing for victory, but the exhilaration and *joie de vivre* of the players can often be far more infectious than staider professional concerts, and indeed the standard is high.

Going east towards Exhibition Road, you pass the monumental façade of the Royal School of Mines, part of the group of colleges known as the Imperial College of Science and Technology, established in 1907 in the true tradition of this region, for theory and for practice—'for the most advanced training and research in science, especially in its application to industry'. With its ancillaries, it fills the whole block between Prince Consort Road and Imperial Institute Road, on your right as you go down Exhibition Road; at the time of writing it is all coming down and going up, the Renaissance Edwardian manner giving way to the current glass and steel and concrete idiom, but among the new the 280-foot campanile (by T. E. Collcutt) has been preserved after a spirited defensive campaign. On the east side of Exhibition Road, agreeably accented by the neighbouring needle-thin gilt spirelet of a post-blitz church (London headquarters of the Mormons), is one of the most charming of Victorian early Renaissance survivors, the Huxley Building of 1868–73, in deep rich red-brown with arcades and loggias.

From here to the Cromwell Road, the mammoth museums proper reign supreme. On the east, the arts in the Victoria and Albert Museum in its ample, regally matronly presence. On the west, Science, in three main departments. First the Science Museum, in a rather dour commercial-institutional style. Arts and sciences were contained in one heterogeneous collection, the South Kensington Museum (which no longer exists as such, so do not write to it, as many people still do), until in 1898 their separation was recommended; the **Science Museum** is now one of the most popular of all, its visitors numbering millions rather than thousands. At the time of writing, its new Centre Block is built but still organising within (the building will ultimately extend through to Queen's Gate on the west) and the switch over from the old display in shoals of somewhat depressive cases, to the new, often very spectacular and exciting methods, very much in progress, so that this very brief summary of guide can only be tentative. As you go in, do not miss, hanging from the ceiling of the stair well high above the hall, the stunning simplicity of the Foucault pendulum demonstrating in serene restlessness the fundamental fact that the earth moves about its axis. Such demonstrations of fundamentals are only relatively rarely to be found in the Science Museum—they tend to express themselves, unspectacularly for the lay mind, in terms of formula. The development of practice—all that passes under the name of technology—from steam to the intricate sophistications of computers—these are the real concern of the Museum, and these indeed are brilliantly demonstrated.

First the basement: the Children's Gallery. This is one of the dottiest, most pleasurable places in London, like a super pleasure arcade but offering also solid instruction. Children and adults alike are usually to be seen, disporting; there are miniature crane grabs operatable; a constant stream of children passing through the busy door that opens magically as the circuit of the photo-electric cell is broken; tape recorder and burglar alarms; the ungrabbable floating golden ball. On the ground floor the emphasis is on power, the story of man's harnessing the forces of nature to supplement his fallible and frail arms and legs. The best way up to the floors above is by sleek slender escalator, for this is the Science Museum. On the first floor the cases house the development of tools, of telegraph and telephone; the story of the reduction of metallic ores to malleable shape. Many exhibits have a taped commentary in a telephone apparatus alongside. On the second floor the climax is a terrific room, a hangar under a big arched roof of steel ribs and neon, with a high airborne gangway running down its centre—aviation. It is a furiously exhilarating arena, with its air thick with frail and dangerous machines, the later and less frail ones no less dangerous, most of them being fighters designed to kill. A man in a balloon basket swings dispassionate among them. The supersonic wind-tunnel goes off every twenty minutes, its intervals plotted by a count-down clock. At the far end is the tea-room; cafeteria service available. There is a weird roofscape from the windows, and the stars may not be as far off as you think, but in the meantime there is tea.

Immediately south of the Science Museum is the **Geological Museum**, seemingly quieter behind a Classical Revival front of the 1930s; inside the geological globe twirls calmly on its axis—there are no buttons here to push, all is silence and slow time. Yet violence of the most fundamental order is precisely what this museum is about, and to the attentive visitor the images it offers, of planets cooling, of immense millennia-long pressures shaping a world, extruding continents and filling the gigantic puddle of the Pacific, conditioning our earth down to its minutest detail, the nature of the dust—these are of haunting majesty and implication. On the second floor you will find a guide to the principal building stones of which London's fabric is made. But what, on a quick visit, people drop to see and dazzle over in the Geological Museum is the long range of cases central in the ground floor, the Gemstones. There you will find them, in the crude state rough and sometimes barely blushed with colour or light—and in the cut and polished state, condensed to their essence, clear and cold as stars in winter or luminous with yet still colder inner light. There they are, jewels enough to break any girl's heart, with their singing names and enigmatic colour—lapis lazuli, opal, agate and chalcedony; amethyst; diamond, ruby and sapphire; corundum, aquamarine and emerald, the peridot, the zircon, and so many more.

Next to the south, and round the corner into the Cromwell Road, is the Byzantine pile of the **Natural History Museum**, the front of which we passed earlier in its green dell. Officially it was 'the British Museum (Natural History)', and its origins are in that cabinet of curiosities that the good Chelsea doctor, Sir Hans Sloane, accumulated in the first half of the eighteenth century and which subsequently became the British Museum (see p. 226) in Bloomsbury. The museum opened here in 1881, already divided into its five departments: Zoology, Entomology, Palaeontology, Minerology and Botany. It forms a classified encyclopedia of these subjects, and in its laboratories behind the scenes the endless task of classifying, ranging, ordering, natural phenomena goes on. There are, for example, a quarter of a million butterflies. The museum is a home also of intensive research and an active promoter of expeditions. On the ground floor, a little way in, you will find, seated in the North Hall, the effigies of its presiding human genii, statues of Darwin and of T. H. Huxley.

The main collections on the ground floor are, to the west, zoology and entomology, and to the east, palaeontology, i.e. fossils. The west wing first—on the left of the entrance. All down the front of this wing a long corridor of illuminated cases displays birds down to the British bird pavilion at the end, where you can see all kinds of British species in dioramas, displayed in settings of their natural habitats. In the galleries north of this, the cold world, relieved first by the coloured corals. Sponges. Arachnids: the malign spider, stripped and revealed as a jewelled mechanism. Behind the clear and innocent glass of the cases, the revelations may appal the lay mind. Possibility of life is revealed on all sides in inexhaustible and staggering variety, all murderous. In the Fish Gallery, sharks, poison fish. The ambitious *Melanocetus johnsoni* in model, twice, before and after swallowing a fish three times its own length. In the Reptile Gallery even the layest of minds is forewarned for the sinister: cobra, viper, rattlesnake, and the lay mind is not necessarily comforted by the guide's reminder that some of their skins are of commercial value. There, blanched and infinitely delicate, the lacy skeleton of a rock python could be a feather boa for a human ghost. All these are of course labelled meticulously, and can be ranged categorically by the orderly and informed mind: a morphology of fish. Yet what astounds, and is not perhaps sufficiently advertised in the Natural History Museum, is sheer spectacle. Go through to the northern extremity of the west wing: the Whale Gallery, surely one of the most spectacular rooms in all London, a heavy body blow at anyone's sense of scale. Above, as though you walked the sea-bottom, ninety-one feet of Blue Whale (or Sibbold's Rorqual—one hundred and twenty tons' worth in real life), afloat among the skeletons of lesser breeds, ribbed immensely, yet toothless. In show-cases at the end porpoises in blue parabolas (they have teeth, but are also of gay and bounding elegance). The whole room is somehow rather mythical, a little dreamy.

The east wing, ground floor, is fossils. Here the time range induces dizziness. Again there is monstrous spectacle, a weird

South Ken for culture.
The congregation of museums
sprang from the profits of the
1851 Great Exhibition. From
beneath the canopy of his
memorial, Prince Albert looks
south over them. He is in bronze,
14 feet high, and holds the
Exhibition catalogue. The
Natural History Museum (*right*)
contains science in a
characteristically ecclesiastical
Victorian shell

The confident face of nineteenth century learning: the portico (1842–7) of the British Museum

anthology of once-living forms all in the end proved wanting. The most spectacular is of course that long room over which hangs a placard—*Dinosaurs* (X), dominated by the giant reconstruction of the skeleton of Diplodocus, 84 feet 9 inches, some fifty tons, that lurched and lumbered 150 million years back.

On the first floor of the Museum (up the stairs at the north end of the main hall—the restaurant is at the top), there are cosier, more modern mammals, stuffed—in the west wing, a stilled zoo in equable artificial light, with elaborately built displays—the okapi in a humid half-lit glade of the Ituri forest: a touching giraffe family conversation piece as awkward and elegant as a painting by Devis; here also the analysis of form in skeletal anatomy. In the east wing, minerals and meteorites, case upon case ranging the endless multi-coloured residue of the cooling of the earth in all its freak and variety of structure and form. The final ascent (up the flying bridge, past a case of mountain goats) brings you to the recently reconstructed Botanical Gallery, kingdom of the plants. This has at its entrance, on folding screens, a herbarium, a practical check list of specimens of some 600 of the more frequent wild flowers of Britain against which you can check your queries. Beyond, complex show-cases demonstrate the nature of plant life, its variety, its ecology; but in the central cases the plant gets vicious—the fungi, and a fascinating (if to the householder horrifying) anatomy of dry-rot. Finally, as if to show that plants, too, can be almost human, the amazing, sensitive intricacies of the carnivorous plants such as the Venus Fly Trap.

The **Victoria and Albert Museum** has two entrances (see map on p. 182): a subsidiary one in Exhibition Road to the west, and the main one on Cromwell Road to the south (it is also well worth remembering on days of above-average bleakness or wetness that there is a covered route to it from South Kensington Station by that weird subway with its grimy glazed tiles and naked electric light bulbs). People tend to get confused about the functions of the Victoria and Albert and of the British Museum respectively, and well they may, for in places they overlap. They grew up independently, and by normal English laissez-faire procedures have never sorted out properly their relationships. However, something of the V. &

A.'s principles may be inferred from its changing names; it began with the Museum of Manufactures at Marlborough House in 1852—what was to be the V. & A. then shaped as the Museum of Ornamental Art. It was thus specifically in the Prince Albertian manner, didactic—for 'the application of fine art to objects of utility' and 'the improvement of public taste in design'. Then it opened as part of the South Kensington Museum, which included as we have seen the collection now in the Science Museum, until at the end of the century what are now known as the two cultures split and the foundation stone of the present building of the arts collection in 1899 was laid by Queen Victoria (her last important public appearance). By then it had become one of the major museums of the world, its didacticism resting on the solid foundations of normal museum principles of selective acquisition, of conservation, research and classification.

In the sphere of the fine arts, the V. & A. holds the national collection of miniature paintings, of water-colours and of sculpture other than classical and modern. Classical sculpture is in the British Museum and modern in the Tate Gallery. Water-colours are of course also in the British Museum (some thousands of Turners among others), as also some not inconsiderable sculpture of the periods officially belonging to the V. & A. Other areas where the two institutions tend to overlap are in ceramics, in Oriental art, in many branches of applied art, but then why not? The Victoria and Albert is not really for oil-paintings, yet, owing to bequests from the Constable family, it is here that you can study John Constable in greater depths than anywhere, and also some nineteenth-century English painters such as Wilkie or Mulready. And leaving aside the staggering holding of the Raphael cartoons, it has other paintings of great importance.

To guide through the collections of the V. & A., in this broad context, is out of the question, but I should perhaps list the categories so that those interested in one or more of them may know that the Victoria and Albert Museum is their place. Architectural details; Arms and Armour; the Art of the Book; Bronzes; Carpets; Clocks; Costume; Embroidery; Enamels; Engravings; Fabrics; Furniture; Glass; Gold and Silverwork and Ironwork; Ivories; Jewellery; Musical Instruments; Pottery and Porcelain; Tapestry; Theatre art; Woodwork. The Library is also the National Art Library, open to the public as the libraries of other museums and galleries are not, and claimed to be the largest in the world on its subjects. All this sounds overwhelming, but owing to the civilised method of display, the museum can be as rewarding to the visitor who has only a day to spare as it can be to the addict who returns again and again. For the latter the study collections, to be found mainly on the upper reaches of the building, offer sheer concentration in which to study a subject in depth and in full detail of variegation; case upon case of Chelsea and Derby figures; silver ranged in the profusion of a silver-dealer's dream. Those with specific inquiries can generally get information from the department concerned by calling on its offices, but you will be much more popular and are much more likely to get the best possible answer from the right expert, if you telephone for an appointment in advance, explaining the nature of your problem. But the general visitor will do best to attack the Primary Collections, a day's tour through which is a practical proposition—but certainly not less than a day for anyone with any interest at all in the arts; there is a restaurant with both a cafeteria service and a rather grander waitress service. I might as well warn you that you will get lost anyway. The building is fairly intricate, but it is not so much that that is the trouble, for it is well signposted—it is more that it is full of vistas off any chosen route, down which entrancing objects will wink and beckon to entice you from any set course. And also almost always there is at least one loan exhibition, sometimes a major one, in progress.

The purpose of the **Primary Collections** is to exhibit 'masterpieces of all the arts, brought together by style, period or nationality': as it were an evolving morphology of the Zeitgeist. Among them the richest and most extensive are the sequences showing European Continental Art, and English Art.

The Continental sequence of rooms opens in room 49—a hushed space holding the relics of nearly a thousand years from late Roman through Byzantium to the early medieval art of the West; the tempest of the Dark Ages has passed, leaving this wrack of small, almost drowned, yet vivid objects. Thence the Gothic (rooms 22–24), quickening in movement, sometimes even seductively yet still all for adornment of the only settled habitation, which was God's, the Church. Then in rooms 25–29, 38 (the famous Hunting tapestries), the awakening of the Renaissance, Italy itself in rooms 16–11, 17–20, including magnificent reliefs by Donatello. Room 21 is climactic with a little yet immensely potent wax model by Michelangelo, a big marble group by Giovanni da Bologna, and the dramatic swirl of the Baroque in Bernini's *Neptune and Triton*. The range opens out downstairs (rooms 4–7) with a greater emphasis on the more decorative arts, through the seventeenth and eighteenth centuries.

The Primary Collection of English Art goes in two stages; on the upper ground floor (rooms 52–58) from Tudor to Early Georgian; from dark oak (note the Great Bed of Ware, mentioned by Shakespeare in *Twelfth Night*) through to walnut; among the furniture and trappings, dusky grottos like aquaria wherein the portrait miniatures shine almost phosphorescent with vivid colour—the Holbeins, the Elizabethan miniatures by Hilliard and Oliver. Here and there inset whole rooms, some salvaged from gone London houses. Then stairs take you up to the continuation (rooms 125–118), late Georgian into Victorian, the work of the great English furniture-makers, Chippendale and Sheraton, the decoration of the Adams (part of Garrick's drawing-room from the Adelphi, by Robert Adam, is here).

Other primary collections are shown, rather more condensed, on the ground floor: China and Japan (44); Continental Architecture and Sculpture; Islamic Art (42) and Indian (41; 47b—here the most radiant girls in London, the two second-century Jain *yakshis* in voluptuous red sandstone); the imaginatively reconstructed Costume Court like a vast shopping arcade. On the ground floor is also one of the great sights of the world, the radiant, majestic and whole harmony of the Italian High Renaissance in the seven great cartoons painted by Raphael for tapestries commissioned by Pope Leo X. But for the London addict I may be forgiven if I linger a moment in room 48 (still there at time of re-writing, but planned for redevelopment), for it is crammed with chunks salvaged from the ever-dissolving fabric of old London's architecture—bits and pieces of this will surprise you all through this Museum, but room 48 has a splendid concentration. A whole row, a positive grammar, of domestic doorways, from Adelphi Terrace, from Great Queen Street. There are shop-fronts, like most of the doorways of specifically human scale and speaking of a now-lost intimacy between shopkeeper and customer; ironwork from balconies—one by Tijou from Lincoln's Inn Fields. From gutted interiors, a staircase balustrade, early seventeenth century, climbing zig-zag high up the wall; a pine alcove from the Old Kent Road (given in praiseworthy piety by the South Metropolitan Gas Co.). There is almost the whole façade of Sir Paul Pindar's house, of about 1600, overhung, bulging with carved wood and rounded leaded glass, from Bishopsgate. Fragments like catch-lines from lost songs; doors that no longer open and that even if they did would give on to nothing but echoes in the mind.

The Primary Collections show the cream of all the departments of the museum in juxtaposition, so that you can see the style of each period informing objects of all kinds, the Rococo broken curve of Meissen china, for example, echoing the drapery in a painting by a court artist. Upstairs, the **Study Collections** concentrate objects according to their kind, and brilliant though the primary displays are, it is in the study galleries that the true museum connoisseur may find his deepest pleasure. But whether you wish to move into such specialisation or not, you should not miss, rather tucked away on the first floor at its northern extremity, the new paintings galleries, and in them especially the unrivalled collection of Constable's work, particularly rich in those swift, immediate oil-studies in which he has no peer.

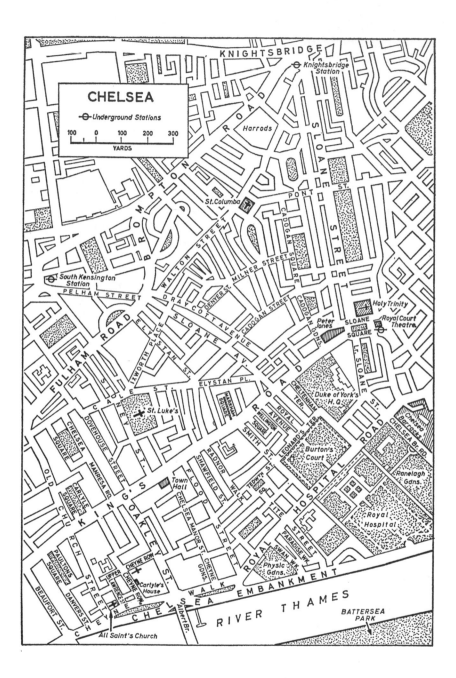

CHAPTER THIRTEEN

Chelsea

✧

'CHELSEA is a singular heterogeneous kind of spot, very dirty and confused in some places, quite beautiful in others, abounding in antiquities and the traces of great men. Our road runs out on a parade running along the shore of the river, a broad highway with shady trees, boats lying moored, and a smell of shipping and tar.' One of the last valid salutes to Chelsea as a detached, rural—or rather riverside—village, that was written by one of the village's most famous residents, Thomas Carlyle, before moving into his long residence at Cheyne Row in 1834. For centuries Chelsea had been secluded from the spread of London by the natural barrier of creeks running north from the Thames (where Victoria Station is now) and by the marshy area of the Five Fields. In its early development it had been far from 'dirty and confused', but rather a 'Village of Palaces', from the time, around 1520, when the greatest of its inhabitants (and indeed one of the greatest of Englishmen), Sir Thomas More, built his house there. The house is long gone and with it such echoes of its visitors as may have remained—Henry VIII, Erasmus, Hans Holbein— but something of its atmosphere is conveyed in More's masterpiece *Utopia*, which has been described as 'but the author's home writ large'. Under the Stuarts and the Georges the big houses in their gardens flowered: Charles II visited Nell Gwynn here (or at least just over the border in Fulham, at Sandford House, where now the gas works blow), and on the banks of the river he built the only remaining palace, the Chelsea Hospital. The Duke of Beaufort had a sumptuous house renovated on More's fabric (where now is Beaufort Street); in the grounds, farther east, of the Earl of Ranelagh's estate later flourished a great pleasure garden around the famous Ranelagh Rotunda that Canaletto painted. About the village, too, the lesser houses began to expand, offering from early on a near retreat for fashionable if not over-moneyed

London writers. Swift walked out and in, to and from London, and in May, 1711, wrote of the sweetness of the air in Chelsea's 'flowery meads', even though 'the hay-making nymphs are perfect drabs, nothing so clean and pretty as farther in the country: There is a mighty increase of dirty wenches in straw hats since I knew London . . .'

Now Chelsea is again famous or notorious for wenches in outrageous garb, but the garb is likely to be the outrage of the avant-garde of fashion, and what might be thought by the innocent to be dirt more often than not is a proud excess of cosmetic allied with a deliberate dishevelment of hair. The salubriousness of Chelsea's air has perhaps always been open to question; about the time that Swift was inhaling the scent of haymaking, the philosopher 3rd Earl of Shaftesbury was moving out from his mansion at 'Little Chelsea' (on the north-west borders, at West Brompton) to higher ground at Hampstead because of Chelsea's 'great Smoake', yet a hundred and twenty years later, in 1821, that generally astringent critic of London, Stendhal, noted that 'London moved me greatly because of the walks along the Thames towards Little Chelsea —there were small houses there surrounded by rose-bushes which seemed to me truly elegiac—it was the first time I had had a taste for such insipidities.'

A little more than a decade later, when Carlyle moved in, Chelsea was already being merged with London, as Thomas Cubitt reclaimed the swamp lands of the Five Fields for Belgravia. 'Steamboats have carried vicissitude into Chelsea, and Belgravia threatens it with her mighty advent,' wrote Leigh Hunt. Yet a very marked village or at least small town atmosphere persisted, even after the building of the new Embankment (1874) severed the intimate connection of the old, wavering, tree-clouded waterfront from its parent river; even after the 'village's' population had jumped from 12,000 in 1801 to 95,000 in 1901 (it has since shrunk by almost a half); even after the opening in 1960 of a supermarket in the King's Road. The atmosphere is of course world-famous simply as 'Chelsea', a word that means a Bohemian way of life in clothes that are not those of ordinary men; a world of beards, pubs, art, junk-shops and studios, of private lives the irregularities of which tend to cease to be private owing to the flamboyance and penetrating articulateness of those who lead them: artists and writers. Painters and authors have indeed been associated with Chelsea fairly steadily since Holbein painted the long-lost group of Thomas More's family about 1527 (a copy has recently come to Chelsea, at Crosby Hall), though the great names mostly congregate there from the eighteenth century on, with Swift, Addison and Steele; the novelist Smollett, then Leigh Hunt and the 'Sage of Chelsea' himself, Thomas Carlyle. George Eliot moved there, if only to die, and furious notoriety came with Whistler and with Oscar Wilde, and respectability with Henry James. J. M. W. Turner, with his hide-out at the end of Cheyne Walk during his latter years in the 1840s, is with Whistler the painter most intimately connected with Chelsea's riverscapes; and Whistler again with D. G. Rossetti and Oscar Wilde are names that evoke most vividly Chelsea's particular aura of exoticism often tinged with scandal.

The aura survives, though its locales shift through the borough. Artists are still scattered through Chelsea, for the studio facilities are excellent; the great artists' pubs in the 1950s became the Queen's Elm and Finch's on the Fulham Road, so popular indeed that the noise was often so great that it was impossible to hear conversation, and the throng so dense that it was equally impossible to reach the bar to get a drink, or even, if successful, to raise the drink in the press to one's lips. But the regulars there are far from being all locals, for Chelsea has long since ceased to be available, as domicile for the impoverished artist. S.W.3 is and has long been a most fashionable address, and the poor have been squeezed out way west beyond the World's End pub; business has moved in in its inexorable drive westwards, and house values have leapt upwards. Whistler's old house, the White House in Tite Street, is not a large house (though bigger than it looks) and even though Whistler had to sell it for reasons of bankruptcy in 1878 for £2,700 six months after he built it, that it should sell in 1962 for a reputed £50,000 would have surprised him. The characteristic smell of Chelsea is now that heady, indefinable zest of money, and the characteristic noise the swish and bang, no longer of the artist's brushes or chisels, but of the interior decorators converting yet another of the pretty-plain bijou terrace houses into a modern residence for a stock-broker, bright as a money-box, with superb plumbing and full central heating. Yet still Chelsea survives, if only just, with an air of casual intimacy that has no rival in London.

Unlike most London boroughs, Chelsea is blessed with a natural entrance, a foyer almost—**Sloane Square**, at its eastern extremity. This is the natural point of arrival or departure: here and here only the Underground touches Chelsea, and here the buses congregate and circle; here is even a taxi rank. And from Sloane Square's west side the main artery of Chelsea, the King's Road between the road and the river, and to a lesser degree north of it up to the boundary of the Fulham Road.

Sloane Square turns, among its chimney-turreted Victorian façades and its busy traffic, about a central paved island with plane trees and one of London's rare fountains; I hope the present system of lighting with strings of coloured bulbs will last, giving a perpetual slightly surprised air of Christmas to the Square's evenings. As a centre it is lively and carries conviction (though like everything else in London one lifts one's pen to celebrate, it is threatened by development— and even before that happens, the Royal Court Theatre has been remodelled, obliterating altogether the spasmodic sound of flushing from the Gents which was wont to accompany dramatic climaxes, though not altogether entirely the rumble of the neighbouring Underground that so often lends an extra infernal dimension to the performance). The Square has, besides theatre and station, a hotel (the Royal Court) of individuality with its own loyal following; a pub (and another pub on the Underground platform); flower stalls, a coffee stall even, and at its western end one of the few London buildings of modern elegance and stylistic conviction from the 1930s, the glass curve of Peter Jones department store, one of the great stores of London, particularly agreeable on the eye when the trees in the square are in their fresh May budding.

With Peter Jones on your right, you can now embark on **the King's Road**, Chelsea village street that wanders westwards with complete architectural undistinction (almost) but a formidable vitality. The use of the word 'village' here begs many questions, and indeed the visitor may reasonably at some points get the impression that the King's Road is Bond Street or, in fact more likely in its latest development, Carnaby Street all over again, re-set in an area still predominantly residential, but the point is that it is still residential even if only mainly for the rich, and at the week-end when Bond Street dies, the King's Road merely swarms the thicker while the traffic seizes up in its narrow flanks; all through the week, moreover, its afternoons are enlivened by shopping mums with prams and darting children. Although an estate agent is on record as saying 'I'm sorry but I think the King's Road will turn into Knightsbridge,' the transition will with luck be drawn out over some years, and the old dining-rooms, the fruit stalls, Mr. Thomas Crapper's renowned establishment (lavatory maker to King George V), and all the old small shops, will linger on a little, though they all fall in the end to supermarkets. Even if junk has become a dirty word at the top of the King's Road, where an antique is an antique and dusted and priced as such, it can just be found at the bottom end, while the antique shops stock an immense variety of quality; if you are interested, a morning or a whole day will be needed as introduction to the King's Road, with pauses for refreshment —the restaurants and coffee-bars are among the best in London, and the place hums with *trattorie* and *bistros*, not to mention pubs (particularly perhaps the cavernous Tudoresque interior of the Six Bells, where once (it was rebuilt in 1900) Rossetti, Whistler and others used to drink). Other shops include excellent clothes *boutiques* especially for the (rich) young female and perhaps even more for the male; one of them at least has opened a *branch* in Bond Street. Thus the shop windows are enthralling even if their architectural settings are nondescript, and the public in its cosmopolitan picturesque as exotic as anywhere in London. And even if the façades, witness of a hotchpotch development in the nineteenth century (after the King's Road was opened up from being a literally private road of the monarch, flanked by nursery gardens and fields), along the road itself, disappoint, there open off the road to north and south a series of most civilly mannered squares and little streets, bright with fresh paint and maintenance and brilliant brass.

The first of these comes on your left (south) some 300 yards down from Sloane Square—**Royal Avenue**, the embryo of a never-completed scheme of William III to drive a direct route to the Thames from his new palace at Kensington. Here you can glimpse the Royal Hospital, to which we will come back from the riverside in due course, and if you go down the avenue into St. Leonard's Terrace at the edge of Burton's Green you will be enchanted by a row of modestly pretty painted Georgian houses. Going on down the King's Road are

Wellington Square on the left and Markham on the right, each
roof-deep in trees, and Smith Street, which seems doll's house
scale. On past the pillars of the Town Hall, with on the right,
in Sydney Street, Savage's St. Luke's (1824), the parish church
built to focus Chelsea's turn inland, very lofty, hugely perpendicular—Dickens was married there in 1836. Oakley Street
is forbidding and impatient with traffic, but, at its far corner
with King's Road, is a little group of austerely excellent
houses, starting with Argyll House, built by Leoni, 1723, in
very chaste brick, and then especially No. 215 (1720), where
lived the composer Thomas Arne (of 'Rule Britannia'), and, a
century and a half later, Ellen Terry. Up Manresa Street on
the right, between the new buildings of the Chelsea Art School,
you can penetrate to the oddly secluded Chelsea Square
(recently re-named—it was yet another Trafalgar), and farther
on down the King's Road Carlyle Square is getting a bit late
and fussy, though still farther on, beyond the crossing of Old
Church Street, **Paultons Square** opens on the left, taking you
back to the discreetly planned charm of the 1830's, house and
communal garden and trees and ironwork in marvellous
marriage (yet only in these last years rescued by a preservation
order from dissolution). Westward from Paultons Square you
are rapidly approaching the end of Chelsea of High Fashion;
crossing Beaufort Street (with care; it is the teeming approach
to Battersea Bridge) at the kink in the road you come to the
Globe Pub, whence there is a straight view between new shops
with houses over, down to the World's End, a gabled and
pinnacled pile of a pub, neo-Elizabethan but standing where
the World's End has stood since Charles II and world's end
indeed as far as many Chelsea inhabitants are concerned,
though the King's Road continues on to the backward drears
of Fulham, past Cremorne Road where briefly in the mid-
nineteenth century flourished the pleasure gardens of Cremorne, and past the crude industrial silhouette of Lots Road
Power Station (whence comes, or came, the power for the
Underground).

North of the King's Road is not so interesting, though **the
Fulham Road**, which marches between Chelsea and Kensington, a little uncertainly as to which it belongs to, has points of
concern; good hospitals, pubs (notably the Queen's Elm,
already mentioned, on whose site Elizabeth I is said to have
sheltered in a thunderstorm under a tree) and some good

shops. The Vale opposite Paultons Square has some trysting values for those interested in British art, as at No. 1 lived the potter de Morgan, and farther down, the surgeon-autocrat of the Slade School, Henry Tonks. But Old Chelsea is housed south of the King's Road, between it and the river, and to get to it the visitor should go perhaps best down Old Church Street. Not much old remains here, but it was, with the parallel Danvers Street, *the* village street before it yielded to the King's Road. Here in houses long since gone lodged that vigorous Jacobite Tory divine, Dr. Atterbury, and Swift ('Paid 6*s.* per week for one sitting-room with confounded coarse sheets'). The stoutest perhaps of Poets Laureate, Thomas Shadwell, died there in 1692, and in Danvers Street lived the discoverer of penicillin, Sir Alexander Fleming.

Old Church Street ends on Cheyne Walk, and on the corner the old church of **All Saints**, the former parish church, holds the microcosm of Chelsea's early history. Finely sited, commanding the river and the new embankment, the church is of painfully fresh red brick (it was blitzed in 1941), but inside the monuments are replaced more or less intact; the most moving in the south chantry chapel is that built by Sir Thomas More for his first wife in 1532; meant to receive later himself and his second wife, it is doubtful if it did, after his execution in 1535 (his head is certainly at St. Dunstan's, Canterbury). The inscription, though a modern restoration, is More's, including the blank space after the word 'homicidis'; in the original draft, which More sent to Erasmus, he described himself as 'a terror to thieves, murderers, and heretics'—but Erasmus objected to the persecution of heretics, and so More deleted them but left, perhaps half mockingly, the blank. More's house and estate, the Chelsea Utopia, have vanished though their name echoes in the bleak length of Beaufort Street; over this tomb his memory hovers even if his body is not there, in not-uncheerful irony, for the body is irrelevant—he wrote the day before he died: 'It is St. Thomas' even and the Utas of St. Peter; and therefore tomorrow long I to go to God; it were a day very meet and convenient for me . . . Farewell, my dear child, and pray for me, and I shall for you and all your friends, that we may merrily meet in Heaven . . .' Close by are two beautifully carved capitals on the responds of an arch, dated 1528 and very early examples (though the traditional association with Holbein is dubious) of the Renaissance idiom in England.

The church is very rich in other monuments, many bearing names still resonant through Chelsea's street titles. A grand intricately strap-worked late Elizabethan tomb to Lord Dacre; Sara Colville (d. 1631) resurrecting in her shroud, a rather rare type of image; Charles Cheyne, Viscount Newhaven, an unusually (for England) uncompromising baroque piece, designed indeed by the great Bernini's son, Pietro, in 1672, and others; also wall-tablets commemorating distinguished locals such as de Morgan and Henry James ('lover and interpreter of the fine amenities, of brave decisions & generous loyalties'). Outside in the churchyard, the great urn designed by J. Wilton for the benefactor of Chelsea, Sir Hans Sloane (who died in 1753 aged 92) survives intact.

East and west from the church goes **Cheyne Walk**, one of the most famous streets of London, fronting bravely on the river, though farther from it than it once was before the Embankment of 1872 imposed its stiff limit, on which the heavy lorries now hurtle, to contain the tide—fortunately much of Cheyne Walk is slightly withdrawn from the Embankment road by a thin strip of shrubby garden, but the smell is of diesel oil rather than of the shipping and tar which Carlyle liked (though he approved of the Embankment's building; progress should not be denied). But the prospect is fine: down river to the tree-bowered pleasure pavilions (and at night, the lights) of Battersea Park on the opposite bank, with the enchanting spider's lattice work of the Albert Bridge's suspension work (built to Ordish's straight chain suspension system, 1873, the roadway bounces upon rhythmic impact, hence the notice at the bridge requesting troops crossing it to break step—long may it defy demolishers); up river the stark industrial landscape of Battersea Power Station, formidable in a winter sunset under a streaky and incandescent sky. Up-river, too, the moored hamlet of house-barges, with its own intimate and often chilly life. Battersea Bridge (1890), a rather chill functional arc, displaces the romantic but unsafe pierlike structure that can still be seen in the works of many painters—including Turner, de Wint and Whistler—who fell for its charms; it was demolished in 1885 following the diagnosis in it of 'a slight curvature to the west'. Over this vista broods Cheyne Walk, terraces of tall houses often behind tall iron railings that temper an expressed desire for privacy with elegance; yet, though still private, they are as clamorous with great names in memory as a wood with rooks.

At the far, unfashionable west end beyond Battersea Bridge (Nos. 118–19) Turner lived at the close of his life under the name of Mr. Booth ('Puggy Booth' to local small boys), in a modest cottage—'miserable in every respect', according to a contemporary. Farther east, the large and distinguished Lindsey House (long divided into Nos. 96–100), once the head-quarters, around 1770, of the Moravian sect in England. Its most famous subsequent resident was Whistler (No. 96) between 1866 and 1878 (when he moved, briefly, to Tite Street); then in Lindsey House the blue and white china collected, and from it the slender dandy with the white lock in the black hair looked on the Thames, and in a famous purple passage noted now 'the evening mist clothes the riverside with poetry as with a veil, and the poor buildings lose themselves in the dim sky, and the tall chimneys become campanili and the warehouses are palaces in the night and the whole city hangs in the heavens before us . . .' (Carlyle noted an allied effect rather differently: 'the gleam of the great Babylon, affronting the peaceful skies'). But Whistler's words almost match his paintings. The Chelsea *Nocturnes*; *Black and Gold—The Falling Rocket* (from a firework display at the long extinct Cremorne Gardens), when shown in 1877, roused Ruskin to accuse him of flinging a pot of paint in the public's face; the equally famous libel action that followed won Whistler a farthing damages and bankruptcy. From Chelsea he threw words as well as paint at a philistine public, in such works as *The Gentle Art of Making Enemies*, and words, too, at unrelished rivals, at Oscar Wilde, urging him 'to cease masquerading in the streets of my Chelsea' in idiotic clothes. Whistler lived in many places in the borough, and died there (at No. 74 Cheyne Walk) in 1893, though he is buried in Chiswick.

Moving eastwards to No. 93 (of 1777)—here Mrs. Gaskell was born in 1810, but she moved almost immediately; No. 92 is Adam-ish, and then (leaving Battersea Bridge on your right) Crosby Hall looms in Danvers Street on your left (Mondays to Fridays, 10–12, 2–5; Saturdays and Sundays, 2–5). Now, as hostel of the British Federation of University Women, it is partly of 1926 but partly of about 1475: that earlier part stood for some four and a half centuries in Bishopsgate, originally the house of a rich City wool merchant, Sir John Crosby, until removed stone by stone to Chelsea where it has happy local associations with Sir Thomas More who owned it briefly, in Bishopsgate in 1523–4. It is an ambitious example of late fifteenth-century domestic architecture, the wooden roof (original) of the hall especially fine. Move east along Cheyne Walk past Albert Bridge; at No. 16 (built 1717, but refaced) was D. G. Rossetti, poet and painter, from 1862 almost till his death in 1882 (at that time, avant-garde art lived in Chelsea: solid academic talent centred on Kensington). In that strange menage, decorated with blue and white china and old furniture, loud with the cry of peacocks—subsequent leasers found a clause in the lease added, that peacocks were on no account to be kept—life was at least lived intensely. Rossetti painted and wrote, and drugged his despair with chloral and washed it down with whisky; Swinburne lived with him for a time, and Watts-Dunton's room was so macabrely bric-à-bracked that it was believed to be haunted. The houses continue stately to the end of the walk, with notable ironwork at No. 15 and at Nos. 6–3 (well-preserved early Georgian of about 1717). At No. 4, with its beautiful doorway, George Eliot died in 1880.

If you go back on your tracks now, westwards, for a last look, walk through the shrub garden strip that separates the Walk from the Embankment; the grave houses move past through the flicker of the branches, for all their variety a most urbanely civilised sequence. In the garden, opposite Rossetti's house, a fountain for him by Seddon; and farther on, a most properly and successful naturalistic statue in bronze, by Boehm, of **Carlyle** seated in his dressing-gown impervious to wind and weather: the 'sage of Chelsea' still vivid in his habitat (orthodox anyway in morals, he was honoured by the borough in his lifetime, by the christening of Carlyle Square in 1872). His vividness rests much on the preservation of his house as museum (for he is still out of favour as a writer), which is almost spookily full of him. To find it, turn up near the statue into **Cheyne Row**, a terrace of more modest, unremarkable houses with a trim village calm; here, into No. 24 in 1834, he moved for uncertain reasons (but, 'Chelsea abounds in omnibi, and they take you to Coventry Street for sixpence . . .'); here, in 1881, in the drawing-room, he died. In this modest bourgeois house most of those huge celebrations of the autocratic hero were written in fierce spate—*The French Revolution, Cromwell, Frederick the Great.* The house (National Trust; weekdays except Tuesday, 10–1, 2–6 or dusk; Sundays from 2) always succeeds in alarming me slightly from the moment I have pressed the door-bell; you are admitted, and there is his stick in the stand and that sombrero-type hat on the peg at the garden door—would you *really* care to meet Mr. Carlyle? The question becomes almost dangerous. On that first floor, in the drawing-room, that stoutly-stuffed arm-chair with the book-rests, where he died; in the basement the pulleys that served for the buckets for the do-it-yourself cold showers, and the kitchen where Tennyson and Carlyle smoked carefully into the chimney to avoid rebuke from the stropped tongue of Mrs. Carlyle. Between the many personal objects, many of them of compellingly ugly vitality, one steps carefully as in a minefield. It is a must for any visitor in London, that house, but it is good to get out of it also, and to go on up and inland a little. At the corner (on the site of one of the studios of the potter de Morgan) the Catholic Church claims its local martyr and saint—Church of the Most Holy Redeemer and St. Thomas More. Across the top runs Upper Cheyne Row, still more modest, still more villagey—almost unreally so: there are white posts, and the roadway expires into a flagged path along two-story cottages. At No. 22, a year before Carlyle, in 1833, there settled in that charming, feckless, reckless, over-familied, courageous and slightly idiotic man of letters, Leigh Hunt; after leaving it, he remembered it as 'full of repose—a little backroom in a street in London is farther removed from the noise than a front room in a country town' (often still true enough today). When Carlyle visited him, he did not think so; he refuted Leigh Hunt's domestic bliss—('a poetical Tinkerdom without parallel'), and catalogued squalor.

Returning to the Embankment, and continuing downstream with the river on your right, past the opening of the Royal Hospital Road on your left, you come to the tall rather agreeably variegated brick façades of the buildings that went up on the new Embankment in the 1870s. Then, behind high iron railings, the closely planted greenery of the Physic Garden (not open to the public), which has been a sort of herb laboratory since 1673; the first cedars in England were planted here in 1683, and hence in 1732 were sent to America samples of cotton-seed from which the huge cotton industry of the States was to bloom. The garden was made over in 1722 to the Apothecaries Company by that voluminous benefactor, Sir Hans Sloane, 'for the manifestation of the glory, power, and wisdom of God, in the works of creation'; Sloane's statue (by Rysbrack, 1737) stands with dignity of robe and wig central in the garden. He was a successful, very moneyed, court physician, and Lord of Chelsea Manor; though responsible for the demolition of More's original house, it is as preserver that he is remembered, for he was a collector of ambitious and omnivorous appetite. He collected much of Chelsea into his property and Chelsea still echoes him in its street names, while out of his collection of manuscripts, works of art and scientific specimens was to grow the British Museum. At the east end of the Garden is Swan Walk with a few biggish and elegant surviving houses from the late eighteenth century, and Paradise Walk; on the Embankment itself (No. 17) notably one of Norman Shaw's most famous and elegantly complicated houses, Swan House (1875), now inhabited incongruously by the headquarters of one of the top private combat units formed since the war against the booming success of the wage-snatch gangs.

The opening of **Tite Street** on to the Embankment is not positively encouraging, indeed rather gloomy, but this, with Cheyne Walk, was for long the most famously inhabited area of artistic Chelsea from the 1870s on; it includes a number of specially built studio-houses, several by the master of that genre, Godwin (33, 29, 44 and the Tower House). Whistler's connection was unwillingly brief (see p. 207), but J. S. Sargent, another American, the brilliant and often sardonic portrayer of Edwardian England (see the excellent representation of his work in the Tate) was based for many years at No. 31 until his death there in 1925; at No. 33 Augustus John received a long line of distinguished sitters. Behind the far from glamorous façade of No. 16, Oscar Wilde lived from the time of his marriage in 1884 until his arrest in 1895, in a decor thought out by himself and Godwin—a decor relatively unfussy, austere almost compared with the clutter of the time, yet which aroused suspicion. Hence the largely delicate dandy shot telegrammic insult at Whistler in the brisk skirmish that followed the latter's *Ten O'Clock Lecture* in 1885; here, on the top floor, Wilde wrote—plays, poems, articles—and from that front door in 1894 the livid invasion of the Marquess of Queensberry was repulsed down the steps. A year later, the debacle, followed by the stripping of the house in a tragi-farcical sale. Sadly, much of the east side has now been demolished.

Back on the Embankment, proceeding still down-stream, your eye will be caught by the tough silhouettes on the other bank of the Battersea Power Station, which (although it can have a rugged appeal at night) by day with its four coarse table legs sticking up in the air and flooding smoke smoothly and potently into the sky, always reminds me of cinema organ music of the 1930s. It is echoed by the four uprights of Chelsea Suspension Bridge, but rebuked now on your left by the grand set-piece of Chelsea architecture, the **Royal Hospital**, standing back behind its flanks of trees and in its green of grass: a long, chaste front with an austere giant pillared portico between the two projecting wings, dark mellow red brick touched at the quoins with Portland stone under the long greenish roof. It has a superb modesty of fitness for place and purpose—as Carlyle noted rather grudgingly and evidently to his own surprise: 'quiet and dignified and the work of a gentleman'. The gentleman involved was Christopher Wren; the building, mainly of between 1682 and 1691, was founded by Charles II as a hospital for aged or disabled soldiers. And there the pensioners still are, in a uniform adapted from the time of Marlborough's wars, dark blue in winter, scarlet with black three-corner hats in summer. A familiar sight in Chelsea; they had a not enviable reputation for scrounging which they are now losing (they can keep their old age pensions), but will often accept a drink in a pub with courtesy and offer in return sharp comment on modern youth, the state of the world, or the problems of longevity ('I keep fit by a routine—a pint of beer mid-morning and evening, same as everyone else, and always have a bath on Monday'—Sergeant Jones, aged 97, December 1961).

On a fine summer morning, the Hospital grounds are as good as anywhere in London for a stroll. In May for one splendid week they break into huge marquees which are ringed outside with bright new garden implements and furniture, wrought-iron, gnomes, etc., and which inside explode like a silent but sweetly stinking firework show, with flowers of all sorts and most seasons—the Chelsea flower show, one of the classic events of the London season, accompanied by queues at Sloane Square station and the upper end of Chelsea a-swirl with bobbing hats as brilliant as the flowers in the marquees. The Hospital building itself should be visited (weekdays, 10–12, 2–dusk; Sundays, 2–dusk. Tips are accepted); in the main ('Figure') Court facing the river is one of the prettiest statues in London, Grinling Gibbons's bronze of Charles II in kilt *à la romaine*; this is decorated with oak on Oak Apple Day in memory of Charles's escape by hiding in an oak tree after the battle of Worcester in 1651, and on the same day the resident veterans go gorgeous into their summer scarlet. The two main wings that project towards the river are the wards where the pensioners have their quarters, oak cubicles off long corridors; the range that joins them, with its clock tower with cupola over the portico, has an octagonal vestibule that is a bit too tall for itself (the marriage of giant orders throughout the building is not entirely successful), but which gives on the east to the chapel and on the west to the Great Hall, both fine rooms. The chapel, panelled and barrel-vaulted, has a tremendously dignified reredos, very rare silver plate, and in the apse a very painterly and hopeful Resurrection by S. Ricci; the Hall is also the dining-room, studded with the names of battle honours and hung with flags. Outside again, in the east and west courts are two fine iron lamp standards.

Eastwards, the grounds of the Hospital join on the wooded, nooked and delled Ranelagh Gardens, where not a trace remains of the apparatus of pleasure which made Ranelagh famous as a centre of entertainment between 1733 and 1805, when for years at a stretch it was visited by almost anybody who was anybody, from Dr. Johnson downwards; it saw concerts (including the infant prodigy Mozart, aged 8, in 1764), masquerades that were forerunners of the Chelsea Arts Balls, fireworks, balloon launchings and other galas. Its focus was a famous building, the Rotunda, which can still be seen in Canaletto's painting of it in the National Gallery.

The Hospital suffered in both wars, and in the second war lost to a V2 rocket notably the Infirmary (where once Robert Walpole's house had stood). A splendid supplement has however been completed: the **National Army Museum** (weekdays 10–5.30; Sundays 2–5.30) in a specially designed building opened in 1971. Moved to Chelsea from Sandhurst, it recounts the history of the British Army from the reign of Henry VII up to the outbreak of the First World War (at which point the Imperial War Museum takes over). The collection consists of relics, uniform and insignia of the army, as well as a number of fine paintings. If you emerge on Royal Hospital Road, and turn right, you have the old burial ground (where Dr. Burney, for many years organist at Chelsea, is buried). You can return to the pulse of Chelsea in the King's Road via Cheltenham Terrace, past the façade of the Duke of York's Headquarters, once also a charitable project (for the children of soldiers' widows) and now a Territorial Headquarters. Begun in 1801 (by J. Sanders), it has an agreeable neo-classic front, which yet, with the serene disposition of brick and Portland stone of Wren's Hospital in mind, seems oddly bitty and unresolved.

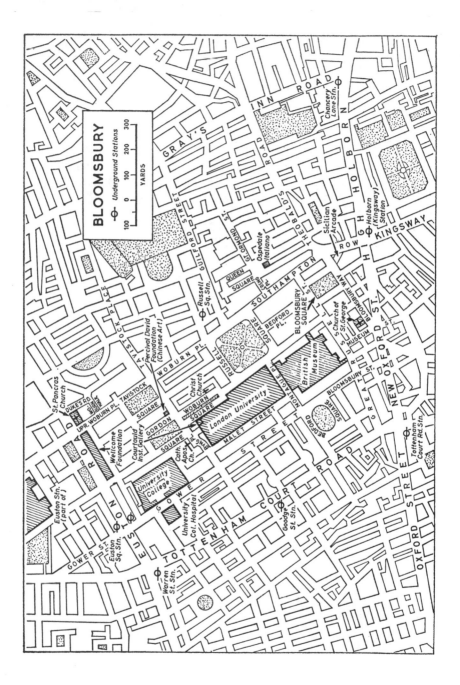

CHAPTER FOURTEEN

Bloomsbury

✈

BLOOMSBURY is for letters and learning, for University and Museum, but a convenient starting point is the big underground junction of **Holborn Station**, that ejects you up its bleak two-tiered escalators into the junction of High Holborn with Kingsway (running south to Aldwych) and Southampton Row, and a prospect in the main of big modern commercial blocks among hurrying traffic of, in comparison, small modern commercial people. But if you go north, up Southampton Row, you will come on your left to an odd architectural folly of 1905, Sicilian Avenue, with colonnades, tubbed bay trees and little shops (some for antiques) suggesting a change in tempo, even uncommercial dalliance; this brings you through into Vernon Way, which leads into Bloomsbury Way, and opposite you on the other side of the road, **Bloomsbury Square**. Though the buildings about this are almost all recent and commercial, the square's garden with its big plane trees and seats survives above a subterranean car park and here was the beginning of modern Bloomsbury.

The name has a certain magic fall, as if of a settling of spent but still fragrant petals, or of russet leaves, on to damp earth (and autumn is indeed the true time to walk Bloomsbury, when the thinning trees unveil the clear elegance of the remaining old architecture of its squares). But the borough of Blemonde, of which it is a corruption, was made over perhaps by William the Conqueror to his vassal Baron Blemonde, and Bloomsbury as such begins only when the Earl of Southampton decided to lay out a square south of his house (long demolished), where you now are, about 1660. John Evelyn came to dinner in 1665, and approved—'a noble Square or Piazza, a little towne'. He also approved the 'good aire'; to the north was the open country. The little town began to grow; the Duke of Montague built a lavish house (site of the present British Museum), and then to the west the great landowning family of the Russells, Dukes of Bedford (whose family names, Russell, Tavistock, Bedford, Woburn still label the area) began to develop a very fashionable fringe north of the west end, in an irregular sequence of handsome squares and roads. In the nineteenth century, fashion began to withdraw ('very unfashionable quarter, though very respectable', wrote a new resident of Bloomsbury Square in 1866). By then the first of the two now-dominant institutions of Bloomsbury was well settled in the British Museum, begun in 1753, and rehoused in its present carapace from 1823. The second, to the north, London University, first in the guise of the discreet and elegant University College, began in 1827 at the north end of Gower Street. But the area was still mainly residential; for lawyers (so handy for the Inns of Court just to the east) and for scholars and writers about their honeycomb Museum. From about 1906, a concentrated and brilliant circle of writers and artists first took their name from Bloomsbury and in due course returned it, enhanced, to the district. 'Bloomsbury', as epithet—and at first in mockery—was applied to a group of whom the most famous were to be the historian Lytton Strachey, the critics Clive Bell and Roger Fry, novelists Virginia Woolf and E. M. Forster. As epithet it implied a somewhat precious mixture of highbrow, arty remoteness from life, of Bohemianism a little dusty, though this did them less than justice.

But the chances of another such group living in Bloomsbury are remote, for the two great institutes of learning, Museum and University, are fast proving cuckoos in the nest and in their voracious growth pushing everything else out of the area. The result cannot be a true campus, for though there are some residential hostels in the district, the University of London is in the main a commuting one, and the danger (already realised in many places) is that it will become the intellectual equivalent of the City, pulsating between nine and five, and a desert in the evenings and at week-ends. At the north end of Bloomsbury Square, Charles James Fox sits, shielded from the morning sun by the premises of the Liverpool Victoria Friendly Society, and looking north up the placid brown brick avenue of Bedford Place (very well preserved, of about 1700), to the companion statue, togaed too, of his fellow-Whig the Duke of Bedford—Whigs and radicals all, friends in their time of the French Revolution, but sculptured for posterity in almost incredibly archaic, neo-classic guise as patricians, which too they also were.

For practical purposes, there is no other course but to divide Bloomsbury into two, as a walk through squares and gardens, and as a visit to the British Museum.

Westwards first, along Bloomsbury Way, brings you to **St. George Bloomsbury** on the right. Up the steepish flight of steps, to the grandiose gloom of the portico, great Corinthian pillars under a great plain pediment, and into the interior—here the axis is south to north, and the altar set back behind two weighty depressed arches borne, again, on Corinthian columns, at north instead of east. Depressed arches and columns, it is by Hawksmoor, 1720–30, and like his St. Mary Woolnoth (see p. 350) orders space with authority into almost solid compression; almost it seems that if you were to remove the casing of masonry like a mould, the air it shapes would still stand firm as a cast in crystal. In St. George, doubts that I have at times that Hawksmoor was no Christian grow stronger; the mood is rather of a Roman stoic order. But St. George is famous really for its exterior, and of its exterior, for its steeple if such it can be called. The tower goes four square enough to a sort of square templet of four pillared porticos with columns, echoing the church's entrance below—but thence diminishes in a still massive stepped obelisk bearing at its peak King George I as St. George. 'Master-stroke of absurdity', Horace Walpole called this, but ideas of decorum change, and you may well find it all now has a compelling surreal logic—it was based (and why not?) on Pliny's description of the Mausoleum at Halicarnassus. Once its effect was still more striking, for the royal supporters, lions and unicorns, crawled about the steps of the obelisk; this was more than the Victorians could bear, and they were removed.

The turning right beyond St. George is **Museum Street** and indeed at once into the Museum quarter: a lively and humming little warren of streets south of the British Museum. For more than a decade, 1965-75, this all seemed doomed, seedy with planning blight, for the voracious Museum was going to swallow it all up—but in 1975, it was all reprieved. Here you can start the nucleus of your own British Museum, in bookshops, in antique shops, on a modest or if you wish immodest scale. In the short length of Museum Street you can buy a nice little piece of silver quite reasonably at S. J. Shrubsole, but if more ambitious you can also occasionally pick up there a rare Wine Cistern for £27,000 or less. Cameo Corner has always surprises in jewellery and oddities; at Craddock and Barnard's you can still get in on the rising market for etchings before they become exorbitant. There are dairies, publishers, more bookshops of all kinds of specialities, a hairdresser, coffee-bars and the Museum Tavern with a cheap and edible lunch. There is a coming and going of scholars of all nationalities, every degree of dustiness, of wild sparkle of spectacle and luxuriance of beard, of every colour and every creed. All dependent on the field of force set up by the great magnet of the British Museum itself, couchant beyond iron railings behind its pillared façade along shady **Great Russell Street**, into which Museum Street brings you.

At this stage we can do no more than note the presence of the Museum (it is anyway impossible not to), to return to it later. It began to build in its present shape in 1823, but the immense columnar façade with its wings came late, in 1842–7. The scale of immensity is difficult to grasp—it would have been given the room it needed to make its full impact if the development of the area south of the Museum had not been abandoned—but, as noted, the abandoning has preserved other qualities.

Great Russell Street runs west to join Tottenham Court Road; towards its end there is, for those interested in modern building, a worthy attempt by the Trades Union Congress on the left, with an Epstein sculpture (and the Y.W.C.A. a little farther on on the right). But our route is first right past the Museum, up Bloomsbury Street, with small brick houses, publishers and the small Bloomsbury boarding houses familiar to countless students, to the opening of **Bedford Square**, calmly and composedly set about its luxuriant central green. 'They'—you, me—have unforgivably let the buses in now, but Bedford Square on a Sunday is still an almost hallucinatory piece of preservation of late eighteenth-century London. It was, in 1775, the first development northwards of Bloomsbury, by its owners, the Russells, Dukes of Bedford, who owned almost the whole area traversed in this chapter and still own this square—hence its survival. Each side is a dignified composition in brick, with uniform handsome doors set in rusticated round-headed archways above a slight but sufficient rise of steps. Now mostly architects, publishers and so on (the Architectural Association is on its west side) it was very grandly residential, and Nos. 6 and 6a once formed the Lord Chancellor's official residence. Lord Loughborough lived there, and later Lord Eldon, that craggy Lord Chancellor —he was especially interested in the wards of court, but his own daughter delighted London in 1817 by eloping from the house (with George Repton, son of the great landscape architect).

Right at the north-east corner of Bedford Square lands you among the uncompromising presence of the British Museum again—its north front, of vast opulent Edwardian fluted pillars (finished 1914: the Edward VII Galleries)—and of the headquarters of the University of London, the Senate House, designed by Charles Holden in 1932. This accumulates in somewhat staid genteel blocks of pale masonry up to a genteel tower 210 feet high. Max Beerbohm, to whom Bloomsbury was antipathetic, was vicious about it: 'bleak, blank, hideous and already vast whited sepulchre'. Truly it does have, particularly on a grey drizzle of a Sunday, something of the quality of a monument to the dead, a kinship to the Cenotaph; architecturally it is a bloodless academic compromise between broad modern blocking and traditional Georgian articulation. And yet, in the shift of time and particularly in contrast with the often much bleaker outcrops in London of post-war building, it begins to take on a little warmth, to become in certain moods almost sympathetic, almost gentle.

The ramifications of **the University** are enormous, and its colleges are scattered between Egham in Surrey to the south-west and Queen Mary's in the East End; it has over 25,000 so-called internal students (nearly half of them commute in at least an hour in each direction) and this number will soon swell furiously. Though relatively young, its schools, faculties, institutes, hostels, proliferate as if to make up for lost time—it received its royal charter in 1836, and London was the last major European capital to get its University. But when it did, its scope was agreeably liberal: 'for the advancement of religion and morality and the promotion of useful knowledge, without distinction of rank, sect, or party' (nor after 1878, of sex; London was the first then to admit women as equals); it has become of course, by virtue of achievement, one of the great universities of the world. The Senate House houses, in the tower, the Library, which includes specialist collections notably of Elizabethan books and music, and also the collection of portraits of writers that once hung above Lord Chesterfield's bookshelves, including Wycherley, Congreve, Addison, Pope and Steele, and the earliest-known version of what may be the only likeness of Spenser.

Going north, you can take according to inclination either of two parallel routes. The western one, Tottenham Court Road, is hideous and teeming and entirely unacademic, with north Soho seeping out from its western side, and the great emporia of furniture on its eastern, especially Heal's and Maples. The eastern route is Gower Street, very long and very plain, its left-hand side a gentle, not disagreeably monotonous terrace of dark brick houses of from 1790 on. The old building of **University College** is on the right near the top of the street, opposite the gaunt spiky dark brick of University College Hospital, but itself like an unexpected reminiscence of gracious living and gracious learning precariously surviving about its green courtyard, wherein two absurd little domed observatories in front of the rather grand main façade: a tall double flight of steps branching back into pillared portico, pediment and dome; by the architect of the National Gallery, Wilkins, 1827–9, and with a strong family resemblance to it, but much more successfully composed. The College includes a collection of work by the neo-classic sculptor, Flaxman; also the most famous of English art schools, the Slade, which has a collection of early works by former students of great fascination—by Stanley Spencer, Augustus John and many others. The College's presiding genius is Jeremy Bentham, philosopher and reformer, who bequeathed to the College, at his death in 1832, among other things himself; there he sits, in a box, which is opened from time to time, his skeleton fully clothed and not unbenign. (Admission generally by previous arrangement only.)

At the top of Gower Street, the welter of **Euston Road** to the right, ringing heavy traffic through north London, and here thicker yet at the approaches to the three main railway termini for the north: Euston, St. Pancras and King's Cross. Opposite Euston is the Wellcome Foundation, with a formidable medical library, and a museum of medical history and science (Monday to Friday 10–5). Then, as if to mark the northern border of Bloomsbury with majesty and religion equal to that of St. George at the south, and with more space to make its massive and eccentric presence felt, the church of **New St. Pancras** in Upper Woburn Place. Much new building is about and the Hearts of Oak Society, that used to create with its bulbous Edwardian baroque such agreeably weird diapason with the church, is demolished. St. Pancras church is Greek, a free variation (by the Inwoods, 1819–22) on the Erechtheum; reflecting the then new respectability and dignity of the area, it was the most expensive church in London since St. Paul's (£77,000) and in its way as massive if less brutally so as St. George. At the west end, over the tall semi-circular columned portico, the tower climbs through three Towers of the Winds; at the east, on each side, stand forth the caryatid tribunes (caryatids for effect; they are terra-cotta about cast iron cores, and their expression compared with their originals—of which you can find one later in the British Museum—seems to be reverting dourly to the Egyptian). I dote upon the tribunes, and from the southern one projects a rather pert flue-pipe. Inside, St. Pancras is a long ruthless drive, a march of low dark wood boxed pews under the flat ceiling and emphasised by the long plainly elegant galleries, to the very dramatic and spectacular close of a gigantic hexastyle, dark polished mottled marble columns touched with gilt, against the pale paint of the apse over the altar.

Following south round the east end of the church, you come into **Woburn Walk**, a stucco terrace with shop windows built in a studied and most elegant design by Cubitt. This seems pure Jane Austen, though a little later, about 1822; properly there are one or two antique shops among them, but the north side is now part of a hotel. This includes No. 5, where W. B. Yeats had his London foothold between 1895 and 1919; a poet of whose work one does not think in terms of either London or Bloomsbury, but of the Celtic twilight, of Byzantium, of the fierce bitter and randy spirit surging against the ageing body's decrepitude. But listen to this song of praise from an A.B.C. tea-shop:

> My fiftieth year had come and gone,
> I sat, a solitary man,
> In a crowded London shop,
> An open book and empty cup
> On the marble table-top.

While on the shop and street I gazed
My body of a sudden blazed;
And twenty minutes more or less
It seemed, so great my happiness,
That I was blessèd and could bless.

So might one sit, mackintosh unbuttoned, the ashtrays full
and rings of wet cups on table, and the green sky of winter
deepening outside into cold night; there is for me almost
more of London in those lines than is bearable.

Woburn Walk brings you to Woburn Place, no place but
the northern end of the main route north from the Strand
at Aldwych, with many hotels. A little south, the road passes
through the eastern flank of **Tavistock Square**; on the left
corner a huge Lutyens celebration for the British Medical
Association (1925), which acts as a kind of trade union for
practising physicians and organises scientific meetings for the
profession. Opposite this, Woburn House, the Jewish Communal Centre with a very interesting little museum on its
first floor (Monday–Thursday 2.30–5; Friday and Sunday
10.30–12.45; closed on Jewish holy days). Dickens lived in
a house on this site between 1851–60, and there wrote
notably *Bleak House*, the novel in which his feeling for a
Gothic London, labyrinthine and fuming with fog, found
perhaps its most vivid expression. And it was in Tavistock
Square that Virginia Woolf (in a house blitzed in 1941) lived
and wrote many of her books. The way back southwards
now you can make by a gentle drift through squares, in a
perhaps slightly introverted mood with the gleam of green
grass, the flicker of tree-trunks and foliage or of the black
dripping branches in winter, and the flicker too of often still
uninterrupted sequences of discreetly polite and proportioned
terrace houses, all moving pleasantly over the eye. But if you
look a little closer, into the windows say, you will at once
perceive the problem of the place, the old problem of architectural preservation, which is the old one of old bottles and
new wine. Proportionable and polite, the old houses are, but
for living in, for eating, sleeping, talking, for being born and
for dying in; their interiors posit a certain basic pattern of
family living. But look through the uncurtained windows now
at the workers, architects, publishers, or most often the staff
of London University. Under hard and efficient lights, they

work among a clutter of tables, stacked files or books ordered and numbered along functional shelves, and almost always this disposition of objects swears horribly with the meaning of the room that contains it, and turns the meaning of the exteriors into sham. If you can solve this problem realistically, Bloomsbury will be grateful. Otherwise, retract your eyes from probing, and proceed with the surface only in mind. And I only hope enough old surface remains to refresh you; the sack of Bloomsbury has accelerated through the last decade.

Note the surviving west side of Tavistock Square, an urbane composition in brick with stucco pilasters, of 1826. Proceed through west to the neighbouring Gordon Square, which was Cubitt of 1820 on, and which, though much rebuilt, in places still holds together about its green. In the south-east corner (No. 53; 10.30–5, except Mondays 2–5, Saturdays 10–1; closed Sundays, Bank Holidays and the first fortnight in September), time off can be taken in the exquisite silences of the Percival David Foundation, a very important collection of Chinese ceramics. A plaque for Lytton Strachey is on No. 51.

Running south from Gordon Square is **Woburn Square**— narrow, almost corridor-like. In 1969 the unpretentious Georgian houses were ruthlessly swept away, but on its north-west corner is the Warburg Institute, spearhead in Britain of the movement, with its emphasis on the classical tradition, on the significance of imagery, that has had such a profound influence in the study of art since the war. Next to it are the Galleries of its sister institute, the **Courtauld Institute of Fine Art** (see p. 246). Its notice board is modest, and its lift like a short prison sentence, but they lead to a luxury of picture-seeing unique in galleries open to the public in London (10–5; Sundays 2–5). It is, to date, quite unaccountably unfrequented, though this is just as well, for if the crowds came how then would fare the carpets, the sofas? The first rooms hold the Lee collection, from the primitives to the Renaissance, also an interesting selection of English portraits and the superb Gambier–Parry bequest. But the major importance of these Galleries is in the Courtauld collection of Impressionist and early Post-Impressionist paintings. Samuel Courtauld (d. 1947), in a period when English appreciation and patronage of revolutionary development in art seemed to have evaporated, was almost a lone English rival of the great American and Continental collectors, and he bought masterpieces—if you like French painting between Manet and Cézanne and Seurat, Gauguin and Van Gogh, a visit is a *sine qua non*. Manet's 'The Bar at the Folies-Bergére', that blonde with a fringe and absent pop-eyed hazed gaze, and the ample crupper reflected in the mirror, is painted still with that broad freedom reminiscent of Hals and of Velasquez (note the still-life of the flowers in the pot among the gold foil of the champagne bottles). Van Gogh has two significant canvases, a landscape of 'Peach Trees in Blossom', painted at Arles in spring 1889, just before he left for the asylum at St. Rémy, and the 'Portrait of the Artist with his ear cut off', of a couple of months earlier while recovering from the fit in which he attacked Gauguin and then cut off his own ear. Close by are two sumptuously melancholy figures from Gauguin's stay in Tahiti—'Te Rerioa' —day-dreaming, and 'Nevermore' (inspired by Manet's 'Olympia'). Degas, Renoir, Bonnard are also here, and the Cézannes of major importance and beauty, including one of the five versions of the 'Card-Players'; a very typical 'Montagne Ste Victoire', in those faceted blues building up its structure in riveting precision. In the blues again of the 'Lake at Annecy', a break-through and break-down of surface and its reconstruction in terms of the logic of a purely pictorial structure—a photographic detail of this, the answering cylinders of tree-trunk and tower, the interlocking triangles, might also seem to be from a Cubist picture, and it was, of course, to Cézanne that Picasso and Braque were to look in their development of Cubism.

Then, as coda, there is Roger Fry's own collection, including also some good French ones, but mainly of his Bloomsbury colleagues' work. In contrast, these English pictures, it must be admitted, are a little sad, a little drab; paintings of painstaking honesty, yet lacking that final ruthlessness that kindles painting into greatness. In comparison with the French, like sticks admirably chosen, skilfully arranged, lacking only the flame.

In Woburn Square again, the exit to the south brings you into the greater expanse of **Russell Square**, with the Senate House of the University bulked large to the west. Russell Square, begun in 1800, was indeed the largest of London squares, but little of its original housing remains (a few houses on the west). The east side presents now an exuberant though sadly dwindling skyline of late Victorian and Edward-

Regency extravaganza: Gloucester Gate (1826) by Nash

EARLY NINETEENTH CENTURY

Opulent
(Nash's Park Square)

Domestic
(Camden Town)

Commercial
(Woburn Walk)

ian hotel building in dark red brick and terracotta; the University has appropriated much of the square, though once it was inhabited by the prosperous upper middle class (for example, Thackeray's Osborne and Sedley families in *Vanity Fair*). The garden was once landscaped by Repton; since the war it has been redesigned and laid out, and now is much enhanced (to my view—there was much argument about this) by ingenious lighting built into the trees. To the south, the statue of Francis Duke of Bedford (by Westmacott) looks down to Charles James Fox in Bloomsbury Square, where we glimpsed him at the beginning of this chapter.

The last of the squares on this walk you will find through a little passage way (Cosmo Place) left off the south-eastern exit from Russell Square, Southampton Row. Queen Square— the Queen being Anne in whose reign it was built (with the north end then and for years left open—is now hospital square, with at least five big hospitals, extending down Great Ormond Street to the east (wherein some very pretty old houses with door-hoods). At the north end, in the otherwise unremarkable garden, a somewhat bruised lead statue that has caused much confusion—generally known as Anne, certainly wrongly, and more probably Charlotte, George III's Queen.

Southampton Row will convey you south back to Holborn Underground Station, but if you are in good strength, the British Museum remains unbroached—for this turn right along Great Russell Street.

CHAPTER FIFTEEN

The British Museum and British Library

❧

As one advances on the British Museum, one may feel calmed by the welcome of its giant portico, and by the terrace among the columns where the readers from the Reading Room walk up and down, pacing, giving a most convincing interpretation very often of their role of profound readers in the British Museum Reading Room lost in profound thought and having a quick drag at a cigarette before returning to their desks. Any such calm is likely, according to my own experience, to be shattered, the moment you are through the revolving doors and into the huge high hall. Even when, as I usually am, bent on some particular errand in the B.M., my first steps inside waver in an agony of indecision, and I am overcome by sheer embarras de richesses, and manifest all the uneasy symptoms of a grasshopper mind.

The beginnings of this mammoth institution lie in the acquisitive habits, aided by considerable wealth, of the fashionable Chelsea physician, Sir Hans Sloane. He bequeathed his collection to the nation, subject to a payment of £20,000 (considerably less than it was worth). The nation took up the offer, passed an act of Parliament in 1753, and appointed a body of Trustees to take charge of Sloane's collection and also of the famous Cottonian Library; the Trustees were further empowered to buy much of another famous library, formed by the Harleys, Earls of Oxford. In 1757, George II handed over the Royal Library, which brought with it the privilege of compulsory copyright deposit, which still holds good—meaning that a copy of every book published in Britain has to be deposited by the publisher free with the B.M. An excellent policy, but one that brings now its embarrassments, for the average intake of books (from all sources) per annum demands more than a mile of shelving space. From these beginnings the collections grew and grew, and still they grow; in the early days in Montague House, public admission was, by modern standards, quaint. By ticket only to gentlemen virtuosi, but by 1810 a ticket was available to 'any person of decent appearance who may apply' three days a week. Montague House gradually dissolved into the present building, the façade of which was finished by 1857, though internal development proceeded for many years after. In 1881 the natural history collections (Sloane's special interest) were separated out and transferred to the Natural History Museum in South Kensington (see p. 191), thus gaining valuable space in Bloomsbury for the remainder. But not nearly enough, and now what was once, as Sloane described it, 'a private cabinet of curiosities' and 'a chamber of rarities', is bursting at the seams, even though a more recent annex has been founded at Colindale to take such things as newspapers. The next move is the separation of national museum from national library. The administrative change took place in the early seventies, and the British Museum is now distinct from the British Library. To the ordinary visitor, however, this change will be largely invisible until the building to re-house the Library a mile away to the north is completed. I have therefore left the two institutions as one in this chapter.

The functions of the British Museum are summarised stringently by the official guide . . . 'May be' (caution at once creeps in) 'may be described as the advancement of learning by the provision of materials and facilities for research, and by the encouragement of the study of literature, history, archaeology and art. Public use of the collections is afforded by the Reading Rooms and services in the Library Departments; by Students' Rooms in other Departments; by exhibition of select material in the Public Galleries; by the publication of catalogues, guide books, and reproductions; by photographic services; and by information given in response to personal inquiry.' Much of the collection is indeed off display—not from any avarice on the part of the authorities, but because the nature of the objects is against display. To consult the hidden parts of the iceberg, the visitor has to assume the port and serious demeanour of the Student, and make an appointment (telephone saves time) or acquire a student's ticket; the latter procedure involves time (for the reading Room of the Library and the Department of Prints and Drawings), but may be circumvented by the simple and public spirited act of subscribing to the National Art Collections Fund, upon the presentation of whose membership card you will be admitted both to the Reading Room and the Students' Room of the Prints and Drawings. The minimum subscription is only three guineas a year, and there are many other advantages—notably that of free admission to all national museums and galleries. In fact both Library and Department of Prints and Drawings always have displays: the Library has both a permanent and a changing one, that of the Prints and Drawings changes—a selection from the enormous range that dwells, safe from light and fading, in solander cases. The National Art Collections Fund card will also admit to the Manuscript Department. One further Department keeps almost all its treasure firmly under lock and key (necessarily, owing to the extreme temptation offered by the objects to light fingers)—Coins and Medals; some Greek and Roman ones are shown, and a very elaborate display of British coinage (first floor), but to consult the collection, you must consult the offices of the Department.

Apart from the Departments already mentioned (Printed Books, Manuscripts, Oriental Printed Books and Manuscripts, Prints and Drawings, Coins and Medals) the main divisions are into Egyptian Antiquities, Western Asiatic, Greek and Roman, British and Medieval (a portmanteau title, embracing in its scope such things as clocks and Chelsea porcelain—here as in some other spheres, the holdings of the B.M. overlap with those of the Victoria and Albert Museum); Oriental Antiquities and Ethnography—the latter (now in Burlington Gardens in its own quarters—p. 82) proving to contain the whole range of fascinating—and, to modern art, semantic—objects of so-called primitive art, from Polynesia to the Congo.

'The collections in the British Museum,' says the official guide again, 'cannot be studied in a single visit'—there is no hesitation at all in this statement, and it is dead right; at some point in any visit to the Museum, everyone of any imagination is likely to be swept by a profound chastening and healthy humility, a despond of sheer ignorance. Knowledge it is true remains (how many books in the B.M.'?—no one can tell you: six million? seven million?), but who can know knowledge in a single life time? One can but make forays, snatch-and-grab raids. Even for the habitué there is at present, and no doubt will be for some years to come, almost always some shock of surprise as one goes through the Museum; another room has closed for re-habilitation here, another one reopened there.

Left of the entrance door lies ancient Egypt, Assyria, Greece and Rome. The latter have been brilliantly re-organised with a breathtaking display opened in 1969 (herald, one hopes, of many changes), but here I can but select ruthlessly and sweep clear through to one of the major treasures. Lord Elgin's great haul from Athens lies beyond double glass doors that sometimes on opening promote a loud, satisfactory roaring as if the winged Eumenides were swarming; the **Elgin Marbles**. These are of course the scuptures from the Temple of Athena built on the Acropolis of Athens in 448–432 BC, the Parthenon, and brought to England from 1802 by the antiquarian Lord Elgin, who sold them, with some difficulty and very considerable personal loss, to the nation. Their history is set out lucidly in the corridor-like room to the left. They were honestly bought by Lord Elgin, though not from the Greeks but from the Turks who then occupied Greece. No one now doubts but that this was a piece of rarely disinterested salvage (if they had stayed *in situ* they would almost certainly have been either scattered elsewhere to later buyers, or half-lost by weathering and neglect). Yet they remain a *cause célèbre*, argued over through the generations as is the cleaning of National Gallery pictures, the friends of Greece maintaining stoutly that they belong morally to Greece and should be returned there. There may even be argument on the subject within the Museum: 'fine studies, accessible to British artists', said a Keeper of Prints and Drawings well over a century ago (J. T. Smith), 'but enduring mementoes of a very unworthy cupidity'. The subject of the frieze, which runs round the walls of the main body of the room, is an idealised rendering of the major four-yearly festival of Athens, the Great Panathenaea. This is the procession—a long movement of incomparable grace and skill, the movement itself best seen in the series of horsemen which gathers momentum, from the initial preparations of those taking part, into canter. In contrast, the fragments of sculpture from the two pediments (to the left, as you enter, the contest of Athena and Poseidon, and to right, the birth of Athena in the round) form a colossal monumental drama, the vitality of the carving triumphant over the losses and breakage of time. Also in the transepts are survivors from the series of metopes, panels originally set on the outside of the building under the lintel, representing the battle of the Lapiths, a people of northern Greece, with the legendary centaurs, carved in high relief. The best commentary on the revolution of Greek art and the quality of its achievement is perhaps simply to come direct to the Elgin room from the Egyptian and Assyrian ones, as if into an explosion of life, even—as in the frieze—of gaiety.

But we must glance at other departments, so back to the Entrance Hall (noting for present or future reference that the refreshment room is down the stairs beyond the Mausoleum Room). All that I have space to do is to look briefly at Books, Manuscripts, and then at the King Edward VII Gallery, which serves as joint display for some of the finest smaller objects from other departments.

For Books a look first at the **Reading Room,** directly opposite the main entrance door: visitors are sometimes allowed to look in, and it is a sight for the seeing, in its seemingly inconsequential vastness, its huge welling up of silent space into the dome. The explanation is that it was the central courtyard of old Montague House, and was originally left as open court in the new building intil in 1857 the librarian, Panizzi, had Sydney Smirke roof it in with that admirable dome—140 feet in diameter (second only by two feet to the Pantheon at Rome) and 106 feet high. It has a very odd sort of outdoor-indoor aura of hush, but if you listen you will hear the Reading Room; it absorbs sound marvellously, and whispered conversations seem to loose themselves, undisturbing, like faint smoke up into the dome, but a low chuntering sibilance is about as though minds were ticking over, over four hundred of them at the desks, into which the occasional harder though still remote thud, is the noise of the metal-bound catalogue volumes against the leather tops of their central shelves. Here books in active brains are breeding books as countless books have bred here for the last hundred years, books by no means always by scholars for scholars. Over there, seat No. G7, is where Karl Marx wrote *Das Kapital.*

Books and manuscripts show selections from their treasures in the group of rooms to the right, as you enter the Museum, of the entrance hall, from the Lindisfarne gospels, or Magna Carta, to Nelson's last letter to Emma Hamilton.

The Students' Room of the Manuscripts Department is towards the eastern end of these rooms but entrance is for ticket-holders only; our way goes north into the King's Library (to house the gift of George III's Library, 1823);

showcases here have oriental illuminated manuscripts, examples of fine bindings, and usually a temporary exhibition of some kind, and a permanent display of some of the great books of English literature, including always a copy of Shakespeare's First Folio of 1623 and a first edition of *Paradise Lost*. At the far end of the room is the Museum's enormous collection of postage stamps.

Hence, by a staircase and a bridge, you come to the new, north, flank of the Museum, opened in 1914 (it can also be entered from Montague Place), and into the long Edward VII Gallery. This used to hold a formidable range of the cream from many of the Museum's departments gathered together. The translation though of the Ethnographical material —ranging from Congo masks and the superb naturalistic Benin bronzes to the dense potency of Aztec relics from Mexico—to Burlington Gardens, has simplified the display, and it is now devoted primarily to the infinitely subtle and serene modulations of Chinese ceramics—a truly magnificent representation which—supported by the superb holdings of the Victoria and Albert Museum and the Percival David Foundation—make of London one of the great study centres of the world for those interested in the arts of the Far East. Further on is, often in sharply contoured contrast, the brilliant vernal colour and pattern of Islamic ware especially from Persia and Turkey.

Above is the Department of Prints and Drawings, with a changing exhibition drawn from one of the richest collections of Old Master drawings and prints in the world, and also the changing display of Oriental Paintings and Drawings. A corridor hence leads back to the First Floor of the main building; in the north wing the extraordinarily prolific witness of Egypt, and of Babylon. The western sequence of rooms leads through Persia and the Hittites into case upon case of Greek vases, and thence into the brilliantly displayed Greek and Roman Life Room (another foretaste of revised methods of display to come in the Museum, with even a live fountain tinkling), and then on to some of the most seductive things in the whole museum—the Tanagra figures and other statuettes. The upper floor of the Museum is very much on the move: entirely new displays have been established, like the detailed demonstration, including some reconstructions, of the most spectacular archaeological find in Britain this century—the

Sutton Hoo treasure, burial furniture of an Anglo-Saxon chieftain about A.D. 600. There is Roman gold, Celtic gold; there is the display of the coinage of Britain already mentioned; the Roman glass Portland Vase and the Lycurgus Cup; the astonishing display of instruments for measuring time, most notably the clock. And so to the top of the stairs that go down to the entrance hall, and before you leave the publications counter, where the postcards will show you what you have not seen, and it will seem as though you've missed almost everything.

In the 1960s the whole future of the British Museum became a stormy and unresolved project. The accepted plan (by Martin and Wilson) for its expansion southward was ruthlessly de-accepted, and a superb and resonant broadside by the Chairman of the Museum's Trustees, Lord Radcliffe, justly entitled 'Government by Contempt', was but an early shot in a long fierce campaign. However in 1975, what appears to be indeed a decisive decision was taken by the Government. The new British Library, comprising the old departments of Books and Manuscripts, will be hived out into a new building to be erected (by some time in the early 1980s?) on a site immediately north of St. Pancras Station. The remaining Departments will sort themselves out in the old building (except presumably Ethnology already translated as *The Museum of Man* to its new quarters in Burlington Gardens) as the British Museum. How this will work out (what, for example, will be staged under the great dome of the Reading Room—*what will happen to Karl Marx's seat at G. 7?*) remains to be discovered. Meanwhile, in the short term, an infill is being built on the west flank, and there amongst other things, the British Museum may be going to have yet another shot at producing a tolerable institutional restaurant.

CHAPTER SIXTEEN

St. Marylebone South

❧

WITH the aid of a little hindsight, a quick glance at the simplest of street plans will tell you much about this area: a rough parallelogram, bounded on its south by **Oxford Street**, on the north by **Marylebone Road**, and west and east by **Edgware Road** and **Tottenham Court Road** respectively. Its inherent orientation is north and south rather than east and west, and it is split north and south by three main arteries: Portland Place, Marylebone High Street and Baker Street. The eastern part, the fringe of Tottenham Court Road, is on the map a fairly tight but not irrational complex, that steadies as you move west into the calm broad grid of late eighteenth-century planning about Portland Place; still moving west, this grid dissolves into the higgledy-piggledy of small interwoven streets about Marylebone Lane and High Street, the oldest, sinuous and still pulsating artery of the area, still, in plan anyway, a village. Then, westwards again, the grid reasserts itself from Manchester Square onwards, but on a rather smaller scale than about Portland Place, a domestic order tidy round Baker Street, Portman Square and Montagu and Bryanston Squares.

Start perhaps at the north-eastern point, emerging from Warren Street underground station, and with eyes averted from the bleak traffic combat area of the junction of Euston Road and Tottenham Court Road. Your eyes will indeed inevitably be drawn upwards, to the presence that now reigns over north London here: the enormous but slender tower erected for radio purposes by the General Post Office. It was finished in 1964, and is 580 feet high, easily the tallest object in London, with a circular revolving restaurant set in its crown at 540 feet—highest place to eat in Europe except for the similar one at Stuttgart. Plunge westwards into **Fitzroy Square**; this, though bomb interrupted, still displays on its eastern side the unified elegance given to it in the 1790s by

ST. MARYLEBONE SOUTH

Underground Stations

YARDS

the Adam brothers, in Portland stone; the north and west sides (plaster) are some thirty years later. From the Square the line of interest leads south, by Fitzroy Street that turns after a while into Charlotte Street, and you are in a region hallowed or pickled more often, perhaps, in the memory of English art. Whistler and Sickert both lived in Fitzroy Street; Constable who lived and died at No. 76 Charlotte Street (thence the line of escape northwards to his beloved Hampstead Heath was clear); Flaxman the neoclassic sculptor was in Grafton Way; Landseer was hereabouts, Rossetti, Holman Hunt and Madox Brown. But the presiding spirit, I always feel, is the landscape painter Richard Wilson, caustic, bottle-nosed and melancholic, perennially broke in near-squalor but evolving out of his alcoholic haze those golden, classically-ordered visions of the Campagna and the Welsh and English countryside. Bacchus brooded over **Charlotte Street**; it is still rich in the altars of booze and food. At its southern extremities, where Percy Street joins it, it is in fact clearly an extension of Soho from over the other side of Oxford Street, but with the emphasis still firmly on food and drink and not on strip-tease. Here are many famous restaurants, ranging from the expensive expense-account boutique of high cuisine through popular but reliable and often exciting old establishments like Schmidt's and Bertorelli's to Greek and Cypriot establishments of remarkable cheapness.

This compact area has the classic Soho contrast of high luxury eating places set in near-slum conditions of housing. But it is being tidied up; Percy Street is now smart, with paint and with plumbing; built in the 1760s, it still has some enchanting doorways of the period among the grotto-fronts of the restaurants.

Moving west, get on to **Goodge Street** where it crosses Charlotte Street; you are on the only through axis of the area, leading straight through Wigmore Street and across to Edgware Road, a mile and a quarter west. As far as Portland Place there is little other than depression north of this axis. Goodge Street becomes Mortimer Street, and you can glance southwards down Newman Street and Berners Street towards Oxford Street. These two roads in the early nineteenth century were also artistic settlements but Berners Street saw also more sinister inhabitants and events—the curiously named Fauntleroy, certainly no spiritual relation of Little

Lord, lived at No. 6; banker and forger, he cost the Bank of England £360,000. The entry of Berners Street into English mythology however was assured by Theodore Hook in 1810 when he perpetrated the strange outrage on a Mrs. Tottingham that has passed down as a classic instance of English humour, heaven help us all. Hook invented the hoax in which the fun consists of sending out some hundred orders to tradesmen to call more or less simultaneously with spectacular and unwanted orders on the victim; goods delivered to Mrs. Tottingham included a hearse. At the top of Berners Street is the Middlesex Hospital; the original foundation stone was laid by the Duke of Northumberland in 1755 (the building was reconstructed c. 1930), and there is a huge and magic portrait of him in the Board Room, if you can wangle your way in, the masterpiece miles above form of the obscure painter R. E. Pine.

Farther west, down Mortimer Street, turn left (south) through Wells Street to Margaret Street, where is **All Saints'**, a church which, however allergic to Victorian Gothic you may be, must nevertheless be experienced. Built by Butterfield, 1849–59, it is a formidable and ruthless soul-bashing statement in harsh red brick, with relentless decoration in carving, mosaic, gilt, and glass; you may not like but you cannot ignore it. Emerging, continue westwards (northwards the prospect is still drear); across Titchfield Street, where cluster the wholesale furriers, cross Great Portland Street where cluster the motor-car dealers, wholesale dress shops, the Royal National Institute for the Blind, the Royal National Orthopaedic Hospital, and if you want, a splendid shop devoted to the ritual clothing in black leather of the motor-cycling cult. Cross—for the moment—Upper Regent Street, and come through to Cavendish Square.

It was at **Cavendish Square** that the suburban development of the fields north of Oxford Street began, the building up of the countryside about the rural village of Marylebone. That was in 1717, when the Tory landowner Robert Harley, later 2nd Earl of Oxford, had plans drawn out for the square, balancing the Whig development of Hanover Square over Oxford Street to the south. The square itself has long lost such squarishnesss as it ever had; a welcome circle of green, with noble and indifferent trees shrining the mid-nineteenth-century statue of Lord George Frederick Cavendish Bentinck, his speech rolled but ready in the hand for the Last Trump. Forgotten now, he was a considerable judge of horses and of men, notably of the young Disraeli (a connection explained, according to the disapproving King of Hanover, 'by his former haunts on the turf, and thus his connection with the Hebrews'). Pierced by constant traffic, the square seems now to be more an adjunct of the huge new commercial buildings between it and Oxford Street; its only relatively early buildings of interest are on the north side, of c. 1770, rather heavily and smugly Palladian, two houses once a convent: between them, at top-deck level of a bus, is suspended against the wall the most successful of all Epstein's sculptural improvements offered to an ungrateful metropolis: a madonna and child in dark bronze, a magic fusion in stark but tender intensity.

Cavendish Square was planned originally with all allied amenities, a market that survives only in name (Market Street at the bottom of Great Portland Street), and a church that is still there, though easily overlooked, along Henrietta Place off the south-west corner of the Square. But do not miss it; **St. Peter's Vere Street**; built by Harley's protégé James Gibbs in 1721–24, it holds within a plain exterior what Summerson has called a 'miniature forecast' of Gibbs's St. Martin's-in-the-Fields, a splendour of elaboration that retains in its diminished, almost toy-like, dimensions a charm that tends to evaporate from the larger surfaces of St. Martin's interior. The names dropped all over this area still echo the pride of the noble families who consolidated it and exploited it through the eighteenth century; the manor of Marylebone was bought by Holles, Duke of Newcastle in 1710; his heiress Henrietta Cavendish Holles married Harley Earl of Oxford, and their heiress Margaret married Bentinck Duke of Portland, and their names and titles still persist in the street names: Henrietta, Margaret, Portland, Harley, Holles, Cavendish, Bentinck, Devonshire and Weymouth, and still too the names of their country estates transplanted: Wigmore, Wimpole and Bulstrode.

But I must turn back to the later development of the area, by the Adam brothers and by Nash. To find the essence of this leave Cavendish Square at its north-east corner by Chandos Street (its name the echo of a project by the Duke of Chandos to build a super town house occupying the whole north side of Cavendish Square, which never materialised); here you will find one of the rare perfect survivals of Robert Adam's London domestic work, **Chandos House** of 1771, a truly urban elegance, beautifully proportioned and discreet, with perfect ashlar stonework and ironwork. And so round the Langham Hotel to **Portland Place.** This once must have been one of the magic focuses of London architecture, for here Nash, in the 1820s pushing his triumphal way of Regent Street up from St. James's Park, shifted key in his progress to include as his third movement the serene splendour of Portland Place, built some forty years earlier in the 1770s by the Adams, and leading up to the grand finale of Regent's Park. The long slow sweep of Regent Street from Piccadilly Circus closed, and slewed left to the opening of Portland Place, at **All Souls,** once vigorously assaulted on all sides as an outrage against all stylistic propriety, now one of the most loved churches in London: a circular porch with columns and, above, a circular drum with columns bearing, like a witch's hat, a sharp conical spike of a spire. It is witty and pretty (pale Bath stone, and inside blue and gold, with galleries) and essentially functional, for its job was simultaneously to end the northwards vista of Regent Street and carry, round its pillared porch, the eye leftwards to the continuation into Portland Place, a most deft modulation. But you have to apply some imagination to the naked eye to make the church perform this trick now. It has shrunk comparatively, as have all old London churches; dwindled in context of beetling 1864 trecento in the Langham Hotel; of the B.B.C.; and of twentieth century commercial in Regent Street, where nothing of Nash, except the plan, remains. The **B.B.C.** that famous building of 1931, makes a not ungallant attempt, with its blunt rounded prow, to carry on the modulation of the round church into Portland Place, but sits sadly and lumpily, a pudding-like monument to good intentions; here is modernism, aerial and all, high-minded pure decorative art with symbolism (relief by Eric Gill), and functionalism, but the cake never rose. The huge later extension did not even try, and in certain weathers succeeds in turning the delicate spike of little All Souls into no more than a snuffer on a squat extinguished candle. But though visually the B.B.C. is tiresome, it impregnates the atmosphere of the whole quarter; it is after all a magic hive, troubling the air with disembodied voices and music from the microphones in its windowless and sound-proof studios, even though it has lost much glamour to its over-weening child, giant television far away west in the great circular building at Shepherd's Bush.

North, Portland Place extends to the green promise held out by Regent's Park. The road itself still has the dignity of its unusual width, but the urbane domestic composition of houses on each side has been mauled almost into extinction; on the right going up, between New Cavendish Street and Weymouth Street, a complete unit remains much as it was originally, though heightened. At the top however, it gives on to Park Crescent, which opens its twin-colonnaded arms, carefully restored, to the Park; this is Nash again, prelude to his pageant of stucco in the Park terraces themselves. Not many of the houses in the Portland Place area retain their original domestic purposes, for they demand domestic staff; offices, embassies and institutions have invaded.

Moving westwards now, along the top boundary of our area, the broad booming **Marylebone Road,** in a way almost boulevard-like under its trees, with buildings tending to be set well back from its edge, but overburdened with heavy traffic— it was in fact the first English by-pass, a clear-way into the City from the west, made in 1757. For clarity we might glance at it now as far west as Baker Street. Set back on the south, just beyond the opening of Marylebone High Street, is **St. Mary le Bone** the parish church, now entirely neo-classic of 1813–17, with an excellently grand porch of Corinthian columns—exploited a few years later by Nash to close the composition of his York Gate on the other side of Marylebone Road. It is not a church that seems to arouse much enthusiasm, a little frigid, too large within for its gentility (note No. 4 of the regulations controlling its churchyard: 'No filthy or verminous person shall use any seat in the Grounds'), but I am rather fond of its airy, if chill, gaiety, invincibly theatrical with its two-tiered gallery at the back, very white and gold, with duck-egg walls and royal blue and gold in the ceiling.

A little farther west down Marylebone Road, on the north side, the famous and enduring refuge for parents with children on wet days, **Madame Tussaud's,** where are the famous characters of history, living and dead, living yet not dead, dead yet not living, in the glass-eyed trance of wax and real clothes. The original Madame Tussaud opened it in the

Strand. She—a little body in a bonnet with sharp steel-rimmed spcctacles—was a shuddery character; the essence of her capital when she arrived in London from France were facsimiles of the fresh-chopped heads of the victims of the Terror. The guillotine—is it real?—is real, and so are many of the objects other than the human figures. As for the latter, they are tamed figures, of power brought helpless within your power as you riddle them with mental pins. The latest innovations include sound and fury, even smells. An adjunct to Madame Tussaud's, slewed alongside under an impressive dome, is the London Planetarium, where in comfort and warmth you can watch the mysteries of the sky unfold above you.

To return to the interior of Marylebone, back at Portland Place, you can move thence westwards through the broad, sedate streets that cross **Harley Street** and **Wimpole Street**; a nice promenade on a fine sunny afternoon, with here and there good Georgian or early nineteenth-century houses surviving in dignity with the faintest but agreable hint of a yawn. Harley and Wimpole Streets are the centre of prosperous medical specialism, tall houses with restrained expressions mostly serving several distinguished doctors or surgeons; the diagnosis, one feels nervously, may not be favourable, but it will surely be expressed to you with the maximum of polite discretion. Medicine has pushed most residents out of these streets.

Beyond Wimpole Street the grid begins to fragment on the old plan of Marylebone village that was; that was, about 1700, still lanes and fields and chapel, a mile from any building development in London, and a sylvan refreshment, with pleasure garden, for excursions from London. Pepys walked there in 1668 ('and a pretty place it is'); later it became more organised on the lines of Vauxhall and Ranelagh, flourished and then as tends to happen in the history of such places, declined to a centre of delinquencies of various kinds, and finally closed in 1778, by which time the village itself was all but swamped already by the advancing of the London tide. Little of early Marylebone remains, other than the agreeable meander of Marylebone Lane into the High Street up to Marylebone Road, but it still serves as village or small town centre shopping area for the district, with promising small antique shops and some very passable small restaurants and contemporary coffee-bars. At the top on the left, a little formal garden marks the place where once was the medieval church which the present church in Marylebone Road replaced; a quiet display of aged and rubbed tombstones, and seats where pensioners simmer on warm days. A little to the south-west of this (approach from the High Street via the modest renunciation of Moxon Street 'late Paradise Street', with little village-like shops and small houses all cream and brown) another church garden, usually loud with children among the tombstones, fighting gallantly to retain some garden grace among recreation ground utilities.

South of this, the broad Georgian grid re-establishes itself westwards; the main east–west artery, **Wigmore Street**, has almost nothing old of architectural interest, but is a big metropolitan thoroughfare for shopping, with a big department store, Debenham and Freebody, specialist shops in medical equipment, and a very rewarding clutch of antique shops about its centre. Wigmore Hall is still a classic site for chamber recitals, where musical reputations can be made overnight (or for that matter, unmade). Off Wigmore Street's north-western end lies Manchester Square, compact, still squarish, with the quiet, dark brick setting off its trees, relatively unbreached by traffic, and laid out in the 1770s; in one corner, a good modern building, the E.M.I., demonstrates for once that curtain wall structures can if tactfully handled, marry into an old context, even when as here it breaks the roof line. But the reason why visitors come to Manchester Square lies behind the heavy rather lugubrious façade of the big house that takes up the north side: the **Wallace Collection** in Hertford House (10–5; Sundays 2–5).

This collection is the biggest and most valuable assembly of works of art ever given to the nation by an individual; it was assembled by three generations of the Seymour-Conways (marquesses of Hertford). The third marquess, close friend and adviser on art matters to George IV, was the prototype on whom Thackeray grounded the libertine Marquess of Steyne in *Vanity Fair*; he made a marriage most trenchant in its wisdom, for his wife was the profitable subject of an unusual dispute. Both George Selwyn and the Duke of Queensberry ('*Old Q*'—for long the dissolute presiding genius of Piccadilly) claimed to be her father, and both, in their eagerness, left her vast sums of money, which helped the

Marquess in his picture buying. His speciality was Dutch cabinet pictures. His son, an eccentric francophile, lived mostly in France (helping to found the famous Jockey Club in Paris), and his is the predominant flavour of the collection, the marvellously coherent interechoing assembly of French art-objects of the eighteenth century of all kinds. He had an illegitimate son, Sir Richard Wallace, who bought well and widely, notably medieval and renaissance objects, and he was responsible for the armour. After his death, at his wish, the whole collection passed to the nation. It was opened in 1900; it is a 'frozen' collection, and, not being added to nor being allowed to lend, has a most reassuringly solid quality, but its variety and its wealth within that variety are astounding; for example, even the native French student of French eighteenth-century art and furniture and *objets d'art* must come to London to the Wallace if he is in any way serious in his study. The collection is linked and united both by a coherent thread of taste and by its setting in considerable part as furniture in what is still recognisable as a private house; curiously—as the collection is relatively so recent—it is in the Wallace collection more than anywhere in London that I have times been most aware of the threat of a possible ghost (the lovely parquet floors, perhaps, which creak at you, or the inexorable tick of clocks). The dominant taste greets you as you enter, and for all the glamorously rejuvenated George IV by Lawrence in the hall, the taste is French—even Charles I, the bust on your left, is French, by Roubiliac, while on the landing of the stairs, the balustrade of which, gorgeous, was once in the Bibliothèque Nationale in Paris, is Louis XIV in exuberant person, by Coysevox. And the stairs take you on up to a boudoir-burst of pink and grey painting by Boucher. Everywhere in the Wallace you will find objects that have in common a high gloss, a brilliant virtuosity of craftsmanship, and very often a sensuality which is, for me, too much on the sweet side. That is of course a matter of taste, and I suspect I am in a minority, and here indeed you can see the French masters of rococo— Pater, Fragonard, Boucher—as well represented, perhaps better, than anywhere in the world. May be it brings out the Puritan in me, but I am repelled rather than elevated by the deliberately aphrodisiac suite of Boucher's in Room XIX, painted originally for the Marquise de Pompadour, no less (her portrait by Boucher is also in the Wallace), to—I quote the official guide—'fan the flames of Louis XV's dwindling passion'. In those large expanses of *potelé* flesh I see rather a hint of bath-salts, but then I am no Louis XV, and of the exquisite artistry of the paintings there can be no question, and their theme, colour and tone are echoed and modulated in a fascinating way throughout the furniture and other objects in this room. In the next room are some of the pictures for which I would gladly give all the other eighteenth-century French objects in the collections: the little Watteaus, and most of all the stupendous 'Music Party'. One of those most rare artists who could pin a butterfly alive, or harness a dream into reality on the frail tough reins of his draughtsmanship; look at the interlocking group of girls who listen to the music, but not too hard if you're in a hurry, for you'll be there for twenty minutes or more. And this is not the only Watteau; there are the other minute gems, and the two big ones, real picnics in arcadia, in the Big Gallery. Beside them Pater, who can be so dream-like if you see him alone, fades like a dream; even Fragonard, even that most famous of Fragonards, the pop-eyed girl kicking her shoe with such delicate indelicacy off over the crouching man below (I challenge any normal male not to identify more strongly with this character than almost any other character in paintings), seems not quite crisp enough and yet not quite dreamy enough, beside the Watteaus. But look also in the big gallery at the four Rubens sketches, and you will see works of the same order as Watteau's, but to a larger rhythm and without that almost audible ripple of melancholy music that haunts all the Frenchman's work. In the big gallery indeed, beautifully hung and lit, you will find many paintings of a stature that overrule any possible squeamishness of taste: Rubens, tall glowing Van Dycks, two great Rembrandts, the rich and mysterious group of the 'Centurion Cornelius', and the most tender, very late, portrait of the artist's son, 'Titus', the young luminous face under the red hat, the eyes loaded with still luminous shadow, holding as it were a question to which the only answer his father could give is the son's own image back again, but burdened now with all the father's profound apprehension of mystery. Compare, against the involved passion of this painting, the cool tonal detachment of the three pictures by Velasquez, the sombre figure of the 'Lady with a fan', the brilliant but still cool observation of the childish panache of the boy 'Baltasar Carlos in the Riding School'. Or consider the dusky and troubled radiance, the tossing olive-greens and greys about the pinkish radiance of flesh, in the great Titian of 'Perseus rescuing Andromeda'; the naked Andromeda, if you think for a moment in front of her, will demonstrate, I hope, my point about the Bouchers more clearly than words can hope to do, for in Titian's treatment of the nude there is certainly sensuality, but vital and uncorrupt and charged with amazement. This is one of the seven great mythological scenes, the *poesie*, painted by Titian in his old age for Philip II, and it once belonged to Van Dyck; an early acquisition in the collection of the Seymour-Conways, but later relegated to the attics while the Bouchers flourished. There are the two big Watteaus, a Poussin; there are very famous pictures of more arguable stature: the Hals, the best known painting in the collection, to which it yields a handsome annual income in reproduction fees, the so-called 'Laughing Cavalier', a brilliant but heartless characterisation. Look, not at his hat and clothes which are a miracle of technical laundry in paint, but at his face; he is not laughing at all, and at any moment that sub-R.A.F.-type moustache will twitch, he will touch you for a five-pound note, and then sell you an unreliable second-hand motor car. There are the soppy Reynoldses, most famously, the faded 'Strawberry Girl', still good for coos, but expendable if you but look at Reynolds at his greatest, as here in the shadowy 'Nelly O'Brien', where charm is captured with a magisterial reticence and subtlety. She like the Pompadour was in the profession of commercial love; portraits of such women were as popular with the collectors here as were the portraits of sweet children. 'Perdita' Robinson is in the Wallace three times over, by Romney, Reynolds, and Gainsborough; they are all admirable examples of the masters' art though barely recognisable as of the same woman—the Gainsborough whole-length seems more the promise of a woman to come than a portrait, a coloured mist that will presently lift as the sun rises.

Elsewhere in the collection, away from this central grouping of great pictures, the visual conversation between pictures and furniture resumes and continues; flawless marquetry, joinery and carving over the restful surfaces of Louis XV and Louis XVI, the worn rose of the upholsteries, the deep dark oily sheen of the bronzes, the enamel brilliance, blue and green, of the Sèvres china. The Dutch cabinet pictures are of high quality, especially the Steens, de Hoochs and the Hobbemas; here in the same taste are the now underrated little pictures of that nineteenth-century French master of the broadly minute, Meissonier—the best collection in England; here is the *locus classicus* for the study of Bonington, a various wealth of water-colours and oils, seascapes, costume figure-studies and land-scapes. Majolica plates, Limoges enamels, fifteenth-century illuminations further complicate the overall texture of brilliant colour and virtuosity of craftsmanship, shot through with gold. Into this, the steely array of armour on the ground floor may seem to strike a discordant note, but it too (a collection of great importance to specialists), though armour seems more at home in the true armoury of the Tower, is again, in the arabesques, the damascening of its curious surfaces, in key. Do not miss the equestrian figure in fifteenth-century Gothic armour, a stunning contortion of steel, the menace of its up-flung sword matched by the menace of the remarkable spurs. In the mid-seventies, the Wallace became mildly convulsed with the pangs of installation of air-conditioning, and consequently some re-arrangement of the display invigorated by a brisker programme for cleaning pictures. The atmospheric essence of the collection remains happily unchanged.

Outside, and moving westwards again, you are in the Baker Street area. **Baker Street** itself is a main traffic artery, feeding in at (now one way and murderous) speed the traffic from the north, and a shopping centre, loaded architecturally with some monstrous buildings. Sherlock Holmes, we all know, once lived here, more palpable in his fiction than most of the real inhabitants, but he would barely recognise it now. The grid of small streets up and down its flanks is a delight for peram-bulation with a great number of its original pretty-plain modest houses of the late eighteenth or early nineteenth century surviving in warm and varied textures of brick, generally four small-scale stories with polite sash windows with the reveals cosmeticked to white, that typical and deli-cious London trick; they generally hold on their ground floor a small shop, and the whole area, while retaining a warming and cosy feeling of being constantly lived in and used, holds a wealth of small antique shops and galleries of all varieties. It is also interesting to see how, now successfully, now hor-ribly, modern development since the war has answered the rhythmic challenge of the discreet near-repeating pattern of old. Just behind the Wallace Collection is surely the prettiest hotel in London, Durrant's, a very simple but satisfying—eliciting a cluck of pleasure—example of that counterplay of brick against plaster.

West of Baker Street the squares continue. At the south end **Portman Square**, though broached hopelessly by traffic, still preserves its noble droop of old trees and an umbrageous garden (the regulations at the entrance prohibit entrance of all but the smallest dogs). There are some survivors from the original splendid patrician houses on the north side; much of it was originally built in the 1770s by a firm of Adamses unconnected with the great brothers, but on the north-west corner (No. 20) is a most important house by Robert Adam himself, all the more important because the Courtauld Institute of Fine Art (see p. 223), which now occupies it, will admit visitors of serious curiosity. Built 1774–6 for a Countess of Home (ancestor of the Foreign Minister, and known to her brisk-tongued neighbour, Mrs. Montagu, as 'Queen of Hell'), its interior is a brilliant example of Adam domestic decoration, brilliantly restored and preserved. Into No. 21 alongside, the Royal Institute of British Architects (R.I.B.A.) has translated its library with its superb collection of architectural drawings: here in the small Heinz Gallery, they show two or three exhibitions a year, drawn from their own resources or from loans.

Westwards again, beyond Montagu and Bryanston Squares, the district fades, rather seedily at the north end (where is Cato Street, home of a famous abortive conspiracy to murder the Cabinet *en bloc* while dining with the Duke of Wellington) into the elephantine garishness of Edgware Road. Beyond, west and north, lies Tyburnia.

CHAPTER SEVENTEEN

St. Marylebone North—Regent's Park

❧

LIKE the other royal parks within London, **Regent's Park** is part originally of Henry VIII's belt of hunting forest; it developed relatively late as a public amenity, being let to private magnates in the eighteenth century, and only fully planned out from 1811 onwards, when the last lease fell in, by the Prince Regent. His handyman here again was of course John Nash, to whom the fabulous terraces about the park are a monument as St. Paul's is to Wren. It is not, as is the case with so many of the long drawn-out London enterprises in development, by any means as originally planned, but a compromise gradually reached through shifting circumstances in time. It was not planned as a public park at all, but rather as a park-city, a sort of garden-city on a very grandiose scale. Besides the containing terraces about the whole area, which were built, there was to be a circus at the top of Portland Place, another circus in the middle of the park, two crescents at the north end, and twenty-six free-standing villas about, each in its own grounds. And of course a pleasure pavilion for the Prince Regent which never materialised but lingers wistfully in the imagination. As time went on, the plan was drastically simplified. The central circus was abandoned, and the number of villas planned greatly reduced in number to leave most of the ground free for landscaping and for gardens. Of the circus at the top of Portland Place, only the southern half was built, a wide sweep of colonnades of Ionic columns that take you irresistibly onwards and outwards to the verdant invitation of trees, grass and air through Park Square to the Park proper.

Rus in urbe; of this, Regent's Park is the supreme example. It is of course, not rural, nor is it characteristically urban London, but it is a beautifully balanced man-made amalgam of the ingredients of nature and of architecture. It is also touchingly absurd; its plan even is delightful and absurd in

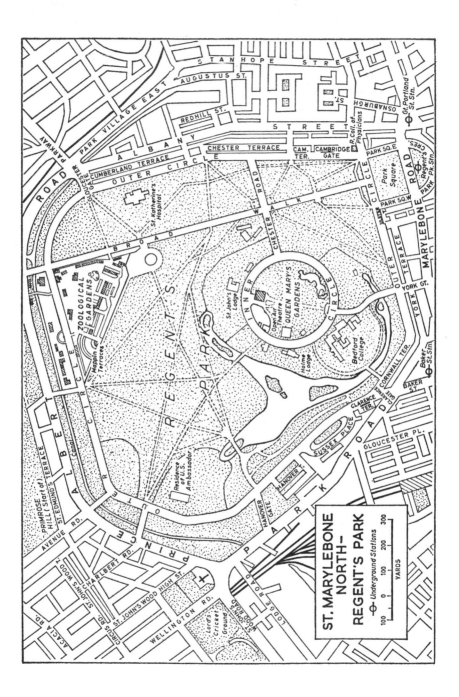

ST. MARYLEBONE
NORTH—
REGENT'S PARK

Underground Stations

100 0 100 200 300
YARDS

its informality: the Inner Circle, geometrically perfect, half-embraced by the faintly octopoid arms of the lake—both contained lop-sided in the arbitrary perimeter of the euphemistically-titled Outer Circle. Nash's terraces that flank the Outer Circle on the east, south and south-west, miraculously preserved from destruction and now restored in a shine of paint, seem palaces.

Proceed through Park Square, with its matched flanking terraces with Ionic columns, its absurd little lodges like Greek Doric dolls-houses; over Marylebone Road, and you are in the Park. The **Broad Walk** opens before you in its aisles of trees, stretching north. But first turn left and west along the edge of the park; the terraces pace with you, each self-contained, each with its own rhythm, flickering through the trees. To walk here, with no aim, is the most relaxing enchantment I know in London, with the terraces glimmering on one side and the tree-fringed waters of the eccentric lake on the other. Here you may still surprise a starched nanny, piloting an enormous pram; more often, in charge of small children bent on self-immolation in the lake, are exotic foreign helps uttering shrill broken cries at their charges like displaced birds. In summer the boats move erratically over the water, and all through the year the birds shoal there, almost as various as in St. James's Park—even more various according to some, who say that goldfinches nest in the park and even claim to have seen kingfishers. The islands certainly teem with birds. The water itself was once that of the Tyburn, that complicated stream that is said to have watered Hyde Park and St. James's as well, but which now, reduced to sewer, flows unsung enclosed in a pipe. It is associated not only with the gloomy gallows site of Tyburn or Tye Bourne proper, but is generally said to be the source of the odd name of St. Marylebone—St. Mary by the bourne.

If you turn inwards, across the footbridge over the water opposite Clarence Gate, past a huge flower bed which is stiff and vibrant with tulips in the spring, you come past the back of Bedford College (a women's college of London University, and a sober modern array of warm brick among Nash's plaster) to the Inner Circle, which contains Queen Mary's Gardens; these are entered through pompous gates in black and gilt iron, and comprise an agreeable, intensively tended sequence of formal gardens, almost miniature in scale within the park as a whole; in the eastern part a lily pool with a Japanesey rock-garden island which is crammed with small conifers and miniature alpines. It has also a miniature mountain, some rather dubious statuary, and the open-air theatre, which has been battling along with the English climate during the summers since the 1930s. But its real splendour comes in June when the batteries of roses for which it is famous, dense in the flower beds, burst upon the astonished London air; then on a warm day you will find old ladies and lovers almost afloat on the fragrance. Round the edge of the Inner Circle there is a miscellany of buildings, some original including the pretty Holme Lodge (annexed to Bedford College); St. John's Lodge which is being rehandled, but has or had a most elegant garden within pleached limes; and offices of the Parks Department of the G.L.C.

Thence back eastwards to the beginning of the Broad Walk, which is the continuation line of Portland Place and, particularly in May when the chestnuts are in bloom, of majestic splendour. Here I attended the most satisfactory wedding lunch of my life; there were four of us, and we ate cold chicken and scored near-misses on pigeons with champagne corks, and then the bride, her lunch hour being over, went back to work. The Broad Walk is perhaps the best promenade of all; as you come clear of the thickets of the Inner Circle that shelter it on the west, the grasslands of the park open up to the north, and on the right the Nash terraces, taller and more elaborate than those to the west, accompany you. First, however, come the exciting new Royal College of Physicians building (1964), and Cambridge Gate (a Victorian intrusion in fussy stone instead of stucco). Then Nash's Cambridge Terrace, severely plain and a bit odd; the long and it must be confessed, rather tedious extent of Chester Terrace, and then the fabulously picturesque **Cumberland Terrace**, with a huge projecting centre block with giant columns and a pediment very busy with tender Empire females, startlingly bleached in their white against Wedgwood blue, in the predominant cream of the stucco; on the skyline too, it bears statuary (very crude seen close to, but most effective from afar). Meanwhile in the Broad Walk you have passed the pompous dolphin fountain, transplanted here for some obscure reason from Hyde Park, and are approaching a cosier monument that is also more functional: a drinking fountain in Victorian Gothic with crocketed gables and odd oriental overtones—*gift*, says a plaque, of *Sir Cowasjee Jahangir* (*Companion of the Star of India*) *a wealthy Parsee Gentleman of Bombay as a token of Gratitude to the People of England for the protection enjoyed by him and his Parsee fellow countrymen under the British rule in India . . . 1869*. It is pleasant to think of Sir Cowasjee. On the north side of the fountain a medallion displays a surly sacred humped bull under a palm tree, which signals surely the Zoo. And there indeed to the left you can see looming up like lava relics of some minor earthquake the curious concrete silhouette of the Mappin Terraces. But meanwhile on your right you have passed a strange Gothic-cum-Tudor intrusion in mellow brick among the pale Nash terraces; built in 1829, it nevertheless also conforms in its plan, which is basically Palladian, to the general classical yearnings of the area, but it reflects a far older institution. Until recently it was St. Katharine's Royal Hospital, the oldest religious foundation, established in 1148 by Matilda, Queen of King Stephen, by the Tower, but moved thence owing to the more pressing needs of commerce, when St. Katharine's Docks were excavated in 1825. Its hospital moved back to the East End in 1950, and the buildings are now a little Denmark in London, its chapel the church of the Danish community in London.

There follows a final range of Nash stucco in the Ionic mode, **Gloucester Gate**, and the procession closes with Gloucester Lodge towards the north-east corner of the park. In all seasons, a walk by the terraces will both elevate and soothe the spirits with incongruous magic, in drifting rain even when they turn ghostly, and damp but undiminished footballers in coloured shirts flicker ritually on the grass between them and the Broad Walk. In spring, when the trees haze with a mist of a vivid green across their pale surfaces, and the park bulbs break against the renewing grass in naked colour, the façades are stage scenery for idyll; in high summer they withdraw a little behind and above the heavy foliage, but I still like them best on a frosty afternoon in winter, placid behind the spidery bare branches like a calm reflection in the still but resonant air; on the west, allied with a sheen of water, wheeling gulls and the brilliant fungoid orange of the weeping willows; to the east, glowing supernaturally in the setting sun.

The **Zoo** was in on the Regent's Park scheme very early, from 1828 onwards; it now occupies some 35 acres, a fantastic maze evolving northwards from the Mappin Terraces under and over the Outer Circle Road and the Regent's Canal (cf. p. 419). It is the crowning folly of the Park, and impregnates, literally, the whole district about the north end of the Park. For both nose and ear, this is the most stimulating district in all London to live in. The heavy odour, as one walks past the gates on a hot August afternoon, may fell the most hardened traveller with an all but unbearable nostalgia for the East (I do not personally, find Zoo odours repulsive but I note that in Baedeker's 1889 edition, the 'unpleasant odour' was then 'judiciously disguised by numerous flowers'). The sounds also within the Zoo are self-evident and in places, as with the cockatoos, lift the top of the head, but to know their true magic you have to live hereabouts. Then, in the hush of a long lie-in on Sunday mornings, your dreams may be most strangely shaped by the ringing rise of whoops from the gibbons and the shuddering roar of lions, mingled with a church-bell or so and the imperious farewells of trains from Euston on the main line to the north. To attempt in any way a guide to the Zoo here would be vain (the guide they sell incidentally is an unusually handsome and helpful specimen of its kind), particularly as it is at the moment of writing in the throes of a re-shaping that will take some years, but the reader should be warned that the Zoo, for a mere initial probe and orientation among its riches, needs at least a whole afternoon.

North of the Zoo is the abrupt heave and lift of **Primrose Hill**; its abruptness gives it unreal eminence (it is only 206 feet high) and from its top there is an astonishing view to the south over London; the view on a clear day right across to the hills of Kent and Surrey used to be controllable by an indicator which pointed out the landmarks. This survived the war, only to be destroyed by vandals in the 1960s.

CHAPTER EIGHTEEN

Thames

✒

LOGICALLY, I should have started with the Thames; the Thames was there before London was, and the Thames is why London is where it is. The Thames is the great divide of southern England, as it is the major entry from the sea. Coming in from the Nore, a wishful exploiter of virgin England would push on through mile upon mile of desolate marshland about the gradually narrowing estuary until he sighted on the north bank a little hill, a swell of ground rising from the river, a defendable proposition with both natural entry and natural defence provided on its south flank by the Thames itself, and on its west flank by the tributary river Fleet. Here also the Fleet and the little Walbrook provided natural harbours, and here the spanning of the river by a bridge was practicable.

Here inevitably the Romans built, and lapped the hill with a wall, and crossed the river with a wooden bridge, only a few yards east of where London Bridge still is, with a bridgehead on the south bank at Southwark. Then they defined London as centre by shafting out the great spokes of the Roman roads across the country from it, and within the limits of the wall they built, for well over a thousand years London waxed and waned and waxed, fed always by the silvery lifeline of the Thames. The Thames is still the lifeline, but the huge, centuries-long, expansion eastward for twenty-three miles, down river from the twin harbours of Fleet and Walbrook, halted after the war. Now indeed the gradual evacuation of the old docks, quays and warehouses, from London Bridge to beyond Greenwich, is almost complete. London is still one of the greatest ports in the world, but its business, following the revolution of shipping methods brought about by container techniques, is now concentrated far to the east. Instead of ocean-going ships, barges, tugs, and the fretty skyline of innumerable cranes—now only empty waters, huge sky, and

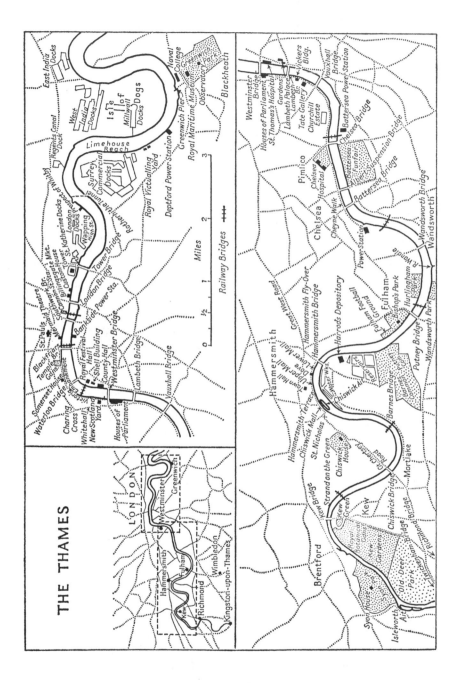

THE THAMES

East India Docks · Regent's Canal · Regent's Canal Dock · West India Docks · Isle of Dogs · Millwall Docks · Naval College · Greenwich Park · Greenwich Pier · Royal Maritime Museum · Observatory · Blackheath · Limehouse Reach · Surrey Commercial Docks · Rotherhithe Tunnel · Royal Victualling Yard · Deptford Power Station · London Docks · St. Katherine Docks or Wapping · Wapping High St. · Tower of London · Custom House · Billingsgate Mkt. · Tower Bridge · London Bridge · Cannon St. Station · Southwark Br. · Southwark St. · Terminal · St. Paul's · Temple · Coin St. · Blackfriars Br. · Bankside Power Sta. · Royal Festival Hall · Shell Building · County Hall · Westminster Bridge · Lambeth Bridge · Vauxhall Bridge · Waterloo Bridge · Somerset House · Victoria Embkt · Charing Cross · Whitehall · New Scotland Yard · Houses of Parliament

Railway Bridges +H+

Miles
0   ½   1   2   3

LONDON · Hammersmith · Westminster · Greenwich · Kew · Richmond · Fulham · Wimbledon · Kingston-upon-Thames

Westminster Bridge · Houses of Parliament · St. Thomas's Hospital · Lambeth Palace · Lambeth Gardens · Tate Gallery · Churchill Estate · Vickers Bldg. · Vauxhall Bridge · Battersea Power Station · Chelsea Bridge · Pimlico · Chelsea · Royal Hospital · Battersea Funfair · Albert Suspension Bridge · Battersea Bridge · Cheyne Walk · Chelsea · Power Station · Wandsworth Bridge · R. Wandle · Wandsworth · Fulham Power Station · Hammersmith Fly-Over · Hammersmith Bridge · Harrods Depository · Fulham Football Ground · Bishops Park · Hurlingham Park · Putney Bridge · Wandsworth Park · Great West Road · Hammersmith · Hammersmith Mall · Upper Mall · Lower Mall · Dove · Town Hall · Wks. · Chiswick Ait · Barnes Bridge · Barnes Common · Green West Road · Chiswick Mall · St. Nicholas · Strand on the Green · Chiswick Eyot · Chiswick House · Chiswick · Grove Park · Kew Bridge · Kew Green · Kew · Mortlake · Brentford · Royal Botanical Gardens · Chiswick Bridge · Old Deer Park · Syon House · Syon Park · Isleworth Ait · Richmond Bridge · Twickenham Bridge · Richmond

riverbank vistas dissolve and reform as you watch.

Londoners, however, still think of the Thames as a working river—not yet for ornament, or for pleasure and recreation—only far west, somewhere around Putney, do Londoners begin to play on the Thames. In the City if you see a Londoner lolling on a bridge, he will not probably be simply idly enjoying Thames-side as Parisians savour the Seine, but watching other people work—one of the great London past-times. If you try to linger over the secrets of nearly two thousand years over the glinting water on London Bridge at half past eight in the morning, you risk being trampled to death by the blind rush of workers on their way to their offices. And no one would dream of fishing in the Thames, though once, for centuries in fact, it was a living larder for London. Harrison in 1586 lists the fish that lived in it—only carp perhaps were a little scant, but 'What should I speake of the fat and sweet salmons, dailie taken in this streame . . .' As for swimming—whether you use the Thames for suicide, or to save a drowning man, you are likely to require the ignominy of the stomach-pump. Anti-pollution measures are working, however, and some foolhardy fish are even venturing back.

But the Thames was, too, perhaps the main highway for Londoners for centuries; from Westminster to the Tower and back again, kings and queens came by water in the painted and gilt state barges: they travelled the Thames alive and dead—the Thames bore Elizabeth I's funeral, as later it bore Nelson's and, in 1965, Churchill's. By Thames-way came the Lord Mayor's procession, a host of ceremonial barges, and on Thames-bank lived a whole race of watermen, the water-taximen celebrated for repartee and insolence. There was music on the river, the voice of Pepys melodious over the waters all littered with broken moon on his way back from the gardens of Vauxhall; or more ceremonially, the splendid surge of Handel's Water Music that so delighted George I that he heard it three times over. Recently this has a little revived, and westwards in a summer dusk you may hear from beyond a bridge the stomp and stutter of pop groups, and then see the lamplit launch come through crowded with jigging figures of the young.

It is still only from Thames that one can see Thames properly. Unfortunately this restricts the visitor to the season between May and September, for in the winter the pleasure boats cease. However, when they are running, they run frequently, at about half-hour intervals; the home pier is by Westminster Bridge, whence you can get a boat going east to Greenwich, or west to Kew, Richmond and Hampton Court. The new hydrofoils are quicker—perhaps too much so. There is only one vital precaution to be taken; the traveller should always take it for granted that the temperature on the water is at least ten degrees below that on firm land, and should dress accordingly; field glasses are also a rewarding accessory.

Let us first go east, to Greenwich—this can happily fill a day, with lunch at the National Maritime Museum or one of the Greenwich pubs; the actual boat trip takes about forty-five minutes.

At once, as one gets on the boat, there is an enormous amount of sky: an oceanic sky, from low on the water far bigger, it seems, than from the bridges. From Westminster Bridge just behind you, on a fair September morning in 1803, Wordsworth recorded what is perhaps the most famous of all London views:

> Earth has not anything to show more fair:
> Dull would he be of soul who could pass by
> A sight so touching in its majesty:
> This City now doth like a garment wear
> The beauty of the morning; silent, bare
> Ships, towers, domes, theatres and temples lie
> Open unto the fields, and to the sky;
> All bright and glittering in the smokeless air . . .

Even then perhaps it depended on how you looked at it; two decades later, on a dark night, Heinrich Heine, no mean poet either, stood on the same spot in despair, dropping hot tears into Thames 'which has already swallowed up such floods of human tears without giving them a thought'. But Heine was perhaps too sentimentally sensitive to take London, and the view is still in almost all weathers grand in scope, immense, though St. Paul's is hidden from you now by courtesy of Shell Oil, and you can see how the new skyline is already composed of squared-off chunks. The component buildings that make up the river front have already been mentioned in chapters on the various areas from which they are accessible

THE THAMES. Parliament and Westminster Bridge across the river at dusk. And looking east across Waterloo Bridge to St Paul's and the changing City skyline

Left, florid Edwardian (1911), a lantern on the gates to Green Park
Right, late Victorian swell, a lamp-post in Northumberland Avenue
Below, a seat, Victoria Embankment, picturesque and uncomfortable as a camel

so I must pass over them swiftly here as does the passage of the boat.

On the first stretch, the view is not unhandsomely contained by Whitehall on your left—redbrick of Scotland Yard, then whitish masonry of Ministries and the wild black pinnacles of Whitehall Court, all rising from the tree-tops; on the right the Scandinavian-looking palace of **County Hall,** chill grey stone starred with chill green, with its romantically steep black roof, yielding to the new slabs, very clean still, of the new Shell buildings and the green turtle roof of the Festival Hall beyond. All this is perhaps properly somewhat pompous; beyond the stumpy legs of the black iron railway bridge to Charing Cross, the river swings right and almost due east under the great white face of the Shell-Mex building with its cold clock; on the South Bank the new buildings of the development mass strongly. Ahead then the slim, pale and stream-lined grace and strength of **Waterloo Bridge,** finished only in 1945, and a worthy successor to what was London's most beautiful bridge. It took some sixteen hundred years for Londoners to get a second bridge across the Thames after the Romans first spanned the river to Southwark; that was Westminster Bridge, finished in 1750 (its present replacement is of 1862). Waterloo came early among others, in 1817, 'a colossal monument worthy of Sesostris and the Caesars', built by the engineer John Rennie. When it came down in the 1930s, its 70,000 tons of granite, craigleth, bramley, blue pennant and york stone were dumped in a field near Harmondsworth, whence they are still gradually being turned into ornamental fireplaces: the noblest stone bridge in the world, it was called.

Through Waterloo Bridge, on your left the last stretch of the Victoria **Embankment,** and along it in pleasurable dignity, the long ripple of the columns of Somerset House, giving way to the green of the Temple Gardens, and St. Paul's visible above. The Embankment was more than a visual tidying up, of course; it made room out of the river itself for the new City–Westminster throughway, and housed stretches of the Underground Railway and, more important, gave space for a rationalisation of London's sewer system. For Thames was also for centuries London's sewer, fed by its tributary streams which were also sewers, and it had for long been famous for its smells before a bumper year, 1858, produced with the aid of a hot summer and low rainfall a stifling stench of such overwhelming strength that action had to be at last seriously contemplated—it was known as the 'Great Stink'. The tremendous engineering operation that gradually got under way afterwards dealt more or less with the sewage problem, but Thames did not at once grow sweet again, for the pollution from industrial and other sources still increased, and only by the 1950s were some able to claim that pollution for the first time was on the wane—but other problems still breed as civilisation marches onwards, and the strontium level (fed from the atomic piles of far-off Harwell) is diligently checked.

And now, even opposite the decorum of this last stretch of composure, Thames side begins to revert to its working clothes. As on the left the **Temple steps** mark the end of Westminster and the beginning of the City, the characteristic texture of working Thames proceeds eastwards, wharf and warehouse. Past the old mouth of the river Fleet on your left, into the dark of three bridges laid heavy across the water at **Blackfriars** in a sturdy chord of architectural dissonance; a touch of painted gaiety on your left is the Mermaid Theatre on **Puddle Dock**, then to the left, where once the brick black warehouses rose cliff-sheer, a new development heaving up between river and St. Paul's; on the right the smoking stacks of Bankside Power Station, and like dolls' houses in contrast, a tiny stretch of late seventeenth and early eighteenth century with bright twentieth-century paint on the doors. And through **Southwark Bridge**—Shakespeare's Globe Theatre was once on the right—the heavy iron shadow of Cannon Street railway bridge, and then **London Bridge**.

No one knows how many wooden bridges preceded the first stone bridge over the Thames, built between 1176 and 1209, but the latter became one of the sights of Europe, with its houses built all across it, its chapel dedicated to St. Thomas of Canterbury and the fortified gates at each end, the spikes of which were ornamented with the decapitated heads of traitors. The houses came down about 1760, and the bridge itself in 1832, being replaced by a fine sober one in dark granite, built by the Rennie family. The old bridge had nineteen narrow arches, and these with their protective piers formed a barrier to the tide, almost a weir, and shooting London Bridge when the tide was running strong was a risky business. London Bridge, netting the ice floes, also enabled the Thames, in an exceptionally hard winter, to freeze over, and when it did London celebrated with frost fairs on the ice, with booths, sideshows and barbecues (even, in the famous frost of 1683–4, the roasting of an ox); the last was in 1814, and Thames has not frozen since the old bridge came down. Now, yet again, London Bridge has come down again; sold for hard cash in 1968 to the U.S.A.—but its replacement already spans the river on the old site.

Below London Bridge the Pool of London begins; on the left, the City shows a river front with some final ceremony: the big platform of **Billingsgate** landing-stage on its dark piles, with the twin gold fish weather vanes glinting high above on the Market; the Custom House behind its trees; then the stone fortress of the Tower bulked behind its grey wall, and the bricked-in mouth of Traitor's Gate, whither so many came by water to their death. On the right, may still be disarray, where once were dark warehouses, cranes, and ships unloading. For recompense, the veteran warship of 1939–45, H.M.S. *Belfast*, is anchored in mid-stream—a museum now, approached by launch from Tower Pier. And there may be, shrouded with tarpaulin, those characteristic Thames craft, the middlemen lighters—long and clumsy-seeming hulks that you may still sight, swinging eight and ten at a time up the river. Beyond the Tower, the end of the first reach of the Pool of London is framed by the triumphant Victorian watergate to London, **Tower Bridge,** built 1886-94; for all that its gaunt Gothic towers ('steel skeletons clothed with stone', as the architect said) overween the Tower itself, the Bridge is a rather warming expression of London pride, and a silhouette familiar to all, almost as the city's trademark. Its very efficiency is popular and impressive, for everyone knows also that the two vast bascules, each of about 1,000 tons in weight, that swing up open to let ships pass in a minute and a half have not failed once in their duty since the bridge was built (the pedestrian way, 112 feet over the water, was however in a way too successful, in its open invitation to suicides, and had to be closed). Through it to the east what is for me the quintessential Thames opens up, the widening waters claim the sky and reject any further constriction by bridges. From now until Greenwich the banks are in strict and intimate service of the river.

It is though now a service of ghosts. You may still see warehouses, rising sheer from the gleam of water, doors open to the empty air, gaping for the feeding cranes that cling like bats to the brick façades, but you will be lucky to catch more than a single ship or two, unloading from opened bellies. Yet in the loose grip of the dark piles of the wharfs, the river is of course still live—sky and water move, the river rising and falling its twenty odd feet each twelve hours in the massive impetus of the tide. There is always movement— if no longer the big ships, still the occasional tug and the nippy police launches, the tourist launches.

On the left the big captive wet dock system has already begun. In these, the water level was controlled by locks and pumps, and a stable platform of quiet water provided whence the big ships can be unloaded free from the tide, but also relatively free from river-thieves. Up to 1800 shipping moored in the open stream was a sitting prey for well-organised professional bandits—the River Pirates, who would cut ships adrift at night, and gut them when they ran aground; other gangs known as the Light Horsemen and the Heavy Horsemen, and the Mudlarks who raided at low tide. Much if not most of their operations were carried out with the connivance of corrupt crews, and about 1800 the annual loss was around £800,000 a year. The new docks were built therefore with security very much in mind, hence their architecture has overtones of fortress if not of prison (the London Docks were built, 1800–5, by Asher Alexander, famous for his prison buildings at Dartmoor). On this route we shall glimpse only three of the five major dock systems; the other two, the Royal Victoria and Albert and King George V, and Tilbury, the major passenger port for London, miles away by Gravesend, are far beyond our reach. Yet it is there, to the far east, that London's future as a port lies, in the newly mechanised container-system docks.

Immediately on the left past Tower Bridge are **St. Katharines Docks,** built by Telford 1825–28, joining on to the **London Dock.** Behind the new (1974) Tower Hotel was once housed wool, wines and spirits; tea, spices, marble; tobacco, rubber, sugar, coffee. The miles of wine vaults under the London Dock warehouses were famous, full of great casks where the wine matured at an even temperature of 60 degrees. The wine oddly did not impregnate the atmosphere with its bouquet, though otherwise a tour through the warehouses was a banquet of odour. But you had to go in to savour it; hereabouts on the river itself the nose tends to be swamped by a coarse blast from the tanneries on the south bank. At the middle entrance to the London Dock, the old dock-town of Wapping suddenly shows through in a glimpse of trees and domestic brick, a reminder that Wapping High Street here runs through between docks and river, with a number of steps cut through down to the river. The most famous of these are Wapping Old Stairs; in a pub there, the notorious hanging judge Jeffreys, who decimated the rebels at the Bloody Assizes after the failure of Monmouth's rebellion in 1685, was trapped in a pub when on the run after William III's revolution in 1688—he died later in the Tower. On the south bank, too, a glimpse soon after of the waterside town of Rotherhithe showing through; a pub, the Angel, with balcony overhanging the water and a little group of ramshackle looking houses, including the former studio of Anthony Armstrong Jones, later the Earl of Snowdon.

On the north bank a warehouse front with the letter E marks the site of **Execution Dock**, where violence came to a swaying halt in the bodies of sailors hung in chains, washed ritually three times by the rising tide. Most famous of its victims was Captain Kidd in 1701. Kidd was officially chartered to scour out pirates on the high seas, but is alleged to have turned pirate himself. Suspicion still is live that his sponsors may have been more interested in the profit he showed rather than the way he got it—his trial anyway was a classic of suppressed witness, but Kidd it was who hung. And then on the left, more cheerfully, the famous tourist haunt of the Prospect of Whitby, indubitably an old smugglers' pub and if over-tidied up now (and with prices correspondingly raised), still a good place to eat, with an admirable sweep of Thames commanded from its romantic balcony. You find it by land at the far eastern end of Wapping High Street.

The river is swinging you slightly north now; an odd sight of tidy municipal park on the right, and under the water here was built the first Thames Tunnel in an engineering epic during which the river broke in five times between 1825 and 1843. Limehouse Reach begins with Chinatown hidden away to the left, and on the right as the river turns widely south, the great timber area of **Surrey Commercial Docks**; desolate they closed in 1970, and the great stacks of teak or bright yellow soft-wood are missing. At the very top of the bend on the north bank is the entry to the Regent's Canal system that you can also meet in the Zoo. And now you sail almost due south down Limehouse Reach, the first stage of a great loop that creates the peninsula known as the **Isle of Dogs,** which is in fact turned into an island by the cuts of the Millwall, the West and East India Dock system across it— bananas, sugar, grain, and hardwood especially. At the bottom of this loop is our destination, Greenwich, but true to London secrecy it is not the pomp of Wren's famous façades that close the longest vista, but the great chimneys of Deptford Power Station on the south bank. Before it come the Royal Navy Victualling Yards in handsome red brick; here from Henry VIII's time were the Royal Docks, where were built many of the ships that beat the Armada, and where Sir Francis Drake was knighted by Elizabeth I on the *Golden Hind.*

As the boat swings round the bend, **Greenwich** comes in sight, with its hill behind, beyond the power station. But there is an, as it were, hesitation in the view, a tracery, at once so delicate and so fraught with memories of the past, that it seems an hallucination: the mast and spars, the web of rigging of the old tea-clipper, the *Cutty Sark.* She is indeed dead, stripped of her sail and preserved in the sanctuary of her dry dock, now an educational centre for the Merchant Navy and a museum you can visit. Hard by her, but minute in contrast, Francis Chichester's *Gipsy Moth IV* in which he sailed solo round the world. Along the riverside beyond her, in dramatic change of key, the splendour and the pomp of a royal salute, whitish stone massed deep behind coupled columns, colonnades and pediments, and lifting twin dark domes to the sky. And royal Greenwich is most easterly of the Thames-side palaces that star the river—Westminster, Kew, Richmond, Hampton Court and beyond to Windsor. At Greenwich was Bella Court, in the early fifteenth century the manor of Humphrey Duke of Gloucester, first royal patron of the humanists and creator of a great library here; Margaret of Anjou named it again, *Placentia,* and it was a favourite palace of Henry VII and of Henry VIII, who here was born, married two out of six wives, and signed the death warrant for a third, Anne Boleyn. The old palace decayed badly during

Cromwell's time, and the present building was created not as a palace (it was too near the river for William III's asthma), but as a naval hospital, the maritime equivalent to Chelsea Hospital, by Mary II; the architect, from 1694 on, was again Wren, though many others, including Hawksmoor, Vanbrugh (the giant orders of the north-west flank are early work of his), Campbell and Ripley later worked on it. The plan is of four great quadrangles set in the angles of a cross; the building is no longer a hospital though very much in use as the Royal Naval College. Its rich chapel and the famous Painted Hall can normally be visited in the afternoon; the latter, used as dining hall by the College and surely the grandest place to eat in London, is very simple, very complex and highly dramatic. The drama is of elevation, controlled up the entrance steps, thence lifting the spirit into the beautifully ordered proportion and space of the hall that closes at the end on a second lift of steps; the complexity comes in the painted decoration that swirls all about walls and ceiling, Sir James Thornhill's masterpiece, demonstrating the triumph of the Protestant succession—it was twenty years in the painting, and features William and Mary, Anne and George I.

The buildings are a fine place to move about among, on a sunny day, in the variety of lights and shades, the expectancy of the great colonnades. As a composition overall, however, the group lacks most curiously its resolution; the main axis of drama is from the river northwards up between the quadrangles, which are deliberately stepped-in, narrowing the view intently for climax between and beyond the two flanking domes. But there, where should be exclamation, is a low white house of the most chaste discretion, and beyond that, tiny on the skyline of the crest of the hill, silhouetted a figure of a cloaked man—the modern statue to General Wolfe, but somewhat irrelevantly related, in cloak and hat, to a well-known sherry advertisement. In fact this river front, splendid in its own proper pomp, is a salute by his successors to the first great English master of classic architecture, Inigo Jones, who, in 1616, designed that white house for James I's Queen, Anne of Denmark, and if the salute tends (as salutes can) to obscure the object of veneration, you can see the house plain in its purity by crossing the road; it is now linked by two long, air-full, open colonnades to east and west to two wings that are much later but support it successfully with sober decorum.

This group forms the **National Maritime Museum,** one of the youngest (1937) of London's major museums but the most superbly sited and housed. The Queen's House, from the front, seems a pure square, with rusticated basement, a double flight of stairs turned elegantly up to the *piano nobile*; tall windows disposed 2:3:2 and a simple balustrade above. Its simplicity was revolutionary at the time in England, where the 'Jacobethan' prodigy houses with their fantastic frontispieces and abundant ostentation were still building busily. In contrast Inigo Jones set up as measure, the 'sollid, proporsionable . . . and unaffected' style of Palladio, and set a standard of quality and discretion to which English architects were to refer back again and again until the mid-nineteenth century. The Queen's House, however, has an odd quirk—it was really two buildings flanking the main Dover road, and joined across it by a bridge: the two additional bridges at each end that make it into the square were added later by Jones's son-in-law, Webb. Inside, the great showpieces are the perfect cube of the hall, with its balcony round the top (though the original painted ceiling by Gentileschi was long ago removed and placed, somewhat cut down, in Marlborough House—see p. 65), and the staircase, a circular well with a most beautiful stair with tulip-scrolled baluster climbing up its void. Here the Museum houses its early portraits—from Drake and Hawkins on—and ship models; it is particularly rich in the work of the Dutch marine-painters, the Van der Veldes. In the wing at the west end of the colonnade are the library and the display of the eighteenth-century maritime history of England including a remarkable representation of the early work of Sir Joshua Reynolds, and Hogarth's vivid 'Lord George Graham in his Cabin'; this culminates in the room of Nelson relics. The Navigation Room has a fascinating glittering show of instruments, and in Neptune's Hall are uniforms, ship-models, figureheads and some of the sumptuous state-barges that once enhanced Thames pageantry. The Museum is open 10–6, Sundays 2.30–6; and in the summer months the restaurant will provide lunch or tea (licensed).

The way back to London can be by boat, by train (Maze Hill Station to Charing Cross), or by bus from close by the landing pier, to Waterloo. But Greenwich would reward a little further lingering: a very pretty little town, in the decorum of the early nineteenth century and with a church, St. Alfege, by Hawksmoor and John James, of formidable almost Baalbekian assurance. Up the slopes behind the Museum, the Park climbs to the former Royal Observatory (founded by Charles II in 1685, and now an extension of the Museum, though Greenwich still sets British Standard Time), and north of that is the wide and windy expanse of Blackheath, a classic rallying point for those like Jack Cade about to assault London, and now fringed with some very agreeable domestic architecture.

The boats going west, up river, from Westminster Pier, go much farther than those going down river; it is in fact $3\frac{1}{2}$ hours to Hampton Court if you go all the way. The last boat that goes through to Hampton Court usually leaves about noon, but if you want to spend time there, it is best to catch a considerably earlier one. By way of compensation, the westwards boats are bigger, and their bars are licensed to sell alcohol.

The boat slides through the flattened arches of **Westminster Bridge** (see p. 256), and along the river flank of the Houses of Parliament, where on a fine summer afternoon you may sight, on the river terrace, M.P.s giving tea and wisdom to little flocks of their constituents. For the first stretch, the banks are quiet, without roads; Parliament gives way to the trees of Victoria Tower Gardens and to the south, the arcaded blocks of St. Thomas's Hospital (gradually giving way to a new building) are followed by the irregular grey of Lambeth Palace. The present Lambeth Bridge is newish (finished in 1932); beyond it on both sides the Victorian embankments take over. On the south bank from the big brick lump of Lambeth Bridge House (headquarters of the Department of the Environment), a stretch of post war commercial building of somewhat aggressive expression does not suggest that once here were the first of several Thames-side pleasure resorts: Vauxhall Gardens, popular from Charles II's time till George III's. Pepys went there a lot in the Garden's first popularity—'to hear the nightingale and the birds, and here fiddles and there a harp, and here a Jew's trump, and here laughing and there fine people walking is mighty divertising'; it boomed again in the eighteenth century, with masquerades, fireworks, concerts, and as a general rendezvous. On the opposite bank, from former marshland sprouts the immense

tower of the new Vickers building, followed by the bulbous
Tate that has become squat in the tower's shadow.

Beyond **Vauxhall Bridge** (in its present shape of 1906), there
follows the fringe of Pimlico dominated by the wintry concrete of the new Churchill Estate of blocks of flats, confronting
across the river the glinting acres of roofs of Nine Elms
Market, whither Covent Garden has migrated, and Battersea
Power Station, with its spiky black front of crane and gantry
devouring black coal at the rate of thousands of tons, feeding
it back from the barges into its gigantic brick console and
breathing softly forth from its four great chimneys the
whitest of white-washed smoke. Under the iron railway
bridge that supplies Victoria, to **Chelsea Bridge** (of 1937);
gardens on the right that were Vauxhall's eighteenth-century
rival, Ranelagh: then set back, the decorum of Wren's
south bank, the boskage of Battersea Park, where in the fifties
and sixties a modern equivalent of the pleasure gardens of
Vauxhall or Ranelagh flowered briefly, went seedy and
expired in 1975

Under the delicate web of **Albert Suspension Bridge** and
through under heavy **Battersea Bridge,** and the elegance of
Cheyne Walk on the north bank is cluttered by the Chelsea
house-boat colony, and fades again into power station, and
on both banks, Thames goes back to industry, with Fulham
beyond on the north and Wandsworth on the south. Beyond
Wandsworth Bridge, the tributary, sweetly named but utterly
abused by industry, of Wandle comes in sadly and almost
unnoticed. On the right a touch of green is Hurlingham Club,
with a fairly grand columned front of about 1760; once the
centre of the game of polo, but now a private 'country' club.
Another touch of green on the south bank is Wandsworth
Park; a railway bridge, and you are coming round in sight of
Putney Bridge, massive between its two church towers, one on
each bank. Here with a cluster of moored pleasure craft,
launches and sailing boats, the sporting Thames begins, and
here the annual boat-race between Oxford and Cambridge
starts. On a Saturday about Easter every year (since 1856, and
sporadically before that from 1829), the two eights set out in
conditions normally of ferocious chill, and row flat out for
four miles and 374 yards west to Mortlake. The banks all the
way are lined with people, and behind the two boats a

cavalcade of launches and steamers proceeds with enthusiasm creating a minor tidal wave. The popular appeal of the event continues apparently unabated, and is worldwide.

At Putney also, one generally sights for the first time white swans in number, those splendid ornaments of Thames. They are protected (though not alas against contamination by oil) and private; they belong either to the Queen or to the City Companies of the Vintners and of the Dyers, and the latter on a morning in late July set off in boats on an exercise still more mystic than the boat-race, known as 'swan-upping'; the swans are rounded up, the Vintners claim theirs by nicking the birds' bills twice, the Dyers once. From Putney if you wish, you can also start to walk; inland, Putney Hill leads up (past the house of Swinburne, whom my mother still remembers as a familiar figure walking frailly about the Common saluting babies in prams) to Putney Heath and thence to Wimbledon Common and acres and acres of common land. But you can also from here, by a largely riverside walk, get some seven miles away to Kew, starting along the north bank from Putney and crossing over to the south at Hammersmith; it is one of the best walks in all London, long-famous.

Beyond Putney Bridge, on the right, Bishop's Park, so called because behind was until recently the palace of the Bishop of London; then the stands of Fulham Football ground with the arc-lights rising tall at each corner like totems, and then as far as Hammersmith Bridge an industrial sequence of some splendour. On the left, however, after the fussy front of the Star and Garter Hotel, the boathouses with their sloping ramps down to the river, the towpath runs between water and water, Thames and big reservoirs (which if you come in by air from the east, stooping through cloud towards London Airport ten miles away, may give you a startling and erroneous impression that London is a city of lagoons). A flamboyant château-like brick building is actually Harrods Depository, famous as a landmark on the boat-race course, and glorious from the west in a winter sunset when its windows catch fire. **Hammersmith Bridge** itself (a suspension bridge, by Bazalgette, the engineer, who was responsible for so much of the central embankments of the Thames, 1887) has a poor press from purists; big, with a touch of Louis XIV and gilt in its turrets, but it assumes charm on longer acquaintance; threats of demolition fail constantly to materialise. A little inland from it on the north is one of the most handsome pieces of British architectural engineering completed since the war, the Hammersmith fly-over which carries the Great West Road over Hammersmith Broadway.

From Hammersmith Bridge, reservoirs continue on the left, but they are disused and on to the site Dean Colet's great educational foundation, St. Paul's School, moved in 1968 from the red-brick building on Hammersmith Road into which it moved in 1884 from its original site of 1509 by St. Paul's Churchyard. The north bank is well worth walking, following the river as it sweeps round in a big loop southwards (here, incidentally, you can well appreciate the extraordinary scope of Thames tide, brimming the banks at high water, shrinking to almost a trickle in a waste of gleaming mud at the ebb). Lower Mall has a handful of handsome eighteenth-century houses with balconies behind trees (limes that stink very sweet in July, and a catalpa), among boathouses and pubs with tables out over the footway (the Blue Anchor though recently remodelled still has that rarity, a pewter bar); then a view of Hammersmith Town Hall, faintly Scandinavian but sturdy in deep red brick, over a garden from which it is separated by the racing traffic of the Great West Road; immediately beyond, a famous pub, the Dove, with a riverside terrace. In Upper Mall more good houses and a splendid magnolia; and William Morris's Kelmscott House. Hammersmith Terrace beyond is favourite territory for artists and there lived and died the doyen of the Thames, Sir Alan Herbert.

Hammersmith Terrace leads through into **Chiswick Mall,** a longish stretch with some most delectable houses, especially perhaps Strawberry House, very delicate, and Walpole House, grand and bland behind its fine railings (and behind, an iris garden that on rare occasions its owners open to the public); but the virtue of the Mall is in its ensemble, its irregular façade knit into the riverside by balconies, wisteria, gardens, and more little gardens between river and road; intimacy of water and land is emphasised at the western end, opposite Chiswick Ait, a forlorn islet where swans congregate and a notice says forthrightly DANGER—RIVER, where the high tide fairly regularly invades the unembanked road, withdrawing in a litter of driftwood. The Mall closes westwards with the church of **St. Nicholas**; this is rich in monuments; do not miss one of the not so famous ones, the enormously little mausoleum to the painter de Loutherbourg (d. 1812), for its long inscription is the happiest expression of civilly elegiac sentiment that I know. The church is, however, especially famous for the urn-topped tomb to William Hogarth, buried here in 1764, reconciled with two great antagonists of the preceding generation with whom he engaged in crisp battle as a young man—the Earl of Burlington and his henchman, William Kent, both buried in the church itself. If you are on foot, you will find evidence of all three still well above ground by swinging inland up Church Street, which is village lane of story-book picturesqueness but lands you slap into a furious roundabout of the Great West Road; follow the signposts to London Airport, and a few yards up on the left is Hogarth's House (open in winter 11–4, Sundays 2–4; in summer 11–6, Sundays 2–6), a late seventeenth-century house quiveringly preserved on the traffic's brink in the shadow of a big new boot-polish factory; here are relics and a good selection of engravings.

Hogarth was the most militantly—even chauvinistically—patriotic of artists and resented fiercely the dependence of so many English patrons on foreigners. Lord Burlington and Kent, arbiters of taste in the early eighteenth century, depended on the Italian classic principles of Palladio and employed many foreigners—the argument has now become academic, and need not deter anyone from delight in the achievement of the English Palladians which you will find manifest in Chiswick House (the north gates to this are a little beyond Hogarth's House). This with its park affords the most elegantly sophisticated public amenity of London. The house itself (1725–29), built to Lord Burlington's plans and detailed within by Kent, is in fact a miniature Palladian villa, square with domed lantern, porticoed with columns, though with marked accents that are English and eighteenth century (Rysbrack's statues by the steps of the architectural household gods, Palladio and Inigo Jones, are far more vivacious than either of their originals would have allowed). The effect is of a toy party house for grown-ups, and the interior, bomb-damaged, has been brilliantly restored, and the original portraits include a painting by Dobson of Inigo Jones (a gateway by him, removed from Chelsea, is in the grounds) and one by Kent of the brilliant poet of the Burlingtonian cause, Alexander Pope. The gardens are no less important and still more seductive, for this, with its carefully controlled asymmetry of water and trees, undulating ground set with statuary, was the first of the great eighteenth-century gardens to be modelled more or less on the principles of claudian landscape painting. On foot to regain the river from Chiswick House, leave by the great iron gates to the south and follow Alexandra and Chertsey Roads and so over Chiswick Bridge to the south bank.

Reverting to the boat, from Chiswick the river swings south in another big loop, under **Barnes** Railway bridge and then sports fields to your right and the river front of Barnes village on your left, and so round and almost north again to **Chiswick Bridge** (where the boat race crews flop in exhaustion at the end of their course).

From here on I must, in my allotted space, condense mercilessly, for we are already miles from central London, though the main sights on the way to Hampton Court are some of the most attractive recreations that London offers to her citizens. **Kew** is the first of them. It is preluded by a pretty strip on the north bank of riverside village, Strand-on-the-Green, mostly smallish houses and nearly all fenced insecurely against a flooding river by little concrete stiles of steps, with lots of boats about (Chelsea must have been rather like this before the Embankment). The steamer pier at Kew is on the south bank just before the bridge, and before you come to the gardens you pass Kew Green; in the churchyard are buried Gainsborough, and also Zoffany, the German born painter of late eighteenth century conversation pieces, whose house over at Strand-on-the-Green still bears his name.

Kew Gardens are rewarding at all times of the year (they are easiest reached by land by the District Line to Kew Gardens Station), not least in winter when you can be certain of tropical warmth in the great glass-houses; but spring and early summer are the period of their great splendour, when the bulbs and the flowering trees, acres of them, refresh the senses of Londoners jaded by the grey rigours of a city winter. It is a very big stretch of green (some 280 acres), but more than a pleasure park: in fact a branch of a government department, rather unexpectedly, the Ministry of Agriculture. Its official name is the Royal Botanical Gardens, and as such it goes back to George III's mother Augusta, who started a botanical garden there in 1759; since 1841 it has been, as it were, the state's institute for botanical research. On the north bank is Brentford, depressed in the aura of its gigantic gasworks (a rather splendid water tower in brick though, excellent specimen of Italianate Victorian waterworks campanile), followed by an opening of broad green in the midst of which a rather dourly four-square house, with corner turrets and battlements, is **Syon House** (by land, easiest by train from Waterloo to Syon Lane). Once a monastery, then from soon after the Reformation the home of the Percies, Dukes of Northumberland, it was entirely rehandled by Robert Adam from 1766 on; its interior is one of the most grandly elegant in England, particularly the Grand Hall in black and white marble, stucco and statues, and the very under-named 'Ante-room', most grandiose in that cool sumptuousness of Adam's style. Syon House opens to the public between May and September but on a rather eccentric roster of days; it is advisable to check before visiting, but on a hot day its grounds, with a view of boats sailing, magically through watermeadows, are splendid. When at Syon, do not miss Syon Lodge, a fantastic showground of garden sculpture, acres of it, the premises of the dealers, Crowthers.

Twickenham and **Richmond** Bridges, and on your left the sharp rise of Richmond Hill; thence for two and a half miles the expanse of Richmond Park almost as far as Wimbledon Common, famous for its deer and its ponds, and now, on its far eastern edge at Roehampton, for the most successful of post-war housing estates, tall point blocks lifting between the trees. **Richmond Park** is royal, and Richmond itself still has the gateway to the vanished Richmond Palace built by Henry VII, where in 1603, Elizabeth I died on a great pile of cushions, fading slowly like a spent fire, Gloriana, till she lay grey. The view of the Thames Valley from the hill is famous, and provoked many artists, Turner of course but also Reynolds to a rare excursion into landscape, and Richmond is full of good houses. Twickenham is on your right now, with Marble Hill, a Palladian house built for George II's mistress, the Countess of Suffolk about 1725, and later occupied by another royal connection, the secret wife of George IV, Mrs. Fitzherbert; it has a small park, and is now open to the public; the building has been restored. Then Strawberry Hill (1749–

76), Horace Walpole's 'little plaything house' that popularised and gave its name to that particular style of fancy neo-Gothic. On the south bank, the house and grounds of **Ham House**; the house itself, which is open (a branch of the Victoria and Albert Museum), is probably the best preserved example in England of grand Restoration interior decor, carried out when it belonged to Charles II's formidable if unattractive (see his bloated portrait here by Lely) minister, the Duke of Lauderdale; if the style seems lavish rather than elegant (especially after Syon House), it is lavish in no mean way. The easiest approach from London is probably by District Line to Richmond Station, and thence on a Kingston bound bus as far as the Fox and Duck at Petersham. On the river itself, a halt at Teddington Lock, end of the tidal reaches of the Thames, and generally saluted by a hopeful if apparently unrewarded band of anglers by the weir. The next stop is Kingston, royal again, the Kings' Stone (now outside the Guildhall) being the Saxon Coronation Stone where seven kings are said to have been crowned. It has an agreeable river front, a busy shopping centre with an excellent and enormous department store, Bentall's.

Finally, the last loop of the river brings you round along the watermeadows of **Hampton Court**. The Palace was built from 1515 for Thomas Wolsey, Cardinal and statesman, on a scale of splendour that Henry VIII finally found unendurable for an alleged subject. Wolsey, already in his decline, thought it tactful to give it to Henry, who accepted it but did not stay Wolsey's fall. It was then (1529) grander than anything Henry owned, as the satirist Skelton had noted ('Hampton Court hath the preemynence'), but he set about adding to its rich red brick and making it grander yet, and lived in it a great deal—there are many associations with most of his wives in Hampton Court, including the reputed ghosts of two of them: Jane Seymour, who died there in giving birth to Edward VI, and Catherine Howard. Elizabeth knew it; for Charles I it served both as home and prison. William and Mary again started work on it, and from 1689, Wren was busy there adding the handsome manner of the Fountain Court and the south and east fronts on to the brick. Mortally involved with Louis XIV in political and military combat though William was, Hampton Court and its gardens under him acknowledged the influence of the Sun King's civilisation—there is more than a hint of Versailles in the additions. The Georges did not use or expand Hampton Court very much, and in 1839 Queen Victoria opened the state rooms to the public, and they have been open mostly ever since (from 9.30—Sundays 11–6, May to September; closing at 5, March, April and October—Sundays 2–5; closing at 4, November to February, Sundays 2–4; the simplest approach by land is by Green Line Bus, 716 or 716A, from Hyde Park Corner). The early brick work, mellow red with blue-black diapering, is a delight both to eye and to touch, and the richness of detail throughout can be barely indicated in a mere paragraph. The range of interest is great too, from the Tudor kitchens of enormous size whence one could feed an army to the astronomical clock over the Anne Boleyn gateway, made by Nicholas Oursian in 1540; from the Tudor brick which for all its symmetry is still typical late Perpendicular Gothic (though ornamented with roundel heads of emperors, by da Maiano, 1521, which are truly Renaissance) to the urbane stateliness of Wren's pale façades to the claustrophobic intricacies of the Maze (said to have been planted in William III's time). The gardens are of a particular luxuriant formality, lawns, aged yews, walks and lily ponds, and tremendous herbaceous borders.

As for the pictures—when the Duke of Würtemburg visited in 1592, Hampton Court was already 'embellished with masterly paintings'; some of those he saw are probably still there, but added to them are royal portraits of the next two centuries, and paintings acquired by Charles I from the Mantuan collection (including the Giorgione 'Shepherd with a Pipe', a terrific Titian of 'Lucretia', Tintoretto in all his swirling abundance in the 'Nine Muses', and so many more, a remarkable series of paintings by Domenico Feti among them). From Charles II's time, Lely's famous 'Beauties', fashion plates of lazy voluptuous flesh, succeeded by the much severer, more remote tall anatomies of the ladies of the more prudent court of William and Mary, by Kneller. From George III's time there comes a brilliant representation of the colourful painterly talents of the Venetians, the Riccis, while some of the very early pictures are due to the pioneering taste of the Prince Consort though the little Duccio 'Crucifixion', so small yet in its monumental stillness one of the grandest paintings in England, has been lent to the National Gallery. These and so many more, set out in a sequence of state rooms ranging from small panelled closets to sumptuous state apartments painted by Verrio or Thornhill or Kent, constitute one of the major English art galleries, and beyond, in the Orangery, is one of the great masterpieces of European art, Mantegna's cartoons for the 'Triumph of Caesar', battered and faded but recently most subtly restored, of indomitable majesty and authority.

CHAPTER NINETEEN

Covent Garden

✿

THIS chapter is in the main for the stage and for vegetable memories—for Covent Garden. It can, at this moment, be written only in those terms, although already in 1974 its vegetable and flower market had moved out. What will happen to Covent Garden is being precipitated from hundreds of planning battles, but whatever it is it had better be good, for Covent Garden, as market, is a quality of London that cannot but be sorely missed. If you start at St. Martin's Lane, the first emphasis is on stage, but there is a curious prelude. St. Martin's Lane is the old direct route north from the hub of Charing Cross, and was built up by 1613. Its southern end was however chopped about first by the creation of Trafalgar Square and then in 1887 by the wide surgery that opened up Charing Cross Road, which both took over St. Martin's Lane's function as a main road and to some extent preserved it, like a subsidiary canal. On the island in the wide irregular space north-east of Trafalgar Square which the junction of these two roads created, between St. Martin's-in-the-Fields and the front of the National Portrait Gallery, one might start this perambulation with a salute to the spirit of the latter-day English martyr, **Edith Cavell**, the Red Cross nurse who at dawn on 12 October 1915, was shot by a German firing squad in Brussels. In heroism she is not alone, but in her dying she welded herself into the living conscience of English history with four words: *Patriotism is not enough.* Into the fabric of London itself she is also welded in a monument of some incongruousness (by Sir George Frampton, 1920)—it has been claimed as the ugliest in the city. She, in pale stone, in the severe fall of her nursing cape, is impressive, but she is set against a lumpish cross of grey granite, that challenges the form-seeking eye, and defeats it. If you look down through an iron grille in the pavement by her, you may find a caption of surreal matter-of-factness printed black on white on a sort of brick vault below—it says: NURSE CAVELL—

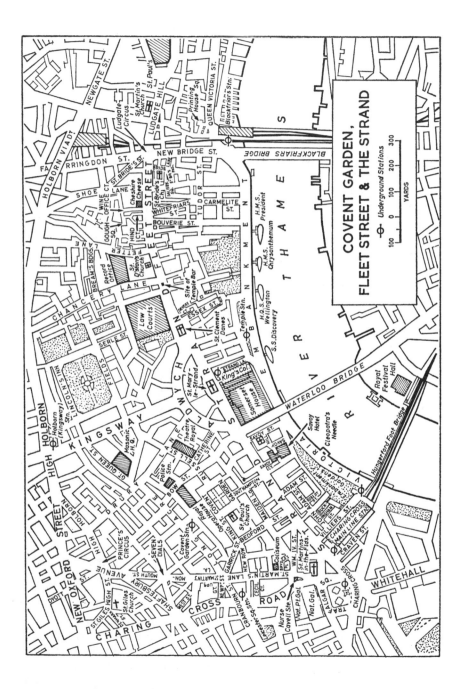

COVENT GARDEN,
FLEET STREET & THE STRAND

NO SMOKEING (*sic*), but a suspicion that just under the surface of London there hums a busy if non-smoking breed of illiterate troglodyte gremlins can be dispelled by reflection—this is simply part of the drainage system built into Charing Cross Road when it was first made. Yet sanitation is not enough either. Over the road east of the statue is the new main West End Post Office, not entirely happily adjoined to the school that flanks the churchyard of St. Martin's and that has a façade of elegant Regency dignity; but inside, the Post Office is a huge improvement to London's amenities with the longest post office counter in Europe and open all through the twenty-four hours (even if it is still possible to queue there just as long as at the old one).

St. Martin's Lane itself is fairly narrow, its west side mainly recent (a backside of Charing Cross Road) but on its right, east, side, despite the brash galumphery of the Coliseum, there is still in the middle stretch eighteenth and early nineteenth century brick of domestic scale (No. 31 is even late seventeenth century) over the shop fronts, and there tends to be a nice coming-and-going around St. Martin's Lane. The Coliseum is the first thing that hits you, all columns and terra-cotta stucco and a big globe heaved high in the sky (the globe was made to revolve, but owing to legal niceties is only allowed to give the illusion, with the aid of lights, of revolving). It was built in 1902, and big, to beat Drury Lane, with a three-part revolving stage, three tea-rooms, a roof-garden, even a pillar-box in the hall; it was for variety and spectacle, for shows like the *White Horse Inn*, and even for Diaghileff (whose ballet ran three seasons here)—but London's biggest theatre after seeming briefly to sell out to Cinerama, is now (one hopes permanently) opera. Other theatres cling still to real live actors and a waft of grease-paint over the footlights—the Duke of York's, the New Theatre (and through in Charing Cross Road, the Garrick and Wyndham's)—with a supporting cast of eating places ranging from a Lyons to classy Italian (Laguna, on the right at No. 50), English traditional (Gow's, No. 37); French (Beoty on the left beyond the New Theatre; Chez Solange in Cranbourn Street), and the famous fish of Sheekey's in St. Martin's Court. But the gem of St. Martin's Lane is a pub, the Salisbury, generally fairly loaded with theatrical and literary types or people who look as though they *ought* to be theatrical and literary types (there is a kind of cool assessing stare I associate with the Salisbury);

the Salisbury is a national monument—and is, I hope, officially listed as such—of the late Victorian pub, all glass and glister, with quilted alcove seats scooped into the walls, svelte bronze nymphs flowering into electric light bulbs, Guinness on draught and a good cold counter.

The Lane is further fed by its tributary alleys and courts, from Brydges Place just by the Coliseum, unremarkable in all except its sheer blank narrowness, to Cecil Court on the left, a pedestrian precinct for book browsers and bric-à-brac addicts. On the right of the Lane, Goodwin's Court, an alley containing a little row of late eighteenth- or early nineteenth-century shop fronts with potted bay trees; then a plaque marks the site of Chippendale's workshops, active here between 1753 and 1813, setting a coolly elegant standard of furniture that was to become, perhaps a little misleadingly, the symbol of a whole civilisation. New Row, also on the right, is the local shopping street, in shabby brick and with a roadway one car wide, with ironmonger, butcher, etc., but also the Jazz Centre and a shop where they sell carnival masks and a super coffee-shop; it expands into the glossy windows of Moss Bros. at its far end, proverbial for hired formal clothes, whether tails or morning coats, hunting pinks or court breeches.

From a little way up St. Martin's, modern London obtrudes, the distinguished slab of **Thorn House** (1960, by Spence & Partners of Coventry Cathedral)—one of the best newish structures, chastely grey, chaste in its proportions and in the proportion of its subdued detailing to the whole, with a rather gallant—and vast—abstract bronze by Geoffrey Clarke crashed on its eastern cliff as though a prehistoric cicada wrecked in a gale. From the south, Thorn House is agreeably offset by the sturdy fuss of a late Victorian pub, the Cranbourn with busy boozy pinnacles. Now renamed the Frigate, it is where Garrick Street and Long Acre come in from the east, and Cranbourn Street and Great Newport Street from the west. **Garrick Street** has, fifty yards along its right, the Garrick Club (all in honour of David Garrick of course, whom we shall meet in a few pages), a palazzo type building of the 1860s wearing its dirt with high pride; it is especially for those with theatrical interests, has a famous and very numerous collection of theatrical paintings (particularly strong in the work of Zoffany and Samuel de Wilde) and is well worth getting invited to—it has a famous long table, where diners sit informally in what can be a remarkable democracy. Long Acre is a much older street (Dryden lived there for a time; so did Oliver Cromwell), but became mainly the premises of Covent Garden wholesalers. In Great Newport Street, to the left of St. Martin's Lane at this junction, a blue plaque on a smart, black-tiled front records the presence on this site of Sir Joshua Reynolds between 1753 and 1761, when he was establishing his commanding reputation and before he moved into Leicester Square (the site is now the Arts Theatre Club, the productions of which, avant-garde and often of bludgeoning free speech, would not have pleased Sir Joshua's notions of decorum).

To the left here (West Street) are two more theatres, the St. Martin's and the Ambassadors; there is also a famous theatrical restaurant, the Ivy. But St. Martin's Lane itself is continued undeviating but more narrowly northward, only now called **Monmouth Street**, once proverbial for its old clothes shops.

Monmouth Street is interrupted by **Seven Dials**, a conjunction of seven streets, and originally an early and grandiose piece of town planning (Evelyn went to see it in 1694—'7 streets make a star from a Doric pillar'). Almost a century later, word got around that treasure trove was in the base of the pillar with the seven dials; it came down, and though nothing was found, was not put up again until in 1820 it was re-erected at Weybridge in Surrey. Meanwhile the area had decayed greatly, and it is as part of the notorious rookeries, the raddled slums of the St. Giles area, that it is characteristically reflected in Dickens, in *Sketches by Boz* of 1834. Earlier, Hogarth had in fact used it as setting for his Gin Lane. It was then at least a focus, but when Charing Cross Road and Shaftesbury Avenue, cleared through the slums thirty years after Dickens wrote, created a new circus at Cambridge Circus a few yards away, Seven Dials became even more literally exhausted, and so it is still, for all its new shiny garage and the prow of the Cambridge Theatre, though as sort of living relict there is a minute street market of four or five stalls between it and Cambridge Circus.

Monmouth Street continues, sliding then into the northeast extremities of Shaftesbury Avenue which ends here in a vast roundabout (here the old fantastically inconvenient public convenience is replaced by a traffic-girt patio of flowering tubs—such is progress). This end of Shaftesbury Avenue (for the west end, see p. 52) looks even more like a failed French boulevard, with its gallant but thin trees and even a real French Hospital. But fifty yards west from this roundabout, up St. Giles High Street (impossible to imagine the village of St. Giles-in-the-Fields of which this street was once the high) is still the church of **St. Giles**—as if marooned in the big new buildings of the triangle between Shaftesbury Avenue, Charing Cross Road and New Oxford Street, but still sending up a brave signal in its sturdily handsome spire. It was once a lazar-house, founded by Henry I's Queen, Matilda, but the present building is of 1731–3, by Flitcroft, a very Palladian protégé of Lord Burlington, but though signed (a most unusual feature) very prominently by Flitcroft with his name over the doorway, it will seem very familiar if you know James Gibbs's churches, particularly St. Martin's-in-the-Fields. Its churchyard is now rather a good garden, particularly perhaps at the week-end when near empty and you can sit among rose-beds, children's swings and shadowy trees, and admire the York stone paving and the tomb chests that stand about, their lapidary inscriptions yielding slowly to obliterating weather and anonymity (all one can make out on one is . . . THE LIFE OF . . .). But one tomb, restored opposite the church's west end, astonishes the eye with its salute:

HOLD, PASSENGER, HERE'S SHROUDED IN THIS HERSE
UNPARALLELD PENDRELL THRO' THE UNIVERSE
LIKE WHEN THE EASTERN STAR FROM HEAV'N GAVE LIGHT
TO THREE LOST KINGS . . . .

Richard Penderell (d. 1671) acted as guide to Charles II in the famous flight after the disaster of the Battle of Worcester. The interior of the church has a rather staid dignity of French grey and blue, red columns and brown woodwork, but some very satisfactory detailing—see how exactly and justly the galleries marry into the columns. There are a great many memorials and in the church a rare congregation of poets' ashes. The memorial most will seek out, in the south aisle, an inscription in blurred gold on black, is to Andrew Marvell (1678). Man and poet of impregnable integrity, with a direct and brilliant power of words that the centuries have in no way diminished:

The grave's a fine and private place
But none, I think, do there embrace . . .

It used to be the custom for condemned criminals on their way to Tyburn to be given a cup of ale at St. Giles.

Outside the church again, round the shrubby churchyard to the north-east, is a very grandiose lych gate in classical masonry of 1804, now without function but including in it a wooden relief of 1687 of the Day of Judgment. The linking road with Charing Cross Road is of singular nondescriptness to look at, but its equally nondescript staircases multi-branched with offices may be to sudden fame and wealth if you are under twenty, have a loud voice, rhythm, and a gimmick; this is **Denmark Street**, better known as Tin Pan Alley, home of the London pop music business. But our way lies east, involving circumnavigation of Prince's Circus which is not charming, though off it on Dyott Street (on the corner of New Oxford Street) is what I regard as the true home of the London umbrella, a handsomely old-fashioned shop, Smith's; Prince's Circus also has its theatre, which has recently changed its name to the Shaftesbury in an attempt to shake off a persistent run of bad luck, and also, inset in a brand-new office block, the only public swimming pool in central London, the Oasis. Here High Holborn begins, where was a village or hamlet as early as Domesday; first right off it is **Drury Lane**. One may advance into Drury Lane with high hopes and lively old echoes in the heart—perhaps of that odd Roman tombstone with a Greek inscription that was found there: *Good Dexios, son of Diotimos, farewell*—or perhaps of Pepys on his way to Westminster on the first of May, 1667: 'in the way meeting many milkmaids with their garlands upon their pails, dancing with a fiddler before them; and saw pretty Nelly standing at her lodgings door in Drury Lane in her smock-sleeves and bodice, looking upon one; she seemed a mighty pretty creature . . .' Pretty Nelly was of course Nell Gwynn, one time orange girl of Covent Garden, actress, mistress of Charles II and mother of Dukes. The north end of Drury Lane is quite lane-ish, with a little antique shop or so, some coffee-bars, pubs, but the roads which lead off it and are labelled with the names of former local celebrities—Dryden, Betterton, Macklin—are all nineteenth century. A big crossing comes, with Long Acre from the west, and Great

Queen Street from the east; the latter was built up in the early seventeenth century and called 'the first regular street in London', but only one or two late eighteenth-century houses survive in the gigantic presence of Freemasonry, the head-quarters of which dominate the southern side.

Farther down Drury Lane, turn right into Russell Street along the great flank of Drury Lane Theatre with its range of midnight blue cast-iron columns. The big entrance to the theatre opens on to Catherine Street on your left but go on a few yards to the junction of Russell Street and Bow Street; Russell Street ends to the west in the glass and green-painted iron conservatory-like prospect of Covent Garden, while up **Bow Street** to your right you can see the portico, with its giant Corinthian columns and pediment, of the Royal Opera House; opposite that is Bow Street Police Station. It is an excellent vantage point whence you can scan memories of much of the history of English theatre, literature, literary life, and of the 'order' in London law-and-order.

The 'Russell' of Russell Street comes from the Russells, Dukes of Bedford, who owned the land of the present Covent Garden area north of their town house on the Strand, and who from 1630 began to develop it in the first planned urbanisation in London. Thirty years later, by the time of Charles II's Restoration in 1660, the development was fairly complete, and into it came the theatre, revived by Charles II after ex-communication by the Puritans, and with the theatre the literary acolytes and actors who tended the muse. About the theatres flocked its devotees, not only Nell Gwynn. Wycherley lodged in Bow Street, and there, too, briefly in 1742, young David Garrick, Macklin and Peg Woffington maintained a theatrical threesome (Woffington was a good London girl who liked her cup of tea strong—she was rebuked by Garrick for extravagance in brewing it 'as red as blood'). There were many others, and those who did not seem to be resident often virtually were, in one or other of the famous coffee-houses. The best known was Will's, on the opposite corner of this junction of Bow Street and Russell Street, where for near forty years John Dryden held sway as the arbiter of literary England. Pepys saw him there in 1664 'with all the wits in town'; a little before Dryden died in 1700, the precocious half-crippled boy of eleven, Alexander Pope, also glimpsed his hero at

Will's. But the most celebrated moment in the history of Russell Street came in the 16 May 1763, when at a bookseller, Davies's, Boswell was introduced to Dr. Johnson.

Of all this nothing remains, but Bow Street Magistrates' Court may perhaps be taken as monument to the greatest of Bow Street's former actual inhabitants—Henry Fielding. It was in Bow Street that *Tom Jones* was written (published 1749), and he was, too, of course the author of a great many plays. It is not so often remembered that he was one of the great reforming magistrates of London; it was he and his brother, the blind Sir John (one of the first to tackle the problem of juvenile delinquency), who were the first magistrates at the newly opened court in 1748 and who made the Bow Street Runners, forerunners of the Metropolitan Police, famous.

A closer look at the two great theatres before we go on to the Garden. The Theatre Royal, Drury Lane, in its present shape is a great, handsome but sparely classical box of 1810–12 (by Benjamin Wyatt—the porch and the long colonnade down Russell Street are a little later), and foyers and staircases inside are of matching ample dignity. It is the fourth on the site; the first, where Nell Gwynn played, was burned in 1672; the second was by Wren, and saw Betterton, Colley Cibber, Garrick, Sheridan, Kemble and Mrs. Siddons, and an attempt on the life of George II in 1716. It was rebuilt (the third theatre) in 1794 under Sheridan's management, and in 1800 a madman took a potshot at George III from the stalls; this building burned in 1804, in a famous blaze that gave its owner, Sheridan, occasion for various stoic jests that have passed into legend—'Surely a gentleman may warm his hands at his own fireside'.

The rival concern in Bow Street, the **Royal Opera House,** Covent Garden, is sited with agreeable incongruity, towering over the Floral Market of Covent Garden alongside (both by the same architect, E. M. Barry). The first building began in 1731 when John Rich leased the site from the Duke of Bedford (whose family still cannily retains the site). In 1808 it burned down; it was rebuilt, and again burned down in 1856; the new building, that stands now much as it was, was planned especially for Italian opera, and its history since is more or less the history of the opera in England, and it is now firmly backed by state subsidy as the national home of opera and ballet.

Russell Street ends to the west in Covent Garden proper, the square or piazza where for centuries was London's main vegetable, fruit and flower market. Then, Covent Garden's day used to begin about midnight, as the lorries began to come in; crates, sacks and nets unloaded under the harsh lights until about five or six in the morning the market was in full swing, with the Covent Garden porters, a hardy and specialised breed, heaving produce around as wholesalers disposed of it almost by the ton. Then the air was dense yet lively and clean-tanging with the blended odours of mixed vegetables and fruit, the cobbles were ankle deep in straw and husks, and the Floral Hall was ablaze with massed flowers and exotic fruit. Market business was mostly over by around nine in the morning, when through its leavings, its organic fragrances, came treading delicately the sober-suited office workers. In November 1974, the market ceased to be, translated south of the river to its new tailor-made up-to-date premises at Nine Elms, while its old home was ceded for the time being to that insidious invader of most great cities in the twentieth century—planning Blight. The Floral Hall has been annexed by the Opera House, and awaits only adaptation into the enlarged opera planned and lacking only money. The former Central Market Building (1828) standing in the middle of the piazza is saved from demolition, restored, and seems to be going to be a shopping arcade. Part of the Flower Market is to become (subject again to money) the National Theatre Museum, moved thence from its allotted home in Somerset House before it had even got there. When you read this, Covent Garden may, or may not, be, a rejuvenated area, humming with new activities, and its market, its fragrances, its former din and bustle, only echoes in the memories of those who knew it before 1974, although its business through the centuries has set a probably fairly enduring stamp on the physique of the neighbourhood.

Only in the north-western corner do you find traces of the place's first splendour as an open piazza; there, the flanking houses echo the original arcades of Inigo Jones's conception of the 1630s, though not themselves original. The design originally was a rectangle open on the south side and probably with glimpses down through trees and the great Strand-side houses of the noblemen to the Thames (as you can still catch a magic gleam of the river beyond the Strand down Southampton

Street); the north side was enclosed by terrace houses with a sort of arcaded loggia, and on the west Inigo Jones built **St. Paul's, Covent Garden.** The story of the church's conception is famous; the developer, the Duke of Bedford, was not anxious to spend a great deal on it, and suggested to Inigo Jones that something not too far off a barn would not come amiss, whereupon Jones promised him the grandest barn in Europe—and gave it to him, and at considerable expense. And so (though its fabric is renewed) it still stands with a formidable, plain and solid majesty foursquare under its great massive eaves—barn-like it is, but a divine barn.

Already by the end of the seventeenth century Covent Garden was the most important London market for fruit and vegetables. So it came to dominate not only the market area but all the streets around, growing ever bigger, drawing in more and more traffic to itself, and so, gradually, choking itself to death.

To visit St. Paul's interior go west either by King Street (No. 27, the Westminster Fire Office of 1856, is a splendidly ornately handsome front) or by Henrietta Street. The big gates into the churchyard are in Bedford Street, and the interior of the church almost disconcertingly plainly bleakly grand. There is a formidable roll of the famous buried here, artists like Grinling Gibbons and that opulent painter of the Restoration, Sir Peter Lely. Wycherley is here, carried from across Covent Garden, and on the south wall a silver casket holds the ashes of Ellen Terry. Here, too, J. M. W. Turner was baptised in 1775. Turner was born in **Maiden Lane**, a narrow passage just to the south off Bedford Street, at his father's barber's shop, now long since gone. Maiden Lane, however, still has, if by now you are seeking refreshment, the old-fashioned theatrical restaurant Rules, and just round the far corner, in Southampton Street, the very rich, grotto-like, deep deep red of Boulestin's, where the food can be as good as anywhere in Europe.

CHAPTER TWENTY

Fleet Street and the Strand

✴

THE main route from the City to Westminster has always been via Fleet Street and the Strand,[1] for nearly a thousand years perhaps. In 1315 complaints were made about the condition of the road, but the Strand end was not paved until 1532.

Within its medieval walls the City of London grew overtight, and one of the places it bulged and spilled outwards was at Ludgate, which closed its westward extremity above the channel of the river Fleet—the Fleet started at Hampstead and met the Thames at Blackfriars. From Ludgate westward these extruded parts of London crept down to and over the stream and up the other bank as far west as where was Temple Bar; here the jurisdiction of the City ended and that of Westminster began, and here, too, Fleet Street ends nominally though it is continued undeviating by the Strand. The area between the old Fleet channel (now occupied by Farringdon Street) and Temple Bar is very densely built; through it Fleet Street itself runs clear, but the narrow roads and concealed courts and alleys that congregate about it seem still to reflect a medieval pattern. The Fleet itself is said to exist still below surface in a tube of some kind; in its early and middle days it was handy as a common sewer; a little later it was broadened into a canal, and the barges went up from the Thames as far as Holborn. From 1765 on it has been more or less covered, and now no longer discharges into the Thames. It had in its time a bridge, a market and a very famous prison (abolished 1846; the railway viaduct runs over part of its site), which was also by some kink of constitution a place where you could get married without a licence, and 'Fleet marriages' were notorious. West of the Fleet and nearer the Thames was another place of correction, Bridewell, which you can see in action in the fourth plate of Hogarth's *Harlot's*

1. See map on page 276.

Progress; its site is marked by an elegant façade in New Bridge Street: its offices, built about 1805. But the two major products for which Fleet Street was and is famous are lawyers and the printed word. To the law, which with some precision divides the area in a broad but semi-private strip running north and south, we must devote a separate chapter (the Inns of Court, see Chapter 21), but to the printed word we can come at once.

Fleet Street is synonymous with the London Press and we should start, naturally, with inspection of the senior member, *The Times*. This great and glorious organ was founded in 1785. Its conservatism was lightened after its acquisition by Lord Thomson: though its fresh presentation pained its more elderly clients, it improved its circulation. For a century or so, it resided in Printing House Square, then in 1962-3, the paper shed its old skin in favour of a new glossy one. This you can still see if you start this walk at Blackfriars Bridge, and look thence at the bottom of Queen Victoria Street through the opening of the railway bridge. But though this still suits the Sunday *Observer*, *The Times* found it handy for a bare decade, and then moved far up Gray's Inn Road into a building of indifferent distinction. For all this, *The Times* remains definitely quite definitely a National Organ if not the National Organ; the daily paper, as it has chosen to style itself since the war (by actually advertising, a first shock for some older readers)—the Paper for Top People. Also known as The Thunderer, it has a weighty voice in its leaders; its role as critic of national government and morality if self-assumed, has now achieved sanction by custom and by history: what it says is, whatever its critics may say, noted. The Editor of *The Times* is also beyond doubt a top person in the same category of authority as the Governor of the Bank of England used to be, as the Archbishop of Canterbury. His paper prints, besides the news from its formidable far-flung army of correspondents, births, marriages and deaths of those who matter, a famous agony column, Court arrangements, a very useful programme of events of each day, besides much else. Its paper also is of toppish quality, and not the best for lighting fires with, but its crossword should be conquerable by the time you have reached your office in the morning. Its correspondence columns are a resonant sounding-board of national opinion, but *The Times* herself is nominally above party.

But I have lingered overlong, so move inland now up New Bridge Street, once the channel of the Fleet; to your right its banks rise quite sharply to climax triumphant (over the railway viaduct) as the dome and pinnacles of St. Paul's ride the air, accented by the dark needle steeple of St. Martin Ludgate in front of them. At Ludgate Circus (the rich Victorian symmetry of which was broken by bombs), Fleet Street starts its westward course, but better to engage in its tributary warrens before you reach the Circus. Third left off New Bridge Street (passing before you get there the old offices at No. 14 of Bridewell Hospital, with an early nineteenth-century stone façade of the most quiet authority) into Bride Lane which swings up (up from the valley of the old Fleet), very narrow; it climbs round to the right to join Fleet Street, with the east end of St. Bride's Church rising from a plateau above it, but rather turn left up a cranky flight of steps, into St. Bride's Passage which debouches into Salisbury Square.

This, though Fleet Street is only a few yards away, has the characteristic air of withdrawn seclusion of the little courts off Fleet Street. It is enclosed, tightly, by a hodge-podge of modern building, but one house (No. 1) indicates in its sedate brick an older, early eighteenth century, scale and decorum. Not as early as the square's name which records that once here was the town house of the Earls of Salisbury, but as early as Samuel Richardson, that stout little comfortable printer (his works were here as well as his house), father of the English sentimental novel.

He was buried in **St. Bride's**, and my favourite approach to this is through a tunnel in the buildings on the east side of the Square (to the right of the off-Fleet Street façade of the great news agency of Reuters); at the end of the tunnel is only a narrow falling of light, for it frames at its far opening the porch, excellently solid and comfortable with its pediment and with its inhabitants' name in lapidary: DOMUS DEI. The porch is only six feet from the next building, and above it goes up, praise be, praise is, that wonderful many-tiered spire, one of the happiest of Wren's many happy spires, and his highest (226 feet; built 1701–3). This is still from many points of view a London landmark, its five octagonal stages lifting their 'madrigal in stone' high over Fleet Street; it demands bells, the spire, and now again it has them, though a carillon muted in deference to modern ears that, bruised by constant traffic,

LEGAL LONDON. *Above*, the lawns and planes of Lincoln's Inn, with the Stone Buildings (1770's); *below left*, Kings' Bench Walk in the Inner Temple; *right*, the Law Courts in the Strand

can no longer bear the virile clamour of triumphant bells. Only you cannot see the spire properly from the precinct of the church, for this is so narrow that it projects the spire like a hollyhock that escapes from a pressure of undergrowth. In the tight little churchyard, among the stones laid against the wall of the church you will find one for Richardson, Samuel and others. The church that Pepys was baptised in (his family lived in Salisbury Square), was burned out in the Great Fire of 1666; rebuilt by Wren (with a regular plan for once allowed him by the site, a five-bay box) by 1678, gutted again by fire in the bomb-hailing night of 29th December, 1940, and then by 1957 restored again, largely at the cost of its great neighbouring newspapers as the true and proper 'Cathedral of Fleet Street'; inside among the new-smelling blonde oak, the black and white pavement, the new white and gold of the lofty barrel vault, great newspapers and great journalists are remembered on the labels of the pews (including one for Edgar Wallace); but the shape is as shaped and window-pierced by Wren, deeply and cunningly sculpted at the top with its bull's-eye windows groined in (avert your eyes from the feigned apse), and do not on any account miss the porch under the tower, which is pure Wren though prophesying and outdoing Hawksmoor in its massive purity of arch and dome. Do not miss either the crypt, in which post-war excavations revealed the foundations of earlier churches, and even a Roman pavement of mosaic and a heap of spent oyster shells and Richardson's coffin. And also, a national scoop worthy of Fleet Street, 'the skeletal find of the century', a chronological anthology of skeletons of the seventeenth and eighteenth centuries, now classified as a 'national archive' and gratefully welcomed as 'an important addition to the armamentarium of crime control methods'.

Outside again, there are the small, almost bleached plane trees (almost French, as if under them you could play *boule*) and the lighting may still (just) be by gas, but fifteen yards or so to the north is Fleet Street.

Emerging on this via St. Bride's Avenue, you are immediately confronted from the other side of Fleet Street by two of its leviathans, Lord Beaverbrook's palazzo in black glass and chromium of 1932, very period, home of the *Daily Express*; its foyer with black gold and silver would beggar most of us and certainly description, *gefrorene Wurlitzer*. It succeeds in making its neighbour, the *Daily Telegraph*, in likewise 1930 period but Greek with a strong dash of Egyptian, look gravely pompous and as if concealing a hiccough. This is the 'street of ink' (but look down it eastwards, to St. Paul's on Ludgate Hill beyond, afloat in the air), and on it and about it are the giants of the British Press; south down Bouverie Street to the offices of the *News of the World*, without a close study of which the national habit of scandal can never properly be grasped: the *Daily Mail*, *Evening News*; north of it, up Shoe Lane, the *Evening Standard* shooting out its bright vans; gone farther north, remote from Fleet Street in Gray's Inn Road, are the main Thomson Empire, *Times* and *Sunday Times*, and also the *Guardian*, but the megaton fount of words is in the *Daily Mirror* building, an enormous new multi-cellular structure banded with red at the top of Fetter Lane on Holborn. The organs controlled from this building are said to command (dailies) over 21 million and (journals, especially women's weeklies) over 43 million readers; thence are controlled also two national 'Sundays', the *Mirror* and the *People*. But it is not only the national press that inhabits Fleet Street and its environs; there, too, are the important London offices of the provincials, from the *Birmingham Post* to the *Irish Independent* and the *Methodist Recorder*. The area is naturally rich in pubs, still here generally called taverns, City-style, and in cafés, some open very (for London) late, catering for the thirst of journalists. It is a busy street, and busier still in a frenetic way at night (most of the big papers arrange tours for visitors, by arrangement; you need to allow time in advance for this as they tend to be heavily booked, but it is well worth while). In architecture it is bitty, its façades belaboured with signs, and in dress it tends to the shoddy—the travel-stained mac of the Fleet Street journalist is no fiction. But Fleet Street is also a potent magic—towards midnight, say, with a not very distant press thumping like a liner, to be sitting yawning in a café over tea reading tomorrow's paper.

But for the day-time seer needing a sight, the excitements of Fleet Street are mostly the extraordinary little courts that hive off it. These, famous though some of them are, agreeably permit discovery, for the entries to most of them are small and narrow, a mere opening through a building. Immediately west of the *Daily Telegraph* in Wine Office Court is the famous hostelry, the Cheshire Cheese—according to legend Boswell, Johnson and company dined here, and if firm record of this is hard to come by, propinquity at least is in its favour as we shall shortly see; it is also a justly popular eating-place for tourists, rebuilt in 1667, very picturesque, though prices have jumped since Johnson's day. Still going west up Fleet Street, the next court to the right is Hind Court; here engage. Dark walls high above you; a minute coffee-house tucked in a corner; a bomb site, and high on a wall, authoritatively, ANCIENT LIGHTS. A swing left and you are in Gough Square (actually L-shaped) and following on to the end of that (its roofline kept fairly consistently to a four-storey level in brick), there is **Dr. Johnson's house** in dark brick almost leaning in the far corner (open generally on weekdays from about 10.30 to 4.30; admission charged). This is a late seventeenth-century house, not grand, and here the Great Cham lived between 1748 and 1759. Johnson, who came to London only at the age of 28, a gawky and lumbering provincial from Lichfield, is surely the immortal patron spirit not only of literary London but of more than that—*No, Sir, when a man is tired of London, he is tired of life; for there is in London all that life can afford.* Granted by the chance due to genius his Boswell, he lives on undiminished, the pattern of the man-of-letters engaged in human society, and a professional the weight of whom Fleet Street has yet to see again. 'There is nothing which has yet been contrived by man, by which so much happiness is produced as by a good tavern or inn,' and wherever he was civilisation flowered like the green bay tree, himself the tree tended by a most remarkable congregation of genius—Burke and Goldsmith, Sir Joshua Reynolds, Charles James Fox, David Garrick (his former pupil from Lichfield) and Boswell; the Burneys, the Thrales. Prints of all these now hang around the rooms of his house. Downstairs it is darkish, the panelling painted dark floor to ceiling, but upstairs lighter; the rooms seem smallish for his great bulk (though on the first floor the panelled partitions can fold back to make one room of the whole story). The stairs, rather coarse and clumsy in detailing, are utterly convincing; one can feel him climbing them with somewhat groping deliberation on his way up to the big attic floor, which is where the Dictionary was written, and everywhere you can see his painted shadow in the copies of Reynolds' portraits of him.

Coming out of the house, turn right into Johnson's Court, not called after him though he lived here too, between 1765 and 1776; more brick, and by day the metallic champing of printing presses—a rather haunted desert, this Court, with staircases descending into the ground from the pavement and a thin brass strip set in the footway apparently at a venture with a strange device—'Portion of land this [but which?] side of brass strip is private property.' This brings you back to Fleet Street.

On west down Fleet Street, and we are entering the precincts of the law, though to begin with these are well concealed behind the fronts of Fleet Street—you could easily miss, on the south side, the timbered front and then the sober façade in stone through both of which entry can be gained to the Temple. Otherwise there are notably pubs: the Wellington; that cool and odorous retreat El Vino; the famous Cock Tavern; to your right Fetter Lane goes north, looking promising with a glimpse of trees at its first bend at the east end of the Public Record Office, but beyond is a barren newness and the vertical catacomb of the *Daily Mirror* building. You are nearing the end of the City now, and the last church is **St. Dunstan's in the West**—the great fire of 1666 stopped a few doors east of this and the church, unlike St. Bride's, was not burned. It was, however, entirely rebuilt about 1833 in the Gothic; in the old church, the poet John Donne was vicar from 1624 till his death in 1631, and Izaak Walton was vestryman from 1629–44; Walton besides writing *The Compleat Angler* (published in St. Dunstan's Churchyard, 1653), wrote Donne's life and must have heard those sermons that are now one of the intricate glories of the English language: 'a Preacher in earnest, weeping sometime for his Auditory, sometime with them; always preaching to himself, like an Angel from a cloud, but in none . . .' The exterior has a plaque for Walton; from the earlier church there survive also the statue of Queen Elizabeth of 1586 (perhaps a bit beautified in the eighteenth century) that once stood on Lud Gate, and a very famous grotesque oddity described already by Strype about 1720 (fifty years after it was made): 'two savages or Hercules, with clubs erect, which quarterly strike on two bells hanging there'. The clubs still strike, as you can see if you manage to coincide with the quarter, but there was a hiatus in their continuity, for when the church was rebuilt, they were

sold (and Charles Lamb wept—he was another famous local
and Londoner, living in the Temple, where we shall see him
later); the clock went to Lord Hertford's villa in Regent's
Park and only came back to St. Dunstan's in 1935.

Some yards farther east from St. Dunstan's is the opening
of Chancery Lane (to be considered also in context of the
Law, see p. 308) and shortly beyond that a strange memorial
in the middle of the road, crowned by an exotic dragon or
griffin in bronze, marks the spot where was the **Temple Bar**
till 1878, when it, a handsome gateway in Portland stone,
ascribed to Wren and bearing statues of James I and Anne
of Denmark, of Charles I and II, migrated to Waltham Cross;
it was too meagre for the traffic. 'Temple Bar'—to cite Strype
again—'is the place where the freedom of the City of London
and the Liberty of the City of Westminster doth part; which
separation was anciently only Posts, Rails and a Chain . . .'
(the actual westward gate of London on this route was of
course Ludgate); here on formal occasions, when the monarch
wishes to enter London from Westminster, there will be fan-
fares and parleys and a handing over of the sword of London
by the Lord Mayor to the monarch and a gracious handing
back of the sword by the Monarch to the Lord Mayor—a
little ceremony that underlines the independent traditions of
the City *vis-à-vis* the Crown. The present memorial was
hideously expensive (over £10,000 in 1882), but is scarcely
noticed by Londoners; the statues of the Queen and the
Prince of Wales (Edward VII) are rather ominous, but the
little bronze reliefs are spirited and lively, and at least the
heads of the executed are no longer stuck upon the top as they
were on old Temple Bar (up to as late as 1745).

And so the City passes into Westminster—Westminster, as
Cunningham wrote in 1851, that 'loves to spend lavishly what
London has laboriously earned'. The transition is not immediately apparent; the two are linked on the north by the
continuing pinnacled and fretty neo-Gothic façade of the Law
Courts (see p. 308), but on the south No. 1 Fleet Street,
though it looks like a West End club, was the premises of
Child's Bank; the original Child's has been absorbed by a
clearing bank far to the east in Lombard Street, but it was
one of the great London banks, the first to issue printed
bank-notes (in 1729), and dealing with clients of the calibre
of Cromwell, Nell Gwynn (their early ledgers have receipts

from her, signed with a clumsy crawling and winning EG, 'Ellen Gwyn—Her Mark'), Marlborough and John Dryden.

But almost at once, the Strand divides on its westward course about the monstrous island of the Aldwych; just before it does so there are on the south Devereux Court, with a famous pub, the Devereux, and then **Essex Street**. This last is an agreeable semi-cul-de-sac, closed at the bottom by an archway through which steps go down in the direction of the river; it was developed by that enterprising post-fire speculator, Nicholas Barbon, about 1675, and still has narrow, tallish brick houses with stone bands here and there to give you an idea of the kind of building that went up in that great spurt of building. But the magic in this area comes perhaps from the echoes of its names, Devereux, Earl of Essex; the estate that Barbon was developing had been Essex House. To get a glimpse of the setting of this estate one must close one's eyes, delete the present press of commercial building and tell oneself what may seem almost a fairy story: 'In ancient times the Strand was an open space, extending from Temple Bar to the village of Charing, sloping down to the river, and intersected by several streams from the neighbouring high grounds which in this direction emptied themselves in the Thames. In after ages, when the residence of the court at Westminster had become more frequent, and the Parliament was held there, the Strand, being the road thence from the City, became the site of several magnificent mansions belonging to the nobility and clergy, most of which were situated on the south side, and had large gardens extending to the water's edge . . .' Not that the Strand was always so idyllic; high men of high power and higher temper lived in those places. Up from that slope where now runs the sedate Essex Street, on a winter Sunday morning in 1601, the mutinous and hysterical Essex, last and most comet-like of Elizabeth's favourites in the pride of his thirty-four years against her near-seventy, came clattering out with his friends to ride against the City, up Ludgate Hill with the cry of 'For the Queen! For the Queen! A plot is laid for my life!' To return later, in the dark, in ignominy; to die under the axe three weeks later at the Tower.

Of that there is only the name on the street wall to rouse echoes. Westward, the vast masonry fortress of **the Aldwych** stands as if it had always stood, so solid, lightened a little only by its banking plane trees; but it dates only from 1900, a piece of town-planning to close the axis of Kingsway to the north, and including Australia House, India House and Bush House (headquarters of the B.B.C. Overseas services). But between it and the southern side of the Strand, and in the middle of the Strand, in file each breasting their way against the traffic stately-pretty as great swans, swim those splendid sisters, St. Clement Danes and St. Mary-le-Strand. Truly, they do swan the Strand, spires high for admiration, and within them, each one, a sanctuary of peace all the more still for the whirl of traffic outside.

The easternmost, and biggest, is **St. Clement's** (the 'Danes' are hazy in myth), rebuilt by Wren on an old ruinous church, 1680–2, and very rare in Wren's work in that the aisles were continued round the east end, a sort of ambulatory and apse; the spire in its gracious soar of diminishing octagonals was added by Gibbs in 1719. The church was gutted in the war, and its famous bells that sing in nursery rhymes ('Oranges and lemons, Say the bells of St. Clement's') cracked though the spire stood; now restored, not quite as it was, but not at all bad, big, airy, new-smelling and vibrant with light from the big double-tiered windows under the barrel vault; the lower stage, aisles, pews and gallery in dark wood, and above the lift in cream and gold of the restored plasterwork. It is now much cherished, the official church of the R.A.F., with crests of the squadrons cut in slate set in its pavement, and a dazzle of brilliant little hassocks in petit point hanging in the pews. The bells too are restored. This was **Dr. Johnson's** parish church; he was wont to sit in the north gallery ('I shall never forget the tremulous earnestness with which he pronounced the awful petition in the Litany—"In the hour of death, and in the day of judgment, good Lord deliver us" '—Boswell, Good Friday, 1773). He is celebrated in a statue of which I am not fond (outside the church at the east end looking down to Fleet Street); it is modern and seems to me to make him look small which in no way he was. West, between St. Clement's and Australia House, is Thornycroft's bronze memorial to Gladstone (1905), his person rising eloquent from a cluster of four virtues. The steps are a pleasant place to rest for a moment on a sunny day, looking back at St. Clement's lifting its spire from its girding trees, even though official vandalism has now removed from you one of those nostalgic granite troughs of the Metropolitan Drinking Fountain and Cattle Trough Association.

West again round the south flank of Aldwych; the old, almost romantically seedy, south side of the Strand yields to mammoth developments, and the bits of old are hard to find; at last looking, the so-called 'Roman bath' (antique anyway, probably mainly Tudor), a fifteen-foot-long enigma fed by a sturdy spring with a flow of 2000 gallons, that *was* in a little alley off Strand Lane, eluded me completely. One of the new developments is the expansion of King's College, but there follows, going westward, more importantly though oddly unobtrusive in the Strand frontage what was meant to be (and indeed is, but on its river front) one of the show set-pieces of London architecture: **Somerset House.** The palace begun here in 1547 by the Duke of Somerset, Protector or Regent of the infant King Edward VI, was architecturally of major importance, though much argued about; it seems to have been the first building fully imbued with classical principle; later it was very royal, Elizabeth lived here as princess, and the Queens of James I, Charles I and II; here in 1658 a somewhat uncelebrated event took place when Oliver Cromwell was crowned—if only by proxy, in the wax effigy used for his standing in state before his funeral, Cromwell was nevertheless posthumously crowned with a royal crown and invested with orb and sceptre. The building was replaced by the present very official range about a vast courtyard built by Sir William Chambers, 1776–86, specifically designed to house various public administrative offices and institutions. The Admiralty, the Royal Society, the Antiquaries, the Royal Academy were once here (the last two now in Burlington House, see p. 41). It houses, *inter alia*, the national archive of wills, which you can consult for a mere 50p a will (though Shakespeare's is now in the Public Record Office) and in its eastern extension (by Smirke, begun 1829) one of the London University Colleges, King's. Some of its spectacular interiors were to be used for the National Theatre Museum, but the latest proposition is that they shall be devoted to the display of paintings by J. M. W. Turner. The main courtyard should be looked at; it is a very carefully worked out, very academic scheme, with sculpture thoughtfully and tastefully disposed about, and balustrades and columns, and space, and it all curiously leaves one with nothing to say except, 'Well, there it is then . . .'

Meanwhile, let us go back to the middle of the road, where **St. Mary-le-Strand** on its island cleaves the motor-cars. The old church was pulled down by Protector Somerset and the stone used for Somerset House; the new one was the first of the fifty churches ordered by Queen Anne (her statue was made for its façade, but never got there and is said to be that in Queen Anne's Gate, (see p. 149). It was built by James Gibbs, 1714–17, and though his commission changed during building, it is perhaps his masterpiece, most consistent in charm and most lovingly wrought in detail. He was just back from Rome, and the massive detail on the façades (you should walk all round it, for it is to be encompassed by the eye), the deep-cut of niches and pediment, rustication, Corinthian pillars and balustrade, is very Roman in quality and feeling. The front is delectable, descending from triangular pediment over the second stage of columns, to the rounded porch with its columns, to the spread, like the last effort of a slow sea movement on a shallow strand, of the rounded, shallow and worn pale steps; about them in June are roses. Inside it is a small but all-of-a-piece church, the traffic noise warded off by blank walls at the first storey, and light allowed by the big round-headed windows in the second; very tidy, a big central aisle marching to the brilliant blue windows of the apsed end, and a zing of incense (it must be high), and a shallow arched ceiling most richly coffered with roses, foliage and cherubs' heads among flowers; the old pulpit remains, cosily squat and bulbous. And the church's seclusion, among the traffic brushing its walls, is inviolate as a fortress. Outside, the spire goes up rather thin, but very delicate in diminishment above the clock.

After St. Mary's, Aldwych comes sweeping south in its arc again to rejoin the Strand at the meeting with the approach to Waterloo Bridge (for which, see p. 257); here there is many a solid traffic-jam, but beyond the Strand continues unified again in its second phase on its way to Charing Cross. Tests have indicated that this is among other things one of the noisiest places in London. On the right-hand side is the vast and ever popular Strand Palace Hotel, one of the Lyons chain and carried out in that odd Lyons facing stone that looks like a processed cheese. There is Stanley Gibbons, hub of the philately business and almost as old as the postage stamp (its founder was born in 1840, the year Rowland Hill introduced the postage stamp). There are theatres, the Vaudeville, the Adelphi; there is the glister of Mooney's Irish House, but the aura of music-hall gaiety that used to pervade the Strand at gas-light is gone. For the connoisseur of the City-type alley there are two excellent melancholy ones running up to Maiden Lane, slots deep in the dirty brick, each with its gas-lamp, each loaded with its half-concealed pub, and in the second one an entirely unexpected pomp of a baroque façade housing the Corps of Commissionaires.

The other side of the Strand is perhaps more glamorous; at the Waterloo Bridge end is Simpson's, the traditional eating-house for old English cooking, vast roasts under still vaster shining dishcovers wheeled to and fro by expert carvers; and then there is the **Savoy**—'a handsome building on the road to Westminster, situated on the banks of the Thames'. So it was described by the fifteenth-century chronicler Froissart; then it was a palace, built in 1245 by Peter Earl of Savoy (uncle of King Henry III's wife) and used by him as, among other things, a kind of marriage agency, as you will see from a notice outside the present Grill Room (one of the famous eating spots of Europe, with its splendid view over the Thames): here Peter 'lodged the many beautiful ladies whom he brought in 1247 from the courts of Europe before marrying them to his wards, a large number of rich young English nobles'. It fell into neglect; then was endowed by Henry VII as a hospital in 1505 (for the relief of a hundred poor people, a function which it surely no longer fulfils, though only officially dissolved in 1702). It became a warren of lodgings, but with a right of sanctuary frequently abused, a famous refuge for 'debtors and disorderly persons', until its last traces were swept away when old Westminster Bridge was built. The hotel now on its site, one of the great hotels of Europe, was built in 1889, by the enterprising Richard D'Oyly Carte, and was revolutionary: it had, not only six lifts, but a bathroom to every bedroom. Its approach, in typical London style, is tucked away but most effective. Limousines and taxis stoop in from the Strand under the shining aluminium fascia of its entrance, surmounted with the skirted and helmeted knight; you may note that the cars here drive on the right-hand side of the road, the only place in Britain, I think, where they do—a special act of Parliament was necessary, but the Savoy got it. The approach includes also the entrance to the Savoy Theatre, in a former version of which D'Oyly Carte staged in dazzling sequence between 1881 and 1896 the famous operettas of Gilbert and Sullivan. The old chapel of the Savoy was round the corner (Savoy Street) but the chapel now on its site is modern (1864), and, though the Chapel of the Royal Victorian Order and used for tolerably grand weddings, is rather dim and sad, much oppressed by its surrounding buildings; an old brass there celebrating the death of a Mr. Gosling in 1586 remarks:

> So well inclined to poor and rich
> God send more Goslings to be sich.

Former inhabitants of the Savoy, including Simon de Mont-fort and (as prisoner) a king of France, John of Valois, are too many to mention, especially of course since it has been a hotel, but the visitor I like to think of is Claude Monet, sitting up there in one of the bedrooms high over the river, evolving one of his shimmery shifting visions of the Thames.

Farther west down the Strand, abandon it—left down Adam Street, and the name Adam announces that you are in what was one of the delights of late eighteenth-century planned London: **the Adelphi**. The site was Durham House, held as town house by the bishops of Durham; by Sir Walter Raleigh ('I well remember his study,' wrote Aubrey, 'which was on a little turret that looked into and over the Thames, and had the prospect which is as pleasant perhaps as any in the world'); but all vanished when in 1768 the brothers Adam acquired the lease, and on the site built a grand and elegant scheme—the first embankment of the Thames, the first attempt to present a composed magnificence to the river. Central in a terrace of houses lifted on arches high over the water lived the actor David Garrick, but fashion did not rally solidly and consistently enough, and by 1872 despoliation had already begun; only fragments now remain. Near the top of Adam Street there is a house with a gentle but firm curve in, and then through Nos. 9 and 8 you read through to No. 7, which closes the vista from the west up John Adam Street and gives you some idea of the calculated and subtle intricacy that this area once had: a tall house in dark brick, but looking out from an open mask of pale plaster that limns the shallow triangular pediment, stresses the horizontals, runs in filigree

ornament down the four giant pilasters down the centre of
the house, and consolidates on the front of the ground floor,
with its delicate fanlight over the doorway; extra accents are
supplied by black ironwork on the balconies. Walpole made
a famous and spiteful comment on the Adelphi—'Warehouses,' he said, 'laced down the seams, like a soldier's trull
in a regimental old coat.' One sees what he means, but also
how malicious it was. The basic structure is indeed plain, but
shapely plain with the bare fineness of good bones, and the
shallow surface decoration set across it is like a cosmetic most
exquisitely applied, with perfect tact and decorum to trans-
mute a well-bred but homely girl into a woman of brilliant
smartness: the essence in fact of the best sophisticated town
architecture.

There is a sturdier statement on the corner opposite (No.
18), turning the corner into John Adam Street, and in John
Adam Street the **Royal Society of Arts,** stronger and deeper
shadowed behind its four fluted columns under the pediment,
has only the arched window recess on the first floor and the
entrance accented in light plaster and paint. This was founded
in 1754 for the Encouragement of Arts, Manufactures and
Commerce, and is still going strong; its interior is still intact
and recently restored (not open, but the inquirer of serious
curiosity will generally be allowed to see if business does not
forbid). The Library has its Adam columns and fireplace, the
staircase its iron balustrade, and in the lecture room on the
first floor is the great effort of that genius manqué of English
History painting, James Barry, on a theme anticipating
Victorian didactics: the progress of civilisation (painted
1777–83).

The opposite side of the road is entirely taken up with the
sour, bleak-ribbed commercial building set up in the 1930s in
place of the original central terrace, but from the far side of
that you can at least look down into the tops of the trees in
the embankment gardens below and over the river, and realise
how steep is the fall from the Strand to the bank. Robert
(i.e. Robert Adam; Adelphi comes from the Greek 'adelphoi'
meaning brothers)—Robert Street has one or two original
houses, but has lost others very recently (by order at governmental level, countermanding a G.L.C. preservation order);
Nos. 1–3 had a whole row of distinguished inhabitants—
Thomas Hood, Galsworthy, Barrie; in the vanished central

terrace lived, besides Garrick, G. B. Shaw and Thomas Hardy. The site of Rowlandson's house in John Adam Street is marked by a plaque; farther west, though a big new development separates them from the Strand, there are still old streets running down to where was the river before the embankment and where now are gardens. Buckingham Street has especially nice old houses with doorhoods; Pepys lived where now is No. 14 between 1685 and 1700, and before that (1679–85) at No. 12, which though altered is still basically the house he knew. 'Buckingham' records that this was once the estate of the assassinated favourite of Charles I, George Villiers, Duke of Buckingham, and of his rake-hell playwright son the 2nd Duke (Dryden's Zimri); the whole little clutch of streets commemorated them—George Street, Villiers, Duke and Buckingham Streets, and (modestly), Of Alley, now scandalously retitled 'York Place formerly Of Alley'. At the bottom of Villiers Street, Charing Cross Underground with attendant stalls, coffee and flowers and the cry of the paper sellers, and on the left the opening into the Embankment Gardens, where in summer in the bandstand the band plays and people close their eyes in deck-chairs; here you may catch a gorgeous bandsman in red and blue with dress spurs, stooped severely over a xylophone. Over the river is the Festival Hall, and about you in the gardens is a plethora of late nineteenth-century statues, including a whole-length Burns in bronze of compelling awfulness; Wilfred Lawson of temperance fame (would not have got on with Burns); monuments to both Gilbert and Sullivan, and a very fetching one of 1921 to the Imperial Camel Corps with a miniature camel and all. Over on the brink of the Embankment, where the cars rush headlong but few walk, is the granite needle, pinkish under its grime, known as **Cleopatra's needle**. It has alas nothing to do with Cleopatra, but is one of a much travelled pair (its mate is in Central Park, New York) from Heliopolis, of about 1500 B.C. Given in 1819 by Mohammed Ali, the Viceroy of Egypt, it only reached England after many adventures in 1878; its hieroglyphs record the deeds of Thotmes III and Rameses II, and leaning over, looking into the swirling mortal tide of Thames one can think of transiency and of Thotmes and Rameses. But before leaving the Gardens, the Watergate at the bottom of Buckingham Street should be seen: the last vestige of the Villiers house. Long ascribed to Inigo Jones, it was perhaps designed by Balthasar Gerbier, a massive tripartite arch of considerable distinction; it was what it is called, the gate to the house from the water, which has now been pushed away from it, far from it, by the nineteenth-century embankment.

Back in Villiers Street there are steps leading up to the footway over Hungerford Bridge that shakes as the trains from Charing Cross go over it. A little farther up, actually in an arch under the railways, is the Players, a club theatre where the staple fare is Victorian pantomime done with furious gusto, audience participation, and much swinging of beer tankards. And then still farther up, a dive free from Villiers Street into one of the railway arches—once dim, cool and cavernous though now all shops, but if you are lucky echoing with accordion music (it used to be haunted by the violin of an old, old man, but I fear he comes no more); it smells a little damp, and also perhaps of beer, for up the steps at the end is a pub that has a bull's-eye-window commanding the passage. But the steps up bring you back to the realities of Craven Street, and up past a long row of plain eighteenth-century houses, to the Strand again, to Lyons Corner House; on your right is **Charing Cross Station** for Kent, but the station's vigorous nineteenth-century Gothic fret has been subdued by a top icing of flat, synthetic-looking modern (for the Cross in the yard, see p. 93). This end of the Strand has been widened, and there is indeed a very great deal of road, enlivened by combat of pedestrians with motor cars, which at rush-hours the pedestrians tend to win by sheer weight of numbers as they storm the station for home. On the north side, on the backside of South Africa House, with St. Martin's spire rising beyond, is inscribed a memory of a great coaching house—Golden Cross House. This was the great all-change stage of West London, and here, you may remember, Mr. Pickwick met up with Messrs. Tupman, Snodgrass and Winkle, and hence, after some difficulty with the pugnacious cabman, the Pickwickians set forth upon their journeys to the tune of Mr. Jingle.

CHAPTER TWENTY-ONE

Legal London—Inns of Court:
Temple to King's Cross

✤

CITY and Westminister meet and seem to merge, as we saw in the last chapter, where Fleet Street becomes Strand, at Temple Bar. As you proceed from east to west or vice versa with the heedless impetus of the traffic, this seems undeniably so. Yet in physical fact, exactly there, at the junction, the City is separated from Westminster by, not a no-man's-land, but a lawyer's sanctuary, some three-quarters of a mile, running north from Thames at Temple Steps through to Gray's Inn's garden end on Theobald's Road: the four great Inns of Court, which together form what is virtually the English University of the Law. Pierced they may be from east to west, both by Holborn and by Fleet Street, yet their entrances are so discreet that the innocent traveller in a bus would not know they exist at all.

Their origins are explained succinctly by G. M. Trevelyan in his *History of England*: 'As the English universities developed colleges, so the English lawyers built their Inns of Court. During the reigns of the first three Edwards they grouped their halls, libraries, and dwelling places in and around the deserted groves of the Templars. Their place of public performance lay two miles farther westwards, in the shadow of the royal residence, where they were royally accommodated in Westminster Hall. . . . But the lawyers slept, dined, and studied in their own Inns of Court, half-way between the commercial capital at London and the political capital at Westminster, a geographic position that helped the English lawyer to discover his true political function as mediator between Crown and people.' And so still essentially the Inns remain, a bewitching anomaly in the thundering wheel-borne town, a warren of courtyards, passage-ways and gardens, each composed like a college of courts; with chambers off steep staircases, communal dining-hall, library, common rooms and chapel. They are still the examining body of

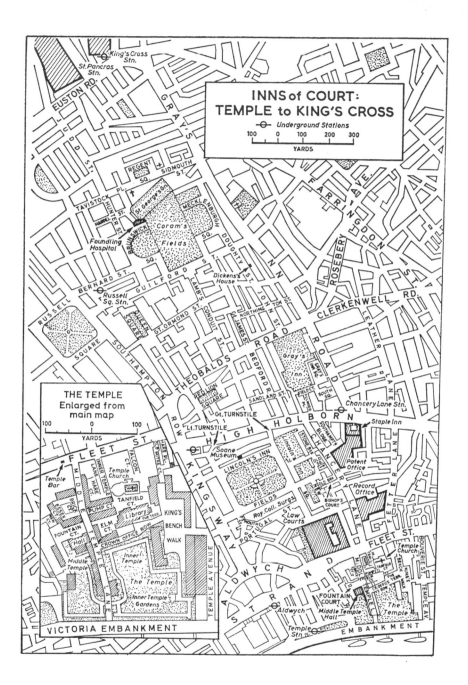

INNS of COURT:
TEMPLE to KING'S CROSS

⊖ Underground Stations

100   0   100   200   300
YARDS

THE TEMPLE
Enlarged from
main map

100   0   100
YARDS

VICTORIA EMBANKMENT

the Law and they alone have the power to admit aspirants as advocates in the courts of England and Wales, even though as is now normal the student actually studies elsewhere. (Residence at Inns of Court for the student has become vestigial but still formally essential, and he has to keep terms by the process of eating three dinners each term in his Inn's Hall, before he can qualify and be 'called to the Bar'—he does also of course have to pass examinations.) And although most chambers are now occupied by barristers and solicitors there is still a very residential atmosphere in the Inns, and, generally in the top chambers, you will often find private inhabitants just living there in blessed seclusion as Charles Lamb or Oliver Goldsmith once used to. Each Inn has its own gradually evolved, largely unwritten, constitution, governed by its senior members, the 'Benchers', under the Treasurer; each has its own discipline and each guards very jealously its corporate loyalties.

Let us start this cloistered perambulation at **Temple Station** on the Embankment, where you turn left down river. To begin with, there are temporary distractions from the Law. At the bank are moored four ships of agreeably archaic aspect. The far two, H.M.S. *Chrysanthemum* and *President*, are naval training ships; the next, the *Wellington*, is the premises of the only City Livery Company to own a floating hall, the Master Mariners, and the nearest, westerly, one, masted and rigged for sail, its black wooden hull feet-thick against ice-floes, is the *Discovery* (visitable daily, 1–4.45). This was Captain Scott's research ship, but *not* the one that took him on the final expedition to the Antarctic when he and his companions died in the blizzard with a stoic gallantry plotted calmly to its end in Scott's own diary (now in the British Museum). Nearby are the Temple Steps, the Temple's own water gateway (and by it on the pavement, on a plinth like a relic, one of the noble Embankment seats, of excruciatingly uncomfortable magnificence, slats on two camels couchant in cast-iron). On the inland side we pass a little garden with statues; and two brave and shining dragons in red and aluminium (salvaged from the demolished Coal Exchange and set up here in 1963 to mark the boundaries of the City and of Westminster and perhaps the City's guilt); on the left the lawns of the Temple go up from under the fringe of plane trees; and then comes the Temple gateway. This is elaborately Victorian but leads you into the narrow slope of **Middle Temple Lane,** banked close by brick on either side, with gas lamps and the Inn doorways painted with the names of their occupants. Middle Temple is to the left of the lane and Inner Temple to the right, but no visible boundary is drawn between them. First right under an arch, and Inner Temple gardens stretch away behind railings (for Templars only) to the river; the little memorial fountain down to the south east is for Charles Lamb. The boy, later to become perhaps the supreme exponent of the English humorous essay, and a character whose radiance still warms today, remained always devoted to the Temple—'the most elegant spot in the metropolis', and later had rooms in Inner Temple Lane overlooking Hare Court. One of his most famous essays, 'The Old Benchers of the Inner Temple', is devoted to it. The statue that we glimpsed earlier is inscribed 'Lawyers were children once'. Sharp left immediately, through a tunnel and up steps into Elm Court; though the brick here is all post-war, you can already feel the agreeable change of texture, shift of levels, and sense of seclusion combined with surprise, that are so potent in the Temple. The south-east exit from Elm Court brings you to the Terrace and into the big open space of **King's Bench Walk,** closed to the east at the end of the Temple precinct by deep, rich façades of old brown brick with opulent doorways (Nos. 4–6 are late seventeenth-century). It is a fine place, even though unwisely cars are allowed to park there, with a broad view down the gardens to the Thames and the happily incongruous eye-catcher of the OXO tower on the far bank. West again through into the paved yard of Tanfield Court, with the Master's House (rebuilt after bombing, following its original shape of 1667, like a little country house) set up above behind railings and its own little lawn; on the left is the Library and the rebuilt **Hall** (visible on Saturdays and all day in August and September; other times normally between 10 and 12 and 3 and 4.30). Then on the right in warmish stone, **Temple Church,** which serves both Inns. The most immediate oddity about this is that the chancel (known as the 'Oblong') yields to a circular nave (the 'Round'). The latter is one of five surviving circular churches (modelled on the Holy Sepulchre at Jerusalem) in England, three of which like this one are connected with the Templars, an order of military knighthood connected with the crusades. This area was their headquarters in England, and it is from them that its name persists; they were dissolved in 1312, and the ground was subsequently leased to the lawyers, well before it is first mentioned as an Inn of Court in 1449. In the Round (of about 1185) of the church, you can still find the Templars in effigy, set very low on the paving, cross-legged, battered, figures of the twelfth and thirteenth centuries, ravaged and eaten out by time as if by moths, yet of formidable forlorn potency. The whole church was gutted to the bone in the Blitz, but has been brilliantly restored. The Oblong was later than the Round—1240 about, but in very pure, positively exhilarating airy Early English, with steep vaulting springing from quadruple grey-green Purbeck marble shafts. The monuments have been restored, and the reredos, made in 1682 under Wren's supervision, brought back from exile; at the west end is the tombstone of the great jurist John Selden, with a lapidary inscription seen through a glass lid let into the floor.

North of the church (the porch of which is sunk into the slope of the hill), a stone slab is set in the ground about where it is believed Oliver Goldsmith was buried, and Inner Temple Lane, with nice overhanging sets of chambers and very precipitous staircases, leads out to Fleet Street. Our way however, goes back west from south of the church, through the rebuilt arcade into Pump Court and so through to Middle Temple Lane again. Here a little below you to the west opens off Fountain Court, with planes and a circular pool with a single jet of water frail under catalpas; the south wall of this is formed by **Middle Temple Hall,** and of this enough was left by bombs to rebuild it much as it was (times of visiting as for Inner Temple Hall), with its panelling, its splendid carved oak screen, and the tremendous double hammerbeam roof. Shakespeare's company is said to have staged *Twelfth Night* there on 2 February 1602. In the late sixteenth and seventeenth centuries, the Inns were famous for the splendour and the quality of their masques and entertainments; many with no special legal vocation were members—Raleigh, John Pym, Clarendon; Congreve and Fielding, Cowper and R. B. Sheridan; de Quincey and Thackeray.

North from Fountain Court is Brick Court where Oliver Goldsmith died in 1774 at the former No. 2. In the Temple you can wander, and get lost, for hours, on a weekday among a briskish coming and going of dark-suited, sleek-headed lawyers, but the Temple holds only two of the four great Inns.

If you leave by Middle Temple Lane, you come on the Strand through a sober late seventeenth-century stone gateway, into the normal fury of London traffic. A few yards east, the entry to Inner Temple Lane looks, to the untutored critical eye, bogus, as does most early half-timbered black and white work; it is however, perfectly good, of about 1610, overhangs and oriels, like Staple Inn that we shall see later (p. 316). It has moreover an excellent chamber of the period on the first floor, with an elaborate plaster ceiling with PH for Prince Henry, the brilliant, ill-starred elder brother of Charles I (open weekdays 1.45–5; Saturday to 4.30).

From the Temple entrances, in spite of Fleet Street you are still in sight of the Law. To your left an immense Gothic stone frontage, extending almost from Temple Bar to Aldwych, is the **Law Courts** (or, properly, the Royal Courts of Justice); they were consolidated here, the buildings designed by G. E. Street, from their former site around Westminster from 1874 on, belatedly but logically enough. The move brought everything into a tidier concentration (though the final court of appeal is still at Westminster, in the House of Lords); tidiness, however, is not the aptest epithet for the buildings themselves, composed in a massive thirteenth-century manner, though very skilfully plotted up the slope, with a fine use of skyline and nobly extravagant in their handling and large breaking of space—the main hall is 238 echoing feet long and 80 feet high, and the ecclesiastical black fleche a landmark. And the detail—note the massive, luxuriant and beautifully made ironwork—is always good. It now serves the Court of Appeal, Chancery, Queen's Bench, and Probate, Divorce and Admiralty (public entrance to the courts when sitting is by the main entrance, though for high drama of the big criminal trials you have to go to the Old Bailey (see p. 386).

Our way lies still with the law, up **Chancery Lane**, which now in spite of coffee bars has a solidly Victorian air; offices, legal specialists in books, wigs and gowns, and the world famous book-auction rooms, Hodgsons, now owned by Sotheby's. The monument of Chancery Lane is the high institutional grey stone of the **Public Record Office**, built between 1851 and 1896 and running right through to Fetter Lane to the east: the national archive especially of government documents and of legal ones. Its search rooms are full of scholars, busy as miners at work on the raw ore of history, extracting dates, names, payments: hard facts from the crabbed hands of centuries-old accounts, rent-rolls, legal depositions (among one such was found one of the very rare signatures of Shakespeare, 1612, now shown in the Museum). The search rooms are not for the casual visitor, though students with a serious question are always welcomed and provided with a student's ticket, and the staff are very helpful. But you must know what you are after. Its holdings are infinite in their variety, and the guide to their mere categories runs to two volumes and 669 pages. However, it has allowed as it were some of the cream in its great vat to float to the top, skimmed it off, and displayed it in its Museum (open Monday to Friday, 1–4 only). The entrance is on the left in the main entrance arch, and the Museum itself, a little sunk, is on the site of a former chapel in a house that Henry III founded in 1232 for converted Jews; from this survives a serene Renaissance effigy (Dr. Yonge) probably by Torrigiani. There is a series of glowing showcases in the centre and others round the wall. The dark beige linoleum hushes footsteps, and in a faint humming and ticking of controlled atmosphere the imagination can open wide over aged and fading scraps of paper. Their resonance within the remembering mind can be terrific, and the range of documents extends from the Domesday Book of 1086 to modern times.

On the other side of the road from the Record Office, is the Law Society in an agreeable classical building of 1831, headquarters of the solicitors and with one of the best law libraries of the world. Going farther north on the same side you come to a gatehouse that seems to fit well enough with dominant Victorian–Tudor–Gothic of Chancery Lane, but is in fact of 1518, though with later windows but still with its old oak doors. Through this lies Lincoln's Inn, third on the northwards route of the four great Inns of Court. **Lincoln's Inn**—which Lincoln provided it with its name seems uncertain—has been on this site since around 1422 (when its records begin). The first courtyard through the gate, Old Buildings, has the Old Hall, the Chapel, and buildings of brick with doorways on to those romantic stairways off which are the lawyers' chambers, in Temple collegiate style. The Hall is of 1490–2, with a good carved screen of the early seventeenth century, and one of Hogarth's incursions into history painting in grand manner, 'St. Paul before Felix', which shows copious signs of ability and industry and little of Hogarth's splendid zest. The benchers rebuilt their chapel in 1620, and John Donne preached the consecration sermon in 1623; the chapel was a victim of the First World War, an early air raid casualty, and then lost some of its glass, but much of the old high pewing remains. It has an open undercroft, by the pillars of which lawyers used to do business much as stockbrokers did by the pillars of the old Exchange.

Through the west gate of this courtyard lie more Tudor brick buildings, and then to the south the big, very handsome New Square, of the last decade of the seventeenth century, about a big lawn with trees. Almost all solicitors' chambers— in this courtyard Dickens worked for a bit as office-boy aged fourteen, and took so decisively against the law: one of his most spectacular episodes, Jarndyce v. Jarndyce in *Bleak House*, is sited in Lincoln's Inn Old Hall. The precinct of the Inn, relatively little touched by second war damage even if a precocious victim of the first war, can still be almost Dickensian in atmosphere, and there is a certain sort of legal person, in bowler hat, black jacket a little dusty, striped trousers concertina-ing at the ankles and over wrinkled shoes, and a general expression of pinched antique gleam, that I seem only to see in Lincoln's Inn. Notices at the gates insist: 'The Porters and Police have orders to remove [note *remove*] all Persons making a noise within this Inn.' And calm there truly is, only enhanced at times in summer by the sound of the band tuning up in Lincoln's Inn Fields to the west. To the north are the main gardens, opening through the picturesque contrast of the nineteenth-century Tudor of the New Hall and Library to the west and the Palladian chastity of the range of Stone Buildings (1774–80, by Sir Robert Taylor) to the north-east. The lawns are famous, closing in evenly and smoothly on to the giant boles of the equally famous plane trees; lawyers and public pace, and you may even sight a baby moored in a perambulator; at the end are terrific traditional herbaceous borders, with iris and delphinium. The gardens are open to the public at lunch time: halls and chapel can be visited generally by asking at the gate of a porter (tips are in order). But really Lincoln's Inn is to walk about in and meditate. Its greatest old bencher is surely Sir Thomas More (the Inn owns a beautiful miniature version of Holbein's portrait of him). Other former associates include Donne, Oliver Cromwell (according to legend anyway), Lord Shaftesbury, even David

Garrick who registered on 9th March 1736, Canning and a host of great lawyers.

The arched western gateway of Lincoln's Inn leads on to **Lincoln's Inn Fields**, which on a Saturday or Sunday, placid in its trees, can seem almost an extension of the Inn, but which on a weekday is busy with people and littered with the noisome motor-car. It is somewhere between a large square and a small public park, with tennis courts, bandstand where at lunchtime in summer military bands warble, flower beds and some splendid boscage. A long battle to preserve it from development by the builders began about 1613, when James I appointed various gentlemen including Francis Bacon, to have it 'laid out in walks', and was settled by a decree of Oliver Cromwell in 1656. The walks where now the lunchtime office workers stroll have seen odd sights: the mock procession of Thomas Sadler and friends with the insignia of the Lord Chancellor of England which they had just stolen from him, in Charles II's reign; the butchered end of William Lord Russell, known as 'the Patriot', executed after the Rye House Plot against Charles II, in 1683. Until enclosed in 1735, the place was notorious for beggars, side-shows and thieves. The south side is dominated by the Royal College of Surgeons, the body that examines and licenses surgeons. Their craft was originally allied with that of the Barbers, and they formed one company, the Barber-Surgeons, until the surgeons split off into their own dignity in 1745. The very noble giant Ionic portico comes from the building by Dance of 1806 on, but the building has at various times been expanded about this feature and looks now a little, perhaps, mumpish about it. The College's great treasure, besides its library, is the Hunterian Museum (to see which, apply in advance to the secretary); this was bombed, but rebuilt, restocked in part, and is now brilliantly shown, anatomical specimens shining and gleaming in organic contortion in the showcases, looking sometimes like rare and precious ores and at others like a three-dimensional Paul Klee—for the student, one of the most important collections of its kind. Its nucleus is John Hunter's own collection, a major pioneering attempt in this field; Hunter himself (d. 1793) was the greatest pioneer also of scientific surgery. Even if you are allergic to the more intimate details of the anatomy, pickled, the College will also reward you with some excellent paintings, including the newly restored and most fascinating cartoon for Holbein's group of Henry VIII and the Barber-Surgeons (with Henry seated larger than life like an oriental potentate), portraits by Hogarth and Reynolds among others, and paintings too of anatomical oddities, giants, famous dwarfs, and straightforward racial studies; animal paintings by Agasse, and especially three beautiful paintings by George Stubbs that Hunter commissioned, including a rhinoceros, a baboon and an albino Macaque monkey.

Farther along towards the south-west corner of the Fields, some prettily elegant houses, and at the corner, Portsmouth Street takes you down to the Old Curiosity Shop, an antique shop the claims of which to be Dickens's original are dubious but which is, here, a surprising and pleasant survival of seventeenth-century village street building. The west side of the Fields, though somewhat overhung in places by the commercial backsides of modern Kingsway beyond, offers great architectural interest, notably in Lindsey House (Nos. 59–60), built in 1640 by Inigo Jones or someone very close to him, a beautiful example of a classic restraint of opulence; its neighbour (Nos. 57–8) is a compliment paid to it (by Henry Joynes) nearly a hundred years later when Jones had become the patron saint of the Palladians.

On the north side of the Fields, which includes Canada Walk, the houses mostly remain in their old single units, though the fabrics range from the early eighteenth century to the 1930s. The focus is on No. 13, which with its neighbours on either side is united into a single composition with yellow brick about a shallow projecting bay that always gives me a faintly Moorish feeling, though it bears at the top very precise Grecian souvenirs in the shape of copies of the caryatids on the Erechtheum. This is **Sir John Soane's Museum** (Tuesdays to Saturdays only, 10–5, closed in August); one of the smaller London museums, but anyone who leaves London without seeing it has missed a remarkable experience. You go up the steps and in the narrow hall you sign the book, and the attendant will, with luck, positively usher you through the door on the right (the staff at the Soane seem to have a tradition of delightfully tactful courtesy). This first room is two, divided by two piers which are also bookcases: there may be at first a slight sense of vertigo produced by sheer congregation of objects in extraordinary variety—books, busts, bronzes, Greek vases, white architectural models, tables, chairs, mirrors—and also by a certain elusive ambiguity in the boundaries of the room, a rejection of any suggestion that a room might be a closed box. Thus in the Library (the space beyond with its recessed windows looking on to Lincoln's Inn Fields) the ceiling is dropped, with hanging arches in front of mirrors built in over the tops of the bookcases; in the northern part, the Dining Room, round mirrors set in the angles of the ceilings reflect the room in diminished perspective. This something of unease may be strengthened, as you find your bearings, by the non-arrival of your host—so strong is the impression of an ordering if quirky individual present; and the carpets are rather worn, the narrow leather-padded furniture much used. Even though your host will not come, for he died in his eighty-fourth year in 1837; yet he still presides, over the fireplace in the Dining Room, in one of Lawrence's most brilliant characterisations. The portrait may have, as ensemble, that typical Lawrentian social gloss that I doubt is apposite for Soane, but the face is superb, with its compressed mouth, its gleam of high intelligence and sensibility, a kind of taut yet most reasonable dottiness—and elusive. This man is a major luminary of English architecture, yet typically escapes popular fame; his surviving work in London is on the periphery (the restored Dulwich; the manor at Ealing) and his major work, the Bank of England (to which he was architect for forty-five years) sabotaged (see p. 326). Only here, in his home, does he survive in central London.

Soane, as architect, is normally classified as neo-classic, and specifically, neo-Grecian, but in his own house such docketing may seem almost irrelevant. Here one is as if poised in a nervously delicate, indeed neurotic, balance against the conflicting assaults of claustrophobia and agoraphobia. The place is a grotto, encrusted with bric-à-brac, labyrinthine with what seem, at the first groping, dead ends. The ornament is of casts and fragments of mixed classic and medieval ornament, of Egyptian, even of American; of work by his artist friends; of a scold's bridle, Tippoo Sahib's chairs, Christopher Wren's watch, Napoleon's pistol that was once, too, Peter the Great's; masks, busts and models by Soane's friends Banks and Flaxman. Yet everywhere, as in the Library, there are hints of escape, expectations around the corner. The dropped ceiling of the Library is typical, and throughout the treatment of ceilings tends as if to deprecate the notion of a ceiling as a sealing, a mere lid. From the Dining Room you pass through two minute highly ornamented rooms, the Little Study and the Dressing Room, but then to left and right the space, not opens up, but extends to left and right (Soane here took in the back parts of the houses on each side of No. 13) through a grove of Corinthian columns and crepuscular dimness where plaster and marble gleam. Left, a central dome lifts over a round gap in the floor; beyond this a cast of the Apollo Belvedere presides with outstretched arm, the tutelary deity of English classical taste, but down through gaps you look into ancient Egypt on the floor below, the open sarcophagus of Seti I, of about 1370 BC; in the lucent alabaster of its depth hovers the outline of the goddess Nut. (This was Soane's finest coup; he snapped it up for £2,000 after the British Museum had felt it beyond their resources, and threw a three day reception to celebrate.) If now you go down to basement level you find yourself in the full Gothick fantasy: Crypt, Monk's Parlour, and a view through a window into a mythical Padre Giovanni's cloister, wherein a colossal grotesque tomb is inscribed ALAS POOR FANNY (who was Mrs. Siddons's favourite dog).

But the main popular draw of the Soane is paintings, and the main concentration of these is in the Picture Room, back on the ground floor near the top of the steps from the basement: a small room, apparently not more than fourteen feet long—but it is all a trick: the walls on the south open, to reveal a hidden recess and more pictures. There are architectural drawings and paintings in the mood, ruin-scapes by Piranesi, Soane's own projects, but the famous ones are the twelve paintings by Hogarth: his 'Rake's Progress' of about 1733, and the later set of four, about 1754, 'The Election', which Soane got from Garrick's collection in 1823. They too are in the mood: the 'Rake', a progress of the young heir from the first glory of his inheritance, through dissipation to the final naked and fettered ruin of flesh and spirit in Bedlam (but No. 6, the Gaming House, with its raging despair of hands flung up against the sky, is perhaps the most apocalyptic), and 'The Election', a satire on democracy in action at the choosing of its best and finest specimens, is also a study in the grotesque animal appetites of man. As in all Hogarth's satirical work, the secret of their enduring fascination and vitality lies in part in a paradox, in the marriage of that line, of such elegance, sureness and life, with subjects of such repulsiveness. Hogarth's own intentions were avowedly moral, to teach and to reform through the eye; I doubt whether anyone's morals are much bettered by a good look at Hogarth, but the clarity of one's eye, one's appreciation of the twentieth-century tragi-comedy, is surely enhanced by his vision of the eighteenth century. Elsewhere too, there are more paintings: in the New Students' Room at the west end of the ground floor, three Canalettos, including one glorious crowded expanse of the Grand Canal, and in the Ante-Room thence a rather unexpected shadowy haunted Watteau. The Ante-Room leads through into the Breakfast Room with the most remarkable of Soane's remarkable ceilings—a sort of canopy pitched within the room, of wood with a little lantern above, all resting on four precarious pin-point corners (also a portrait of poor Fanny by James Ward). From the Hall stairs lead up, past the cunningly lit slot of the Shakespeare Recess (wherein lurks a cast of the Stratford Memorial bust of the Bard), to the Drawing Rooms on the first floor; here in presses are kept the very important collection of architectural drawings, from those by the Elizabethan John Thorpe, to Wren, Adam and Soane himself. Among the objects in the table cases is one of the most beautiful illuminated manuscripts in London, a breathtakingly accomplished example of Italian Renaissance miniature painting by Giulio Clovio about 1540.

Outside, the way east along the top of Lincoln's Inn Fields leads to the entry to Great Turnstile (this, and its counterpart Little Turnstile at the west end, record the old turning styles that kept the cattle in when the Fields were still pasture); on the corner, in a building almost quaintly old-fashioned in its columned windows and glazed brick, are the offices of the leading weekly of the Left, the *New Statesmen* (with an ancillary shop where the excellent Ganymed reproductions of paintings are sold). This passage takes you through into **High Holborn**, the northern parallel to Fleet Street and like it a major throughway from City to the West. Much here is very new—for example immediately opposite you, State House (1961), with its big Barbara Hepworth sculpture, its windows stacked tidily among the hangers of its green-black uprights in sixteen stories. But the dominant presences of High Holborn are still rather older, the palaces of Insurance, of which the Pearl dwells down to your left in pale polished granite giant columns and giant cupola of 1914, with a galaxy of bronze lanterns and bronze St. George within.

Following High Holborn east, across the top of Chancery Lane you find on the right Southampton Buildings, which included one of the most astonishing London confections in tormented terra-cotta and majolica, of 1895, later a branch of the Westminster Bank, and now vandalously demolished and replaced by an unremarkable anonymity; by the Patent Office, where are registered the plans of new inventions ranging from the highest genius to the wildest lunacy, a gate opens into a court and quiet, the noise and glint of a fountain, and cloistered brick again—**Staple Inn**, one of the former Inns of Chancery, founded in 1545, rebuilt in the eighteenth century, bombed, rebuilt again. In the first court, through a passageway, Dr. Johnson was at No. 2 in 1759–60 and there is said to have written *Rasselas* within the spare time of a week to pay for his mother's funeral. The character of this court, cobbles and York stone, trim brick and plane trees—is still sedately eighteenth century, well-restored, but as you come through back into Holborn and look up behind you, the street front of Staple Inn presents a dazzle of black and white timber and plaster, gables, overhangs and oriels, most astonishing in Holborn (which looks like and is a sort of prelude to Oxford Street); yet though like Inner Temple entrance it looks too good to be true, and though it is of course restored, this façade is basically the real thing, one of the last survivors of such Elizabethan work in London, going back in part to 1586.

Staple Inn stands at the junction of High Holborn, west; Holborn, east; and Gray's Inn Road coming in from the north; also at the beginning or end of the City, a boundary marked here by stone obelisks, the Holborn Bars, on each side of the road. Our concern now is really with the most northerly of the great Inns of Court. Gray's, but from Holborn Bars you can see to the east the second great Holborn palace of insurance, the immensely severely-expressioned red brick Gothic of the Prudential, most famous of such companies. Beyond this you can also sight a department store, mighty Gamage's, now scheduled for demolition, and alongside Gamage's flank, in Leather Lane, is a rather pleasantly nondescript left-over, street market.

To find **Gray's Inn**—you can easily miss it from High Holborn, but note, track down No. 22 (and if possible go in and use, Henekey's, a winebar of some majesty in dimension, and with a nobly old-fashioned display of wines in the cask); next to this, rather reticent and unlabelled, a chaste stone gateway and passage leads into Gray's Inn. It was a school of law by the fourteenth century and its list of members and benchers is long and of great distinction: from Henry VIII's great revolutionary bureaucrat, Thomas Cromwell, to Elizabeth's, Lord Burghley; the Caroline martyr Archbishop Laud, and from the opposing cause, the Parliamentary regicide John Bradshaw; up to Lord Macaulay and Birkenhead, better known as F. E. Smith. But the *genius loci*, and a formidable one, is Francis Bacon, Viscount St. Alban, Lord Chancellor, statesman, great inductive philosopher and master of the lapidary word—if you open the first edition of his undying *Essays* you will find them dated 'from my Chamber at Graies Inn, this 30 of Januarie 1597'. He was Treasurer of the Inn, and kept chambers here from 1576 till his death in 1626, and still presides in effigy on the lawn of the first court, South Square—a modern bronze by F. W. Pomeroy, in panoply of Lord Chancellor's robes, wounded in the right shin by enemy action, but unshaken. Gray's was badly bombed, and Hall and Library are completely rebuilt, but the Hall screen is still the original late sixteenth-century one, made within a few years of the first performance in this Hall of Shakespeare's *Comedy of Errors* in 1594.

Gray's Inn Square, the second court through to the north, also bombed and restored, has the entirely rebuilt chapel but holds still among its planes and grass a very calm and dignified echo of the late seventeenth century. To the west is Field Court, and thence to the north, the gardens, lawns and trees, very venerable and calming even if the association of the older of the catalpas with Bacon's green fingers is optimistic rather than factual. But Lamb, devoted Templar though he was, avowed them 'the best gardens of the Inns of Court', and before him Addison walked here, and Pepys with Mrs. Pepys when it was a walk of high fashion. (Now open to the public on weekdays, June–July 12–2; August–September 9.30–5.)

If you leave Gray's Inn by its western gate into Sandland Street, a singularly spacious road of brown brick touched with red opening up to the right is Bedford Row, still very much in the 'altogether reverend and law-breathing' mood that Lamb diagnosed in Gray's Inn; excellent urban architecture of about

1700, now mainly lawyers' offices. It is continued over the traffic barrier of Theobald's Road (pronounced 'Tibbalds'— once the way out to James I's palace of that name) by Great James Street, a little later (c. 1720–30) but even prettier with its many door-hoods on carved brackets. Right and then left up John Street which becomes Doughty Street, and on the right No. 48 is now known as **Dickens House** (weekdays, except Bank Holidays, 10–12.30; 2–5).

The house itself is a modest three-bay unit, in a dark, sooty brick, with three stories of tall windows with pale reveals, unremarkable in the pleasant if monotonous terraces of similar early nineteenth-century houses along the road. Dickens lived here in the early days of his marriage (after his move from Furnivall's Inn, now vanished from Holborn) from March 1837, until late 1839, when a growing family forced him into larger premises—these were at the top of Marylebone High Street in Devonshire Terrace, where he was for twelve years and wrote many of his most famous books, but which was demolished in 1958, leaving No. 48 Doughty Street as sole survivor of his London dwellings. Here he wrote the end of *Pickwick*, and then *Oliver Twist* and *Nicholas Nickleby*. The house belongs to the Dickens Fellowship, but was acquired only in 1924 by when it had naturally passed through several hands, and that intimacy of person and house that is so marked in Carlyle's Chelsea house can never be quite recaptured. There is, however, a fascinating assembly of relics covering his whole life.

A few doors up Doughty Street, on the other side, at No. 14, Sydney Smith, that most unsanctimonious of canons of St. Paul's, lived between 1803–6: one of those rare wits whose jokes keep their savour—of Macaulay (who lived for a time close by to the west, in Great Ormond Street), he remarked that he 'had occasional flashes of silence which make his conversation perfectly delightful'. Smith was also a confirmed Londoner: 'I have no relish for the country; it's a kind of healthy grave. . . .' Doughty Street leads into the green and trees of Mecklenburgh Square, the east flank of which, an austerely noble composition in stucco and brick of about 1812 (by Joseph Kay) is worth lingering a moment on. Then, turning left, round the railings of a big expanse of grass and play-grounds, to the top of Lamb's Conduit Street: the conduit was an Elizabethan innovation, and though gone for some two hundred years, is presumably remembered in the charming statue of the lady with an urn at the top of the road among the public lavatories. Just down the road is **the Lamb,** a wonderfully preserved late Victorian pub in brown and green, with boarded ceiling, true settles, photos of theatrical figures (when they *were* figures); round cast iron tables, oil lamps (electric now but still passably dim), and a very rare boxed-in bar with snob-screens, and often, thrown in free, a not unpleasant sprinkling of Bloomsbury intelligentsia.

At the top of the road, opposite the statue with the urn, part of the gate of the old **Foundling Hospital** still remains, in front of the grounds now known as Coram's Fields (where, if you keep to the rules, you may roller-skate). The Foundling Hospital itself was demolished in 1926, but its offices were re-housed in Brunswick Square, which you reach by following on round the railings to the west and north. The Square itself was much bomb-damaged (it forms a symmetrical pendant alongside the Fields to Mecklenburgh Square over the other side), but on the north side, past the new School of Pharmacy of London University, you come to Captain Coram, seated in bronze under the canopy of a vast plane tree, outside the offices of his foundation. Coram, a bluff, rubicund sea-captain, was seared when he lived at Rotherhithe by the frequent sight of 'deserted infants exposed to the inclemencies of the season, and through the indigence or cruelty of their parents left to casual relief or untimely death'. A man of determined and imaginative philanthropy, he founded the Foundling Hospital to relieve this situation, in 1739; it is now no more as such though still very active as a benevolent institution; that its fame has endured is mainly due to Hogarth, one of the original governors, who had the happy idea of persuading artists to give pictures to it and of opening its gallery and court room to the public. These became in the reign of George II a most fashionable rendezvous and attracted much useful alms. And both gallery and court room are still there, rebuilt into the new building as they were, and may be seen on Mondays and Friday between 10 and 12 and 2 and 4. The fact is not advertised, but press the bell and the staff are most courteous. At the bottom of the stairs a scale model shows the old Hospital, a sad loss to London's architecture; at the top of the stairs hangs one of the most famous portraits in the history of English painting—'the portrait', said its author, Hogarth, 'I painted with the most pleasure, and in which I particularly wished to excel, was that of Captain Coram. . . .' Rubicund indeed, and redder yet in his splendid coat, the founder sits there in unassuming splendour: it is a brilliant transposition of the court-manner of Van Dyck into harmony with a stoutly bourgeois if not plebeian character. The Long Picture Gallery has some more conventional state portraits and also the score of Handel's 'Messiah' and Hogarth's punch-bowl. The best pictures are in the Court Room—a lovely room, all dark red with white plaster arabesques and the light shimmery from the plane trees outside—with notably a most delicate, magic view of the entrance to the Charterhouse in sun and shade by the young Gainsborough.

The west flank of Brunswick Square is now laden with a vast ziggurat-ish residential and shopping centre in flying concrete, and the dominant character of this neighbourhood of eighteenth and nineteenth century building is threatened up Hunter Street and thereabouts, to the north. There was a little row, soot-black, of brick houses in Hunter Street near its beginning. No. 54 (now demolished) was where Ruskin was born in 1819, that prophet of the Gothic to whom in no small part Victorian London owes its shape. Leave Hunter Street first right, down Handel Street, and you come into what is I think the most elegiac of all London gardens: **St. George's,** once the cemetery of St. George's, Queen Square. It has now lovely lawns, and trees, and flower beds: head stones ranged along the walls; and in autumn when the leaves fall at the still, clear close of an afternoon, one might almost come upon Thomas Gray in composition. The great pale table tombs, some lurching sideways as if wrecked on the sward, stand about, and among them, a very tall, startlingly white, obelisk. The north exit from the gardens brings you to Regent Square, where the Blitz left for decades elegiac decay—the gutted hulk of St. Peter's, grecianly ruinous with its great portico and pillared tower guarding a ravaged void (it was by the Inwoods, the rare Greek revivalists, who built St. Pancras Church also), survived miraculously for years, but is now only a memory; north and west are bright modern flats.

North again from Regent Square up Judd Street will bring you to the driving traffic and architectural higgledy-piggledy of **Euston Road**, untidy as a dock-area about the three great

Wren's Monument, to commemorate the Great Fire of 1666. The relief
has Charles II in Roman kilt and Restoration wig "affording protection
to the desolated city and freedom to its rebuilders and inhabitants"

GOTHIC AND GOTHICK
The fan-vault of Henry VII's
Chapel (about 1512) in
Westminster Abbey, the most
elaborate and daring example of
this most English climax of Gothic
architecture, solid stone carved
and engineered into an aerial web

Wren's St Mary Aldermary (1704)
— the earliest Gothic revival in
London

termini of Euston, St. Pancras and King's Cross. Euston, which owned perhaps the most monumental of all nineteenth century London structures, the great Doric arch, has lost it to the demolitioners since this book was first written, and has re-arisen as prime example of a style dubbed by John Betjeman as 'faceless efficient'. But look east, and there (one hopes) will still be the great Gothic phantasmagoria of **St. Pancras Station** (1868–74, by Scott), high as a cliff crowned with pinnacled castle in a Grimm's fairy-story, drawing up with complete confidence into its sky-assaulting rage of turrets the whole shabby, unresolved hotch-potch of the station area (if you think I exaggerate, see St. Pancras on a clear gold even-ing when the sun kindles it from the west). Its value to the London skyline is inestimable, and even more so as the rigour of concrete and glass envelopes more and more of London. When Euston's rebuilding is complete, St. Pancras may cease to be a station, and its future functions seem obscure; they must not include that of serving as victim for the demoli-tioners. And do not, for all its blaze, be blinded quite to the merits of King's Cross, that Lewis Cubitt built in 1852, most functionally, in two great arches of simplicity, to close the railway tracks from the east. And here, at King's Cross, down subways of remarkable complexity, you can find your way to the Underground and almost anywhere in London.

CHAPTER TWENTY-TWO

Bank

꙰

THE password for this operation is simply BANK. Not necessarily 'the Bank', or 'Bank of England', but, with a certain magisterial aplomb, BANK. To get there is easy, for Underground transport and buses converge upon it as on a magnet. To get your bearings at first sight, it is easiest to use the subways, whence emerge by an exit to the Royal Exchange. Here a long wedge of pavement thrusts west into the traffic, upon which you can orientate. Behind you (east) the grey steps rise to the many-columned portico of the Royal Exchange; on your right (north) is Threadneedle Street and walling its north side a great massy grey wall of masonry girds the Bank of England; inside the wall, the columns and topping balustrade of which do not relieve its air of unwelcoming introspection, the Bank heaves up its bulk skywards, showing rather aggressively colossal pillared porticoes at about third or fourth-storey level, safe where no one can get at them. The Bank, known familiarly nearly for two hundred years now as the 'old Lady of Threadneedle Street', looks a bit broody, but then the eggs on which she sits, in her deep vaults, are literally of gold, ingot upon ingot. Her wall sweeps severely round to the north-west all along Prince's Street. The third road of the junction is then Poultry, running due west opposite you, whence the poulterers have centuries since yielded to the banks, and there at once, clad in rich masonry of the 1920s and 1930s, representatives of two of the Big Four senior banks (National Westminster and Midland, the others being Barclays and Lloyd's); throughout this area, almost every fifty yards or so, you will find some branch of one of the Big Four, standing like a bastion, reassuringly solidly and expensively housed, in the shifting currents of money which is the life-blood of the district. The Headquarters of all the Big Four (they were Five, but they seem steadily to be amalgamating) are here, and the Midland's now opposite you in Poultry:

not unsubtly grandiose (by Lutyens, 1924), ceremonial—crowned even by a low discreet dome. Mammon here as elsewhere has swallowed up religion: somewhere on this site was St. Mildred's Poultry, a little Wren church demolished in 1872, and also Tom Hood's birthplace.

Proceeding anti-clockwise in the count of streets,[1] running south-west is Queen Victoria Street, a Victorian improvement cut through to Blackfriars about 1867, but bombed to bits. Then the entrance to Walbrook, running south to the Thames a quarter of a mile away, is hidden by a bluff of more masonry that looks in danger of erosion by traffic, so close: a heavily rusticated, rather defensive ground story, with compressed steps up to a giant portico of Corinthian columns crowned by a pediment in which figures demonstrate quietly the Dignity and Opulence of the City, London treading firmly on Envy and introducing Plenty. This is the Mansion House, the residence of the Lord Mayor of the City of London, all in Portland stone. Then from the south-east, King William Street (another improvement, cut through from 1829 as artery to the then rebuilding London Bridge), and the legendary bankers' street, Lombard, come in together at Bank; lastly, immediately on your left Cornhill runs almost due east (once for corn but now also for money). Just by you, on the Exchange pavement, the Duke of Wellington in dark bronze high on his dark bronze horse (Chantrey's last work, 1844) looks rather out of context lacking troops (and also lacks stirrups): but he gave English commerce freedom from major wars for a century.

The three major buildings briefly glimpsed in this orientation stand for three major elements in the make-up of the City. The Exchange—for general commerce, for trade, for, in fact, exchange; the Bank—for the fact that the City still claims to be the greatest money-market in the world; the Mansion House—for the City's long tradition of stubborn corporate independence which it still maintains, for its pageantry, its rich hospitality. Each needs a rather more detailed scrutiny.

The **Mansion House** first (it is generally visitable on Saturday afternoons but on written application to the Secretary only). The building itself is Palladian in inspiration, built to the designs of George Dance the Elder, 1739–53, though later its skyline was somewhat altered; it contains at the top the

1. See map on page 334.

Lord Mayor's private apartments, and behind the great colonnade of Corinthian pillars, in the *piano nobile*, what are indeed a truly noble suite of state-rooms, a richly sumptuous example of eighteenth-century décor, including the 90-foot long Egyptian Hall. The traditions behind the Lord Mayor go back centuries before this building to about 1191, when Prince (later King) John recognised certain rights of the City; since then the City as an entity has always been a major force to be reckoned with in the affairs of the nation, accumulating slowly its thickly encrusted dominion of wealth, privilege, independence and ritual, of power. The actual administration of the square mile of the City, the chores of local government such as rates, sanitation, and so on, rests with the Court of Common Council of the Corporation of London, elected by the qualified voters of the area. A future Lord Mayor will have probably though not necessarily served on this; he is actually elected by the Liverymen and by the Aldermen. Liverymen are the members of the City Companies or Guilds, those entitled to wear the robes or *livery* of their particular craft; aldermen are the elected representatives of each ward (that is administrative division) of the City, and the future Lord Mayor will be both a member of one of the Companies, a Liveryman, and an Alderman, and also before his election will have served a year's term as one of the Sheriffs (an older office than the Mayor's, first recorded some 1300 years ago). On Michaelmas Day the Liverymen, wrapped about in their colourful furred gowns, meet in the Guildhall and select two aldermen by vote, from whom the Court of Aldermen make the final choice; there follows on the second Saturday in November the world-famous Lord Mayor's show, an archaic pageant that has drawn crowds (for years it went in ceremonial barges by Thames) for centuries: the rumbling coach, hedged by pikemen in half-armour, with the red-robed, be-feathered, be-gold-chain-swagged, new Lord Mayor for the year proceeds to the Law Courts in the Strand to present himself to the Lord Chief Justice (who represents the Monarch—the procession used to be to Westminster to the very person of the Monarch). For a year indeed the incumbent of the office of Lord Mayor of London ranks second within City limits only to the Monarch.

All this ritual (the Lord Mayor's coach, for example, carved and gilt, painted by Cipriani, and in high fashion when built in

1757; weight four tons, powered by six horses) may seem archaic and obsolete, but for the City the Lord Mayor is a very lively and potent symbol still; outsiders may note that he dines frequently and lavishly, makes over a thousand speeches in his year, has lace frills in full fig and real turtle soup, and spends vast sums of his money as well as the City's. But also he embodies the history and the still-enduring confidence of the City's belief in itself and its achievement as merchants and venturers, and its independent solidarity—and not without romance, for every Lord Mayor in some degree evokes the most famous of his predecessors—Sir Richard (Dick) Whittington, four times Mayor before his death in 1422, and imperishable as the small boy who heard at Highgate the message of Bow Bells, and turned again, to conquer London.

Then the **Royal Exchange**, hard behind you. It is the third on the site; the first was founded in 1565 by one of the greatest figures in English commercial history, Sir Thomas Gresham (see p. 346), who was piqued by the splendour of the merchants' building in Antwerp; his building burned with London in 1666, and its successor burned again in 1838. On the present building (by Sir William Tite, 1842–4), the campanile still bears aloft Gresham's crest, the great gilded vane of a grasshopper (eleven feet long) salvaged from the second fire. The tympanum over the massive range of columns bears a staid scene of lady Commerce supported by the Lord Mayor, an Alderman, a Common Councillor, and merchants of many races, with the inscription, piously selected from the Psalms by the Prince Consort, 'The Earth is the Lord's and the Fulness thereof'. At the entrance there will not always be indications of welcome, though rubbed brass plates announce that here be the Royal Exchange Assurance (a company that has been here in fact since 1720, though the company that claims to be the oldest insurance company in the world, The Sun, 1710, is just up Threadneedle Street, on a site whence it expelled in 1841 the Wren church of St. Bartholomew-by-the-Exchange). But go on in, to find the merchants all gone. The wall arcades and the great covered courtyard (with an old rough floor of Turkish honestone surviving from the earlier building) where once you could find the greatest in the City busy are empty, and no exchange business has in fact been carried on here in public since 1939.

It houses exhibitions from time to time (and showed most of the Guildhall Museum till 1968, when the fragments of past London moved on their way to the yet unbuilt Museum of London). There are also late mural decorations by various artists illustrating in picturesque detail incidents from London history; some Victorian regal statuary (and an unexpected, fierce, colossal bust of Abraham Lincoln by A. O'Connor, 1930)—but at the moment, the Exchange seems somewhat uncertain of its function.

Emerging from contemplation of this shrine to commerce of the past, the smooth pavements outside, the solid masonry, may seem a little less secure. Look across again to Poultry— there under the National Westminster Bank was found in 1929 a neolithic axe; round the corner by Prince's Street in the same year, the Roman spite known as the London Curse, a rough piece of lead marked (twice): *Titus Egnatius Tyrannus is hereby solemnly cursed, likewise Publius Cicereius Felix.* But, lapped behind its wall all along Prince's Street and round Threadneedle Street, the **Bank of England** appears indifferent to any hint of hubris or decline and fall. She was founded at the beginning of the age of reason in 1694 by a shrewd Scot, William Paterson, largely to raise money for the revolutionary and embattled administration of William III, in return for which (while still a privately owned company) it received certain privileges. Hence over the years it has become the Government's Banker, until in 1946, by a Labour Government, it was nationalised and its capital stock transferred to the Treasury; the Old Lady (the Bank was alluded to by Sheridan in 1797 as 'an elderly lady in the City of great credit and long standing') has, however, remained, according to expert witness, remarkably unmoved by the event, buttoned up behind her wall. A nod from the Chancellor of the Exchequer (but maybe it was the Bank who told him to nod) and the Bank Rate alters; the Bank controls the National Debt; it alone issues paper money, and likewise holds in sold gold a great clutch of ingots at £5,000 apiece, the national gold reserve. The Bank is the banker of the other British banks, the great balancer. The bank is public, but very very private; you may advance into the entrance hall (a little way up Threadneedle Street), observe its servants in tails of pink and waistcoats of scarlet, glimpse the central court beyond, but farther you are unlikely to get. Withdrawing, you can study her external phy-

sique, her dour expression. That stern girding wall, so chastely
severe, survives from Sir John Soane's building; built 1788–
1808, the Bank was perhaps his masterpiece, a stately and
brilliant sequence of domed halls and courts, the destruction
of which in the rebuilding of 1921–37 has been claimed by
Pevsner as 'the worst individual loss suffered by London
architecture in the first half of the twentieth century', and not
lost to enemy bombs. Now it has penitentiary rather than
fortress air, but penitentiary de luxe. Still, though the Bank
lack a coherent grandeur, it has mass (and an extension, post-
war, at the east end of St. Paul's, as big again), and seems
solid enough; her nights are secured (since the Gordon Riots
of 1780) by a detachment of the British Army which used
to tramp phlegmatically in from barracks in the West End
every evening between five and six, somewhat confusing the
traffic. These are the only state troops that the City will toler-
ate within her limits.

Round and about, within a hundred yards you will find
many other ingredients of City life. A prime specimen of the
City Companies has its premises here, in Prince's Street just
up on the left; Grocers, once a comfortably opulent building
in Neo-Dutch-Tudor of the 1890s, was gutted by fire in 1965,
but the Company itself goes back to about 1180, and is the
second of the Great Companies in precedence, and typical
enough of them. There are twelve major Companies (Mercers,
Grocers, Drapers, Fishmongers, Goldsmiths, Skinners,
Merchant Taylors, Haberdashers, Salters, Ironmongers,
Vintners and Clothworkers) and over eighty lesser ones, with
a total of over ten thousand members, the liverymen who select
the Lord Mayor. The Companies have developed of course
from the medieval craft and trade guilds. Their present use-
fulness may not be immediately apparent; the public usually
sees or reads of them as they go about some archaic or picturesque ceremony like the Vintners walking to church in
procession, preceded by two wine porters in smocks and top-
hats clearing the way with besoms, or the Stationers distri-
buting cakes and ale in the crypt of St. Paul's of an Ash Wed-
nesday; or reports of great dinners stiff with white shirts and
clanking with decorations in murmurous well-fed, well-wined
assembly. But they still exercise considerable power; if you
want to be somebody in the City civic hierarchy you must first
be a liveryman. Much of their great wealth is deployed upon

charitable and educational purposes; some of the great public schools of England were founded by the City companies (Oundle by the Grocers). Their meeting-places were almost obliterated by the Great Fire of 1666, and many again were destroyed in the blitz, but most have resurrected. None of them are open to the casual visitor, but most of them will admit a serious inquirer by previous arrangement, and for all that their fabrics have suffered they are worth seeing, not only for the treasures they harbour in plate, in formidable official portraits—but also for their rather awesome atmosphere of material well-being. Yet perhaps the most telling thing about the Companies is that they are there at all even vestigially— in other European countries the Guilds died, but the English dearly love an institution.

Then there is also religion. **St. Stephen Walbrook** will best serve as example, for it is by the master designer of the City's churches, Sir Christopher Wren, and also the Lord Mayor's parish church. Even today, hardly anywhere in the City will you be more than a street away from a church, but the density was originally far greater. In the Great Fire eighty-seven churches were burned, and in the following thirty years only fifty-one of them were rebuilt; these were later thinned out by pressure of business, and then, hideously, by the blitz. This fading of the church does not, however, simply reflect a triumph of Mammon, but also the simple disappearance of the City's parishioners. All these churches were parish churches at a time when the City was both worked and lived in, and the size of some of the parishes indicates the astonishing density of the inhabitants—St. Ethelburga in Bishopsgate was supported by a parish of three acres, an acre less than the area covered by the Bank of England's single building in Threadneedle Street. About 400,000 people work in the City now, coming in like a tidal wave between 8 and 10 a.m., pouring out again between 4 and 6, but only about 5,000 live there; to walk the tributary narrow streets and alleys about the Bank area at the week-end is a somewhat eerie experience. There is hollow emptiness as though the last trump had sounded, and every door, even many of the churches, will be closed against you; if you look for food you will be answered by empty milk-bottles. Thus the great hour of the City churches has become the lunch hour, when they spring to life with services, with concerts, and the time to visit them is between Mondays and Fridays between 11 and 3 (some but by no means all are open all day (see pp. 477–8).

St. Stephen, to serve here as prime example of the City churches, stands almost immediately behind the southern end of the Mansion House, on Walbrook. Typically, the exterior is plain, almost drab, a box simply, one might think from the outside, from which to force the fancy flower of the spire. You go in up a rather abrupt flight of steps (abrupt, because this was the bank of Walbrook, the stream that ran—and still runs, but in a deep pipe now—down to the Thames and about which the Romans built densely); at the top 'through a vestibule of dubious obscurity . . . a halo of dazzling light flashes at once upon the eye; and a lovely band of Corinthian columns, of beauteous proportions, appear in magic mazes before you . . . On a second look, the columns slide into complete order, like a band of elegant young dancers, at the close of a quadrille'. Thus the most eloquent of Wren's admirers in the early nineteenth century, Elmes, saw it, and thus, restored from war damage, it still forms and reforms within itself with perfect intricacy as you move about it. In its beautifully resolved complexity, St. Stephen is not typical of Wren's City churches, for it is the most elaborately ambitious, the most Baroque, of them all; built between 1672 and 1679, Wren designed it while involved with his early designs for St. Paul's, and St. Stephen is, in small, a variation on the same theme, the marriage of the un-English central dome with a traditional English church plan of nave with aisles, chancel and crossing transepts; in St. Stephen, moreover, this is contained within the plain oblong of the 'hall' church which in the late seventeenth century was the logical answer to the needs of the Anglican liturgy for a parish congregation. Wren himself summed these up: 'in our reformed Religion,' he wrote, it was essential 'that all who are present can both hear and see'. It was not enough for Anglicans, unlike Romanists, to 'hear the Murmur of the Mass, and see the Elevation of the Host'; English churches should 'be fitted for Auditories'. The altar tends to be, relatively, unemphasised, subdued in front of the richly carved wooden reredos, on which are written loud and clear the Paternoster, Decalogue and Creed; the pulpit, often very richly carved, with stairs and decorated canopy or sounding board, is as much emphasised, for the sermon (as you can check from almost any Sunday entry in Pepys's Diary) was the great excitement of church-going. The congregation's relish seemed to Dr. Johnson in the next century indeed improper—'There prevailed in those days an indecent custom; when the preacher touched any favourite topic, in a manner that delighted his audiences, their approbation was expressed by a loud hum, continued in pro-portion to their zeal and pleasure. When Burnet preached, part of his congregation hummed so loudly that he sat down to enjoy it, and rubbed his face in his handkerchief.'

In St. Stephen everyone can hear and see perfectly, for all its complexity. Upon the oblong of the plan, the columns create nave with aisles, transepts and chancel, a cross-shape marked more firmly in mid-air by the rich architrave that links the scrolly tops of the columns. But it is then perhaps that the most entrancing feature of the church comes, as the arches spring from the octagon formed by the eight central pillars and modulate into the hemisphere of the dome. As architecture, St. Stephen for me offers a purer pleasure even than St. Paul's: as a resolution of a problem it is of almost abstract lucidity and elegance, yet also the most subtly sensuous delight—it is a church you must move about in, as though in a sculpture turned outside in, to see it shape and re-shape itself, and move among its flooding light.

Though formally richer than almost all the City churches, as I have suggested, otherwise in texture and in mood St. Stephen is fairly typical. Restoration still has to re-gild the roses of the dome, and the pews (of which Wren anyway seems not to have approved) were already removed in a Victorian clear-out, but there is, salvaged from the blitz, still a wealth of that dark carved wood that works like a sonorous yet lively bass register against the cream or near-white plaster and the gilt of the City's churches. The popular association of almost all such carving with Grinling Gibbons is reasonable enough as it is nearly all in his manner—a perennial harvest offering of fruit and flower, of ripe curve, of ripe and naked children—though in fact a number of skilful hands were employed. Here you can see the children dancing on the top of the sounding board of the ample pulpit, and there is endur-ing vitality in the sinuous carving of altar rails and pulpit steps, and a burst of splendour in the gallery and organ to the west. None of Wren's churches are sombre, and in many of them a sudden assault and piercing of sunlight will even provoke gaiety—a quality that has disturbed many more puritanically-minded Englishmen who have complained forthrightly that in them they do not find God. It is true that the chubby children more closely resemble pagan *putti* than angels, and true perhaps that the buildings are not numinous in the awful way that the groves of Westminster Abbey, for example, can be, haunted and charged in depth and shadow by mystery. It is true also that their furnishings are often worldly—the splendid iron swords-stands, for example—but that God or divinity at least, is not apprehensible in them I will never admit. They are the expression of an enviable confidence of spirit: that God, if as yet unfathomed, must ultimately be fathomable to human reason and faith in conjunction, that He is the final resolution. Of such a faith, logical yet inspired, the resolution of St. Stephen in its cool clarity is a just reflection, and a true expression of the spirit not only of Wren himself, but of that brilliant generation of which he was but one luminary, and which included Newton. Its confidence in a divine order permeated through to congregations of less demanding intellectual order, and even a century later you can find Boswell expressing it in his manner: in July 1763, he went to St. Mary-le-Bow, 'the true centrical church for the bluff citizens. I had many comfortable ideas . . .'

Typical, too, is the evaporation in Wren's creation of the earlier churches of St. Stephen; they go back in fact to before 1100. The first building was on the other (west) side of Walbrook; the second, burned of course in the fire, on the present site, was of 1429 and John Dunstable (d. 1453), so-called father of English harmony, was buried there. But now it is all Wren, and you would never guess that the architect actually buried there is that brilliant successor to and in some ways reactor against Wren, Sir John Vanbrugh (d. 1726). 'Lie heavy on him, earth, for he Laid many a heavy load on thee,' runs a famous malicious epitaph on Vanbrugh, but Wren, though unwittingly, provided his younger rival with a canopy that is in its majesty all light.

I have lingered thus long in St. Stephen because it provides introduction and key to much that is common through the City churches; we shall visit most of these churches, those that still stand, later and much more cursorily. They have in common a remarkable coherence of character, though the variety within this coherence is equally remarkable. The unique character comes simply from the fact that while Wren doubt-less played not much more than a supervisory role in the de-tail of many of the churches, it was still his one mind and imagination that designed some fifty of them after the holo-caust of 1666, a challenge and an opportunity offered to no other architect in history on such a scale. If the exteriors as I have noted are sometimes unremarkable, this is probably because, in the dense context within which he had to build, they were often simply not visible, apart from their façades; externally they flower in their spires, which Wren certainly conceived in almost choreographic terms about the overriding dome of St. Paul's itself. This spire-scape has gradually sunk from view as London over the last two hundred years has grown up in height of building among it; you can only see it now in old topographical paintings, most admirably in those of Canaletto or of Samuel Scott or Marlow. But on the other hand, particularly against the great blank of gridded glass offered by much of post-blitz architecture, the individual charm and variousness of the spires is perhaps even enhanced, as you can see, coming out of St. Stephen, in the delicate idio-syncrasy of its tiered steeple in the setting of the mammoth Bucklersbury House on the other side of Walbrook, and the other new massive building that has gone up by the church's eastern flank.

Back in front of the Mansion House, your eye, conditioned now by St. Stephen, may well be wounded by the lack of co-herence, the bittiness of the central hub of the City of London about the Bank of England: almost by its sheer lack of hub-ness. True, there is a certain response of Bank to Exchange to Mansion House in that all show grand columns to the world, and there is a constant and massive onslaught of traffic, but that is about all. But this view will nevertheless tell you by in-ference something of what to look out for in the City, and what not to look out for. The stuff of this central area particularly is woven of the elements we have noted: the banks and insur-ance offices, the brokers' offices, the rich portals of the City Companies; the spires, the still and sumptuous splendours of the church interiors. The essential texture that all these create is not to be found in the main traffic arteries, but in the lanes, courts and alleys that thread off them—very often foot-ways only. The townscape of the City is registered by one angle-shot after another, and the viewing range is likely to be not more than fifteen or twenty yards, or less. London as a whole is reticent generally about its sights; the City within London is positively secret. Yet it is fabulous to walk about in, and is capable of endless surprise. In the next chapter I have tried to trace a route which, while it scarcely ever wanders more than a quarter of a mile away from the Bank, will thread together an extraordinary variety.

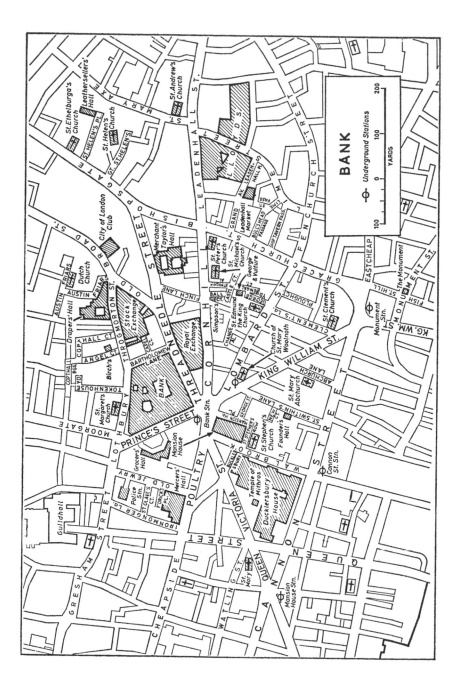

CHAPTER TWENTY-THREE

A Circuit about the Bank

❧

IF sound in wind and limb, assault the **Monument**.

Reaching the Monument's base is no problem: it has its station on the District Line, or a No. 13 bus will take you almost to its foot. It sticks out of the steeply sloping ground at the junction of its own street and of Fish Street Hill, and indeed thrusts heavenwards out of a rich odour of fish (you can see Billingsgate Market from its foot, at the bottom of Monument Street). It is open for climbing from 9 to 6 (4 in winter) and, on Sundays between May and September only, between 2 and 6.

The Monument celebrates, in a not untypical London mood, catastrophe: the Great Fire of 1666. A massive Roman Doric column, freestanding on its square plinth, built 1671–7. Its original design was more markedly in the complementary mood of *resurgam*: Wren first drew it out with brass flames flickering all the way up it, and a resurrecting phoenix at its apex—the final gilt urn that tops it he seems not to have approved. The base has a spirited Baroque allegorical relief by the Dane, C. G. Cibber, showing London destroyed and London restored—Time lifts delicately up the ravaged lady London from her ruins; Plenty and Triumph attend, while Charles II in Roman kilt urges on others, an architect included, to the task of rebuilding. The Column as sited looks somewhat haphazard, but is as commemoration almost finickally precise: 202 feet high, it is said to be 202 feet away from the spot in Pudding Lane to the east, where on the night of 2nd September, 1666, the fire broke out, to burn for five days, to consume utterly some 436 acres of the City's fabric, including about 13,000 houses and 89 churches. Its progress is vividly recorded in the pages of Pepys and of Evelyn.

The ascent up the interior should be made. It is 311 steepish steps on a cramped spiral, but you tread in the footsteps of

legion upon legion of Londoners and visitors through the last
three hundred years, and should you pant, Addison was there
before you panting, stopping several times to recover breath.
And at the top, flooding the strait platform, there is a huge
sky, and London cluttered below, disorderly about the broad
shining wander of Thames. The immediate area laid waste by
the Great Fire you can gauge—from this side of the Tower of
London on the east to just beyond the tiered spire of St.
Bride's Fleet Street, way west of St. Paul's dome. Though
small in the huge saucerful of greater London between the
Kent and Surrey hills to the south and those of Hampstead
and Highgate to the north, the fire-swept area is big enough,
and within it you will find hardly a trace of pre-1666 London
above ground: the City's antiquity, its middle-ages, its Elizabethan timber and plaster work, were burned out. Even of the
immediate post-fire rebuilding, almost nothing has survived
with the noble exception of Wren's churches, and little even
from the eighteenth century except for a few more churches
and some public buildings.

The fabric of the City building is really Victorian (Dickensian still in places) and Edwardian—and the Edwardian style
in the City goes right up to 1939, for the City was very reactionary about modern architecture. Yet it is built on a street
plan which is basically still very much that of medieval London, for though Wren, Evelyn and others drew out logical
town-plans for a new London almost before the ashes of the
Great Fire were cold, they were impracticable in terms of the
politics, the possible, of existing property and available
money. It is the peculiar mixture of massive wrought Victorian and Edwardian façades, of bleak, cliff-like, Victorian and
Edwardian backside, often almost in conflict across narrow
lanes, concentrated in pressure one upon the other, that for
me produces much of the nervous and exciting tension of the
City. And this is still true, though from the top of the Monument you can see further radical changes made since the war:
the monuments to the second great catastrophe to ravage the
City raise their squared and shining heads to the sky, the glass
and steel office buildings that are everywhere going up on the
sites devastated by blitz between December, 1940 and 1944.
Indeed, the City is changing more violently, more radically,
than at any time since the Great Fire. Sometimes it may seem
(at London Wall, for example) as though it is sloughing a

complete reptilian skin for a new one. It changes literally from the pavement up: the old York paving stones beneath your feet, idiosyncratic in size, each weathering like an old face and cracking, when it cracks, with sharp decision, they are yielding to standard oblongs, sometimes pinkish, of synthetic stone (that crumbles dissolutely when it cracks). Brick and Portland stone give way to metal and glass (often oddly amorphous in character for all their precision of grid); gas, which still lingers in the City lamps, gives way to electricity, and at a winter's dusk in the new buildings shoal the dead-bright fluorescent tubes. Away to the west the 500-foot Post Office mast by Tottenham Court Road mocks St. Paul's dome, looking like a giant's spindle, a component part of some mammoth mile-high city still to be built. Time perhaps to come down from the Monument; the most direct, plumb-line descent from the top has been vetoed for over a hundred years by the cage, so many used it as the last convenience of despair; so back down the dim spiral, where you can cheer on, if rather smugly, those labouring upwards.

The way I now suggest is a day's threading through, and around and about, the heart of this area that was burned and built again and bombed and built again, to give some idea of its intimate texture, of the heart of its confusion; it is also, should you love Wren's churches, a glorious church crawl.

First up **Fish Street Hill** from the Monument to one of the big traffic junctions of the City that has first to be navigated: from your right comes in Eastcheap (where once the meat market now at Leadenhall was sited); reading round from it are Gracechurch Street; then the crossing of King William Street that comes in on your left from London Bridge and throbs north-west to the Bank; finally running near due west, Cannon Street; the last two are largely Victorian throughway improvements (though Cannon Street was once Candlewick Street, from the candle-makers who lived and traded there, and the Grace of Gracechurch is probably 'grass' for a haymarket of sorts—all over the City the street names thus record former concentrations of trades). All banked deep with the masonry of commerce now, and lethal with diesel fumes and wheels, not for lingering.

Go left into **Cannon Street**. The second turning off this to the right is Abchurch Lane, and in it is **St. Mary Abchurch** (? from Up Church), by Wren, 1681–6. And as near to a domestic habitation, God be welcome, as you will find in much of the City, such a comfortable brick box, stone-dressed, behind what was its graveyard and is now a simple space to sit in, with seats, and a tower with a little lantern and the most delicate of lead spires. Inside, with endearing pretension, it has a shallow dome with Virtues, slightly clumsy (but then they so often are), generally ascribed to but certainly not by Sir James Thornhill; the dome seems almost hitched in, one support being a stray pillar (the site is not quite square). But the woodwork is the thing, and the gorgeous reredos really is by Grinling Gibbons (his somewhat urgent demands for payment for the 'olter pees'—his English was not strong— still survive); for the hallmark of Gibbons's quality look at the lightly lively swags of flowers, so vital it seems that to-morrow they must fade. The pulpit still has its steps, the font has a cover with a little niched pavilion, though the kennel for Christian dogs under one of the pews has gone.

Back in Cannon Street, the next turning to the right is **St. Swithin's Lane**. St. Swithin itself (by Wren, 1677–85) was just beyond this, but was blitzed and wiped from the face of the City. Set in its face was a stone known as the **London Stone**; the Elizabethan antiquary Camden took it to be a 'military, like that in the Forum at Rome, from whence all distances are measured', and in Shakespeare's *Henry VI* the rebel Jack Cade strikes it with a staff to mark his lordship of London. Centuries of such bruising have reduced it to an unremarkable umpish anonymity. It has been replaced on its old site in a new building, the Bank of China.

Going up St. Swithin's Lane, you can glimpse through a building on the left the minute former churchyard of St. Swithin, now a garden big enough to hold a couple of benches; then, No. 13, a fairly lush Victorian porch into Founders' Hall (one of the minor City Companies), but New Court, the head-quarters of the Rothschilds, most legendary of banking names, has been sumptuously rebuilt.

All new from here on. Left into **George Street** (for St. Mary Woolnoth, the church facing you at this cross-roads (see p. 350), left again into the narrow crack taking you round the back of Mansion House and between it and St. Stephen (see p. 328) into **Walbrook**. On the other side of Walbrook,

Bucklersbury House fills up with square shiny precision its square acres; but walking around it into Queen Victoria Street and following it down, there in the angle of the brand-new building is the Roman Temple of Mithras. Excavated in 1954, it is getting on for 1,900 years old; now, moved and set up on its little plateau in the arms of the shiny modern building, it is like a *memento mori*, the skull in the portrait of a man in his prime. What remains is as it were the ground plan in relief of a sixty-foot long temple with columns and a triple apsed end; the sculpture found with it is at present in the Guildhall Museum (see p. 396). The Mithraic cult, worship of a sun god that came from Asia Minor to Rome, become very much of a military free-masonry among the legions, who took it to the end of the Empire; it was a tough and virile cult, with emphasis on ordeal.

Huge areas of Queen Victoria Street were flattened by bombs, but over the last decades, as the new buildings have gone up, the Victorian survivors seem to have flowered in a new youth in contrast, so various, so rich in detail and in the broken play of light and shadow. And beyond the west extremity of Bucklersbury House, over the street at the corner of Watling Street is an older survivor, the tower with pinnacles of **St. Mary Aldermary**. The tower, which survived the Great Fire, is probably much as it was rebuilt about 1510, though revised in shape slightly in 1701 and again in the nineteenth century (the finials of the pinnacles are even in post-war fibre glass). The interior, however, is a remarkable specimen of Wren's adaptability (1681–2); the money for rebuilding seems to have been given on condition the church followed the former design; the result is Wren Gothic, and St. Mary has been claimed as the 'earliest true Gothic Revival church in London'. It makes a delightful concoction: a big, light, church with twin aisles, roofed with a filigree fan-tracery with little saucer-domes set in. It is more like icing than the functional sinews of true stone fan vaulting (it is all in plaster), and further succulence is added by a nostril-dilating haze of incense, for St. Mary is high (even if not, judged by density of smoke and number of candles, as high as St. Magnus). It is now one of the so-called 'Guild Churches', without a parish but serving the weekday needs of City workers.

North from St. Mary up Queen Street: a gorgeous shot of

the dark dome of St. Paul's riding the sky between the smooth flanks of post-blitz buildings along Watling Street on your left. Up Queen Street, a typically City narrowing view, as if rather grudgingly allowed you, to the eighteenth-century Gothic front of the Guildhall (see p. 394). At Cheapside turn right and then almost at once left into the little slot, large enough to take one slender lorry perhaps, of **Ironmonger Lane** ('so called', noted Stow, 'of Ironmongers living there, whereof I read in the reign of Edward I, etc. . . .'). First building on the right is the Hall of the greatest perhaps of all City Companies, the **Mercers**: blitzed, now rebuilt traditionally, with a discreetly handsome door that extrudes a canopy on grand occasions, but now also with a practical roll-up garage door next to it. On this site Thomas Becket, martyr and saint, is said to have been born about 1118, and on it there was founded by his sister, about 1190, a hospital which came under the patronage of the Mercers. After the Dissolution they took over the chapel; here is a most beautifully poignant figure of the Dead Christ, probably of the early sixteenth century (entrance usually only by appointment).

Shadowy, narrow, not more than 150 yards long, holding a little hush among business, with light-catchers angled out from its walls, Ironmonger Lane was of the essence of the City. Now tidied up, it conceals under No. 11, probably a late eighteenth-century house, a Roman pavement which the owners will generally kindly show to a visitor. Off to the left, struck sterile through the buildings into King Street, a still narrower slot in white glazed tiles called beyond doubt Prudent Passage. To the right, with a motor scooter or two parked outside, a hint of a garden, trees, and a church tower rising sedately among. This was Wren's **St. Olave**, demolished in 1888. Now the tower is simply the somewhat grand entrance to a house. St. Olave's Court takes you east through into **Old Jewry** (the London ghetto before Edward I expelled the Jews in 1290); a little wider this, but with two remarkable little courts off it. Turn right out of St. Olave's Court, and twenty yards down Old Jewry, is Frederick's Place, and you are back in the eighteenth century, very trim; on each side brick houses, with painted ironwork, butted into the tall backside of Mercers' Hall. There are cobbles, there are even torch extinguishers, and in all a haunting dream of urbane domesticity, of what much of the City must have been like when the great

Adam brothers developed this little court as a speculation in 1776. Back in Old Jewry (turning left up it) near the top, a glimpse of a concealed court that seems now most Victorian, Dickensian—Fagin might pop out; but what will in fact not pop, but stately plod, out is likely to be a policeman for here is the headquarters of the City of London Police, topped by the crested helmets and with red and white arm-bands which distinguish them from the Metropolitan Police. This is a further reminder of the City's independence.

Right at the top of Old Jewry, into Lothbury and almost at once the big traffic crossing where Prince's Street goes north into Moorgate; from here the east side of Prince's Street and the south side of Lothbury are stonily enigmatic with the Bank of England's girding wall. From a plain façade, **St. Margaret Lothbury** lifts a white tower and a dark lead obelisk spire. The interior is not to be missed. Rebuilt by Wren from 1686, it is spatially simple, a nave with a south aisle now arcaded off, but has become almost a museum of its own and of other, now destroyed, churches' furnishings, with, dominating all, a gorgeous great screen with a weighty central pediment and a vast spread eagle, supported on the most exquisitely delicate twisted openwork balusters that look as if they should snap under an eighth of the weight they carry (it is imported from All Hallows, Dowgate). The pulpit is again a formidable piece of carving, its tester frilled with swags, birds and lively cherubs, and came from All Hallows also. The communion rails, as also the reredos in the south aisle, come from St. Olave's, whose abandoned tower we passed in Ironmonger Lane, and is all contemporary. The cover of the font, with a dove with bough rather trapped in a lovely lean-to of cherubs, is also St. Olave's, while the bowl, often ascribed to Gibbons himself and certainly of the most urbane sophistication, shows in its pale reliefs the dove again returning to an Ark like a Restoration man-o'-war without masts, and a very pretty Adam and Eve. Also, a rarity in City churches, some good busts. It makes up a most sumptuous rich assembly, aptly, for St. Margaret is the parish church of the Bank of England.

Immediately next to St. Margaret is (No. 7), a Victorian building which in its vigour of 1866 Venetian Gothic, its almost manic (yet beautifully finished) exuberance of decoration, always refreshes me, and is a splendid foil to the Bank's wall opposite. Follow round this building into the foot-passage of **Tokenhouse Yard**, deep in banks. At the week-end there will be no one, and if you come then you might pause, for an echo of that other disaster that swept the City three hundred years ago, the Great Plague of 1665:

'Passing through Token House Yard in Lothbury, of a sudden a casement violently opened just over my head, and a woman gave three frightful screeches, and then cried, "Oh Death, Death, Death!" in a most inimitable tone, and which struck me with horror and a chillness in my blood. There was nobody to be seen in the whole street, neither did any other window open; for people had no curiosity now in any case; nor could any body help one another; so I went on to pass into Bell Alley . . .' The voice is Defoe's. He was not in fact present, but recreating the scene in that brilliant and enduring report, *The Journal of the Plague Year*. One who was courageously present, when the Court and most officials had fled to the country from the rumble of the death carts and the cry 'Bring out your Dead!' was Pepys, and in his Diary as nowhere else you can catch the atmosphere of lurking disaster in which nevertheless those who stayed went on living.

The end of Tokenhouse Yard looks like a cul-de-sac; however, there, next to the door of No. 12 at the end, you will find an opening that looks like a private way into a house; push through it but not too impetuously or you will go through the window of one of the characteristic little gents' barber shops of the City at its end. Turn right here to **Copthall Buildings,** currently being demolished; Copthall Avenue goes off to your left, with a jazzy building with gilt fins looking startling new (all this area is broodily overshadowed by a monster tower that the Drapers' Company has developed between Copthall Avenue and Throgmorton Avenue). Copthall Buildings turns sharply right by a left-over little brick house with a stucco porch, and here you may begin to be claustrophobic, but pushing on, you will probably see a parked car or two so there must be a way out, and Copthall Buildings leads into Angel Court, the angelic host perhaps being represented now by branches of Midland, Westminster and Barclays. Here was till 1974, on a near-miniature scale, windows set in black wood, one of the famous chop-houses of the City, Birch's, advertising still (and with what elegance of lettering, gold on frosted glass) *Jelly (Invalids)—Wines—Liqueurs—Iced Punch—Soups.* Heedless the City bent on mammon tends to destroy its own character. So through to **Throgmorton Street.**

If you have come on a weekday, the maze which you have, I hope, just navigated, will probably have been busy with pedestrians, men in black suits, and often brolly and bowler: brokers, jobbers and business men, and usually moving briskly, for the air here is the yeasty one of the Stock Exchange. Among them you will probably also sight a stately top-hat or so, and their wearers are likely to be bill brokers, directors of one of the City's discount houses, who still daily pad about from bank to bank, contemptuous of the telephone, borrowing a few thousand from those who have it loose and lending it forthwith to those who need it (and of course brewing a profit for themselves). Throgmorton Street itself, as you turn left into it, used to seem, for all that it is one of the most famous streets in the world, still partly medieval so to speak in its Victorianism. Narrow, with a rich fretty texture, gas lamps on brackets, its façades used to yearn together from opposite sides of the street and to exclude the unnatural sky. It still possesses some nice comforts for business men: Slater's Bodega with its name in mosaic, shops for cigars and a branch even of the Bond Street chocolate-makers, Bendick's, and on the left-hand side through a doorway flanked by two vast caryatids is the Hall of the big Drapers' Company, which has tucked away in its invisible gardens a mulberry tree said to go back to James I.

The **Stock Exchange** itself used to have a neat, very blind façade, running down most of the south side of Throgmorton Street and doubling round the corner along the north side of the beginning of Old Broad Street; very sober, with just a gloss in polished granite here and there. From 1967, this changed dramatically, as, by phases, the old building was bashed down, grubbed out, and in its place has grown its contemporary replacement. This is of average tediousness—an attempt to give it visual accent, in the shape of a soaring finned tower on the Old Broad Street Corner, is not unspectacular but difficult to admire from near its base as round that swirl the usual pedestrian-searing hurricane that high-rise buildings breed. The enlightened habit of the Stock Exchange, began in 1953, of maintaining a viewing gallery for the public still holds however. Here, you can watch the 'floor of the house' in action, and there are guides to explain the technicalities.

At the corner of Throgmorton Street and Old Broad Street, a lane, Austin Friars, goes off on the left to the Dutch Church, once an Augustinian Priory, but made over by Edward VI in 1550 to Dutch and other Protestant refugees. It was bombed, and is now rebuilt entirely. Just up Old Broad Street on the right you can glimpse the City of London Club, neo-classic (1832), in stucco among the bank masonry, very like a West End Club. Following down the wall of the Stock Exchange, you will come to the junction with Threadneedle Street, and so left (with the entrance, No. 30, to the biggest of the City Companies, Merchant Taylors' Hall, chartered in 1327 but gutted in the war and rebuilt) up to the corner of **Bishopsgate**, where on your left the former National Provincial Bank queens it in the large majesty of 1865 (by Gibson), eloquent with pale statuary on its roofline. Now National Westminster, its façade is being preserved, if somewhat shrunk by a 500 foot high-rise development going up behind it. Up some 150 yards of Bishopsgate, bank upon bank, and then cross the road to the minute St. Ethelburga, that almost crouches between its massive neighbours with a plain but stubborn face of common rag-stone, an expression tempered by an absurdly toy-like square bell-turret on top. It reads, from the pavement up: door late fourteenth century; window fifteenth, turret perhaps eighteenth century but weather-vane 1671; its modest little interior is similarly of all periods, for we are now just north of where the Great Fire stopped. A more remarkable survivor, back down Bishopsgate on the same side (past St. Helen's Place, a close containing the Hall of the Leathersellers Company), will be found in **Great St. Helen's**, a passageway that expands into a plot of green, with trees; slightly sunk at the end, St. Helen. Grey stone, with two big fifteenth-century windows, and a most subtle suggestion of embattled gabling undulating under a pretty seventeenth-century bell-turret. It is not a small church, but in 1969 was reduced to seeming doll's scale by a high, sleek Manhattan-style tower beyond it.

Down the steps into the entrance, and a world that seems miles away from the banks outside; in a dim religious light of Victorian glass, under the low-pitched wooden roof, the church seems big, slightly lopsided, and of mysterious space—then as your eyes adjust, very rich in texture, brooding upon its antiquity. It is really two churches: the nave of one, the north (on your left) was the church of a Benedictine nunnery, built about the beginning of the thirteenth century on to the parish church to its south. The two churches were then separated by a more solid screen than the present columns (of about 1475), and it is curious to imagine the two congregations seated in their near separation. The nuns were not always too discreet; once they were rebuked for waving over the screen and another time instructed that 'alle daunsying and revelyng be utterly forborne among you except Christmasse...' They vanished, of course, at the Reformation, and the parish absorbed both churches. The lopsided impression comes from the fact that the original parish church is broken into two, nave and chancel, and has also a transept to the south. The church was somewhat refurbished in the mid-seventeenth century, and some very sumptuous furnishings date from then: the plain shaped but very pretty font in coloured marbles (1632), the dark carved door casings, and in the chancel a very rare, elaborately carved wooden sword rest of 1665 (almost all City swords rests are in iron, as is the second one here). There is also a wealth of fifteenth- and early sixteenth-century monuments (and a few recent ones—an enigmatic plain tablet just right of the door to Fanny Gamble, d. 1907: *Faithful over a few things*). Some nice angular brasses mainly in the transept, which is full almost in Westminster Abbey style with monuments, also with the bulge of the organ. There, too, unusually good late fifteenth-century alabaster effigies, John de Ooteswich and his wife, also Sir John and Lady Crosby, he a very successful Grocer but wearing knightly armour (his very ambitious house stood close by, but is now to be found, part of it, in Chelsea—see p. 207). But the characteristic quality of achievement of the memorials of St. Helen's is set by the tombs of the Elizabethan and Jacobean periods; it was then that England, hitherto on the fringe of the Continent and poorly placed to play a dominant part in European commerce, found herself central in the world of the great oceans of the new continents opening up; aided by the temporary decay of Flanders, then by Drake's victory over the Spanish, the London merchants began to establish that grip on world commerce and finance that they have never entirely lost. Some of them are here; they were not always pleasant—that gaudy (Westminster Abbey style) monument, with strapwork, arches and much bright paint, to Sir John Spencer (d. 1609) and his wife, for example; 'Rich Spencer', Lord Mayor, and mean. But just beyond, a wall monument to Alderman Richard Staper (d. 1608) has an epitaph that might have been written by Hakluyt: . . . *Hee was the greatest merchant in his tyme, the chiefest actor in discoveri of the trades of Turkey and East India, a man humble in prosperity, payneful and ever ready in the Affaires Publique, and Discretely Careful of his Private* . . . Of such flesh and spirit was the best in the City made. There are others, with voluminous families kneeling about them. A curious tomb is that for Sir Julius Caesar Adelmare (1636), Lord Chief Justice; on the plain black marble-top, a trompe l'oeil deed in marble, with the seal broken, recording that he had paid his debt to nature. And alongside him, very fittingly here, the great Sir Thomas Gresham (d. 1579), housed in a sumptuously plain marble tomb, with fluted sides and black top in restrained, truly classic detail, and of beautiful quality. A rarely apt memorial to a true Renaissance merchant prince, it makes the other monuments look somewhat gauchely provincial. Gresham was born into the City's purple, both his father and uncle being Lord Mayors, but he himself became not merely one of the leading Londoners, but one of the important men of Europe: courtier, statesman, diplomat, besides merchant and great financier. He helped largely to restore the credit of the English crown under three monarchs, and his hand is behind the moves that shifted the centre of the cloth trade to London, that pushed out the privileged merchants of the Hanseatic league, that led London to displace Antwerp as the commercial capital of Europe. The Royal Exchange was his personal creation, and when he died he provided for Gresham College, an educational foundation dispensing free lectures. His name is immortal in the City.

Before you leave St. Helen, note the modest little tomb chest in the middle of the floor to William Kirwin, 1594, with its Latin inscription: 'To me who have adorned London with noble buildings the fates have afforded this narrow house . . .' On the sides, incised, pale wraiths of likenesses of himself and family. Emerging, you will see on your left the high bronzed tower of the Commercial Union Building: sail (on the crisp down-draughts) between this and the also new P. & O. building to the corner of St. Mary Axe on Leadenhall Street. Here is **St. Andrew Undershaft,** a plain grey church mainly about 1530; the shaft it was under was the Cornhill Maypole, finally destroyed after the curate of St. Katherine Cree had denounced it as a heathen idol in 1549. It has some good monuments: a big one to Lord Mayor Hammersley, unusually lively for its date (1636). Hans Holbein lived in this parish (he died of the Plague of 1543), and is commemorated by a tablet, but the true local shrine here for Londoners is the famous monument to the first and still in many ways the most attractive of her topographers, John Stow, who published his *Survey of London* in 1598 and died in poverty in 1605; he is shown half-length, with pen in hand, industrious as ever, and every year the current Lord Mayor renews the pen in his hand.

Leadenhall Street is a big thoroughfare with the usual banks, but here too a very strong emphasis on the offices of the great shipping companies. Over the road a little to your right is the great underwriter of their risks in the perennial battle with the hazards of the sea: **Lloyd's,** one of the most famous institutions in London which took root like other institutions in a coffee-house towards the end of the seventeenth century. This, run by Edward Lloyd, was in Lombard Street. The pre-war building fronts on Leadenhall Street and runs down Lime Street, across which a bridge connects to the post-war building on the other side; the entrance here looks rather like that of a largish aseptic railway station, but if you can get in (entrance by introduction from a member only) it is well worth it. The big 340-foot new main 'Room' is a spectacle as is that of the Stock Exchange; in the centre is the Lutine Bell which is struck once for news of disaster and twice for good news (the *Lutine* sank in 1799 carrying near a million and a half of gold which Lloyd's had underwritten). Nowadays risks are spread among syndicates and combinations of syndicates of the 5,000 members, and the business extends far beyond maritime insurance, even to underwriting hurricane risks in America. The local deity of Lloyd's is Nelson, who at Trafalgar in 1805 destroyed the French Navy; relative peace at sea, which Lloyd's even more than most people have reason to appreciate, lasted thereafter for a century. His relics enshrined here include the logbook of the frigate *Euryalus* with the record of the immortal pre-battle signal: *England expects* . . .

The area around Lloyd's is normally milling with pedestrians, brisk insurance brokers and underwriters about their business, with something of the same air of an office extended into the open as the Stock Exchange. But down Lime Street turn first right—into one of those changes, entirely unexpected, of mood and tempo, at which the City is so expert; you are in **Leadenhall Market,** centred about its big two-storied, cross-shaped iron and glass shelter; splendidly and robustly Victorian, with copious decoration. Originally for poultry, from the fourteenth century, the market is now very general and in fact a shopping centre of small shops with all necessities of life, with cheap cafés and some excellent pubs—the Lamb at the market crossing, with its dining-room above, corn sprays on the windows and opulent lamps, is famous. The whole area smells rich of life, of meat and fruit, of ironmongers and vegetables. It has been busy since Roman times, and, from the market west, deep in the ground, there are traces of the huge central London basilica about which the Romans probably centred their commercial life; it has been estimated as over 500 feet long. The alleys going west—Bull's Head Passage or Ship Tavern Passage—take you into Gracechurch Street; right here brings you up to **St. Peter** on the other side at the corner of Cornhill, and you are well back in Great Fire area, for this church is Wren again (1677–87). It has a singular elegant doorless façade on Gracechurch Street, and round at its back the red-brick tower hoists up a little dome and an obelisk, topped over-all by a ten-foot St. Peter's key, from among two great plane trees in a tiny dusty churchyard. Inside it is biggish, with a tunnel vault and aisles, a fine pulpit, but in the furnishings most notably one of the only two chancel screens in Wren churches (cf. St. Margaret Lothbury), designed, according to contemporary witness, by Wren's daughter.

Thirty yards farther down Cornhill (otherwise mainly banks, including the big headquarters of Lloyd's Bank), another Wren church, **St. Michael's,** with a tall Gothic tower sometimes called Wren's last work (finished 1721) but actually designed by Hawksmoor; the interior was ravaged in the nineteenth century by 'restoration', and almost the only surviving furnishings are the font and a most elaborately expressive pelican in her piety (close by the entrance). Thomas Gray was baptised here, and the church has his walking stick; he was born in 1716 a few yards farther down Cornhill, where a modern plaque with a portrait is set into the Union Discount Company's premises—the *Elegy in a Country Churchyard* does not here, for me, come readily to mind.

Immediately past this, insert yourself into the masonry in the slot of **Ball Court** to find facing you the cheerful front of one of the most famous of City taverns, Simpsons; if you do not go in, on down a still narrower slot, left into Castle Court (bigger, two can walk comfortably abreast) and an even more famous tavern, the **George and Vulture**. Chaucer knew the George (the Living Vulture was a separate inn up to the Great Fire), but the tavern is above all Mr. Pickwick's and the City Pickwick Club still meets here. An excellent view from here, over a wine-shop and St. Michael's Alley, of the sun-catching pinnacles of St. Michael's tower. In St. Michael's Alley in 1657, a youth from Smyrna, Pasqua Rosee, 'obtained leave to pitch a tent and sell liquor'—the first coffee-shop.

If you follow round the George and Vulture you come into George Yard, which looks minute now in the shadow of Barclays' headquarters but was a most important coaching terminus, and this brings you to the legendary street of the bankers, **Lombard Street** (Lombards from Italy became the London specialists in finance after Edward I expelled the Jews). A few yards up to your left on the far side of the road is the opening to Plough Court, whence all traces of Alexander Pope's birthplace, other than a commemorative plaque, have long vanished, but immediately on your right is another Wren church, **St. Edmund the King**; its tower in Portland stone has a rather gay, larky, lead lantern and spire—it is difficult to see this from the depths of Lombard Street, but you can sight it from the old churchyard at the back. The church is unorthodox in that it runs south and north instead of west–east, the altar being to the north.

Lombard Street is sedate now, sumptuous in the rich surface masonry of banks, and the traces of the famous coffee-houses between its eastern end and Cornhill, in Change Alley, are all gone. Change Alley now is a crosswork of sterile ways, sunk among seven-storey backsides of banks all glazed in white tiles, like a giant's lavatory. But there in the early eighteenth century most stock exchange business was done, and there at Jonathan's or Garraways even amateurs or hopeful incompetent poets liked to have a flutter; thus Pope wrote to a friend there in 1720, the year of the great financial crash known as the South Sea Bubble, asking to be remembered to John Gay 'for anywhere else (I deem) you will not see him as yet . . .' It was at No. 16 Lombard Street that Edward Lloyd had his coffee-house whence sprang Lloyd's of London. Some banks still have the agreeable medieval habit of indicating their presence by a sign hanging out over the pavement, and outside No. 68 is a large and beautiful gilt grasshopper—the house is said to have belonged to Gresham though it is now Martin's Bank (the oldest in England, founded in 1563). The London Clearing House (in Post Office Court on the other side of the road), is where the major banks daily balance up their claims on each other; some £700 million is said to change hands daily. The south side of Lombard Street joins King William Street upon the massy prow of the Guild church of **St. Mary Woolnoth**; the wall, Lombard Street side, with its great clock bracketed out, is famous among architects. Its three great arched recesses are cut deep and emphatic into the stone, as though the very mass and toughness of stone had challenged an imagination of fierce vigour to combat; the front of the church, with its heavy rustication, ascends as if in the process of dividing into twin towers, and triumphing indeed in its two separate sturdy turrets. It is by Hawksmoor, 1716–27; its interior is a cube with a taller oblong borne at each corner by three Corinthian pillars set central in it, very rigorous in its volumes, culminating in what is almost a squared version of a dome. It is all white and gold, with dark furnishing and big dark reredos with baldacchino, big pulpit; the disposition of these has gone slightly awry in restoration when the galleries were removed (the doors for these lead enigmatically now on to air).

The site must be worth thousands if not millions, and many attempts have been made to sweep St. Mary away. About 1900 the Tube got in underneath; the entrance round on the left is not to the tomb any more—the dead were evacuated to

Ilford—but to Bank Station. An old doorway with cherubs' heads survives with an exhortation to lift up your hearts, but the more recent notice is a warning not to loiter under threat of prosecution.

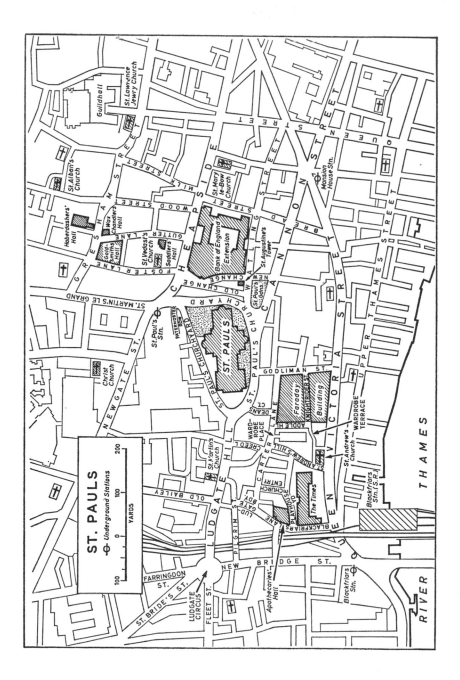

CHAPTER TWENTY-FOUR

St. Paul's

❧

THOUGH the spires of Wren's churches sink gradually from sight as the multi-storey office blocks slab denser on the bomb-sites, the dominant feature of his greatest creation, St. Paul's Cathedral, is still dominant too, over all the western skyline of the City of London; that beautiful dome, second only in Christendom to St. Peter's. If you come from the West End in a bus, you see it clear from down Fleet Street, dark and lucid on a fine spring morning after rain, with a flash of sun on its gold cross, or on a misty September day as if afloat. From Ludgate Circus, it is bisected by the sharp, dark obelisk spire of St. Martin Ludgate. But I would not go first to St. Paul's, but rather stalk it through the jungle about it, the under-growth.

If you start from Ludgate Circus, **Ludgate Hill** forms the main approach to St. Paul's poised at its crest, but the ap-proach in typical London fashion arrives askew on a curve at its focus, besides being barred in mid-air by the shabby old brick railway viaduct. It was mostly bombed; the new is up on the left and fairly complete all round the north of St. Paul's, but right of Ludgate Hill are still the bomb-sites, the ground plan of cellars deep in the hillside, parked with cars and here and there tufted with blitz weeds. Somewhere there was La Belle Sauvage Yard, with a famous inn; near it were the premises of the Master-Craftsman Grinling Gibbons, the great wood carver, whom Evelyn claims to have discovered in romantic neglect in a lonely hut in Deptford marshes in 1671 and then to have introduced him to Wren, so starting that long and fruitful collaboration that we shall see in St. Paul's. The old City Wall came down from the north on the contour of the hill a little north of present Old Bailey, and its eastern Lud Gate (where doubtless to begin with the Romans had a gate; it was demolished when most of the City gates were, about 1760) was just this side of **St. Martin Ludgate.**

St. Martin goes back in myth anyway to the Welsh hero Cadwallader, but the present church is very much post Great Fire, and very much Wren's, an excellent prelude to St. Paul's. It has a most civil vestibule with two sets of stairs (note how they cope with the slope of the hill-site), and through the great dark carved screen, the interior rises very tall from the dark wood furnishings into the coloured light of the windows; four tall Corinthian columns shape the Greek cross of tunnel vault in the ceiling above, and the crossing is accented by a splendid great brass candelabra; the woodwork is almost all richly good and contemporary, and over the font a pretty pale pelican. The church has a rare seclusion of sanctuary that the threatening ground bass of traffic from Ludgate Hill only succeeds in heightening.

Its façade is a noble composition: the three tall windows, and the lines of the tower lifting from pavement level through them, then lofting between its scrolly volutes pale to the shadow of its cornice, to the dark bulb, the delicate iron balcony, the open arcade whence the final exclamation of the lead spire goes up. To see this you need to cross the road, and thence is a fine sight of St. Paul's façade to the east. To the south, Pilgrim Street takes you twisting down to Ludgate Broadway (all of fifteen feet broad), into Blackfriars Lane, cobbled, with a glorious view of St. Bride's over the bomb-sites west, pale as a bleached willow herb spire from over Fleet valley. Blackfriars is the site of the Dominicans' church and friary built in 1276, demolished at the Reformation; down on the left, a doorway leads into a little secluded court-yard, the charming Hall of the **Apothecaries** Company, miraculously unbombed, of 1684 revised in 1779; it owns some handsome portraits. Round its southern corner into Play-house Yard and an elusive echo of Shakespeare, for here on the site of Blackfriars was the Blackfriars Theatre, where Shakespeare probably played. Even *The Times* has left the site. Left up Church Entry (a narrow crack with the derelict churchyard of gone St. Ann's with a dusty acacia and a warning not to throw dirt) and right along **Carter Lane**. This (provided it survives—it is under threat) is mainly standard nineteenth-century office and storage building, but a little to the right off it, enclosed like a pearl, Wardrobe Place, a tiny square: York stone about an oval of cobbles, the glazed white tiling of City backside contrasting with early eighteenth-century brick, gas lamps, planes and spindly acacias among little pots of flowers and dustbins. Wilfully characteristic of City texture, quite unexpected, and delectably unreasonable. Farther down Carter Lane, up to the left, in Dean's Court, another one: the Deanery, behind a brick wall with double gateway with pineapple tops and shadowy in the canopy of two immensely tall planes, a sedate brick building (a doorway is often ajar and you can peep at its front—it is one of the very rare domestic houses certainly by Wren, 1670). The streets to the south of Carter Lane have some pretty eighteenth-century brick survivors.

Down steeply to **Wardrobe Terrace** and the north flank of St. Andrew by the Wardrobe, a Wren church gutted in the blitz and restored; Wardrobe Terrace (the Wardrobe was as it were the Crown's depot for furniture, furnishings, armour, etc., moved to this area from the Tower but burned out in the Great Fire) takes you through to **Bell Yard**; on the corner is still a Bell pub, and from a Bell pub here in 1598, Richard Qyney surscribed a letter: 'To my loving good friend and countryman, Mr. Wm. Shakespeare deliver thees'—the only letter to Shakespeare known. Shakespeare owned property in the Wardrobe area. But now from the Bell an awesome vista through a canyon of twentieth-century brick with flying glass and iron bridges over, no more than an interruption in the mammoth telephone headquarters of Faraday House now, though still labelled Knightrider Street. It is impenetrable (for security reasons) but somewhere along it is a tablet to Thomas Linacre (1460–1524), the great physician who founded here, in his own house, the College of Physicians. At the end of Bell Yard left up Godliman Street; on your right to the east the bombs, that so happily missed the richly various little warren we have just been through, blasted all, and all is hygienic newness, but at the top of the road St. Paul's lifts up from its trees.

Here, from in front of the noble south portico with its semi-circular pillared porch, the weathered statues high on its pediment above, and above again the great drum striped with pale columns over its internal shadow, the dark dome, the pinnacle with the golden ball—hence you can perambulate the eastern end of St. Paul's. Its setting is all new or awaiting renewal: the welcome if over-respectable garden with its pleached trees and its water; the bomb-shattered little hulk of

St. Augustine has gone, but its tower remains, entrance now to the very new Choir School. The tower once held a name plate CHANGE, which read after the blitz as a lamentation but recorded the streets of Change and Old Change, an area where a hundred years ago were 'calico printers and Manchester warehouseman' but which has now solidified eastwards into giant office blocks about Watling Street and Cheapside. The brick building, vast, with a wide curve answering the apse of St. Paul's is the Bank of England extension, and offends me with drear traditionalism. The curving roadway that actually flanks St. Paul's, full of buses, is nominally **St. Paul's Churchyard**, once the most famous name in English publishing and book-selling—from shops here much of Shakespeare was published, but after the Great Fire the book-sellers moved north, many into Paternoster Row, until the blitz when once again the books about St. Paul's burned and fragments of burned paper snowed black on Ludgate.

It is more rewarding, rather than scrutinising this in detail, to keep your eye on the dome while walking about it. This is almost my favourite City pastime, best on a Saturday afternoon or Sunday, when traffic perils are diminished, and under a blue dome of sky fleeced with light clouds; thus you can make St. Paul's work, its rich façades shifting and changing in gorgeous measure about the slow revolution of the dome against the sky. In winter you do this right round St. Paul's but in summer the planes to the north are too dense in leaf.

From the junction of the Churchyard with Newgate Street, St. Martin's le Grand and Cheapside, you can see three of the most splendid of Wren's spires in attendance upon St. Paul's dome; to the west the slender, most delicate, triple-tiered squares of columns ascending as they diminish into the sky— the steeple of the gutted Christ Church, built by Wren on the foundations of the chancel of the huge Franciscan church that was there till the Reformation. To the north, very spirey in contrast, one of his simpler-seeming, but in fact perhaps most subtly elegant work, St. Vedast, balancing diminuendo the play of pierced window in solid stone, of convex curve against concave. And to the east down Cheapside, not tower or spire so much as the idea of campanile wrought out in stone, the most beautiful of all, **St. Mary-le-Bow**. As you go down towards it, it rises more proudly now than before for the street has been widened back from it. From the pinnacled top of the square tower springs a rotunda of pillars, and the lines of these are drawn beautifully upwards through the balcony above and curving in into a second cluster of pillars, merging into the ejaculation of the slender obelisk spire; at the top, poised as by magic, a little ball and still above that the vane, a splendid dragon (some nine feet long).

Bells are built into the legend of St. Mary, though it was the one bell that must have recalled Dick Whittington to London from Highgate—'the great Bell of Bow'; the qualification for a Cockney is to be born within the sound of Bow Bells—it ended with a great chime of twelve bells that came crashing down through the tower in the blitz—now they are back, their new career opened by a peal from Prince Philip in 1961. 'Le Bow' comes from the eleventh-century arches of the former church in the crypt; Wren's church, built between 1670 and 1683, was as if a proving piece of his rapid maturity as architect; gutted in the blitz, it has been rebuilt—the old churchyard, set back from Cheapside, has become a most contemporary piazza, with a new statue of Captain John Smith of Virginian fame (rescued by the romantic Indian princess, Pocahontas). The two doorways at the base of the tower are in quality, with their lushly lazy cherubs, their burden of carved fruit, and their massive beautifully pro-portioned frames, the best things of their kind in London.

Cheapside seems to have been for centuries as it were the sparking-point of the City; its history is starred with acts of sudden and bloody violence, and swept by the running flicker and blaze of riot. Edward II was ill enough advised to appoint the bishop of Exeter as *custos* of the City in place of the lawful Lord Mayor; the bishop was dragged by the hair of his head by the City mob from St. Paul's down through the mud to the Standard, and summarily beheaded; the rebels Wat Tyler and then Jack Cade also took toll of their victims there. The riots were liable to be quarrels among locals—in a famous one of 1339, there was a tremendous battle among members of the Skinners and Fishmongers Companies, but there were also a number of more sinister xenophobic explosions, of which the most notorious came on the 'Evil May-day' of 1517, when the jealousy of the City against foreign merchants burst out into a bloody riot. Such outbursts tended to start in Cheap-side simply because it was the focus, the concentration of City life; it was above all open and very various market ('Cheap' comes from the Old English 'cyppan' to bargain), and echo of the concentration of merchants about survives in the street names of its tributaries, Bread, Milk and Wood Streets, Ironmongers Lane. As late as 1850 it was still a shopping-centre that rivalled those of the West End; now it is a lunch-time shopping area for City workers, scoured by the blitz and rebuilt, its memories almost obliterated, the mess, chatter and vital colour evaporated from its smooth surface, its residents long gone. On Sundays it is desert, and even on a weekday, of a fine summer's morning, its characteristic noise in a little court off it may seem to be the chatter of the typewriters singing each to each over the ground swell of the traffic, the clack of a typist's high heels as she crosses the yard with a pot of coffee. Yet here were poets and writers: Sir Thomas More was born in Milk Street in 1478; John Milton in Bread Street in 1608 (and had but a short walk to St. Paul's School down Cheapside) perhaps within hearing distance of the most famous of meeting-places of poets, the Mermaid Tavern, where Shakespeare and Ben Jonson might meet, also in Bread Street. Bread Street now lies near-dead in the clutch of the civic pomposity of the Bank of England extension and any bread you get there is likely to be pre-sliced, and pale with hygiene. But there is one touch of romantic poetry in Cheap-side, in the living fabric of a great plane tree that lifts high over the corner of Wood Street—older perhaps than any building surviving on Cheapside, except St. Mary-le-Bow.

A slight digression north up Wood Street, brings you to Gresham Street (after Sir Thomas, see p. 346); here there is a nice view to the east of the church of St. Lawrence Jewry to the east, and northwards up Wood Street of the simple but pretty tower of St. Alban, Wren's Gothic; the church itself, gutted, has been demolished. West along Gresham Street, a clutch of City Companies, mostly rebuilt after the blitz (Wax Chandlers, corner of Gutter Lane; Haberdashers, corner of Staining Lane, farther up which the Pewterers), but the Gold-smiths, between Gutter and Foster Lanes, are still housed in the very handsome, solid, palazzo built for them by Philip Hardwick in 1835, with crisp and gigantic detailing.

At the bottom of Foster Lane, on the way back to Cheap-side, the restored interior of **St. Vedast** is worth looking at. St. Vedast, a rather rare saint in England, was the fifth-

century Bishop of Arras who converted Clovis (Foster of
Foster Lane is a tortuous English bastardisation of the name).
Burned in the Great Fire, the present shell was Wren's cheapest
church, for he was able to use some of the earlier walls, between which Herrick had been baptised. Gutted again in the
war, it is now the Guild Church of the Actors' Church Union,
and aptly elegant, with black and white marble floor, pews
ranged sideways like a college chapel, and a decorated ceiling
bright in gold and silver (aluminium, actually); some of the
furnishings are old, and the reredos, once in Wren's vanished
St. Christopher-le-Stocks, has been brought back from
Essex. But the great beauty of the church, as already indicated
(p. 356), is the spire.

Hence you can walk across to the north flank of St. Paul's
among its deep trees. Just abutting on the near corner of the
present choir of the cathedral, stood the resonant open-air
pulpit called St. Paul's Cross; from before the thirteenth
century, the three annual folkmotes (meetings) of London
were held there, and it became almost the sounding board of
England, of church and state alike; thence bishops harangued
royalty, though royalty at least sat under a shelter against the
wall of the old cathedral; hence papal bulls were promulgated,
and proclamations made—'a kind of Times newspaper',
Carlyle called it.

The Cross was torn down in 1643, and the present pillar
with statue of St. Paul that commemorates it only put up in
1910.

And so round the north side of the Cathedral, where the
new building of the nineteen-sixties has replaced the old
nineteenth century shops and the blitz wasteland beyond.
White and sleekly slabbed, with pedestrian ways clear of the
ground, and slotted north to south to give room for the
presence of the dome to tell, this new development has aroused
much opposition, yet its rectangular sharp gridding is no bad
foil to the baroque mass and surge of St. Paul's. And St.
Paul's itself, new-washed, has acquired both new clarity of
detail and an even greater splendour.

The **west front**, rising up from the steps beyond that oddly
indeterminate statue of Queen Anne—what *is* she doing with
her sceptre?—is rich enough. The frontispiece has two stories
of coupled columns, eight couples below, four above, and
above that the triangular pediment with sculpture (conversion

of St. Paul) inset and statuary above (by Francis Bird); on either side rise the towers, the clock in the southern one, with columned turrets of an intricacy that surpasses anything in the City steeples. And these of course flank with splendour the splendid dome; they are 212½ feet high, but the dome rises high above them to 365 feet. The serenity of the dark of the dome, rising from the rotunda of pillars, seems absolute, resolving the movement of the west front into peace, and bearing the little pillared lantern, the golden ball, the golden cross. The portico is actually richer, has more movement, than Wren may have wanted; he would probably have liked a simple row of gigantic columns clear to the pediment. As it is, the double-storeyed nature of the whole exterior is emphasised; this disturbed the conscience if not the eye of the nineteenth century, for there is nothing behind the upper storey wall; but it is only partly there for picturesque reasons, for it has also an architectural function, the weight of the walls acting as buttress.

The usual entrance is on the right of the portico, but with luck on a fine day, you will find the central doors flung wide—and so, ideally, you should come to St. Paul's on the main axis of its symmetry, and preferably on a slow tide of sunlight from the west. Inside, a coolness that calms the nerves yet crispens the mind, pervading an immense composure and harmony of space. Between the arcade of the aisles—pale grey stone, sharp foliage of the carved swags, gilt-railed balcony, and shallow saucer domes set in white above—the nave processes to the chancel far beyond, there changing key, dark below with the old wood of organ and choir, and glister of gold mosaic above, through to the focus of the high altar set against the eastern apse, pure gleam and shine of gold in its twisted baldacchino. If you go with this vista, a little way up the nave, you feel rather than see the immanent dome, and then its surge, and its majestic embrace and containment of space in contentment.

Somewhere on the fringe of the crossing, it may be good to sit a little.

St. Paul's is the cathedral of the See of London, founded in 604. The first building on this site was built for the first Bishop, Mellitus, appointed from Rome by Augustine. The cathedral burned in whole or in part, first in 961, again in 1087 and in 1135, but the building that the Middle Ages

One of the best-known of City taverns, Simpsons, typically concealed in a narrow, deep-sunk court, with gas-lighting and, more rarely, the sun

MALE PRESERVES
The Court Room, Grocers' Hall. Late Victorian with an Elizabethan flavour, housing opulent traditions from the Middle Ages onwards. The overmantel is from the Old Hall of 1682 (note the polish on the table)

The Library in the Travellers' Club, Pall Mall. Of a rather livelier elegance than most clubs, with classical echoes of the Grand Tour (the frieze is copied from the Bassae, Phigalia)

knew was in progress through the twelfth to the fourteenth centuries. It was one of the great Gothic churches of Europe: cruciform, with nave and chancel some 560 feet long within (longer than Wren's building), with a tower with great spire (burned down in 1561) central over the crossing. Old St. Paul's was a major national centre, with its rich and precious shrines, its pilgrims, its buried kings (who included Ethelred the Unready) and its chantries, but for Londoners it became also a sometimes over-secular meeting place, almost a conveniently-covered extension of Cheapside Market. The nave became known as Paul's Walk; as early as 1385 ball-playing had to be forbidden there, and in 1560, a bishop could describe it thus: 'The south alley for Popery and usury, the north for simony, and the horse-fair in the midst for all kinds of bargains, meetings, brawlings, murders, conspiracies, and the font for ordinary payments of money, as well known to all men as the beggar knows his bush.' Worse desecration came in the Interregnum of Cromwell, when shops were set up in the portico, and the nave served as barracks for cavalry-men and their horses. With the return of Charles II, investigations began again into the problem of restoration, and in spring 1666 Christopher Wren produced his first design, but in September the Great Fire struck. With the rest of the City, from Cheapside to the Thames, from near the Tower to beyond the Fleet, St. Paul's burned. 'The stones of Paul's flew like grenadoes, and the melting lead running down the streets in a stream,' recorded Evelyn. At night, a schoolboy two miles away in Westminster could read a miniature edition of Terence by the light, and leaves of books stored in the crypt fell as far as Eton. When the fire died, there remained 'a large heap of stones cemented together by the lead with which the church was covered'.

Wren produced various designs for rebuilding, rejected by committee opinion, before the so-called 'Warrant' design was accepted; the vital clause in that agreement was that Wren was free to modify it as the building progressed, a clause of which he took full advantage. The first stone was laid in 1675; the last in 1710, when Wren was seventy-eight. In the course of building he suffered perhaps more than might be expected in the complicated progress of so vast an enterprise, and something of a persecution of him began in 1697, when his salary was withheld on the grounds that progress was too slow. Yet it did proceed. Charles II died, and James II had his eye on the building as a desirable new central shrine for the hoped-for conversion of Britain to Catholicism, hopes broken by the Glorious Revolution of militant protestantism under William III in 1688. All through the last decade of the seventeenth century and the first of the eighteenth, England under William and then under Marlborough led Europe in arms against Louis XIV, but the cathedral still grew. Wren's connection with it lasted till 1718, when a grateful nation dismissed him from his post as Surveyor of the Works, not without threat of prosecution as well, and the next year an additional trimming was completed which he did not want: the balustrade round the top ('Ladies,' wrote Wren, 'think nothing well without an edging'). But from his retirement at Hampton Court the old man could still visit St. Paul's as he loved to do, and sit for a while under the dome, until his death in 1723 at the age of ninety-one.

The principles that guided Wren, as he wrote looking back when he was eighty-five, were those of 'the best Greek and Roman architecture' ('and if I glory it is in the singular mercy of God, who has enabled me to begin and finish a great work so conformable to the ancient model'). Accordingly his ideal was a regular cross (Greek) plan, from the crossing of which on eight regular arches should surge the dome; his Great Model (eighteen feet long, in wood, preserved in the library) of 1673 is an elaboration on that basis, and was duly rejected by conservative opinion as unseemly for traditional Anglican worship. His problem therefore, was to marry a dome on to a basically Gothic plan with a long nave. The plan that was accepted had in fact a shallowish dome with a heavy lantern above, all topped by a tall spire (very like St. Bride's); happily, by his escape clause, he was able to modify this, which looks almost grotesque in drawings, into the present exquisite balance: the large rhythm of semi-circular arch, of saucer dome, moving outwards from under the great hemisphere through nave and chancel, aisles and transepts, contents the eye, and fuses the whole.

Almost overnight Wren seems to have summoned up a team of craftsmen of the necessary talent; there is certainly small hint of such quality before the Great Fire. Besides the famous immigrants, the Dutchman Grinling Gibbons, and the French wizard in iron-work, Tijou, there were the Englishmen, the Strongs, master-masons, Edward Pierce, Jonathan Mayne, and Francis Bird. In his office Wren had, as clerk of the works, also an architect who was a genius in his own right, Nicholas Hawksmoor (and the office was busy: while Wren was building St. Paul's, he was also designing and supervising fifty other churches in the City).

Before we start to walk about the church, look up at the dome as the central arches lift through gold to the Whispering Gallery, the drum with its carved apostles, the painted dome itself closing into the opening high at its top, through which you seem to glimpse a dome beyond the dome, yet another empyrean. The dome is in fact three in one: the inner surface that you see, painted with scenes from the life of St. Paul by Sir James Thornhill; then, from the outer rim of that, from all points invisible, rises a brick cone that takes the weight of the lantern above, and from which, on a timber structure, the outer, lead-covered, dome is stretched almost like an umbrella on its ribs.

By the south-west entrance, under the clock-tower, is the geometric staircase, not always readily accessible but to be seen if possible, a most elegant spiral of steps cantilevered out and ascending diminuendo from the eye, with a lovely iron railing by Tijou.

In the body of the church, the sights are of three basic varieties. The first, which is everywhere, is the detail of the enrichment, much of it contemporary: fruit, flowers and foliage carved in stone and wood, though most of the later work (mainly late nineteenth century) tends to be sadly inert in quality on close inspection. Then there are the monuments. Wren's church was clear of these until 1790, but in the hundred and twenty-five years after that, it was gradually peopled by a giant race of national heroes of martial merit, almost all in cold white marble, and some in a strange naïve sophistication of nakedness, and with a stiffish formality of gesture that contrasts with the large flowing movement of the church. The church absorbs them, large though they be, in its own immense scope. But the third and fundamental sight is the movement of the building about you as you move: the slow and majestic shift of space, sometimes of rich ambiguity, provided by the piers, the coffered arches, by dome and dome. The rare London sun can greatly enhance this with its own wilful counter-point of shafted light.

In the **south aisle** you have at once, in the dark wooden screen (by Mayne, 1706) to the oval chapel of the Order of St. Michael and St. George, a splendid example of St. Paul's carving; farther up, two good and typical Napoleonic war memorials (by Banks: Captain Burgess and Captain Westcott). On a pier of the nave is a replica by Holman Hunt of his best-known painting, 'The Light of the World'—that dim, sweet yet spiky, archetypal expression of Victorian piety, very shocking in mood against Wren's clarity. From here you can best see, in the third bay of the nave's north arcade opposite, the immense monument to the Duke of Wellington, by Alfred Stevens (begun 1856, but finished long after Stevens's death, in 1912). A Victorian neo-Renaissance variation on the Elizabethan catafalque tomb theme, it is uninhibited in ambition and in detail, if derivative, of excellent craftsmanship. In the **north aisle**, by the door, a singularly chill memorial chapel to Kitchener; thence, the oval chapel (of St. Dunstan) with a glorious carved screen pairing the chapel opposite in the south aisle; and thence as you go towards the chancel the grandest of Victorian presidents of the Royal Academy, the Olympian Lord Leighton, very senatorial in fluent gleaming bronze (by Brock), and more soldiers. In the **north transept** (restored from bomb damage) are predominantly the military, though one of the most elaborate (by Rossi, 1815) is a colossal celebration of Admiral Lord Rodney, posed as if for a photograph between History and Victory. In the **south transept**, the naval emphasis, with Flaxman's Nelson (finished 1818), the most impressive, but Admirals Lord Howe and Collingwood almost as lavishly celebrated. There is a touching monument of Sir John Moore of Corunna being lowered into the grave, and, by the transept door-case (lovely wood carving), a comfortable conversation piece of two friends, Generals Pakenham and Gibbs. Among all these the painter J. M. W. Turner, though his meagre physique is blown up to heroic scale, is rather out of context.

In the **chancel**, under the glittering nineteenth-century encrustation of the roof, the choir stalls and organ offer the richest efflorescence, luxuriance, of Grinling Gibbons carving, wreaths and garlands, cherubs and angels, an inexhaustible delight to the eye. The organ itself is by Schmidt, commissioned in 1694. Handel liked to play here, and with the organist, Maurice Greene, was locked into the church, 'in summer often stripped unto his shirt, and played away until 8 or 9 o'clock at night'. At the end of the choir, the baldacchino over the high altar is new, replacing the blitzed Victorian reredos, and much more in key with Wren's mood, though its richness of black and gold is still a little harsh. At the arches of the entrances to the chancel aisles, are Tijou gates, and very beautiful black and gold screens by him at the eastern end. The chapels remade since the war are (north) to Modern Martyrs; (behind the altar) the American Memorial Chapel to the armed forces of the United States; and (south) the Lady Chapel. The monuments are now ecclesiastical, and among them (south aisle) the only complete survivor of the monuments in Old St. Paul's: the macabre figure (by Nicholas Stone, 1631) of John Donne, poet and Dean of St. Paul's, standing huddled in his shroud on an urn. The conceit, grim yet vivid as a flame in a cold draught, is worthy of his poetry, and even the account of his 'sitting', naked in the shroud, while still alive, is unforgettably preserved in Izaak Walton's Life of him.

The monuments seen so far are but monuments, divorced from the dust of the men they commemorate, and that is one reason why they lack the poignancy of those in Westminster Abbey. The true grave yard of St. Paul's is below, in **the crypt** (entrance from the south transept, sixpence)—low, with massive piers, extending all under the church above, and said to be the biggest in Europe. As you come down into it, almost at once on the right you will find that simple black slab: *Here lieth Sr Christopher Wren Kt. . . .*, and above it on the wall the inscription composed by his son with its famous phrase: *Si monumentum requiris circumspice*—a phrase repeated now in the pavement above under the dome. Beyond this is Painters' Corner, and it is here and not at Westminster that you will find the memorials to English artists, beginning with that excellent import from Flanders, Van Dyck; Reynolds, Lawrence, Turner, Constable and many others. At the east end under Old St. Paul's was the parish church of St. Faith; the present chapel (1960) on the site is of the Order of the British Empire and a trifle genteel perhaps for its setting in its gilt, pearl grey and rose pink. But the central presences, to the west and under the dome itself are those twin conquerors whose triumphs in the early nineteenth century secured peace and prosperity for Victorian London and whom

London in gratitude loved to celebrate: Nelson and Wellington. Here their bodies rest, well and awesomely sealed in massive splendour; Wellington in an immense and brutal sarcophagus of Cornish porphyry carried high on a base of granite; Nelson, romantic to the last, in a beautifully severe black marble of classic Italian Renaissance style—and so it is, for it was made by Benedetto da Rovezzano for Cardinal Wolsey, appropriated for his own purposes by Henry VIII, but remained empty until Nelson's body ended its long journey here in 1805 from Trafalgar; inside it, he lies, in a coffin made from the mainmast of the French flagship, *L'Orient*. At the west end (past some sad fragments of pre-Great Fire monuments from Old St. Paul's) is stabled the eighteen-ton funeral chariot that bore Wellington to St. Paul's in 1852.

After the descent, ascent. This is from the main body of the church, in the south aisle, and goes in five stages; though if you go all the way, you must be prepared for 627 steps. The first stage is up a broad and easy spiral, to the **South Triforium Gallery**, which acts as a little museum with architectural plans and relics; among them remark the cast of Pierce's bust of Wren (the original marble is in the Ashmolean Museum, Oxford), perhaps the finest baroque bust made in England and showing the sensitivity, an eagerness in movement, of one side of Wren's genius vivid in his face—and against that contrast the engraving of Kneller's painting of him as an old man, still keen with intellect, but the mouth now tight: the great architect in the polite and formal fashion of his time. Off this is the library, with admirable woodwork. The next part of the climb brings you to the guide's delight, the **Whispering Gallery** with its odd acoustics that enable you to hear a whisper uttered the other side of the dome as though it were spoken next to you; this gallery runs round the interior of the base of the drum and offers an odd mixed-up perspective of the church below with strange glimpses of the intimate parts of the organ in the top of the arches about the crossing; looking up, you can see Thornhill's paintings in the dome perhaps too clearly—Wren wanted mosaics which were too expensive. Thence, by a much tighter, steeper spiral to the **Stone Gallery**, the walk that girdles the top of the drum outside, and from here you can see all over London. If it is a clear day and you are still strong in leg, it is now worth the final stages (which also cost a further entrance fee) to the

Golden Gallery, at the top of the dome and at the bottom of the lantern, whence the view is dizzy, and so lastly into the Golden Ball itself.

St. Paul's is, I think, now more warmly loved in London than at any time in its history, at least by all those who lived through the second war, for it was on the night of 29 December 1940, when London burned, that the image of the dome with its cross held high above the tumultuous smoke and the glare of flame was seared into Londoners' imaginations: the image of survival.

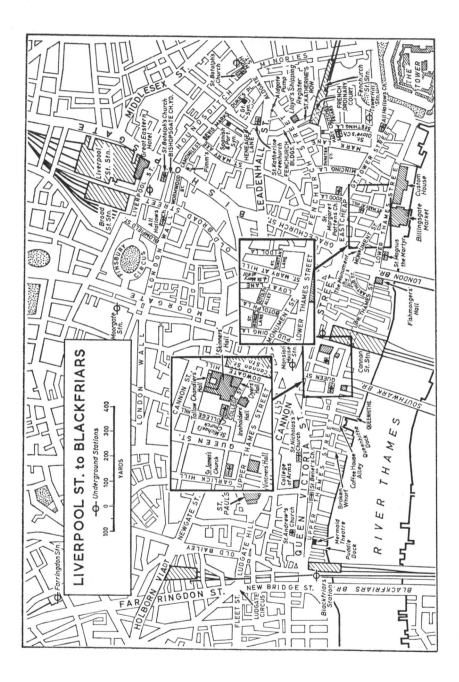

LIVERPOOL ST. to BLACKFRIARS

⊖ Underground Stations

YARDS

100 0 100 200 300 400

CHAPTER TWENTY-FIVE

Liverpool Street to Blackfriars

✺

THE last three chapters have been perhaps over-circuitous for the taste of some. I would now advise a point-to-point between two railway stations (which are at least easy and obvious for access and departure). The route is still through the City, involving banks, offices, churches, alleys—the east and south flanks of the City—but also with warehouses, fish, and the wet smack of Thames air: but the route is, especially, for smells. For Edward Fitzgerald, High Victorian London stank 'all through of churchyards and fishshops', and an element of this persisted in Ian Fleming's nostrils in 1960, when he diagnosed the dominant as 'fried fish and Players'. In fact the eddies drift and change all the time, with ephemeral felicities such as coffee, the smoky autumn tang of a hint of fog, pavements suddenly fragrant with rain, but all tend to drown in the remorseless fume of diesel-powered traffic. This you will not entirely escape on this route, or any other London one, but there are sudden pungencies that dispel even diesel.

Liverpool Street Station has the City's one big hotel, the Great Eastern, hung unexpectedly with dim lush portraits of Restoration beauties. To the west, Broad Street Station, with a long flanking cliff of unfeatured brick (but with an outside staircase arcaded as if for monks) is daily increasing in value as a survivor from an older City texture. Left at the west end of Liverpool Street takes you down Blomfield Street (with a glimpse to the right of trees in Finsbury Circus) to London Wall, and left down this a very pretty view of the tower of **All Hallows**, topped by its open cupola. The narrow little garden along the street, with its flowers, seats and five precious trees, is in fact backed by the wall of London, a short stretch of medieval work visible, and Roman below ground (the shape of the church's vestry is determined by an old Roman bastion). Before the Reformation anchorites lived here in an 'anker-hole'; the church was rebuilt by George Dance the Younger in 1765, blitzed, and restored as City Centre for Church Art. The restoration has made the most of the most elegantly sophisticated interior; it is a long hall with apsed end, in fact lavishly decorated but with an effect of the most chaste economy—very eighteenth century in contrast to Wren's interiors. The pulpit, clinging to the wall, has a surprise entry by a door from a stair from the vestry, whence the preacher must have been able to burst dramatically upon his audience. The decorum of the exterior, brick and Portland stone, contrasts agreeably with the new rigid and rectangular development on the corner of London Wall and Old Broad Street.

Left into Old Broad Street and first right through a narrow opening into Bishopsgate Church Yard; deep among office fronts, then past an unexplained Moorish extravaganza no bigger than a kiosk, and into the churchyard of **St. Botolph's,** the only green spot in the area and very popular, with seats, lavender, even a tennis court, and cast iron lamp brackets arched over the main walk. The church hall, in low and civil red brick among the overweening offices to its rear, has a schoolboy and girl in niches of 1821, when it was an infants' school. The church, rather stolidly large with a handsome tower, was rebuilt in 1728 in rich dark red brick with stone dressings; the inside is staid and rather comforting, with long low dark pews, galleries, all among white and gold and duck-egg blue. St. Botolph is celebrated for the frank variety of the entries in its registers, which reflect the milling vitality of old Bishopsgate, thus: baptism—'Bennett reput daughter of John Allen, which John went with Sir Francis Drake, to the Indiains, in which tyme this child was got by a stage player'; burials—'A Portingall, wether beaten', 'Tittie Totattie, that colde not speake'.

Bishopsgate was a main road north out of London in Roman days and still is; the gate, demolished finally in 1761, stood just south of the Churchyard, between Wormwood Street and Camomile Street (the area south of this is being vastly developed, and a famous City chop-house, Pimm's, has already fallen victim). Camomile Street to Bevis Marks is an uneasy, indeterminate area, between City and East End, and still very Jewish in atmosphere. Sephardi Jews began to resettle in London under Oliver Cromwell (whom they still acknowledge with gratitude) for the first time since their expulsion in the Middle Ages.

The still remaining and sumptuous expression of their prosperity by 1700 is to be found in Heneage Lane off Bevis Marks, in the Spanish and Portuguese **Synagogue** built for them (by a Quaker, Joseph Avis) in 1701. There is no comparably preserved synagogue in Britain, and it is particularly fascinating in context with Wren's City churches—the plan, a plain oblong, with galleries borne on Tuscan columns, is similar to many of them and the rich woodwork carved by the same craftsmen. The Ark might be a reredos, but opens of course to show the scrolls with their silver bells, and the air is dense with the dipping branches of gleaming Dutch brass candelabra, still with candles. The bigger, Great, Synagogue of the Ashkenazim (originally mainly from central and eastern Europe) is back in the extension of Bevis Marks, Duke's Place; this was founded in 1690, but was blitzed and left only a wrecked shell. It is a little mournful this area still, and to be kindled by the warm vitality of London Jewish life in action you have to go through to the streets parallel to the east—Houndsditch, where Strype recorded in the early eighteenth century 'brokers, joiners, braziers, and such as deal in old clothes linen and upholstery', a street market now expanded two hundred yards farther east to Middlesex Street better known as the famous Petticoat Lane (see p. 412).

From the end of Duke's Place, **Aldgate High Street** broadens out east to the vanishing perspective of Whitechapel High Street and the East End. On the left, the obelisk spire of another St. Botolph (Aldgate), a somewhat stolid church of 1744 by the elder George Dance, refurbished in the late nineteenth century and now with a very odd ceiling like an extremely expensive embossed white wall-paper with figures, but also memorials to some eminent victims of Henry VIII: Thomas Lord Dacre, and Sir Nicolas Carew, beheaded in 1537 and 1538. On the other side of the street is an excellent antique pub, a little overfurbished with brass whatnots of an olde variety, but genuinely of the late seventeenth century, the Hoop and Grapes (No. 47), with a wooden bay-window, and dark brown beams within, and barmaids with bow ties. Ald Gate itself (demolished 1760), was important apart from the fact that Chaucer lived some eleven years actually in it, for this was the main route out of London east, and still is. A little west of the gate inside the walls was a well, later a pump which became proverbial and is still there, on the corner of Leadenhall and Fenchurch Street, though irreverently screened by traffic direction-boards.

Fifty yards down Leadenhall Street to the west, is the long flank and tower of **St. Katharine Creechurch** (i.e., Christchurch; a big Augustinian Priory here, founded in 1108, vanished at the Reformation); the tower is of 1504 (with a little eighteenth-century cupola), but the body of the church is of 1628—a rare period for English churches, and inside indeed it is the most odd pretty transitional object, very light and airy, nave and aisle with no chancel and the feeling of late Gothic perpendicular, yet articulated by round Italian columns and with plaster lierne tracery on the ceilings. Very gaily restored now to a Contemporary colour key, with the arms of seventeen City Companies repainted and flashing in the ceiling bosses, it looks brilliantly phony as if a stage set. It has an organ of true distinction by the famous Father Schmidt, 1686, standing out over the west end on handsome columns. It is now very busy as the H.Q. of the Industrial Christian Fellowship, which has involved boxing off part of the aisles with office partitions, behind which the typewriters chant. It is especially associated with Charles I's archbishop, Laud, who consecrated it with the high and elaborate ritual associated with him but profoundly distrusted by the puritan body of the English people, who in the end had their revenge when Laud was beheaded on Tower Hill—his manner of celebration when consecrating this church was part of the evidence held against him at his trial. He is remembered here in a chapel in the south aisle (with a copy of Van Dyck's portrait of him); there too, is an unusually touching Elizabethan effigy to Sir Nicholas Throgmorton (d. 1571, Ambassador to France and Chief Butler of England, after whom Throgmorton Street is named)—what is unusual is the movement of the head, turned to the side as though in sleep he had half-heard the waking call of his name. On the font the arms of Sir John Gayer, some time Lord Mayor, who in 1649 cheerfully founded the 'Lion Sermon' which is still preached every 16th of October to celebrate his deliverance from a lion in the Syrian desert. . . . The flags between the windows are those of neighbouring shipping companies in Leadenhall Street, whose premises we have remarked earlier (p. 347), so over Leadenhall Street and into the almost surreptitious, easily-missed opening of Fenchurch Buildings, and through to

Fenchurch Street. Over the other side of this, to the left, is Lloyd's Shipping Register, built by Collcutt in 1900 and one of the best examples of the rich part-baroque part-Art-Nouveau style. To the right of this, there is a passageway tucked in by a court and fountain, **St. Katherine's Row**. In the garden people sit thoughtless of its origins, which are, as so often with touches of invaluable green in the City, a vanished church (St. Katherine Coleman, already noted in 1838 as 'almost undiscoverable', and finally torn down in 1926).

But do not miss St. Katherine's Row, nor be alarmed when it lands you in the gloom of a great brick vault, white-washed at the sides but with its vaults vanishing from feeble lamp light into dark above. There are cobbles underfoot, and a large notice against the committing of nuisance, but the wonder of this cave is the smell, for its close air is drenched with spices of the east (cinnamon perhaps usually predominating); the vault supports Fenchurch Station above (whence the lines run to Tilbury Docks), and this cave is valuable storage space for spice merchants—but it might well be Aladdin's. In fact it is called, not to confuse the issue, French Ordinary Court.

It brings you blinking and perhaps a little dazed out into Crutched Friars (which is clearer: the name explicable from a vanished friary of the Holy Cross). This is all new, with one trim and elegant survivor from the early eighteenth century just on your right, No. 42, in very domestic scale brick with a pretty door, a valuable reminder of the old scale, when the area was residential. For most of the period (1660–9) when his famous Diary was being written day upon day, Samuel Pepys, up-and-coming young clerk in the Navy Office, lived in Seething Lane, which runs south from Crutched Friars where Crutched Friars becomes Hart Street. In Seething Lane, handily, was the Navy Office, and **St. Olave** is on the corner at Hart Street. The church (St. Olaf, King and Martyr, is Norway's patron saint) is mentioned by 1109; the fabric that stood till the blitz was mainly of about 1450, and much of the stone has been re-used in rebuilding. The churchyard was made famous by Dickens, in his *Uncommercial Traveller*, his 'best beloved churchyard, the Churchyard of St. Ghastly Grim'; the gateway with its ferocious spikes and skull and cross bones that aroused this nickname is however, not an allusion to the Great Plague, but a standard motif based on a design in a Dutch pattern book of 1633 (the gate is dated 1658). The interior is bright and blonde and scented with new oak, though some precious early memorials were saved from the war (an excellent Jacobean one, two figures gay in their kneeling piety, the Aldermen Bayninge Brothers). But if it seems a little empty when you go, you need only open Pepys for the buzz —on the splendid 6th of June, 1666, when the news of the sea-victory over the Dutch came through—'but Lord! how all the people in the church stared upon me to see me whisper to Sir John Minnes and my Lady Pen. Anon I saw people stirring and whispering below [he was in the Navy Gallery, now gone], and by and by comes up the sexton from my Lady Ford to tell me the news, which I had brought, being now sent into the church by Sir W. Batten in writing, and passed from pew to pew.' Even though complaints of dull sermons are frequent, there were often consolations ('but I mightily pleased to look upon Mr. Buckworth's little pretty daughters'). There still, by the altar, is the touching, pretty-plain, rather pop-eyed bust of Pepys's wife Elizabeth (if only she had kept a counter-diary to his!). The closing entry of the Diary, 31 May 1669, is overshadowed by Pepys's fear of his own failing eyes, but it was his wife, later the same year, who was mortally struck down aged only twenty-nine. The marriage, which had lasted fourteen years, is recorded with all affection and normal exasperation in the Diary.

One could produce a longish list of candidates for the title of archetypal Londoner, that would include Chaucer, Whittington, Defoe, Lamb and Hazlitt, Dickens, but I would always plump for Pepys, for in him, in the omnivorous appetite of the Diary, there is an immediacy that seems naked of any veil of literature (after all, even Sam Weller is fiction). Every Londoner can match parts of his own experience in Pepys, his hypocrisies, his failings of the flesh, his pleasures in a drink, in food at a pub, in music, his appreciation of shifting fashion, and can site them still often where Pepys sited them (though there has been a heavy toll of his pubs). Almost the greatest miracle of the Diary is the unboringness of its ordinariness, yet Pepys was otherwise a man of considerable distinction: hardworking, devoted and successful Civil Servant, known as the Saviour of the Navy, and though not a merchant, a civic dignitary—Master of Trinity House, Master of the Cloth-workers (just up the road, on Fenchurch Street; rebuilt, but they have the loving cup he gave them in 1677); intimate of that circle of ingenious—a word typically loved by Pepys—men who founded the Royal Society (of which he was President), and which included Wren, Newton, Boyle, Evelyn (his great friend), some of them major geniuses. Vain he was, but not of that kind of vanity that would make him dream that he would stand in popular affection of posterity above them all; yet were he to know, he would be delightfully delighted.

Thence up Mark Lane, first left through Dunster Court and left down Mincing Lane, with implacable twentieth-century office monsters about you. Mincing Lane should be the cosy home of the mother of tea shops, for it is the centre of the tea trade (tea is still, in spite of the coffee bars, to the Londoner as petrol is to a car), but its expression is bleak beyond endurance. Eastcheap on the right at the bottom is a relief, with an airy view away to your left to the spire of All Hallows Barking with the turrets of the Tower beyond, and sometimes wild architectural manifestoes of Victorian individualism (Nos. 33–35 with tier on tier of Gothic arches, emphatic and undercut as an admiral's eyebrows). Here also (on the corner of Rood Lane) is a plain church by Wren (**St. Margaret Pattens**—meaning, according to Stow, clogs which were made nearby), with a severe, un-Wrenish, but beautiful, plain spire (best view from the north in Rood Lane); its façade composes civilly with a former wineshop (at a still earlier period, the rectory) which boasts an elegant bow window and some handsome Corinthian columns—a lot of the wine trade has premises hereabout. From Eastcheap, Idol Lane takes you sharply and narrowly down the slope towards the river; off it on the left from the blitzed shell of the church and shrubs, rises the tower of Wren's **St. Dunstan-in-the-East,** with a singularly happy conceit of a spire lofted from the junction of four free-standing flying buttresses, borrowed from the Gothic of such churches as Newcastle Cathedral—the church is not to be re-built but the tower will stand. And here you will be already moving in the almost palpable odour of the district, which is Billingsgate, which is fish. West down St. Dunstan's Lane and left down St. Mary-at-Hill will bring you full into focus, squarely opposite **Billingsgate Market**, yellow brick of 1875 with Britannia over it, on Lower Thames Street.

There has been a market and wharf here perhaps since

Saxon times, and it was previously more general, for Stow (1598) 'for ships and boats commonly arriving there with fish both fresh and salt, shell-fishes, salt, oranges, onions, and other fruits and roots, wheat, rye, and grain of divers sorts'. It is certainly now fish (though it comes in by rail and not by river now) and most of all if you come about 6 a.m., when the pavements run wet, and lorries jostle, and the white-coated porters with their special flat hats of leather and wood, heave hundredweights of fish about on their heads. It should be seen, though it is not to everyone's stomach. It is noisy, vital and certainly freespoken, though I have never been able to prove for myself that Billingsgate earns its synonymity with bad language (which it has had since the time of Alexander Pope and before). The language in Billingsgate I have heard is the normal London use of Anglo-Saxon monosyllables and other oaths as natural prefix to any noun. The premises, stalls, caverns, of the wholesalers and fish specialists extend up the alleys all up the hill, and so, up slippery cobbles with fish either side of you (it might be a lane in an old fishing town on the coast), up Lovat Lane to the fisherman's church of **St. Mary-at-Hill**, and into its interior, in some ways the most winning of all City churches.

It is basically by Wren, 1670–6, on the site of an earlier church that went back to the twelfth century (Stow says Thomas Becket was parson here); Wren worked his into the irregular site by cunning use of a slightly unequal cross-shape, which he flowered at the centre with a shallow dome on four Corinthian pillars. My impression, which always abides, that this is closer to the original state of his City churches than any other as now seen, does not stand up to close scrutiny, but it does alone have the old chest-high box pews (all numbered neatly), and the woodwork throughout is formidable. Though much of it is by William Gibbs Roger and dated 1849, and lion and unicorn have 'V.R.' on their breasts, the quality is such that it needs a specialist's eye to distinguish it from the work of Wren's time. The chandeliers are palpably Victorian iron work but again excellent of their kind; the detailing of the dome decoration, off-white with touches of blue for Mary, is eighteenth century, and there is a battery of five particularly splendid iron sword-rests, painted and gilt. On the rich gallery of the organ, at its proper place at the west, a clock ticks; another clock outside bracketed in gold and black on

REFRESHMENT
Lord Mayor's Banquet in the
Guildhall, under Pitt the
Younger, Apollo, Mercury, and
Britannia side-saddle

Bottled beer and draught

Piccadilly Circus. Ten to eleven and all's well, with the taxis moving upon Shaftesbury Avenue, where theatres are emptying and restaurants filling up

the east façade is a famous piece of nineteenth-century expertise—it is driven by very remote control from its works in the tower the other side of the church, right over the roof.

From St. Mary you can sidle along the contour of the slope, through two alleys deep and odorously sinister (Botolph Alley and St. George's Lane) into Pudding Lane, where on that September night of 1666 London took fire. Down this, the Monument to the Great Fire lifting tall on your right (see p. 335), back to Lower Thames Street and a changing townscape, the unhappy reverse of the close, human-scaled alleys of the hill. Hence one of the major monuments of Victorian architecture in London was ripped out in 1962 in the name of road widening and traffic-flow: this was the astonishing glass-roofed, iron-ribbed Rotunda built by Bunning, 1847–9, as Coal Exchange. Here much more will change; east to the Tower will be almost one block of building, though with footways promised hung over the Thames. The Custom House, east of Billingsgate, is apparently to stay; there has been one here since the fourteenth century but the Thames Street front of the present one is almost a demonstration that late Georgian building can be tedious (the river front is much better).

And **St. Magnus the Martyr** will, beyond doubt, stay. You see the church on the left as Lower Thames Street tunnels under the approach to London Bridge to join Upper Thames Street; it is Wren's, built 1671–85 but the steeple later, 1703–5, and the steeple, with its beautiful strong octagonal lantern in stone, dark lead dome and spire, is one of Wren's most formidable. In 1924, by building the great cliff of Adelaide House on London Bridge Approach above, they obliterated the spire from London's spirescape and from the river but it is still magnificent from Lower Thames Street, irrepressible as a flower in spring, surging from its dusty shrubs and indeed succeeding almost in making Adelaide House look a little insecure. The approach to Old London Bridge used to pass in part through St. Magnus's porch, as can still be seen. The interior, known to thousands who have never seen it from T. S. Eliot's unforgettable phrase—'inexplicable splendour of Ionian white and gold'—is still as inexplicable and as splendid yet dim among its slender Ionic columns. As you come in from the debris of smashed crates, straw, and the miasma of fish of Billingsgate it is more splendid still in that it floods the nose with incense, both dense and pungent, and trembles in the eyes with candle-flames. The sensual effect, against Billings-gate's background, is breathtaking. The present church has the original organ basically (1712, and the first swell organ anywhere); in the former church was buried the most glorious of English medieval architects, Henry Yevele (d. 1400), who built the nave of Westminster Abbey; and Miles Coverdale, who published the first English bible, was rector. Some, they say, have also seen a ghost here.

Hence the road goes under London Bridge, but you can climb up on the bridge approach by steps to look at the front of the Hall of the **Fishmongers'** Company, fourth of the twelve great companies; the façade is urbanely grand, of 1831–4, and though bomb-damaged the sequence of splendid stair-case and state rooms inside are restored to full civic grandeur.

West of London Bridge (see p. 258), Upper Thames Street was a narrow working street, essentially concerned, as so much of the City is not, with actual goods; here were and still are to some extent, the wholesalers in furs and skins, the wine merchants, the paper-makers. From the south side rise the high irregular cliffs of dark and dirty brick, the warehouses with direct access to the river and little wharfs, and through them cut the deep blind ravines to the river with strange names like Stew Lane, Broken Wharf, Trig Lane. The river itself, fifty or a hundred yards away, though rarely visible, is always sensible in the air. On the north side, up the side of the hill, the same texture with creeping lanes among warehouses and offices like warehouses was repeated, but with churches and City Halls among it. It was heavily blitzed; part of its fabric stood but much was destroyed and it is impossible now to describe very much as it will be, as it is still rebuilding.

The first dominant landmark west from London Bridge was the long sheer flank of brick of Cannon Street Station, monu-mental, nearly two hundred yards long with its terminal cupolas high over the river. It has crumpled under the demoli-tion hammers as Cannon Street rebuilt. On the river side cars are parked, and weeds thick on the site of All Hallows the Less (but Pepys too, might have seen them three hundred years ago, for the church burned in the Great Fire and was never rebuilt; Pepys walked Thames Street as we do now, hopefully, 'and there do see a brave street likely to be', though we are less confident). By Fishmongers' Hall was once the Shades, a famous pub, the last in London whence the wine was drawn direct from the wood into silver tankards. Yet you can still find a relation on the north of Thames Street, up Arthur Street into the cobbles of Martin Lane and the black wood front of the Old Wine Shades, with its dark wood horse-booths for devoted drinkers inside—and farther up, almost on Cannon Street, a brick tower (of 1852, here once was St. Martin Orgar) absorbed into an office building. Into the tunnel under the recently and drably reconstructed Cannon St. A big multi-storey car park along on the left (rather a good one), but on the right up Dowgate Hill some still-standing old Company Halls: the **Dyers** at No. 10, **Skinners** at No. 8 (they have been on this site since 1295); the present building is seventeenth and eighteenth century), and **Tallow Chandlers** at No. 4, tucked away in a leafy courtyard behind an iron gate. In College Street west of Dowgate, is the re-built Innholders Hall, and then by a very municipalised post-blitz little lawn, the tower of **St. Michael Paternoster Royal**, with a charming three-tiered spire related to those of St. Stephen Walbrook and St. James Garlickhithe, but circular (rather late Wren, 1713). The pre-Wren church was important: Whittington, who lived next door, was buried there in 1423. The 'Royal' of the church's name, however, indicates not blue blood but the purple of the grape, for the wine merchants here did great trade with the vineyards of La Réole in Bordeaux. The church was gutted, but is now complete after restoration.

Over the approach to Southwark Bridge, and just beyond on the left, the nominal headquarters of the wine-trade, the Hall of the **Vintners** Company, basically still of 1671 (inside it has a famous show-piece of Wren-style carving in its staircase). **St. James Garlickhithe** over the road was blitzed but is now restored, Wren of 1676–83, but its spire, like St. Michael's of which it is a variant, again later (1714–17), and this type of spire clearly relates to the west turrets of St. Paul's then much in Wren's mind. The interior is famous for its profusion of iron work, not only sword rests but iron hat-stands, all saved from the blitz. The 'Garlick' *is* for garlic—according to Stow it was sold around here. That particular pungency however, is only in the memory, though some six centuries back it may have been familiar enough in the nostrils of Chaucer who was probably born in this area (his father was a Vintner) about 1340.

To your left, between you and the river, the warehouses continue mysterious and lowering. Down Queenhithe you can penetrate to the slap of water, oily and potent. **Queenhithe Dock** was once a popular port, a rival of Billingsgate until London Bridge barred off the larger craft from it, but still for years after a major stage in the waterway of London traffic (hence Essex slipped furtively back to the Strand after his abortive revolt in 1601). Until recently, the dock looked formidably romantic, decaying orderly about its square of water, where the lighters are still tethered—it was almost Venice, almost Bruges, but specifically London. Close by was the narrowest of all the riverside alleys, macabrely labelled Coffee House Alley, but clearly carnivorous, a slot one body wide in the brooding warehouses. Now most of these structures have been demolished, to be replaced by an office and hotel complex of fairly bland unmemorableness. In the rather isolated buildings which remain, and form one boundary of the dock, the essence of its former character has somehow been preserved. Further along Upper Thames Street, opposite Broken Wharf lifts the glorious tower of **St. Mary Somerset**, clustered with pinnacles—Wren's. The two long derelict Victorian houses flanking it which survived the bombs, have now been pulled down, and the site surrounding the church is to be redeveloped in the future. Set at the base of the church tower (which had lost its church many years before the blitz), there were sited instead with most exact felicity one red telephone kiosk, and—at an angle—one of those green cast-iron City sarcophagi for litter, with its specific restrictions about orange and banana peel (as though the City pullulated with men in bowler hats unzipping bananas). Behind the isolated church tower, on the hill which rises quickly to Queen Victoria Street, where formerly a battlefield of blitzed basements used to stand, a waste which flowered wild with the blitz flowers, is now a group of typically nondescript city office buildings. Opposite the Mermaid Theatre, a cellar stencilled with the leaf of bracken. On the hill above, the tower of bombed St. Nicholas Cole Abbey (restored), and farther left the steeples of St. Benet and St. Andrew in prelude to the dome of St. Paul's itself high on the skyline, inviolate over desolation. The little group formed by St. Mary's tower seemed a monument of all this, as charged with memory as the Aliscamps at Arles. St. Mary's tower will stand, but by perhaps 1980, it will be set no doubt among an immaculate newness of fresh building, and its landscape of war, even the grim warehouses to the south, swept from London's memory.

One last church survives in a mammoth redevelopment cocked into the hill above Upper Thames Street; **St. Benet.** Small, cosy, Dutch almost, in cheerful dark brick with lead spire; by Wren 1677–83. It is now Welsh, Welsh Episcopalian, and it holds close the last particular fragrance of this promenade, a little damp, a little musty, the odour of an old-fashioned country church. It has dark galleries, and always when I have been there the brass lectern has been a little tarnished, and the pews are designed for wounding shins— it is a crotchety and most sympathetic church within. The Heralds have connections with this church, and if you climb up round the steps north of the building, you will be able to see, next the green-roofed, St. Paul's-spoiling lump of Faraday Building (a telephone exchange) on the other side of Queen Victoria Street, the heralds' building, the **College of Arms.** This is a plain but handsome building of the 1670s, brick, with an open courtyard to the street (the fine eighteenth-century iron gates were given by an American well-wisher recently). The college is presided over by Garter King of Arms, and his colleagues have the fairest, rarest titles of England, such as Clarenceux, Norroy and Ulster, Portcullis, Rouge Dragon, Rouge Croix and Bluemantle. Here (for a fee), answers to genealogical and heraldic queries can be got; the specialist library is unparalleled.

Here, where Queen Victoria Street slants down to join Upper Thames Street, hard by Blackfriars Station (with its strange archaic destinations carved into the piers at the entrance—Lausanne, Margate, Herne Bay, Wiesbaden, Leipsic, St. Petersburg, etc.) I can leave you with confidence in good hands. Just opposite the station is the **Black Friar**, lavishly appointed with Art Nouveau decoration, the best pub of its kind in London. If since 1967, and the cutting through here of the underpass to the Embankment, the road has become difficult to cross, it is worth the trouble. A little east, at the beginning of Upper Thames Street, are the gay, low, forthright pillars and foyer of the Mermaid Theatre, a happy post-war venture of actor-manager Bernard Miles, reintroducing living theatre into the confines of the City, and not so far from where Shakespeare once played at Blackfriars. If you go down the theatre's side to **Puddle Dock**, you can get, in its restaurant, a reliable and reasonable lunch with a glass of wine, and a wide view over the Thames thrown in.

CHAPTER TWENTY-SIX

Holborn Circus to the Guildhall

✿

To reach **Holborn Circus** best walk three hundred yards east down Holborn from Chancery Lane station (Central Line) or take any of the numerous buses that go down Holborn. The Circus is immediately recognisable by its confluence of six roads under the gridded cliff of the new *Daily Mirror* building; also by the presence, though somewhat diminished by the latter, of what has strong claims to be the most idiotic statue in London. On a bronze horse on a bronze pedestal among the cars Albert Prince Consort waves, not uncheerfully, a bronze hat in the direction of St. Andrew Street; it is by one Bacon, put up in 1875. Other evocations may also seem a little incongruous:

> My Lord of Ely, when I was last in Holborn,
> I saw good strawberries in your garden there . . .

Shakespeare's Richard III to the Bishop of Ely, whose great town house was just north of the Circus. There John of Gaunt died in 1399, 'time-honoured Lancaster'. Later the Bishops were forced to let it to Sir Christopher Hatton, but retained the right to gather for themselves twenty bushels of roses yearly from its great garden. All that remains of Hatton, Elizabeth I's dancing Lord Chancellor, is the name of the rather dour, even seedy in parts, street running due north: Hatton Garden with no trace of roses. In fact its harvest is now if less fragrant much more valuable, for behind its mostly modest frontages, and in the street even, goes on some of the most important diamond trading in the world. At No. 5, a more romantic memory: a relief portrait recalling yet another of those exiles who camped in exile in London to plot revolution: Mazzini, who lived there in 1841–2 brewing the unification of Italy.

Charterhouse Street, spoked north-east from the Circus, has more solid memories of the Bishops. First left off it,

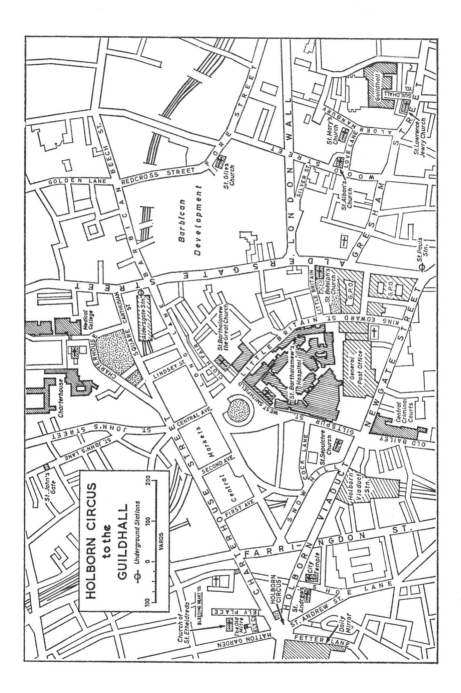

Ely Place (threatened by the developers) is still sanctuary:
police do not enter, even on the premises of the Old Mitre
pub (1546) up the narrow slot of Ely Court, you may not be
arrested. The entrance is surveyed by a lodge and a beadle,
and up to 1939 the beadle used to announce of an evening
that it was ten o'clock and all was well. There are some nice
old houses (for the place has already been 'developed', by a
Mr. Cole from 1773), but the only fragment of the old ecclesiastical palace is its chapel, **St. Etheldreda** (a rare saint,
abbess of Ely in the seventh century; her uncorrupt hand,
attested by a document of some if not sufficient age, was found
in a farmhouse in 1811, and a piece of it is in the church).
It is now one of the very few medieval churches in England
that have reverted to the Catholics, for a Welsh congregation
sold it in 1874 and it was bought by the Rosminian Fathers.
It dates from about 1290, two storeyed like other private
chapels (such as St. Stephen's at Westminster); much restored,
particularly since it lost its roof in the war, but with a sparse
and clean tact that shows the bones and tracery of the structure—very late Geometrical on the yield to early Decorated.

Back in Holborn Circus again, the exit is east on to **Holborn
Viaduct**, a typical high Victorian cutting-through operation of
the 1860s to clarify the traffic that had previously tangled up
in the valley of Fleet below. Its eminence has somewhat sunk,
on its right, the church of **St. Andrew**. This was spared by the
Great Fire but nevertheless rebuilt by Wren, and one of his
biggest churches to accommodate a very big parish. It was not
spared by the blitz of 1941, but is now restored and the tower,
Wren's rehandling of the original fifteenth century one, survived. Chatterton, most romantic of poetic forgers or forging
poets, was buried nearby after his suicide by poison in 1770;
in 1808 Hazlitt was married with Charles Lamb as best man;
in 1817, Benjamin Disraeli, later prime minister, was baptised
at the rather elderly age of twelve, apparently as a reprisal by
his father against aspersions cast on the latter by the Elders
of the Bevis Marks Synagogue. Beyond this, also on the right
and also blitzed and rebuilt, is the City Temple—and rebuilt
very lavishly as the 'cathedral of the Free Churches'. Hence on
to the bridge over the valley, and the bridge itself is worth a
look, very handsome in Victorian confidence, with rich ironwork at each end; some equally handsome Victorian Floren-
tine Gothic palazzi down which were flights of stairs de-

scended to Farringdon Street (two have come down, the other two are threatened). The four bronze statues on the bridge itself are fine (better memorial to the Prince Consort than his statue to the west), opulently personifying Commerce, Agriculture, Science and Fine Art, and all properly inscribed with their identities so that there shall be no mistake. Over the bridge (past the Holborn Viaduct Terminal with its old iron sheds now concealed behind a very glossy front), and along on the left, slewed against the road beyond modern building, a sturdy grey Gothic tower: **St Sepulchre Without Newgate**. The tower is basically fifteenth century, though restored (particularly the over-heavy nineteenth-century pinnacles); the fan vaulting of the porch is original. Inside there is a big, surprising sense of space and light and air, very pleasing though stylistically the interior disintegrates into a rare clash. Generally but probably wrongly given to Wren, it was re-shaped in his time but subsequently much muddled, but it has nice plaster (?) falcons poised for flight at the springing of the arches; a fine font and a still better organ in gold and brown against the prevailing off-white. Much good music is in fact made here, and every 22nd of November they hold a Cecilian festival. Captain John Smith, the famous Governor of Virginia, who was rescued by the Indian princess Pocahontas, was buried here in 1631. But St. Sepulchre has more sinister associations. The famous watch-house to the east (bombed) was built in 1792 to survey the graveyard, which had become the main source of supply for the professional body-snatchers who stored their prey in an inn opposite until they were claimed by surgeons from St. Bartholomew's Hospital (handily just down the road). And in a glass case in the church is a hand-bell, and in the tower the great bell of St. Sepulchre that tolled every night for curfew, and tolled also with appalling frequency as the condemned from Newgate passed on their way to Tyburn. The hand-bell was supplementary, used to rouse the prisoners the night before they were to die; having roused them, the bellman comforted them—'All you that in the condemned hole do lie, prepare you, for tomorrow you shall die . . . Past twelve o'clock.'

The bellman did not have far to walk. Outside the church, on the opposite corner of the road junction, the elaborate Edwardian baroque front (1902–7) of the Central Criminal Court, universally known as the **Old Bailey**, rises to its copper

dome and the skyey gilt figure of Justice (not blindfolded, but
with scales) that is still a landmark of the area in spite of high
new buildings. There was Newgate, the chief prison of London
from the thirteenth century on, and from 1770 rebuilt in a
masterpiece of grim, Piranesian grandeur by George Dance;
the names of the famous and infamous that it housed are
legion—William Penn the Quaker, Daniel Defoe, for example
—in contrast with arch criminals like Titus Oates, Jonathan
Wild (hanged in 1725 and celebrated by Fielding) and Jack
Sheppard, thief and most virtuoso of escapers. It is uncomfortable ground—the road widens, you may note, opposite the
Old Bailey and this was to allow room for the spectators who
used to crowd here (and drink in the nearby pubs like the
Magpie and Stump) particularly after the site of public executions shifted here from Tyburn after 1783. The drama of
justice in action, though not its final executions, are still
visible; parties are shown round the building of the Old Bailey
about 11 a.m. on Saturdays (or weekdays when the courts are
not sitting between 11 and 3), and the public galleries hold a
limited audience when the courts are in session. The important,
headline-catching trials are generally in Court No. 1 or No. 2
(entry from Newgate Street from 10.15 and 2; for trials of
major scandal the queues tend to wrap round the corner of the
building and you have to arrive very well in advance to hope
for a seat).

Hence go north up Giltspur Street; Cock Lane is first on
left (once the only walk licensed for prostitutes within the
City) and high on a wall there is a celebrated little gilt figure
of a boy, exposed naked on a console and clasping his arms
about himself as if cold: the Fat Boy—here according to
legend if not quite to fact, the Great Fire reached its farthest
limit. Then Giltspur Street opens out into **West Smithfield**,
arranged rather jumbly about a central circle of green; rigid
all across its northern end is a hugely long building of iron and
glass, with a slight air of both railway station and seaside pier:
the Central Meat Market of 1886. The long wall running along
your right (east), high but civil, is St. Bartholomew's Hospital.
Smithfield is 'Smoothfield', for century on century a level and
open space, originally just outside the City walls, for the
citizens' entertainment and exercise, for spectacle. There is a
famous account by Fitzstephen of the medieval horse-fair,
and in the nineteenth century London costers were still select-

ing their donkeys there with fastidious expertise; the meat is now dead. From the twelfth to the nineteenth century one of the greatest of English annual fairs was held there in August, St. Bartholomew's, and it was the site of the major cloth fair when England's wealth rested on wool. As place of spectacle inevitably also it became place of execution—in some ways the most dramatic perhaps was that tough moment when the young Richard II faced Wat Tyler and his rebels here in 1381 —when Lord Mayor Walworth drew his great sword and in summary decision cut down Tyler, and the revolt melted away. But Smithfield's ugliest agony is of fire, and the hideous burning alive, in the name of God, of Catholics by Protestants and Protestants by Catholics in the sixteenth century.

St. Bartholomew's Hospital, on the right, is the oldest hospital still to be on its original site in London, founded in 1123, though the present building dates from 1702 (when the very handsome gateway, with its statue of Henry VIII, was built). Within it is busy yet cloistral in atmosphere rather like a university college. It has a hall of great dignity by James Gibbs, and an opulent main staircase in brown and gold adorned with Hogarth's best-known excursions into serious history painting, 'The Pool of Bethesda' and 'The Good Samaritan', quoting here and there from Raphael and Van Dyck—much run down by contemporaries but ('Bethesda' especially) with some beautiful work in them (not generally visitable, but serious inquirers will normally be admitted by previous arrangement). The little church within the hospital is generally visible on inquiry, and is worth a look, in its present very unusually octagonal shape by Thomas Hardwick of 1825. The medical history of the hospital is long and of the utmost distinction: William Harvey, demonstrator of the circulation of the blood and one of the great English empirical geniuses, was its chief physician from 1609 to 1643, and the teaching college, 'Barts', is perhaps the most famous in England.

Beyond, in the north-east corner of West Smithfield, you will see the black and white overhang of a late Elizabethan half-timbered house (restored, but of a very pretty design) over a battered thirteenth-century arched doorway, leading to a church that is, with the exception of the chapel in the Tower, the oldest in London: **St. Bartholomew the Great.** Both it and the hospital were founded by a worldly and eccentric courtier of Henry I, Rahere, about 1123, following a personal religious crisis; it was originally a great Augustinian Priory of the twelfth and thirteenth century, but becoming in due course at the Reformation parochial—and also then proving too large. The great nave was allowed to decay; the thirteenth-century archway was an entrance to it, but where it was you now pass through the picturesque, tree-hung, little graveyard, to the present entrance. Inside is immense, of weighty substantial solidity, admitting light as if magnanimously on sufferance, and hugely off balance: only the top of the cross-shape remains, the former chancel and transepts. The transepts are constricted uncomfortably by modern restoration, but elsewhere restoration has been remarkably successful (it was very necessary, as so much of the fabric had been hewn about for lay purposes—the Lady Chapel was for years a fringe-factory, and a blacksmith's forge was in the north transept). The grand march of great plain rounded column and round arch, with the gallery over—all Norman, though the clerestory above is Perpendicular—to the rounded close of the apse and back, is one of the most nobly satisfying things in London. It is interrupted, in the gallery on the south side, as if by a grace note, by a delicately pretty little oriel bay inserted just before the Reformation by Prior Bolton, presumably as a private oratory and accessible from his lodgings; it is marked with his punning device (an arrow—bolt—transfixing a barrel—tun). The Lady Chapel beyond the apse is of about 1330, much restored. Of the original furnishings not much has survived, but the font is said to be the only medieval one in the City—in it Hogarth (born in Bartholomew Close just to the south) was baptised in 1697. The church is also rich in monuments, especially (north of the sanctuary) that of the founder, Rahere. Retrospective, for he died in 1143 and this is of about 1500, but very elegant, tomb-chest under canopy, and set with little kneeling monks holding books inscribed with verses from Isaiah. Also a nice memento of Sir Robert Chamberlayne (d. 1615), a little kneeling figure revealed by two angels holding the curtains apart. In the south ambulatory a fairly elaborate memorial to Sir Walter Mildmay (d. 1589), one of Elizabeth I's Chancellors of the Exchequer and founder of Emmanuel College, Cambridge, and other good monuments mainly Elizabethan and Jacobean. An odd association of the church is with Benjamin Franklin, who worked here—in 1725, during one the various permutations of the functions of the Lady Chapel when it was used as printer's office.

Immediately north of the church, the road called Cloth Fair celebrates in name the old function of Smithfield; in it Inigo Jones's father was a clothworker, and it still has one splendid, well-restored façade from the seventeenth century (Nos. 41–2, probably post-Great Fire, but note the wooden bay-windows which suggest an earlier date). The north side of Smithfield is the long range of the **Meat Market**, biggest of its kind in England; to be seen at its characteristic busiest and bloodiest of course early in the morning any time between 5 and 9. Smithfield seems to breed its own brand of porters, immensely meaty too, in blood-stained blue or white, hearty, articulate and bustling, and enough at 6 a.m. of a dank day, humping carcases around, to turn even the strongest stomach at least temporarily vegetarian. You can pass through the market to Charterhouse Street; if you take the central avenue it brings you opposite the junction of St. John Street. A hundred yards up this to the left is St. John's Lane, over which is **St. John's Gate**, once again the former entry to a Priory— of the Order of the Hospital of St. John of Jerusalem, known as the Knights Hospitallers. Built about 1148, burned by Wat Tyler in 1381, and rebuilt much in its present shape in 1504. The order was revived in 1831, and moved back here in 1873, and is now (St. John's ambulances) a familiar feature of the London scene. The room over the arch is the Council Chamber; it has various relics of the order and can be visited by previous arrangement with the Curator. Part of the church of the Priory survives, though this involves a slight excursion north from our main route, to St. John's Square, beyond St. John's Lane; this—and other churches of the order: cf. the Temple Church, p. 306—had a circular nave like the Church of the Holy Sepulchre at Jerusalem; the site of this is marked in the cobbles of the square, but it was rebuilt and then the church was blitzed, and rebuilt again; the crypt, however, has excellent Norman work, and the most beautiful effigy of the late sixteenth century in England, though Spanish work presumably and of a Spanish knight of the Order (with the eight-point star on his breast), Juan Ruyz de Vergara, Proctor of the Langue of Castile in the Order of St. John, in serene dignity of sleep with a little page dozed off at his feet.

Reversing back down St. John Street, turn left along Charterhouse Street; this brings you to a green square set off it to the north in an abrupt seclusion: **Charterhouse Square**. 'Neat and comely' it was by 1657, and has remained so, in its time quite a grand address and still with some nice old houses (4–5, are early eighteenth century with later doorways), and a general air of placid coherence. The Gateway to Charterhouse itself on the north (fourteenth century)—the third former priory (Charterhouse is a corruption of 'chartreuse' and nothing to do with charters) that we have met on this walk, all originally founded just on the outskirts of the medieval City. The **Charterhouse** was rather war-damaged, but has been fully restored and is worth visiting (by previous application to the Registrar only; usually by guided parties on Saturdays). It was founded originally by a soldier, Sir Walter de Manny, in 1371 (and it proved a tough community: their Prior at the Reformation, John Houghton (now the Blessed) was quartered for refusing to submit, and one quarter hung on the gate of the priory, but the monks still held out); then it passed to the Howards, but was bought in 1611 by Thomas Sutton, a rich soldier, who left the enormous sum of £200,000 to endow it as a charity. It had two functions, as a hospital for genteel and military pensioners, and as a school which was to become one of the great public schools of England, with a distinguished roll of alumni—there Addison and Steele were co-scholars; John Wesley, Thackeray (it is 'Greyfriars' in *The Newcomes*). In 1872 the school moved to Godalming in Surrey. The foundation's income, now much depreciated, maintains still in the old buildings some forty elderly pensioners (male, and Anglican). The first chapel was in the Master's Court, through the entrance gateway, and there the founder's coffin was discovered during the post-war restorations (he was buried near the original altar). The present chapel is to the north-east (the architecture in general rambles agreeably, and reflects still the lay-out of a mainly sixteenth-century manor) on the site of the original chapter-house, converted after the death of the second founder, Sutton. His tomb is the most spectacular object in it, one of the most elaborate, busy, and in execution, accomplished compilations of mannerist sculpture in England (effigy by Nicholas Stone, 1611), with an extensive bas-relief of the brethren attending chapel. Pulpit, arcade and some of the other woodwork is also of Sutton's time. Note Vanity as a small boy blowing bubbles. The Great Hall (used as the dining-hall) is variously Tudor with a good fireplace, and the Great Chamber, finished about 1571, though badly bombed, has been well restored and is one of the best rooms of its period.

From Charterhouse Square east, Carthusian Street takes you in a hundred yards to **Aldersgate Street**, for centuries the main approach to London from the north. In a house here at a prayer meeting, John Wesley on 24 May 1738, was granted that divine assurance that changed his personal life and the history of the Church in England. In the twentieth century, Aldersgate Street was more or less knocked out of existence in the blitz. Opposite you now is, to the north, the completed Golden Lane development (by Chamberlain, Powell and Bon), and, confronting you, the towers and domestic bastions of the Barbican, the mammoth rebuilding of scores of acres laid waste by the blitz, in an attempt to replant a resident community in the City. Conceived though by no means finished, in the period when high rise buildings were thought to be the stuff of Paradise, the Barbican does not respond to the current slogan of Small is Beautiful. Yet, irrespective of that, few will deny that it is impressive. Almost lost, there survives in its midst **St. Giles Cripplegate** over on Fore Street, lonely in its concrete wilderness, with the great shining slabs of London Wall rising south of it. St. Giles, if you wish to make another excursion off the main route, via the intricacies of Barbican, was an old church, re-built in 1545, spared by the Great Fire but gutted by the blitz, and now rebuilt again. It is famous particularly for the people buried in it—John Speed the map-maker, Frobisher, and John Milton (a bust of him by Bacon; a body believed to be his was turned up in 1790, but most of it had been sold by the next day as souvenirs). Oliver Cromwell married in the church in 1620. In the graveyard you can see three bastions of the old wall of the City of London.

Alternatively if you prefer it you can walk down the western flank of the Barbican, along Aldersgate: then as you reach London Wall, running east (to the left: no 'wall' now, but instead a double carriageway) you see alongside its northern edge the oldest part of the Barbican Development—giant stride of cool cellular giant slabs, six of them, identical in shape. All office blocks, for this is the 'commercial fringe' of the development, and linked by upper level footways along the top of their continuous two-storeyed podium. On a fine day, as you look down the road, the first shutter flash of the impression on your retina may be exhilarating: the shape of things to come. But it *has* come, and you may think, sizing up its seven-league stride, that your own stride is not seven-league, and that there is a not-so-small desert between each block. It's draughty on those podiums, and goodness how small you are.

Actually on the corner of Aldersgate and London Wall, in part of the last tall block to be developed there, you should find the new Museum of London (architects Powell and Moya; scheduled to open in 1975, it really *should* be open by 1977). Here are to be merged the contents (see p. 180) of the former London Museum, shown in Kensington Palace till 1975, and those of the former Guildhall Museum which since the war had shifted uneasily from temporary quarters in the Royal Exchange and elsewhere. The new Museum is to re-display, no doubt in a splendid new arrangement, the treasury of past Cities of London. Still the most exciting are the finds made at the site of the Mithraic Temple, going back to about AD 90: the most substantial Roman discovery made in the City since the war—in 1954 it gathered dense crowds when it was revealed in digging the foundations for Bucklersbury House above Walbrook (see p. 339). Of the mysterious sun-god himself, Mithras, there is a good marble head with Phrygian cap, perhaps from a group of a bull-sacrifice; a marble head of the god of the underworld, Serapis (with a corn-measure on his head), and a rather later (perhaps fourth century), marble group featuring Bacchus, of coarser quality, but the late Roman little round silver box with African animals chasing round it is delightful. There are fragments of Samian and Roman pottery, mostly very mute, very broken, yet flickering the imagination with faint ghosts of those who used them, broke them, threw them away, so many centuries ago in London. There are later fragments too, pieces of the Eleanor Cross that stood in Cheapside (late thirteenth century; cf. p. 95), various fragments of medieval statuary, ornaments, weapons (and a very Italian bronze reliquary head, staring with void eyes, of about 1550 but found in the Thames near Wapping); then, earlier, rare, fragments of the Saxons, of the Vikings; Roman frippery, glass, tiles, figurines, shoes even, sandals—and even a well-preserved predecessor of a bikini in leather.

Going on south down Aldersgate, mostly the old (i.e. Victorian) envelops you again (in Little Britain, off to the right, Mr. Jaggers had his office in *Great Expectations*, while Professor Hitchcock has singled out No. 12 as a mature example of arcaded warehouse design of 1858). And on its south corner, west, a nice little modest little red brick box of a church, **St. Botolph Aldersgate,** small tower topped by small wooden bellcote rather as if for doves; inside there is a delightful late eighteenth-century interior, with coffered apses to east and west, dark wood galleries, and a richly emphatic Agony in the Garden east window of the same period (also a delicate portrait medallion by Roubiliac to Elizabeth Smith, d. 1750). Its churchyard is now a leafy garden holding a charming hush deep in the massive buildings above, with a tiny rill of a very welcome fountain and a large bronze statue of Sir Robert Peel. It has, further, a very odd little arcade with tablets commemorating acts of heroism in humble life, for which the painter G. F. Watts, very characteristically, was responsible in 1887: all are for people who gave their lives in saving life. The Park itself is known as **Postmen's Park,** for the buildings that overhang it are mostly of the General Post Office. This occupies a large area between here and Newgate Street to the south; the Chief Office, King Edward Street, is open twenty-four hours a day, and a statue of Rowland Hill, founder of the Penny Post, is outside; the buildings were much bomb-damaged, as beyond them, to the south-west, was Wren's Christ Church—on the site of the former Greyfriars Monastery—of which only the elegant three-tiered steeple is to be left. Guided tours of the Post Office, with its own automatic electric mailbag railway which runs underground for some $6\frac{1}{2}$ miles, and of the Telegraph Office, can be arranged by writing to the Regional Director, London Postal Region, E.C.1.

From Postmen's Park, retracing a few yards north, engage to the east along London Wall on its south side, bearing right off it very soon into Silver Street (once, of course, for the silversmiths); right down Wood Street and left at the surviving Wren Gothic tower of St. Alban into Love Lane ('Love Lane, so called of wantons', noted Stow in the sixteenth century, but not notable for them now). Thus to **Aldermanbury,** and on the corner there was till recently another Wren Church, St. Mary; a modest little church gutted in the blitz, it made a romantic ruin, especially the beautiful unusually composed shell of its east end. Expertly dismantled, however, the whole surviving fabric was shifted across the Atlantic to Westminster, Fulton, Missouri, where it has been restored as a memorial for Winston Churchill. But a garden has been preserved in its stead, and in it happily too the bust of Shakespeare that once stood outside the church—the editors of the First Folio, his colleagues Condell and Heminge, were both buried here, and in the church Milton married his second wife, Katherine Woodcock, in 1656. Turning south down Aldermanbury, with the new building of the Guildhall Library on your left (opened 1974) incorporating a rich Clock Museum (from the Worshipful Company of Clockmakers), and then left along Gresham Street (see p. 358) to yet another Wren church, that has been bombed but this time fully and lavishly restored: **St. Lawrence Jewry** ('Jewry' from the Jews who used to live around her until expelled in 1290). It was a big, plainish but very expensive box of a church as rebuilt by Wren, its interior furnished with terrific magnificence, all burned in December, 1941. It is once again now very magnificent in terms of spacious light, air and white paint and a very great deal of gold, for it is the place of worship of the City Corporation, whose home of ceremony you will find round the corner of the church's east end (the exterior of which is a serene composition with fine carved ornament).

Guildhall, focal point of the government of the City of London for over a thousand years, is sited with a typical London informal reticence, off Gresham Street, not in a square or a park, but in Guildhall Yard. Yard it is too, the width of the nine bays of the façade (only in the latter part of the twentieth century has the City decided the Yard does not allow enough room to permit proper deployment of pikemen on festival occasions and has proposed to enlarge it, sweeping away the pleasant eighteenth-century wing to the west the replacement, by Giles Scott and Partners, is a free improvisation on the mood of the adjoining façade but in, perhaps, rather a loud voice). The original façade is a charming essay on Gothic and classical, with four fantastic gay pinnacles and an exuberant coat-of-arms contradicting the slightly severe expression of the plain pointed windows beneath (by George Dance, 1788-9); but the big porch by which you enter, with tierceron vaulting, is original of the early fifteenth century (open 10-5; Sundays, summer, 2-5). Immediately beyond, the Great Hall, 152 feet long, is also basically of the fifteenth century, though much rebuilt after the Great Fire and again after the blitz. It is now used for City ceremonial, such as the election of the Sheriffs (Midsummer Day), for the Lord Mayor's banquet after his election in November, but in the sixteenth century was used for important trials—here were condemned the Protestant martyr Anne Askew (burned at Smithfield in 1546), equally the Jesuit Garnet in 1606; Henry Howard, Earl of Surrey, the poet, 1547, and in 1553 poor Lady Jane Grey and her husband. Its most celebrated inhabitants were two wooden giants. Gog and Magog, according to legend imaging the struggle between the ancient Britons and the Trojans. They burned in the blitz but have been replaced by modern versions. Otherwise the Hall has some emphatic sculptured memorials. The earliest is local, of 1772, showing a Lord Mayor, William Beckford, in the act of delivering a sharp rebuke to the Crown on behalf of the City; the later ones are to national heroes, starting with the best and liveliest to the elder Pitt (by Bacon, 1782); others represent the younger Pitt, Wellington and Nelson. The most recent is a seated bronze by Oscar Nemon of Churchill.

Below the Hall is the crypt, with very impressive vaulting in blue Purbeck marble, and to the east the Art Gallery and the Library. The Gallery generally houses a loan exhibition (but owns some interesting statues, the Charles II and John Cutler formerly on the College of Physicians and other statues from the first Royal Exchange). The Library is a first-class and up-to-date source for reference, but also a main source for any-one interested in delving into the history of London, on which it has the most extensive section and a great deal of original source-material, such as records of many of the City Companies. It holds the one book from the original City library bought from a bequest by Whittington, a Bible; Ralph Agas's plan of London in 1591; the Great Chronicle of London that old Stow used—endless material relating to London, like copies of the London Gazette: an edition of 1666, for example: 'The ordinary course of this paper having been interrupted by a sad and lamentable accident of Fire lately happened in the City of London . . .'

CHAPTER TWENTY-SEVEN

South Bank—Southwark to Lambeth

✌

ALMOST all of London south of the Thames I must simply omit. It is no mean omission, for the area is immense and ever-increasing, but it escapes the would-be guide as inevitably as it has escaped the boundaries of old London. There are of course individual sights to stop the visitor and drowned villages ghosting faintly under the surface; some of these I will mention, though with the barest of signals, in Chapter 28, but to form them into a connected route within a chapter is impossible.

The factor that for centuries cut off south London from north is the obvious one: the barrier of the Thames. Though the London watermen kept communications open between north and south from Bermondsey to Lambeth, the only part of the south bank that was properly integrated with old London was Southwark, the southern bridgehead of London Bridge; **Southwark** is indeed as old as London and the inevitable place to start this brief fringe perambulation of the south bank. Here all roads from south and south-east converged on London; the Romans were there, already no doubt with the inns which were to become famous—Southwark was the London terminus for all traffic from the south. Indeed, by 1619, one source could state unequivocally that Southwark's population consisted 'chiefly of innkeepers'. But it was by then already famous for other things. While intimately connected with the City over the other side of London Bridge (and known as the Ward of Bridge Without from 1556) it remained in some essential points independent of the City, and it was in its 'liberties', outside the range of City authority, that the London theatre flourished at the Rose, the Swan, the Globe, in Shakespeare's time. The district was also famous for the church (the London great houses of the prelates of the southern sees, of which the only survivor is away over at Lambeth); for prisons, including the euphonious

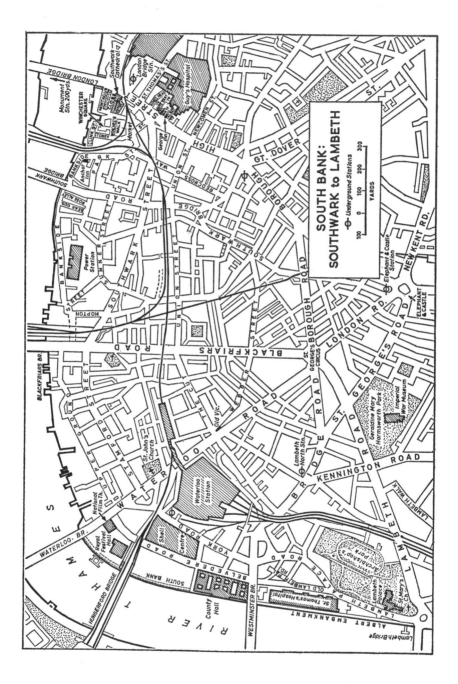

SOUTH BANK:
SOUTHWARK to LAMBETH

⊖ Underground Stations

YARDS

100   0   100   200   300

Clink, which has survived even if in name only as the generic name of all prisons; and for brothels and for Southwark Fair that Hogarth drew in its hey-day.

If you come from the north bank, approach Southwark over London Bridge (see p. 258) (for which the Underground station is Monument). The view from the bridge, brand new though it is, remains still, up and down river, always uplifting, mysterious, escaping. On the south bank the patched, worn front of warehouses, attended by cranes, and above them, to the right of the bridge, rather modestly the square tower with its four steep pinnacles, of **Southwark Cathedral**, our first goal. Somewhat sunk below road level, abutted closely on the north by office buildings and looped in mid-air to the south by the lumbering, clanking railway viaduct, the church thus survives a little staidly, if also somewhat oppressed, amidst an industrial and commercial landscape which is one of the most spectacular—with a *terribilità* worthy of Piranesi—in London.

The Cathedral has developed out of a church founded in 1106, dedicated to St. Mary and known as St. Mary Overie (i.e. 'over the water'?); an Augustinian church with priory, supported by the Bishop of Winchester (then a European potentate in standing), whose town house was close by (and fragments in fact survive in Winchester Square nearby, half-swallowed up in the brick of the warehouses). The Norman church burned in 1212, and the new one was one of the earliest in England in the Gothic; the design is still basically of the thirteenth century, and so too much of the fabric, though the latter has suffered various vicissitudes, and the entire nave is a reconstruction of the 1890s. It is a great cross, with the tower over the crossing carried on four huge piers (each with an unusual, severe flat surface turned inwards); it has a basic simplicity that as you walk round it you may find both chaste and ultimately seductive; beyond the choir perhaps especially, where the retro-choir is not very tall and of four parallel naves all of equal height under the simple vaults, very equal, very placid. The great stone screen behind the high altar in the choir is basically late Perpendicular, given by Fox, Bishop of Winchester, about 1520, but its gilding and its elaboration of statues are all nineteenth century. The charm, however, that will cause most visitors to linger in the Cathedral is not the symmetry of the design but the notable accumulation of furnishings that the centuries have brought together here.

The monuments include a modern one to Shakespeare—it is only a few hundred yards from here to where the Elizabethan theatres flourished; Shakespeare's brother Edmund, Henslowe, Fletcher and Massinger (in one grave), are among his colleagues buried here. There is also a monument to the poet John Gower (1408); a famous effigy to the pill-merchant Lockyer (do not miss the epitaph), and the tomb of Lancelot Andrewes (1626), writer and great churchman. The Harvard Chapel commemorates the founder of Harvard, John, baptised here in 1608.

If you leave the church by the south-west door, you have the immediate choice of two areas either of which, particularly if you are rather late and it is dusk, or worse, deep night, may seem like a temporarily evacuated segment of the Inferno; both well worth seeing for their qualities of horrid picturesque. North and west, the canyons in the brick warehouses, dead-ends, the river the only way out to the north. Winchester Walk, Winchester Square, site of the old Bishop's palace. Clink Street, claustrophobic. But here a whole landscape, that in a few years, will seem both incredible and impossible to evoke, is crumbling: as London's port recedes to the east, the inner warehouses no longer have function. All, by the time you read this, may be modern offices and smart apartments. Meanwhile, you may meditate on prisons. Southwark had seven at one time or another, now all gone, but their atmosphere easily conjured up among the blank warehouses. The most famous of them, Marshalsea and King's Bench, were off the High Street to the south. King's Bench was burned in the Gordon Riots of 1780, though at once rebuilt. According to legend, Henry V as Prince of Wales was confined there; more certainly so were Smollett the novelist, and John Wilkes, and even more certainly, Mr. Micawber. The Clink Prison was not the most famous (and apparently anyway had relative amenities—the Catholic Gerard called his transfer there from the Counter in the Poultry in 1594 'a translation from Purgatory to Paradise'); technically, if ironically for the prison's inmates, the Clink was a 'liberty' under the Bishop of Winchester, but for the English theatre the 'liberty' was very real and the condition indeed of its existence free from the censorship of City of London authority.

South of the church, **Borough Market**, undercut among the railway viaducts, also of high sinisterness at dusk, and like other markets to be caught in its full teeming vitality only in the early hours of the morning. On the east side of the High Street, opposite the Cathedral, is London Bridge Station, into which channel the lines from Waterloo, Charing Cross, and Cannon Street, and whence they leave again for Kent; it is the trundling of these lines, high on their viaducts, that gives the area an extra dimension. Off the High Street, along the south flank of London Bridge Station, St. Thomas's Street; here was St. Thomas's Hospital, moved to Lambeth, where we shall see it later, in 1868. Its church (1703) still survives in a decorum of civil brick, and now is used as the Cathedral's Chapter House; alongside a row of old houses with some pretty doorways, and opposite it another famous hospital, Guy's, with an elegant courtyard open to the road, built from 1721 and founded by Thomas Guy (his statue, by Scheemakers, is in the forecourt), a London bookseller.

Back in the Borough High Street, a few yards farther south, a series of narrow courts preserve the memory of the famous Southwark coaching inns. The King's Head, in King's Head Yard (the building is modern); White Hart Yard. In Dickens's time there were still such inns—'great rambling queer old places with galleries and passages and staircases wide enough and antiquated enough to furnish material for a hundred ghost stories'. **The George** (tucked away in a court at No. 71 Borough High Street, precariously surviving amidst British Transport and in the shadow of tall factory chimneys) is the only partial survivor. It was originally built about a courtyard (as you can see such galleried inns in so many prints by Hogarth and Rowlandson), but only one side with gallery now remains, dating from some time after 1676 (date of the great Southwark fire). Farther south on the High Street, Chaucer's Tabard Inn, where he assembled his Canterbury Pilgrims late in the fourteenth century, was on the site of Talbot Yard. Still farther south, Newcomen Street (with fine carved royal arms of about 1730, once in the gate-house to London Bridge, at the King's Arms, and seventeenth-century bollards) goes to the left, and to the right, opposite, Union Street. First right off Union Street and north up **Redcross Way**. Here you might pause perhaps, though an unpropitious spot, in memory of St. Mary Magdalene—at the crossing of the two roads, under a factory, is what was known as Cross Bones Ground. All this area was once a formidable concentration of brothels (another benefit of the 'liberty' of the Clink) which afforded among other things some financial benefit to the Bishops of Winchester (whores were often called up to the sixteenth century—'Winchester geese'). They seem to have been administered not without some English feeling for fair play (thus a rule of 1162: 'no single woman to take money to lie with any man but she lie with him all night till the morrow'), but charity did not extend to the women when they died. They were not allowed to be buried in shriven ground; their unshriven graveyard was here, by the crossing of these two roads.

North up Redcross Way, under the railway viaduct and over Southwark Street, brings you to Park Street, which runs into **Bankside**. Where the two meet, Park Street bears left and a little way along here, somewhere under the brewery, is the site of the most famous theatre in the world, Shakespeare's Globe, built in 1599, burned in 1613, rebuilt and finally demolished in 1644: most of the late tragedies, including Hamlet, were played here. Bankside itself bears up through warehouses to the river and there goes west, a clear half mile almost to Blackfriars Bridge. No. 1 is happily a famous pub, the **Anchor**, said to be seventeenth century though recently rejuvenated; an excellent place to lunch, with the dramatic view of river and St. Paul's rising above the warehouses on the north bank. Log fires, old wine bottles, and portraits of Mrs. Thrale, the blue-stocking wife of Henry Thrale, the brewer of Barclay's (the brewery that now stands where once the Globe), and of Dr. Johnson their sometime guest. Also more ominously in the public bar, a plaque 4 feet above ground marks the flood high tide of 7 January 1928.

From here Bankside is most intimate with the water; warehouses with cranes attendant on whatever the river traffic may deliver up to them, but among them, a handful of surviving domestic houses of the late seventeenth and early eighteenth centuries. Also (just beyond Southwark Bridge that Bankside passes under) the narrow openings of Rose Alley and Bear Gardens recall the long gone Rose Theatre (where Shakespeare is said to have acted) and the Hope Theatre on the old bear garden. Then to the left, the huge monster Bankside power station, ejecting a plume of smoke, but beyond it

Bankside bears away inland before Blackfriars Bridge, into Hopton Street wherein, in the overweening presence of the warehouses, two charming survivals: a tiny house of about 1700 (No. 61 but derelict in 1975) and the pretty almshouses of 1752. Right at Southwark Street brings you to the top of Blackfriars Road and the approach to Blackfriars Bridge. Stamford Street continues west (now in Lambeth), a rather long 600 yards through some remaining brick terracing, to **Waterloo Road** and the approach to Waterloo Bridge.

To the left down Waterloo Road is a neo-classical church, St. John's (built on wooden piles from 1822, as the district, mostly marsh still, was being developed after the opening of the first Waterloo Bridge in 1817); gutted in the war, it was restored for the Festival of 1951, and is now rather gay inside with angels festive in a very Festive mood. Farther down the road, beyond the railway bridges, is the theatre long famous as the Old Vic (cf. p. 404). On the other side of the road is the many-levelled commuter warren of **Waterloo Station**. Going back north up Waterloo Road and then left into York Road, you will see its operatically pompous main entrance up a vast flight of steps—though minus now a celebrated lion that once topped Watney's Brewery, then (1951) moved here, but now graces the end of Westminster Bridge. Waterloo Station at rush hours, morning and evening, is a good place to observe the hurrying, ant-like, spectacle of London emptying or filling up, an operation performed here to merry music from the loud-speakers. Traditionally the station for stockbrokia, it still bobs copiously with bowler hats, though many of their owners dive direct from the suburban platforms into the depths of the 'Drain', that peculiarly claustrophobic direct line from Waterloo to the Bank.

On the other, river, side of Waterloo Station, cleft by the painted girders of Hungerford Railway Bridge to Charing Cross over the other side of the river, is the area known as South Bank. Derelict after the war, it was stripped down for the 1951 Festival of Britain Exhibition, still remembered fondly as an explosion of gaiety and style in the bleak post-war utility austerity era. Between Waterloo Bridge and Hungerford Bridge there survived from the Festival the **Royal Festival Hall**, a very able and in parts spectacular concert hall (by R. H. Matthew and Sir L. Martin), which now contends with the Albert Hall as the main orchestral centre of London. Its spacious foyers and dramatic staircases were for England a welcome innovation, and some claim its acoustics to be the most perfect in the world; in 1951 it was left uncompleted, but the revision and enlargement of the river front is now done, and ties in better with the other new buildings. Another survivor from the Festival is the National Film Theatre, moved to its present site, tucked actually under Waterloo Bridge, in 1957; this is well worth joining (it is normally open to members only) for anyone interested in revivals of classic films and for seasons of foreign films not generally visible on the commercial circuits. The development of the area farther south hung fire for years, but the **National Theatre** finally opened to much rejoicing in 1976 (in a superbly massed design by Denys Lasdun). The whole area is intricately linked with pedestrian flyovers and riverside walks; two small concert halls opened in 1967; the new Hayward (Arts Council) big exhibition gallery was finished in 1968, and the skyline is hard and brutal with concrete. But earlier commerce had dug resolutely down for two years into the Thames-side clay, and thence had heaved up, over seven and a half acres immediately inland from the South Bank site, the monstrous **Shell Centre,** the largest office block in the United Kingdom, holding 5,000 Shell workers and all mod cons. It was acclaimed in 1962 with a hail of abuse—'visual, sociological and communications disaster . . . a hormone-fed cottage', to quote but one missile —but is beyond sad doubt *there.* From the twenty-fifth floor (up 800 feet a minute in the high-level lifts) for a fee you can get a magnificent view of the London which it has bruised so fiercely. In front of it, towards the river, has risen the National Theatre which was temporarily housed in the Old Vic.

South again along the river is **County Hall**, the headquarters of the Council of Greater London, built (by Ralph Knott) from 1912 on. This used to seem vast, a gigantic nordic château, under its high-pitched dark roof, but now, even with its recent additions on the landward side, it has dwindled almost to the quaint and cosy in comparison with its huge neighbour. Still, it covers some six and a half acres; though the building for the moment seems static, the Council (elected by the ratepayers) is in the throes of reshaping. The interior of the building is visitable and is an interesting specimen of the grandly municipal taste in decor; visitors can also attend sessions of the Council, a sort of miniature parliament. For information, ring the Information Bureau (928-5000 ext. 7430)—or better, visit it; it is a mine of information on all things pertaining to London.

County Hall abuts on Westminster Bridge, and hence the last stretch of this walk can take you along the Albert Embankment, built in the 1860s, and a nice footway allowing inspection of the rippling façade of the Houses of Parliament on the bank opposite. Inland from the Embankment is again all change. Here still is at the time of writing old **St. Thomas's Hospital** (we glimpsed its first site at Southwark earlier in this chapter); in its present shape it lasted about a century, but its characteristic blocks with the rather Mediterranean-looking balconies are now dissolving as the big new building shapes up behind and through it. Beyond it—and this will no doubt look even more picturesque than now when the new hospital is up—is the basically medieval, irregular complex of **Lambeth Palace**, in brick with white facings; squared and castellated gatehouses; long, steeply pitched roof of the hall with its pretty little lantern; real Tudor chimneys and neo-Tudor turrets beyond. At its southern end the grey ragstone tower, mainly fourteenth century, of St. Mary, the parish church of Lambeth. Originally the palace was closer to the water, and the archbishops came and went (where now is a smart pier for the River Police) in the archepiscopal barge (Lambeth, according to some, means 'the loamhithe, or muddy landing-place', and indeed the whole area of the south bank as far east as Blackfriars was long known as Lambeth Marsh; County Hall floats on it on a concrete raft five feet thick). The palace is the last survivor of the great London seats of the bishops along this bank, and Canterbury has owned it since about 1200, Catholic and Protestant alike. Here in 1547, Cranmer did 'eat meat openly in Lent, in the Hall of Lambeth, the like of which was never seen since England was a Christian country'. Eleven years later, here Cardinal Pole died, last of the Catholic Archbishops in the brief Marian restoration, twelve hours after the queen who had welcomed him back from his exile in Rome. From Lambeth, under Charles I, Laud held sway until his fall, and here still the Archbishop of Canterbury has his abode in not unsumptuous wholesomeness. Parties of visitors are taken round, generally on Saturday afternoons (information from the chaplain).

Entrance is through the gate-house, an admirable example of Tudor brick, built by Cardinal Morton in 1490, and so right to the garden in front of the (neo-Gothic) residence of about 1828, though the fig-trees to the west are said to descend from some planted by Cardinal Pole. Beyond the figs, the Great Hall, ravaged under Cromwell and rebuilt by Archbishop Juxon after 1660 in a remarkable and winning Gothic-survival style ('a new old-fashioned hall', Pepys called it); it has a choice hammerbeam roof, but also a certain amount of elegant classical detailing about; there is an important library with some fine illuminated manuscripts. Beyond is the crypt, early thirteenth century, and the oldest surviving part of the Palace, and above it the Chapel itself, of some fifty years later but gutted in the war and now almost all restoration. The fifteenth-century Lollards' Tower, in Kentish ragstone, is really a water-tower but retains its name on the tradition that Wycliffe's supporters were imprisoned in it— Wycliffe himself certainly underwent his second trial for heresy in the chapel at Lambeth in 1378, but the prisoners in the massive little room at the top of the tower were more probably much later—Laudian Episcopalians. The palace has also a rich collection of portraits, a rather fascinating set of variations on the theme of lawn sleeves, from a good version of Holbein's famous dour painting of Archbishop Warham through the admirable Van Dyck of Laud—no doubt the painting that Laud found fallen to the floor in his study one night in 1640 ('God grant,' he wrote in his diary, 'this be no omen,' but perhaps it was, though he still had five troubled years to live before his head fell on the scaffold).

St. Mary's Lambeth, hard by the gatehouse of the Palace, is an ancient foundation but pleasantly rebuilt (except the tower) in 1851 by Philip Hardwick; tall and airy inside with some good old monuments to ecclesiastical dignities; the glass went in the war, but the little Pedlar's Window in the south chapel has been replaced no doubt in gratitude. It celebrates the Pedlar's Acre, which brought in 2s. 8d. a year when it was bequeathed to the church, but realised in hard cash in 1910, when it was sold to the County Council whose building now covers it, £81,000. Here lie among others Captain Bligh of the Bounty, and the two John Tradescants, father and son, perhaps the earliest museum-makers in England, in the seventeenth century—their collection, acquired rather discreditably by

Ashmole, went to found the Ashmolean Museum in Oxford. Their monument has a fascinating exuberance of images of ruin and death.

The exhausted visitor may now get back to the north bank across Lambeth Bridge, but those still in vigour may like to look at something of the interior of Lambeth, to the east down Lambeth Road. Some 600 yards down to the right, among new brick municipal housing blocks, opens off Lambeth Walk, home of the famous dance and site of a busy street market, and beyond that is Geraldine Mary Harmsworth Park, in which was once Bedlam. The first madhouse, Bethlehem Hospital (Bethlehem to Bedlam is an unnerving corruption), was at Bishopsgate Without and then at Moorfields, and had become one of the sights of London (for a good laugh) by the early seventeenth century; many descriptions of it survive, such as Ned Ward's in the 'London Spy', but its stark fury is to be felt in the last of the 'Rake's Progress' by Hogarth in the Soane Museum; in 1815 it was transferred to this park, where it remained until its latest remove to Kent, in 1930, the wings were then pulled down, leaving most prominently, and now a little over-large, the big pillared portico and French-looking dome (by Sydney Smirke, about 1840); into this moved a great array of records of another bedlam, of global conflict of sane men among themselves— the **Imperial War Museum** (open weekdays 10–6; Sundays 2–6). This was founded in 1920, in part as historical record, but also very much as a national memorial to the sacrifices of the First World War. In 1939 its purposes and functions had to be extended, and in 1953 (Korea) again. For those who knew either war, this museum will set off trains of personal memory like fuses. The enemy, stilled now to a lay figure in a clean uniform in a glass case; the grey German uniform looks archaic; and a few yards away from you perhaps a small boy who knew neither war whistling softly under his breath as he inspects with historical detachment the late Messerschmitt 163B.

CHAPTER TWENTY-EIGHT

Points of Interest Beyond

❧

Bayswater. The northern fringe of Hyde Park; gravelly soil with springs now subdued, but this was once the first commercial home of watercress. It was developed in copious stucco as the northern counterpart to Belgravia between 1830 and 1860, but never (for ever the 'wrong side of the Park') became either quite as stable as Belgravia nor quite as grand. It was first known as Tyburnia (being anchored at its western extremity at Marble Arch where was Tyburn gallows). Now that end is high fashion, a north-west extension of Mayfair, with one extremely elegant square (Connaught). Farther west the district waxes and wanes behind the big modern blocks of flats that front on to the Park, and is a classic home of the small hotel and the boarding house and the London landlady ('Nothing like that has ever happened in this part of the house'). Towards its western fringe is the vacuous London sight to slay all sight-seers: amidst a handsome ornate terrace of houses (Leinster Terrace), the façades of Nos. 23–4, uniform in all respects with the others except that they have no houses behind them—false as dickies, more false, to conceal the fact of life offered by the Metropolitan Railway running behind them. The village street of the area is Queensway, with its department store, Whiteley's, some good restaurants, and the only skating rink near to central London. The area gives on the west to Notting Hill and on the north to Paddington.

Bethnal Green Museum. (By Underground to Bethnal Green Station, Central Line; open 10–6; Sundays, 2.30–6.) In what was once one of the most notorious of London East End slum areas, still very depressed in parts. The Museum is an extension of the Victoria and Albert, and housed in an agreeable and interesting building of 1875 (incorporating the iron roofs used for the original South Kensington Museum, and with a celebrated tour-de-force of Victorian sculpture, John Bell's 'Eagle-Slayer', that was prominent at the 1851 exhibition). There is a general collection of paintings, pottery, silver, etc., but also a local collection on the history of the area and of local products such as silk from the Spitalfields weavers; important costumes and an admirable display of dolls and dolls' houses.

Cemeteries. The preceding chapters include many glimpses of the congregations of the dead in Inner London, not least at Westminster Abbey and St. Paul's. But very few are so to speak active, and in many cases the stones have been taken out, and stacked in pale and blank rows about their perimeter like a fence. They become elegiac City gardens—*Et in Arcadia Ego*. Many who eat their sandwiches in them do not even remember what they were. By the early nineteenth century, squalid and noxious, they had become a public scandal and recognised as a danger against the health of the living. Dickens, among others, campaigned against them, and after a Royal Commission, the large-scale, commercially organised, Victorian cemeteries of Inner Outer London were laid out. The first was at Kensal Green (1833), followed by Norwood, Highgate, Brompton and others. Some of these, even if not to all tastes, certainly rank among the sights of London. Kensal Green (by Underground, Bakerloo Line, Kensal Green Station) is perhaps the most extraordinary, with its 50,000 odd graves between the Harrow Road and the railway lines, presided over by the looming gasworks. Royal cachet was set upon it by the burial of two of George III's children (Sophia and the Duke of Sussex); stylistically, the tombs decaying present the decay of Classic into Gothic burgeoning into multitudinous Victoriana. Leigh Hunt, Thackeray, the two Brunels the engineers; Tom Hood, Trollope and the comic sporting artist John Leech are among those who lie here. It is of course interdenominational, the Anglican chapel being Doric and the Nonconformist Ionic; the Roman Catholic Annex (where lies Cardinal Wiseman) is to the west. Brompton also has its devotees, but Highgate Cemetery is more important (entry from Swain's Lane, in two parts, east and west of the road). Laid out in 1838, it is a very remarkable piece of landscaping, especially a strange circular sunk catacomb of Egyptian flavour about a big cedar tree, with the chancel of the parish church of Highgate high above. The most famous grave, topped with a vast somewhat Stalinist bust, is that of Karl Marx (d. 1883), but others include those of George Eliot, Faraday, Christina Rossetti. The modern cemeteries are farther out, and anyway much of the dignity has gone out of death; funerals that once would have been of black and purple slow-stepping splendour now slip discreetly past in sleek black limousines—if not over the speed limit usually not much below it—to the conveyor belts of the crematoria. But many of the old, small churchyards of villages now swallowed up into London, conceal strange vanities—the most extraordinary perhaps the life-size concrete, Arab tent with a medley of Christian and Mohammedan symbols, housing the tombs of Richard Burton, explorer and translator of the *Arabian Nights*, and his wife (in Mortlake Catholic Cemetery, North Worple Way). For Bunhill Fields, see under Wesley's House below.

Clapham. (By Underground, Northern Line to Clapham Common.) This was once an elegant country retreat for gentlemen, south of the Thames, but was a suburb by Thackeray's time, and is now very firmly ensconced within London. The High Street runs downhill from the station; first right down this is Clapham Park Road, and off it Triangle Place, the former location of the Museum of British Transport. In spite of widespread public opposition and controversy, the Museum was recently dispersed to the provinces (mainly York). It is a considerable loss to London, though perhaps one has no grounds to begrudge the rest of England so small a part of the wealth of the capital. North from the station takes you to Old Town and delicate surviving houses of old Clapham (beyond, in St. Paul's Church, one of the best surviving baroque figures in London, memorial to Sir Richard Atkins, d. 1689). Nos. 39–43 Old Town are Queen Anne; farther up, on the North Side of the large, plain, expanse of Clapham Common, are Georgian houses—at No. 29, Sir Charles Barry, architect of the Houses of Parliament, lived and died (1860), and here too, a last echo of the ubiquitous Samuel Pepys, for in a previous house on the same site he died in 1703 (see p. 374). On the opposite side of this corner of the Common, there is a charming enclave in Belgravia mood, remnant indeed of a development said to be by Thomas Cubitt from 1822, Crescent Grove.

Dulwich. (By Southern Region railway to North Dulwich station.) Another south London village, with a blessedly placid green heart still. In Dulwich Village, south from the Station, some good houses, and south again from there (College Road) brings you into rural open spaces. The Park is famous for azaleas and rhododendrons, and much of the rural character is due to Edward Alleyn (d. 1626), famous Shakespearean actor and bear-baiter, who founded here the College of God's Gift, a trust responsible for Dulwich College, a major public school, and, more notably for the visitor, Dulwich Picture Gallery. This is housed in a remarkable Gallery designed by Sir John Soane in 1811–13, a commission with a peculiarly posthumous domestic specification —it was to house its donor, Desenfans and his friend Sir Francis Bourgeois (picture dealers and collectors), and Desenfans's wife, for perpetuity among the things they had loved, so that the gallery incorporates also a mausoleum. Blitzed, and restored, the building no longer quite fulfils Soane's intentions, but his extraordinary originality, his search for pure architecture in modulations of light and of volume, are still striking. The pictures are remarkable. The nucleus of twenty-eight pictures (mainly portraits) left by Alleyn was increased by some eighty more left by William Cartwright some sixty years later. Most of these are artistically indifferent, but include unique and most rare records such as the self-portrait of Shakespeare's colleague and friend, Richard Burbage. The quality, however, was remedied when the great collection of Desenfans and Bourgeois came to Dulwich. By British painters there some good portraits (Cartwright Bequest) by Lely's short-lived pupil, John Greenhill, and by Lely himself; a charming little Fishing Party by Hogarth, and an important group of portraits of the Linley family by Gainsborough and by Lawrence—also some Reynoldses, including a studio version of his formidable Michelangelesque apotheosis of 'Mrs. Siddons as the Tragic Muse' (compare Gainsborough's version of her as a very spry lady of fashion in the National Gallery). The Gallery is very rich in Dutch and Flemish— Teniers, some ravishing Rubens sketches, and Rembrandt.

There are two little Raphael panels; Murillo; and superb
Poussins, but for many the supreme attraction will be the
liquid fantasia of colour and line in Watteau's 'Les Plaisirs
du Bal'. Open 10–6 (closed Mondays), but closing at 5, 1 September–15 October and 16 March–30 April; at 4, 16 October–
15 March; Sundays 2–5 (April and September), 2–6 (May–
August).

East End. A somewhat vague expression, but generally used
to indicate the area lying east of the limits of the City of
London, from the Tower to Liverpool Street Station, and as
far east as the old limits of the County of London; including
Stepney, Bethnal Green, Shoreditch, Hackney and Poplar.
Its traditional associations are with slums (by 1598, Stow
could call Wapping 'a continual street or filthy passage'), the
London poor as described by Mayhew; with the docks and
the huge bleak brick prison warehouse architecture; and with
a teeming vitality expressed in the Jewish street-markets, the
pubs, in the street life, the explosive exuberance at festival or
funeral, in sudden violences. Much of this remains, though
the East End has become the scene of some of the most
extensive development schemes in housing by the London
County Council in the bomb-devastated areas, and the poor
are not so poor (though some districts, like Cable Street just
east of the Tower, will still appal). The East End contains
some well-known sights, set pieces for any London tourist:
Wapping High Street and its warehouses and the Prospect of
Whitby pub; the three great Hawksmoor churches which for
staggering grandeur, surpass his churches farther west—all in
Stepney, St. George-in-the-East, Christ Church Spitalfields,
and St. Anne Limehouse (all war-damaged and the subject of
suitably passionate campaigns for restoration); the most
splendid of all surviving London eighteenth-century shop-
fronts, in Artillery Lane off Bishopsgate; the pubs, on
Saturday nights, or, in the dock areas particularly, even at
midday of a weekday you may find people singing; the street-
markets, most famously Petticoat Lane (Middlesex Street) off
Whitechapel Road, on a Sunday morning, raucous and
pullulating. In curious contrast, a little farther east down
Whitechapel Road, the Whitechapel Art Gallery (weekdays
11–6, except Monday; Sundays 2–6; District Line, Aldgate
East station), in a chunky, aggressive, art-nouveau barracks

by Townsend, has sponsored in recent years some of the most exciting exhibitions (de Stael, Pollock, etc.) in London. Throughout the area there are also surviving here and there, often in a state of most picturesque decay, individual houses and groups of houses from the seventeenth and eighteenth centuries. In my experience, however, the East End, which can become on close acquaintance almost the most exciting of London atmospheres, is the most difficult for tourists, particularly foreign tourists, to 'work' alone. A personal guide is the real answer, preferably someone who has lived in the East End and knows it backwards.

Hampstead to Highgate. High on their ridge to the north, these two retain, more than any others, their atmosphere of off-centre retreats for refreshment and rural repair of spirits jaded by the city. The village of Hampstead boomed early in the eighteenth century, and became almost spa—healthful waters included (Well Walk and Flask Walk), and cherished home of some very famous Londoners, particularly associated with John Constable and John Keats. Now it is closest in atmosphere to Chelsea, but a hill-borne, airy Chelsea, full of pretty houses, painted up to the nines, narrow streets angled steeply up and down, and evidence of prosperous art and intellect (recently the admirable High Hill bookshop bore a notice, 'Children of Progressive Parents admitted only on leads'), and full of money. Go south down the hill from Hampstead Underground Station (Northern Line, with the deepest lift in London), to Keats Grove with Keats House, where the poet lived for that brief but incredibly fertile two years, 1818-20; it is open to the public (weekdays, 10-6), and has many relics of the poet, and a mulberry tree under which he is said to have written the 'Ode to a Nightingale'. Back at the Tube station again, fifty yards west along Heath Street brings you to the opening on the left of Church Row, one of the best streets in London let alone Hampstead, terrace houses of red-brown brick ranged in the most wellbred yet unstuffy and simple felicity, all of about 1720 (or almost all; intruders on the north). The church at the end, St. John's, is gothicky 1743, with many later alterations, and splendid iron gates bought in 1747 from a mansion of almost mythical splendour, the Duke of Chandos's Canons. The impression inside is mainly nineteenth century, but there is a very handsome mid-eighteenth-century pulpit (and a bust of Keats by an admirer from Boston, Anne Whitney, 1894). In the south-east corner of the graveyard lies John Constable. On the right of the church (north) goes Holly Walk, very much up, into a charming warren of little roads and alleys up and down and about the spur of hill between here and Heath Street. The houses, mixing the fairly grand and spacious with the cottage, include Romney's romantic dwelling (Holly Bush Hill), and in the Grove, Fenton House, a National Trust property (open weekdays except Tuesday, 10–1 and 2–5, or dusk; Sundays from 2 only), of 1693, all in a walled garden, with Lady Binning's collection of porcelain and furniture, and also the Benton-Fletcher collection (which used to be at No. 3 Cheyne Walk) of early keyboard musical instruments—including a very early harpsichord of 1612 that Handel once played on. Other houses to look out for are New Grove House (George du Maurier's between 1874 and 1895); Admiral's House; and Grove Lodge (the novelist John Galsworthy's from 1918 till 1933). No. 3 Lower Terrace is where Constable first moved into his beloved Hampstead in 1821. Up Heath Street, cut in above Heath Street, is very villagey, still recognisable as it was shown in a famous Pre-Raphaelite picture, 'Work' by Ford Madox Brown (featuring Carlyle), but Heath Street itself pants with cars climbing up out of London through a very contemporary medley of espresso bars and antique shops. South-east and east of Heath Street (which is the great divide of Hampstead) another cluster of houses jumbled on narrow streets up and down the hill, some of the houses most covetably pretty. In Well Walk (the healing waters of which are commemorated in a little fountain) was Constable's last Hampstead home (at No. 40) from 1826 until the year of his death, 1837. The reason he chose Hampstead, apart from health, was Hampstead Heath, the great rolling space of grass and trees and sky where he painted so often, and which runs to Highgate, east and Parliament Hill to the south. This is simply for walking in, for getting lost in, for lying down in the sun in, and needs no commentary. The main road running across the top at the north (Spaniards Road/Hampstead Lane) goes past the Spaniards, a partly weather-boarded eighteenth-century inn of great picturesque and romantic association. Before that, tucked into a fold at the western corner of the Heath, by its pond, and itself like an island, the odd hamlet called the Vale of Health, where Leigh Hunt took a room after his release from prison in 1816, and on which the great Bank Holiday fair of Hampstead Heath seems to centre. Beyond the Spaniards and south of the main road is Ken Wood House, pale and serene along the terrace over the slope and its own lake with fake, eye-catcher bridge (also a concert-shell for open air concerts in the summer). The house, rebuilt by Robert Adam for the first Earl of Mansfield in 1767–9, has a very typical and sophisticatedly pretty library, with delicate plaster work and ceiling paintings; but more important, it houses a formidable collection of paintings left to the nation in 1927 by the Earl of Iveagh—mainly, in bulk, English eighteenth century; much Romney (a famous one of 'Lady Hamilton' at a spinning wheel), Reynolds, but especially the most ravishing Gainsborough of 'Lady Howe' in a Chinese hat and a dress of shimmering pink, almost shocking, almost edible. But these are not the greatest pictures; there are also Van Dycks, a Cuyp, a most fascinating view of London Bridge in 1639 (?) by a very rare Dutchman, Claude de Jongh; there is the Vermeer of the 'Guitar Player', glinting, cool, full of music, and there is one of the most formidable, most haunting paintings in the world—the great late 'Self-Portrait' by Rembrandt, of the most realistic, down-to-earth yet mysterious and moving majesty. Ken Wood House is open weekdays 10–7, or dusk; Sundays from 2, and offers refreshments in its old coach house, and also in the summer usually a good loan exhibition. East of Ken Wood, Hampstead Lane, or a walk through the heath, brings you to Highgate, again with many pretty houses clustered at the top of its hill, a good park (Waterlow), its famous cemetery (see p. 409), and on Highgate Hill the Whittington Stone, only recent (1821), but as good a guess as any to record the spot where Whittington rested, with no doubt his cat, and heard the bell of Bow ringing out, and turned again. From all the ridge from Hampstead to Highgate, the views over London to the south are extraordinary.

Kensington. The museum-hive of South Kensington is surveyed in Chapter 12, but the area of central Kensington west of Hyde Park needs at least indicating (any bus along the south of the Park going west, or by Inner Circle to Kensington High Street Station). The village street, Kensington High

Street, though also a main route out of London, is busy with shops, including one presiding department store, Barkers. Next door was Derry and Toms; then, for a few years fabulous Biba's that overgrew and burst in 1975. The famous roof garden must not be abandoned. From opposite Barker's, Church Street runs north up Campden Hill and is very rich in antique shops; in architecture rather stodgily middle-aged mid-nineteenth century stucco but with some charming little streets like Bedford Gardens off it. Behind Barker's to the south, Kensington Square, with some good old houses (J. S. Mill lived at No. 18, Mrs. Patrick Campbell at No. 33). About half a mile west down Kensington High Street, on the north side, is Holland Park, where until the incendiary bombs took hold in the blitz, the great Whig dynasty of the Foxs, with titles of Holland and of Ilchester, still maintained a great Jacobean country house with its park all private, almost in central London. It is now public, though still with a lovely air of retirement, still with ornamental geese and peacocks, and among them the children of diplomats playing in all the tongues of the world; also nannies and prams. At the southern end, on Kensington High Street, is the new (1962) exhibition hall of the Commonwealth Institute, with terraces, smooth green water, walls of pale blue opaque glass, and a green roof like a spaceman's party hat. Externally the effect is quite gay and cheerfully unorthodox; internally, windowless, it is not so effective, and one may feel that the architect has allowed the heady notion of hyperbolic paraboloid (which is what the roof is) to induce forgetfulness of the function of the museum, which is to exhibit objects. It is exuberant inside, but almost impossible to get a grip on, in a series of galleries, flying staircases, broken levels; one can never be sure quite where one is, and, constantly groping for one's bearings, loses the display in the overwhelming décor. The Commonwealth Institute (10–5.30; Sundays 2.30–6)—it was founded as the Imperial Institute in 1887—is for the propagation of the gospel of British Commonwealth, and is very much educational, surveying in a series of dioramas and other displays (some of them beautifully and very imaginatively realised, and absorbing, once one has established one's direction in the building), the peoples of the Commonwealth, their various modes of life; the climates in which they live, their natural resources and their industries. Temporary art exhibitions are held in a special gallery, and there are free film shows, and a restaurant. Up in the Park behind it are the melancholy remains of the blitzed Holland House—the west wing and the arcaded ground floor of the south court (and a tea-room in the delightful orangery which is to be remodelled). The house was begun in 1605; later Addison (by virtue of marrying the widowed Countess of Warwick) lived there, and later in the eighteenth and nineteenth centuries (after the Fox family had bought it), it was famous as an intellectual and political hive of energy; Metternich, Talleyrand and Humboldt were often there, and later Gladstone, Macaulay, and G. F. Watts. Immediately east of it, a sparse functional Youth Hostel in not disagreeable contrast, and north and west of it the gardens are a delight. Farther west along Kensington High Street again, to the south, another good, large square (Edwardes) is hidden off it by Earl's Terrace. On the north side of Kensington High Street the ambient roads are no longer stucco, but semi-palatial high Victorian red brick, a great centre for high Victorian art in a very distinctive style of building. In Melbury Road, Holman Hunt died at No. 18 in 1910; No. 6 was built by G. F. Watts in 1876. The curious, now very remote—so much so as to be almost magical—sumptuousness of that civilisation can best be appreciated in the house of the Olympian President of the Royal Academy, Lord Leighton, in Holland Park Road, which is open to the public (weekdays, 11–5); especially its Moorish hall, inward-looking, set with blue tiles by William de Morgan, and with a tinkling fountain.

Notting Hill. (By Underground to Notting Hill Station, Central or Inner Circle Line.) You emerge from a very sleek new underground station, with fluorescent lighting of the kind now replacing the old everywhere and taking the glamour out of the Underground, on to the north side of Notting Hill Gate, one of the first big developments of post-war London set about the main road west from north of Hyde Park. South of Notting Hill Gate is respectable Kensington, and north of it too—to the west, Ladbroke Grove area, is much stucco now becoming very desirable. But this is not an area for accepted 'sights' as such, but for meandering, for sniffing in an urban texture of great variety and sometimes intense melancholy (try a walk eastwards towards Paddington through decaying squares on a cool autumn morning). The visitor however, comes to Notting

Hill usually simply for the Portobello Road market (going north from the station, fork right in Pembridge Road, and first left off that; the market begins about a quarter-of-a-mile down the road). This is certainly the most rewarding street-market for antiques, junk, tat: lamps, cut glass door handles, icons, marble eggs, pictures, jewellery, silver. The merchants tending to the precious, even the louder ones ('Anybody want serving, don't be shy, all cheap and nasty'), are nevertheless, many of them, experts, and know very well what they are selling (a huge amount of inter-selling between them goes on); hence the bargain gets rarer and rarer, but prices are generally fair and even in well-established ware like silver usually somewhat cheaper than in the West End. Wonderful place for Christmas presents, but don't leave it till too late or you won't be able to move in the road for the crowd. Saturday morning is the great time. Off the market, like banks of mud about a glittering stream, deep slum, recently notorious owing to the revelations as to the activities of exploiting landlords such as the fabulous Rachman. The area is a flash point for racial trouble, and some of the most incredible of London crimes have taken place not far hence—like those of Christie the necrophilist (see his appalling tableau in Madame Tussaud's; his house was in Rillington Place, now mercifully granted another name).

Paddington. This was rural until in the early nineteenth century it became terminus first for canal and then for railway (the main line from the West). Try taking the Underground (Bakerloo or Metropolitan Line) to Paddington Station, and thence walk east along Praed Street—typical London transit area, both seedy and flashy—to Edgware Road, turn left (Edgware Road has some claims to be the most horrible road in London) and left again into the Harrow Road. This brings you to Paddington Green, with a wan memory of Sarah Siddons in a statue inadequately derived from Reynolds's portrait of her (see Dulwich); her cottage here, Westbourne Farm, was demolished in 1860. The present church was finished in 1791, small but very complicated with Grecian hankerings. In the church that preceded it, Hogarth was married, and in the church that preceded that, John Donne preached his first sermon. In the eighteenth century, bread was thrown from the steeple for the populace to scramble for, on the Sunday before

Christmas Day. Church and green are now set amidst aggress-ive brick and rumbling lorry traffic, but farther west down the Harrow Road there comes an unexpected and placid colloquy between stuccoed houses, trees and water, known as Little Venice—pale houses of withdrawn distinction, with pilasters and tall, shadowy windows; an area now much sought after by artists and writers (there is an art gallery on a barge, and from the canal basin, in summer, boat trips ply east down the canal to Regent's Park and the Zoo).

Wesley's House and Bunhill Fields. Off City Road (by Under-ground, Northern Line to Old Street). No. 47 is Wesley's House, a plainish three-bay house of about 1770 (open week-days 10–1 and 2–4); here the founder of Methodism lived for the last years of his life, and died in the bedroom in 1791. Much of his furniture is there, and other personal relics; on the north side the chapel (rebuilt in 1899) that he founded in 1778. The entry, rather Grecian, to Bunhill Fields is on the other side of the road; Bunhill is said to be 'Bone Hill'—the main burial place of the Non-Conformists between 1695 and 1852, with the graves of William Blake, John Bunyan and Daniel Defoe among its hundreds—three splendid fighting Londoners. Defoe died in 1731 in Ropemaker Street, just to the south, and in much-bombed Bunhill Row, to the west, Milton spent the last twelve years of his life till his death in 1674, and there finished *Paradise Lost* and wrote *Paradise Regained*.

Envoi

✣

THE preceding pages offer but a selective, personal and highly
fallible guide to landmarks; an introduction to the physique
of London as she stands and as she has stood in the centuries
of her becoming. The present particular difficulty for the
would-be guide to London is precisely that she is now becoming at a faster rate perhaps than ever in her history—I
only hope that, by the time you read this, enough is left to
leave most of it relevant. Buildings, whole blocks of buildings,
included in the preliminary drafts and earlier editions have
had to be removed from this text because they are no longer
there. The Shot Tower from the South Bank, the Euston Arch,
the Coal Exchange; a whole church (St. Mary Aldermanbury)
has finally been exported to the United States, a whole
museum (of the Royal United Service Institution in the
Banqueting House, Whitehall) has been dispersed—where
now the great table plan of Waterloo, and where the Duke's
green umbrella? Hundreds of lamp-posts of curious character
have vanished, and thousands of weathered York paving-
stones given way to composition slabs. The Old Vic has
yielded to the National Theatre, another precious Adam
fragment of the Adelphi has gone. Another St. James's Club
has sold out to the developers (the Junior Carlton), the
Metropolitan Music Hall in the Edgware Road has crumbled
under the demolition hammers (who are your favourite demolitioners?—mine are Wackett Bros.). And now, even
London Bridge has gone—not, as in the nursery rhyme,
falling down but being sold, by a nation of shop-keepers, for
hard currency for re-erection stone by stone in the United
States.

But one could go on endlessly, and anyway the old is always
replaced by something new of which one may not approve
but which exists—a new set. London's stage will go on
changing as the generations pass over it, but it will remain one

of the greatest stages in the world, and some of the old things will remain. They have, after all, washed St. Paul's, and the Horse Guards still clink and jangle through the misty mornings of the Mall; the Royal Victorian Medal (silver) has been awarded to Yeoman Bed Goer Payne of her Majesty's bodyguard of the Yeomen of the Guard, even though the London County Council itself has ceased to exist, replaced by the Council of Greater London. London has always been a stage, always changing, and when she stops changing, then will be the time to up sticks and off. In the meantime, if you must go—though you will surely return—you might do worse than to leave with Mr. Pickwick and Mr. Jingle. The Golden Cross, from which Pickwick set out from Trafalgar Square, is no longer there, but there's a Lyons on its site and you could well all but lose a limb in the traffic now as Mr. Pickwick all but knocked off his head at the archway of the inn as they set off on the first stage down Whitehall and to the west—

'Dangerous work,' said Mr. Jingle, 'other day—five children —mother—tall lady, eating sandwiches—forgot the arch— crash—knock—children look round—mother's head off— sandwich in her hand—no mouth to put it in—head of a family off—shocking! shocking! Looking at Whitehall, sir?— fine place—little window—somebody else's head off there, eh, sir?—he didn't keep a sharp look-out enough either—eh, sir, eh?'

'I am ruminating,' said Mr. Pickwick, 'on the strange mutability of human affairs. . . .'

Appendix

❧

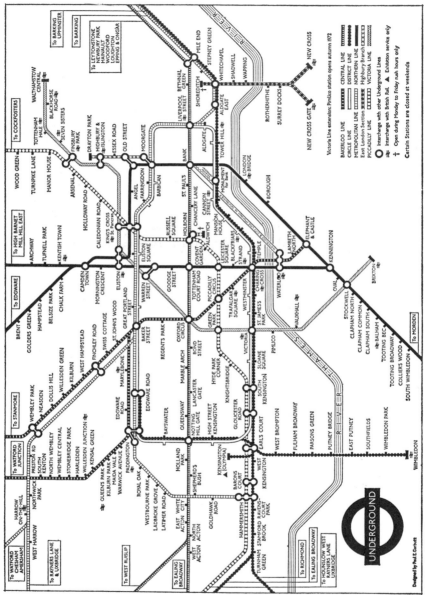

Travel in London

'The increase of London is prodigious. It is really become too large. The consequence is that people live at such a distance from each other that it is very inconvenient for them to meet, and are so crowded that they confuse one another; and it is easier for people who live ten or twelve miles from each other in the country to meet than it is for people who live a few streets from each other in London. . . .'

The comment is not new (it is in fact Boswell's, writing over two hundred years ago in 1772), but, even though London at long last may have started to contract (in population if not in area), it remains as pertinent as ever. The decentralisation of London, its liberal scattering of its focuses of interest, is one of its charms within its stupendous overall centralisation, but it does mean you have to travel. Ever since London's twin poles have existed, Londoners have had to adapt themselves to considerable distances within their capital; Westminster is a good two miles from the Exchange in the City. Citizens have of course, always had the use of their human feet for intercommunication, and the only way to get to know any given area is still by foot. But feet (which emphasise the common animality of men, and also are slow, get tired, get wet, or too hot) have always been considered the lowest and most vulgar form of motion; risen or rising citizens preferred grander means, to begin with the horse. Even as late as 1850, it has been reckoned, there were around 25,000 individual equestrians in the streets of London; today, apart from the riders in Hyde Park and the occasional barbaric clatter of shaking colour of the Household Cavalry, the only equestrians are the mounted police. The other great method of travel, on the City/Westminster axis, was, for almost as long as the horse, the boat. Before the multiplication of bridges, before the road surfaces under the ministration of engineers like MacAdam became controllable in heavy weather, the Thames was not only a main thoroughfare for ordinary traffic but also the great processional way for state occasions.

Through the sixteenth century, private coaches began to proliferate in London streets, until by 1598 Stow could complain of their numbers as a menace: 'the world runs on wheels'. In 1634, hackney carriages were first permitted to ply for hire in the street, and already the traffic problem was officially acknowledged to be in need of control, for in the same year a monopoly was given to a speculator to provide a hire service of sedan chairs, the object being to cut down the number of bulky carriages that choked the roads. Sedan chairs, the short-run taxis of the time, remained in use until the early nineteenth century, when they gave way to the most elegant and romantic of taxis, the two-wheeled hansom. Then the four-wheel hire-vehicle was the growler, and private carriages freaked into attractive variety: gigs, tilburies, dogcarts, wagonettes, phaetons, landaus, victorias and chaises. About 1850 the medley, particularly in the narrow streets of the congested City was formidable; a welter of carriages, equestrians and foot-passengers, a bedlam of hoofs, grinding wheels and axles, cracking whips, permeated by the acrid animal odour of horse-sweat and leather and dung. And then—almost entirely forgotten now—there were the other animals, not only the huge dray-horses, but in the City positive herds of cattle, sheep, pigs converging on the markets; about 1850, a weekly average of around 70,000 of these animals flowed to and from Smithfield Market (only in 1867 was a statute framed to forbid the droving of cattle in London streets between 10 a.m. and 7 p.m.). By then the suburbs had spread like a flood; even before Victoria came to the throne, a number of local stage-coaches, fore-runners of the bus, were delivering 18,000 suburban commuters into Town daily. The engineers had brought the road surfaces up to approximately modern standards to facilitate the passing of dense wheeled traffic, a facility responded to, as always in the history of the roads, by an immediate over-increase of traffic that almost at once destroyed the facility provided. Horse-buses were introduced in 1829, beginning with a route from Paddington Green to the Bank, by the lyrically named Shillibeer. The routes multiplied rapidly. In 1824 the first railway line, Greenwich to London, opened with bands playing at stations, and took a half million passengers in its first year, pouring them into town. Thirty years later, 1854, came the beginnings of the Under-ground, the Inner Circle being completed in 1884. By then horse-drawn tramways were in operation, a speculative venture launched in 1859 by the American tycoon G. F. Train.

The second London line took you from Victoria to West-minster Abbey for 2*d*. By 1900 the tram network was dealing out over 340 million tram-journeys a year, shovelling over 55,000 passengers into the central area each morning before 8.30 a.m. There were the usual experimental forms—steam-trams, traction-trams, compressed-air-trams—before the electric variety won, and seemed set for ever: a romantic form of transport, particularly at night, clanging, masted, a galleon glowing with light down its hissing glissade through the black canals of raining streets. But gone, vanished as if it had never been; by 1960, not a single tram was left on the roads. Gone too, already by then, the cross between the tram and the bus, the trolley with its silent swooping along beneath the aerial axis of its wires; the bus (motor) remains in pre-carious triumph to represent public transport on the surface.

The triumph of the bus is but one facet of the triumph of the motor car, with which London like all capital cities, now wrestles—as vainly, it sometimes seems, as Laocoon against the throttling coils of the serpent. The reasons for this strangulation are clear enough. As London grew in power and pros-perity, its business expanded and multiplied, demanding bigger premises and more of them. But these premises still had to be central to be efficient, and the demand pushed up land values in central London, and then in West London, until it actually pushed out a very high proportion of the domestic population from houses that were no longer econo-mically viable as dwellings. Thus the number of actual resi-dents in the City declined from about 128,000 in 1801 to an incredible 5,000 in 1951—that is of course the extreme case, but the pattern is common to the whole central area, which reached its peak population figure (residents) about 1880 and thence declined to less than what it was in 1801. The central area has become in fact an arena for work, which is filled by the great tide that sweeps in from the inner and outer suburbs in the mornings and floods out again at night. The crisis came through the last twenty-five years with the tremendous in-crease in the notoriously affluent society of private motor cars, using which a single traveller tends to occupy, it has been reckoned, 100 square feet of space as against the 6 square feet that he needs in bus or train. There is simply not enough room in Central London for him. The answer is complex and inevitably slow in realisation, but its aim must be, not to banish the motor-car and admit defeat, but to make the greatest possible use of it compatible with the retention (or rather recovery) of an urban civilisation in which two-footed men, women and children can live and fully 'have their being'. Now, to take a small example, London planning tends to drive the weak and the old to the wall; its imposition of subways often accessible only by staircases is mercilessly inhuman. If you are lame, and for any reason unable to cope with stairs, you must quit London (at Hammersmith Broadway, emerging from the underground you can sight a cinema fifteen yards away on the other side of the road; to reach it without a laboured descent and ascent of very steep stairs, you will have to walk over half a mile).

By 1970 the emphasis in action still seems to be not on intercommunication between human beings, but on the maintenance of 'traffic-flow' which frequently cuts sheer across intercommunication between human beings. New clearways cleave through the suburbs into the city, more and more streets become one way torrents of traffic, and the pedestrian finds it harder and harder and longer and longer to get where he wants to be. But the indications of counter-action are strengthening gradually. Car-parking meters have already severely censored the circulation of private cars in the central areas; multi-storey garages are going up. What is now needed is a closely-reasoned network of super-highways to clarify the exits and entrances to London, and the throughways; these will have to bring motor traffic within easy striking distance of all parts of the central area, which itself may well in the end resolve into a linked series of precincts largely for pedestrians only though with perhaps some form of purely local public transport; the necessary servicing by trucks and lorries would have to be confined to specific hours of the day.

Attempts to repopulate central London have increased since the war, but the flood of commuters from the suburbs will always be immense. For them the prestige and attractiveness of public transport has somehow to be increased, and the reluctance of all governments to spend even a fraction of what they spend on defence (or even for the roads), on the development and probably subsidy of public transport somehow to be overcome. The eighth underground line, the Victoria, was shamefully stuck, until 1963, on the drawing boards since well before the war though its costs are relatively not great and its effect on the relief of London road congestion very marked; it finally opened in 1969. Monorails are not even in sight. But the problem is immensely complex, and moreover its solution has somehow to be married into the history and being of London's physique, developing and enhancing it rather than mutilating its essential character for the sake of one function. Perhaps just as we get in sight of the answer, we shall be confronted by a whole new set of problems as someone at last drives the internal combustion engine into obsolescence (that barbarous source of power, a combination of crude explosions), but with what? transistor driven rucksack helicopters? or powered roller-skates? Time alone and the resource of man will show.

But the real concern of this chapter is neither the how and why of the London impasse of intercommunication, nor its ultimate solution if any, but the more practical aspects of living with it now. If you are going to see London, you cannot do without what are so lightheartedly called its travel facilities; you must come to terms with them, and even, after the first bewilderment of initiation, accept them as an integral part of the spectacle of London. No one can deny that travelling in London is at least an experience.

For the intimate inspection of any given area, as already indicated, your feet are your proper vehicle, though within any given area do not, when crossing the inevitable roads, be carried away by the illusion that everyone else is on foot; in 1960, over 74,000 people were casualties on London's roads. Nor is it now enough for the visitor from the right-hand driving countries of the world to reverse his normal rule of looking left then right; he may well be in a one-way street. To arrive at a given area, to cover a distance over comfortable walking range, is another matter. Bicycles, except for the most intrepid, are out; a bicycle is no platform from which to argue with the towering flanks of a London bus; for me, motor-bicycles and scooters are also out; though they have exciting powers of infiltration in turgid traffic, they too are unstable and their accident rates rise steadily. The private car—particularly, in summer, the open convertible—can be very rewarding, swishing through emptied week-end streets of certain areas of the City and West End as though they were canals, or drifting mothlike through late night London from one floodlit monument to the next, inhaling the nocturnal odours of the city as you go. But normally to drive within London without being driven mad by frustration needs a considerable experience of local conditions within different areas, so that you can retain some sort of control, in mazes of one-way streets, over your direction, and find at the end of it, without endless circling of full-up meters and car-parks, a resting place whence you can take to your feet (most meters anyway will only allow you two hours, and the areas in London where you can park without them are shrinking rapidly). Public transport is the real answer; if you are rich, there are hired cars easily available from a multitude of firms, whose drivers can be left to worry about parking problems, but the normal *luxe* semi-public transport is by the famous London **taxi**.

This, while modifying slowly in appearance, is still of a staid, rather upright, and generally still black wholesomeness, that tends to excite derision at first in the eyes of visitors used to streamlining; but derision usually ends in admiration when the virtues are realised of their capacity, their privacy (the driver contained behind a glass screen), their manoeuvrability with the extraordinary lock that can spin them round in a narrow street without backing, their easiness for getting in and out of, their capacity for baggage. They are not off-the-belt private motor cars making do as taxis; they *are* taxis, and as such, even though the leather has become mock leather and they tend to smell under the evocative ghosts of previous passengers' presence (who smoked that cigar, what lily did that faint perfume gild?) sadly new, they still retain a specialised romance and glamour. One American once told me that he would rather any day travel with a girl in a London taxi than in a gondola in Venice. As taxis they are also cheaper than almost anywhere else in the world, and the tariffs firmly controlled by the meters (though the unwary should watch out after midnight or when taking journeys of over six miles, when the normal rates do not apply—a fact that some drivers are not over-scrupulous in warning their fares about; a price over six miles should be agreed *before* embarking). Their drivers are graduated from an intensive course, and the Londoner expects his driver to know even the smallest streets within the area covered by this book, and is generally still not disappointed (though the old say the drivers are not, like everything else, what they used to be); a tough, long-

suffering if sometimes crotchety, independent body of in-
dividualists. They may or may not offer you a hand with a
baggage, generally not; they will open the door for you
if it is the door on their side and does not involve them getting
out. The only time I remember a cab-driver actually getting
out to open the door was when I asked him to stop and let me
out on a London bridge; he was out and round to the door
in a flash—the last client, he explained, who had asked him to
stop on a bridge had been out and over the parapet into the
mortal Thames before the driver had realised what was
happening—as he said: 'Well, that's life, isn't it? you get all
sorts. But he never paid his fare.' Many of them are mines of
recondite information, but they do not expect you, as do New
York taxi-drivers, to indulge in chit-chat as part of your duties
as a fare; they do expect tips, and the minimum tip would now
be at least 5 new pence, and possibly 10 new pence for a fare
between 50p and £1. A writer of 1850, among General Hints
to Strangers, included this—'If you are in a hurry, and want
to catch a railway train, call a Hansom-cab, and promise the
man a shilling above his fare.' For hansom read just cab, and
the advice is still sound, but owing to inflation rather more
than 5 new pence is now advised (the same writer also stated,
incidentally, that 'Saturday is the aristocratic day for sight-
seeing', but it is alas now the day rather for mass sightseeing,
when the more popular and obvious sights can be so crowded
that they can barely be seen).

But public surface transport will mean for most the London
bus. It was, I think, Mr. Gladstone who first proffered the
often quoted advice that London is best seen from the top of a
bus, and there is some truth in it even though the buses that
he had in mind were roofless, with a clear field of view. But
modern buses, provided you can get the front seats at the top,
will serve quite well, and are of course both warmer and drier.
Handsome and solid and red as fine Englishmen in their
prime, yet chocolate box gay with fluorescent advertisements,
I love London buses though their ways are devious, their
timing erratic and their manners, when full, arrogant. Their
drivers are phlegmatic men, notable for efficiency and surprisingly constant courtesy to other, generally smaller,
vehicles on the road. Their conductors, male and female (the
latter 'clippies' . . .) are, the moment you set foot on their

bus, masters of your fate; they can decide whether the dog with you is the sort of dog they like (and it is advisable to check that this is so before proceeding into the bus), and it is their right if you displease them to eject you from their bus. Inevitably in the stress of the rush hours some of them abuse their powers and turn into pocket dictators, but even so they are the victims of the immense necessary machine that makes London tick—even as you are, whom with an iron arm they bar from entering their bus where there is plenty of room to stand, to leave you though you be ninety and ill and coughing your heart out, to stand again in the pouring rain. It is no good arguing; the conductor is rigid within the rules as a prisoner in irons—no standing in buses except during the rushes, and then only five. Every day at the rush hours the precariousness of what we call urban civilisation is demonstrated, and its essential pretence. The patient queues, herded about the rallying signs of the bus-stops in Regent Street or Oxford Street, are aware of the importance of maintaining some sort of order to contain the threat of Chaos; even though, as the long-awaited bus arrives, the weakest may well get knocked out of place in the rush, the individual and obvious queue-jumper is at once cast out with withering scorn. In the tubes no queueing is possible once on the platforms, and very little quarter is given or expected; the privilege of travelling standing in a carriage as packed as almost any slave-train in history is open for all strong enough to push their way in; the most appallingly pathetic daily sight in London is that of certain generally small, ill-looking, prematurely middle-aged men, who wait on central London platforms as train after bulging train goes through, until at last, glimpsing a seat, with a blind, rodent-like scuttle they plunge through the opening doors into it, knocking women and children aside like nine-pins: self-preservation in naked action.

The ways and the routes of London buses are devious, pleasant to contemplate if you are not in a particular hurry. They thread London through and through, each with its own route and each route with its number; in theory they are spaced evenly along the route, but in practice they tend to coagulate in galaxies of the same number in conformity to some mysterious law. In Piccadilly, if unlucky, you may wait for twenty minutes while buses of every number except 9 sweep past, to be rewarded at last not by one No. 9 but by an armada of them. The vast majority of them are double-deckers, lending both height and a certain monumentality to London's traffic, especially when stationary, panting black diesel fumes, in a jam. Visually indeed they are vital to London's urban landscape, plangent scarlet in the endless vistas of façades that London dirt inexorably subdues to grisaille. Their great exhausts, mingling with those of the lorries and the taxis (now mostly diesel too), add a port-wine-type body to the sour and heady cocktail of the London air, making it more lethal yet. In them you sit close, on the ground floor neither smoking nor spitting, and wearing the buttoned-up mouth of the Englishman on his travels; talking between friends travelling together occurs, and often travellers will thaw to fellow-passengers who reveal themselves as foreigners, but Londoner to unknown fellow-Londoner does not give. Upstairs you may smoke but still not spit, and the atmosphere, on for example wet winter nights with the windows steamed up and a day's concentration of tobacco smoke and wet overcoats is an acquired taste; from the top deck the view sideways is disturbing, a close inspection of first-floor interiors not designed for close inspection, an unauthorised intimacy. Then, out towards the suburbs, veiled sequences of net-curtained bedroom windows, saying no, and the occasional glimpse of the family grouped in devotion about the flickering shrine of the telly. Almost any bus, if you take it for a longish stretch of its route, will convey, as no other medium can, the swiftly changing texture of the city in all its abrupt transitions from high luxury to squalor, a pattern of innumerable spider's webs joined together, with, at the centre of each, a nexus of shops, a tube station, town hall and library. Navigation to and fro across London by bus is a matter of memory and experience; no map known to me does anything except confuse me as far as bus routes are concerned. If in any doubt at all, it is always wise to check with the conductor that his bus is going where you think it is going. One of the most frequent mishaps that afflicts the beginner is to find himself on the right bus but going the wrong way, for all buses cover their routes in both directions, a fact one may well forget in the heat of the moment. Even a compass does not always help; you may be on a route like the 27, the main purpose of which is forthrightly south-westwards, but which at one point can be found proceeding due east.

The **Underground** is another matter. In all guides, in all stations its map confronts you, as lucid, stable and pretty in its
primary colours as a Mondrian, as elementary and workable
as the circuit of the simple crystal-set. Be warned; this map,
like so many works of art, is a triumph of omission, and a
highly platonic vision of the abstract ideal underground, the
Idea of Underground in Paradise. It conveys, accurately, the
sequence of stations on each line, and the points at which they
intersect, where you may change. But any hope that the
Inferno has been purged, cleansed and re-habilitated to act as
the Underground communication system for Paradise will
not last long when you actually descend (we are perhaps even
farther from that solution than Dante was). From the plan
there has evaporated the whole most physical problem of
getting on to those lines so purely drawn; all kinks, all curves
(consider merely its rendering of the river Thames) are ironed
out, and the warren of subterranean footways, lifts, escalators,
spiral staircases unhinted at. Once you are on beam, the map
is admirable; but the fact remains, as people have often told
me, that for the beginner, the apparently much more confused
system of the Metro in Paris is much easier, and indeed I
remember vividly how in the first three months I lived in
London, I kept on finding that I had got either to St. Paul's
or Putney Bridge, irrespective of my wished-for destination
which was never either of those two places.

I am strongly biased about the London Underground,
because it was the first thing in London which, in sporadic
visits from a provincial youth, I fell in love with; it is still for
me the most romantic and mysterious part of London, though
my relationship with it, after years of profound intimacy,
has tempered to a love-hate. An emotion shared, I am con-
vinced, by hundreds of thousands of Londoners, although the
Underground carries far fewer passengers (a mere $1\frac{3}{4}$ millions
daily) than do the buses. The mesh of the Underground web
is much less fine than that of the buses, and so much less
flexible to the needs of the traveller. The farther out from the
centre of London you are, the farther apart are the stations,
but in the centre, within the magic ring of the Circle Line,
you are never out of easy walking distance of an Underground
station; unlike the buses, the Underground routes all radiate
to and from the centre, except the Circle Line, which contents
itself with defining centre. Basically, there are two networks.

The oldest comprises the Metropolitan, the District and the
Circle Lines, the shallow routes, sunk just below the surface,
weaving through vast sonorous tunnels of the original Victorian or almost imperial Roman amplitude, allowing for
engines with funnels and for top-hats, through cuttings walled
with dark red brick, in and out of light and darkness. The
rolling stock is old-fashioned, even the new silver coaches, in
its dimensions, roomy with room to stand and lurch in; its
gait is, compared with that of the tubes, slow and hesitant,
it tends to stop around. At Edgware Road the impression that
the driver has nipped off for a cup of tea is sometimes irresistible; sometimes it saunters, and will pause for reflection for
minutes at a time between stations. It is lovable and archaic,
sometimes dubbed ironically as the last survival in London of
the Middle Ages, and indeed it often seems to be yearning to be
a tram. And its stations are real stations, sometimes with
cigarette, newspaper or sweet kiosks, with stunning Piranesi
effects of naked girders and flights of stairs. At Sloane Square
there are real escalators but also a whole pub, the Hole in the
Wall, recently renovated, where you can during opening times
sit and watch the trains go by, and also again, proceeding at an
angle high in the air above the tracks in a gross iron tube, one
of London's lost rivers, the Westbourne. West Kensington,
in May, is a local festival of purple iris, and by Gloucester
Road, as the train pauses there is a weeping willow raining in
spring its vivid green, as though it were the Cambridge Backs
and madrigals were expected. Some stations are being tarted
up, but others farther out still hold a seedy glory—go west
for example on the Metropolitan, in canyons between the
dusky backsides of Paddington, strung with that rare London
jewellery, multi-coloured washing threaded casually at all
levels, through stations like piers, with peeling matchboarding
and brilliant hoardings—Westbourne Park, Ladbroke Grove,
the new West Indies where the coloured people come and go.
The Metropolitan serves the west as far as Hammersmith,
and ramifies north-west far into suburb country to Watford
and places with sylvan names, Uxbridge, Chalfont and
Latimer, and goes east to Barking. The District roughly
parallels it on a more southern axis, from Hounslow and
Ealing in the West to Upminster, forty-four miles away in
Essex to the east. In the centre they are linked by the schoolboy's delight, the Circle Line where trains go round and round

endlessly; if of an introspective disposition you can settle in here for a morning illegally with a minimum ticket and a good book in comparative warmth, and really get away from it all. According to a persistent if unprovable London myth, some people live on the Circle Line. The great virtue of the Circle Line, for those in transit in and out of London, is that it links all the main-line railway stations north of the river (that is, it is no good for Waterloo. The District Line only ventures south of the river, to the west, two arms extended to Putney and to Wimbledon, and to Kew and Richmond respectively). This shallow near-surface network is the most complex to navigate, for Metropolitan, Circle, and District all at certain stations share the same tracks, and trains have to be chosen with care.

Far below, deep in the earth, below even that other network of sewers and cable channels, burrows the second Underground system, the Tube proper; the five lines— Central, Piccadilly, Bakerloo (no battle, but a combination of two of its principal stations, Waterloo and Baker Street), the ambivalent Northern and the Victoria. Not for the claustrophobic, but, for Londoners who remember the blitz, cherished havens of security, for the tube stations were the best air-raid shelters of all. Tubes they literally are, steel-threaded through the solid earth; their station platforms are not really stations at all but brightly-lit landing and loading bays bulging the darkness at intervals along their length, all more or less identical. The trains are tailor-made for the tube with their arched tops, and low snaking motion; when they emerge into daylight at the extremities of each line, they seem almost to blink, and scuttle the faster like reptiles betrayed out of their element. Their splendid redness is alas giving way to a no doubt more economic silver in the new stock, but though silver like aluminium kettles seems to go dingy, their world is magic. Fabulous as a piece of engineering, fabulous in its sheer day to day efficiency, fabulous in its voracious subterranean indifference, digesting thousands upon thousands of human beings every day and spewing them forth again. The tunnel rumbles in its darkness; from the squat mouth, the train appears, beetling, projects itself into the glare of the platform, which, slowing, it occupies precisely with all its length. The doors sigh unanimously open, and people plunge out and in. Hoarse short-hand cries for

Mind the Doors and *Hurry along please* echo. The doors swing
to again and the train is away, touching nearly thirty miles
an hour before its tail has cleared the platform. A telephone
bell rings wildly, signifying death, breakdown or disaster?
Nobody anwers. The platform refills, the next train comes in.

Tube etiquette need cause no anxiety; there is none, and
these packed carriages offer daily demonstration of the collapse of traditional English chivalry under slow pressure.
Gentlemen offer ladies, for reasons well known but politely
never mentioned, their seats, but in the tubes they usually do
not. There is only one nice point; if, being male, you are
seated, the normal practice is not to rise for a woman (she is
anyway likely to live longer, as statistics prove, than yourself): but if, in a crowded train, you are already standing and a
seat empties in front of you, it is still for some reason normal
to look round to see if there is a woman standing in the vicinity
and, if so, to offer it to her though it is yours by right of propinquity. Conversations are, as usual among travelling Englishmen, rare; they also are difficult, even if one should wish to
indulge. In summer the windows are open, and the racket of
the wheels belts off the tunnel walls into the carriages. Everyone sits as if absent, only the provincials and foreigners be-
traying themselves by their forward crane to follow the
mystic diagram on the opposite wall that tells them where
they are. Otherwise eyes rest on newspapers, half-seeing, or
fully unseeing rest on nothing while heads rock in unison, and
over them, from the low ceiling, the hanging straps sway with
them. Through tubes of darkness, the trains travel each with its
brightly lit load of hundreds; at the stations, brakes shriek
sometimes like human beings; as the doors open the travellers,
most of them as if sleepwalking, emerge and pass swiftly
without bumping off the platforms up stairs marked No Exit.
In the underground halls, streams converge, mingle, cross,
some pouring back into tunnels marked No Entrance, others
embarking on the diagonal shafts that open up to the surface.
Though it may be a station with lifts, which I distrust,
irrationally, to the point of, on occasion, even undertaking
the slow slog up the emergency stairs. Lifts with automatic
doors are my phobia, with their megalomaniac automatic
voices.

Then there are escalators. *Escalators!* Those great and glorious endless belts conveying fodder to and from the trains.

Londoners tread them lightly as a fakir walks on fire; spin down on tip-toe, leaning back; float up, the middle-aged serried on the right (on the right to let the nimble young speed up on the left). Male heads turn to scan the corset advertisements on the wall. The huge heaving grind of the slatted treads jars agreeably under the soles; the rubber handrail moves with a shivering life of its own, sometimes a little faster or slower than the stairway itself. At top and bottom comes the magic flattening out of the steps, the arching up into steps, the smooth slide into the comb-toothed grille as you pass on to terra firma. Sometimes in cracks at the angles of the stairs you glimpse light from below, from some buried engine room. On the escalators lovers, facing each other, sail upwards, motionless but transcendent as gliders on an upward air current. Once at Maida Vale at midnight, I, going down, owned the escalators with a man in a bowler hat going up. In pride and stillness I was going down; in humility, gloved hands clasped in front of him holding his brief case and umbrella, he was going up, and in the rumbling silence we bowed briefly to each other as we passed into the night.

Rush hours can be literally infernal, to be observed once but not to be participated in; do not travel between 8 and 10 a.m. nor between 4.45 and 6.15 p.m. But observe at least once, with, if you can, a Dante-esque detachment, the jungle in action. If you participate you may, as Londoners do, get used to it. Men and women, like rugby forwards, heave and surge into trains apparently already packed as tight as sardine tins; the underground corridors can become at places like Oxford Circus or Holborn so dense with people that walking pace is reduced to a penguin shuffle of half-a-mile an hour; it has taken me a quarter of an hour to change platforms at Holborn. It brings out the worst side of the famous London capacities for endurance of suffering, so valuable in wartime, but criminal at times when it becomes sheer masochism. Rather than stagger office-hours, let us endure the rush hours. Once a train broke down in mid-tunnel; fire broke out, the tunnel filled with asphyxiating fumes. What did the passengers do, asked a journalist. ' "They were remarkable," said a London Transport official. "They did not even complain!" ' It was not remarkable and they ought to have complained; there is often a quality of smugness in our heroism which has infuriated foreigners for centuries.

Yet I find the magnetism of the Underground persists through the years undimmed; for me there is waking and sleeping and there is travelling in the Tube, an extra mode of being, trance-like. Once your course is selected, you cannot abdicate; you are committed to the Tube, and you go, apparently nowhere; the platform at which you arrive is identical with the platform you left even though it has a different name. Where are you going? where one million and threequarters fellow passengers on the Tube are daily going; the faces ranged opposite you in the blank and even light of the carriages, the paler faces reflected in the black glass behind them, your own face travelling with you and nodding at you. If you go to sleep in the Tube, you are likely to have strange dreams. The lines are lethal, and a popular method of suicide. Countless gloves and umbrellas are lost daily, and in 1960 on Leicester Square station platform was found a parcel containing a diamond and a sapphire necklace, the insignia of the Orders of St. Patrick, the Garter, and the Bath. Maybe people too are lost. (The Bus and Underground Lost Property Office is at 200 Baker Street, N.W.1.)

The entrances to stations, at surface level, are unemphatic and at times modest to a fault, though once you know the red, blue and white device of London Transport it is easy enough to spot. The smell is less emphatic than that of the Metro (that hot aroma of garlic, Gauloises and machine-oil), less vital and rich, canned in its own way, but heady too for the addict. It is said that the air is changed by fan pumps every quarter of an hour (5 million cubic feet a minute) and that the average temperature is fairly stable at about 70 degrees. Certainly the draughts are not stable, and from time to time coming round a corner a great gust will flatten your clothes against you with an icy blast. At most stations, tickets may be bought from a clerk at a guichet or from a machine, but unlike the Metro there is no flat rate; the enormous mileages covered make this out of the question. Ticket queues are frequently formidable, but a curious gentlemen's agreement exists between public and London Transport ticket collectors; you can if you wish buy a minimum ticket from a slot machine and pay the rest of your fare at the far end to the collector. The conditions of this understanding are obscure; it is worth noting that the Transport Executive prosecutes 7,000 people a year, but on the other hand I have never had any argument with collectors though you ask for trouble if you have no ticket. The staff are generally helpful and long-suffering, and their ranks recently implemented sturdily by West Indians, sometimes now hilarious. Your ticket is nominally punched when you go in, but it is impolite to insist on this as it means interrupting the conversation or meditation of the officials concerned. What may be called the foyers, the areas containing ticket offices and entrances to lifts or escalators, are often dingy, but in the greater stations sometimes splendid, though Piccadilly (see p. 44) is the finest of all. And throughout the London Transport system, the lettering is a connoisseur's delight, a house-style the functionalism and honest elegance of which is still unmatched in any other comparable concern in the world; it was worked out for the Executive by a brilliant calligrapher, Edward Johnston.

The more intimate and obscure charms of the Underground can only be learned by long acquaintanceship—the short cuts at certain stations, the names of dead stations that flash by unlit in the tunnel. (It is however worth while, if travelling on a Sunday, to make sure before you start that the station you have in mind is in fact open on Sundays—some close.) There is the miniature, nonhuman tube that belongs to the Post Office and whisks automatically loaded with mail between Mount Pleasant, the main sorting office, and the main stations (visitable by arrangement with the Divisional Controller at Mount Pleasant, E.C.1). And I have omitted the most fascinating freak of the Underground, the highly specialised line known as 'The Drain', which conveys the bowler-hatted commuters from Waterloo station (terminus for trains from Surrey, traditional headquarters of stockbrokia since railways began) to the City; a direct swoop in its own peculiar carriages without intermediate stops to the Bank. At the Bank, the most modern of all underground improvements—not an escalator, but the immense travelator, or moving walkway, that throbs city gentlemen to and from their offices at a fair running speed; the story that the dance known as the Twist was originated on it is without foundation, but it is a sure winner for a child's attention. But for me, not even where the most everyday elements of the Underground are concerned, familiarity never breeds contempt. Arriving from a journey away, at one of the main London stations, as soon as I am in the Tube, I am already partly home. That Mr. Meynell whom Boswell quoted nearly two hundred years ago was more prophetic than he guessed. 'The chief advantage of London,' said Mr. Meynell, 'is, that a man is always *so near his burrow.*'

Hotels

The following lists offer a selection only. Fuller lists with details of accommodation and prices are published by the British Travel Association and the British Hotel Association. For Overseas visitors only, the London Hotels Information Service, 88 Brook Street, W.1 (629-5414) will arrange bookings and advice, free. Other booking agencies (fee-charging) are Hotel Accommodation Service (Hotac), 93 Baker Street, W.1 (935-2555); or Hotel Booking Service, 5 Coventry Street, W.1 (437-5052).

Prices rise so swiftly that I have renounced any attempt to list them here. Three stars indicate the very expensive, two the expensive, one the—relatively—cheap.

Mayfair and St. James's (including Piccadilly, Oxford Street and Park Lane)

ATHENAEUM COURT, 116 Piccadilly, W.1 **
BERKELEY, Wilton Place, S.W.1 ***
BERNERS, 10 Berners Street, W.1 **
BROWN'S, Dover Street, W.1 ***
BRYANSTON COURT, 56 Great Cumberland Place, W.1 *
CAVENDISH, Jermyn Street, W.1 ***
CHURCHILL, 30 Portman Square, W.1 ***
CLARIDGE'S, Brook Street, W.1 ***
CONNAUGHT, Carlos Place, W.1 (off Grosvenor Square) ***
CUMBERLAND, Marble Arch, Oxford Street, W.1 **
DORCHESTER, Park Lane, W.1 (over Hyde Park) ***
DURRANT'S, George Street, W.1 (by Manchester Square) **
EUROPA, Grosvenor Square, W.1 ***
FLEMING'S, Half Moon Street, W.1 **
GREEN PARK, Half Moon Street, W.1 **
GROSVENOR COURT, Praed Street, W.2. * *

GROSVENOR HOUSE, Park Lane, W.1 (over Hyde Park) ***
THE LONDONER, Welbeck Street, W.1 **
LONDON HILTON, Park Lane, W.1 (over Hyde Park) ***
LONDONDERRY HOUSE, Park Lane, W.1 ***
MANDEVILLE, Mandeville Place, W.1 **
MAY FAIR, Berkeley Street, W.1 ***
MEURICE, Bury Street, St. James's, S.W.1 **
MOSTYN, Portman Street, W.1 *
MOUNT ROYAL, Bryanston Street, W.11. * *
OLD ST. JAMES'S, Park Place, St. James's, S.W.1 **
PARK LANE, Piccadilly, W.1 (near Hyde Park Corner) **
PICCADILLY, Piccadilly and Regent Street, W.1 **
REGENT PALACE, Piccadilly Circus, W.1 **
RITZ, Piccadilly, W.1 (over Green Park) ***
STAFFORD, St. James's Place, St. James's, S.W.1 ***
STRATFORD COURT, 350 Oxford Street, W.1 *
WASHINGTON, Curzon Street, W.1 **
WESTBURY, Conduit Street, W.1 (corner of Bond Street) ***

Charing Cross, Strand, Covent Garden area

CHARING CROSS, Charing Cross Station, W.C.2 **
HOWARD, Norfolk Street, W.C.2 *
PASTORIA, St. Martin's Street, W.C.2 (Leicester Square) **
SAVOY, Strand, W.C.2 (views over the Thames) ***
SHAFTESBURY, Monmouth Street, W.C.2 **
STRAND PALACE, Strand, W.C.2 **
WALDORF, Aldwych, W.C.2 **

Westminster, Victoria, Belgravia, Knightsbridge

BASIL STREET, Basil Street, S.W.3 (near Knightsbridge) **
CADOGAN, 75 Sloane Street, S.W.1 **

CARLTON TOWER, Cadogan Place, S.W.1 ***
EBURY COURT, 26 Ebury Street, S.W.1 *
ECCLESTON, Eccleston Square, S.W.1 * *
GORING, 15 Beeston Place, S.W.1 * *
GROSVENOR Buckingham Palace Road, S.W.1 *
HYDE PARK, Knightsbridge, S.W.1 (Hyde Park) ***
ROYAL COURT, Sloane Square, S.W.1 **
RUBENS, Buckingham Palace Road, S.W.1 **
ST. ERMIN'S, Caxton Street, S.W.1 **
ST. JAMES'S, Buckingham Gate, S.W.1 *

Bloomsbury area

BONNINGTON, Southampton Row, W.C.1 ⎱   Prices
CORA, Upper Woburn Place, W.C.1 ⎰ by arrangement
COUNTY, Upper Woburn Place, W.C.1 *
GRAND, Southampton Row, W.C.1 *
IMPERIAL, Russell Square, W.C.1 **
IVANHOE, Bloomsbury Street, W.C.1 *
KENILWORTH, Great Russell Street, W.C.1 *
KINGSLEY, Bloomsbury Way, W.C.1 *
MONTAGUE, Montague Street, W.C.1 *
MOUNT PLEASANT, 53 Calthorpe Street, W.C.1 *
PRESIDENT, Russell Square, W.C.1 **
ROYAL, Woburn Place, W.C.1 *
TAVISTOCK, Tavistock Square, W.C.1 **
WHITE HALL, Bloomsbury Square and Montague Street,
W.C.1 *

Kensington

DE VERE, De Vere Gardens, W.8 **
KENSINGTON CLOSE, Wright's Lane, Kensington High Street,
W.8 **
KENSINGTON PALACE, De Vere Gardens, W.8 ***
MILESTONE, Kensington Court, W.8 **
PRINCE OF WALES, De Vere Gardens, W.8 **
ROYAL GARDEN, Kensington High Street, W.8 ***

South Kensington

ADRIA, 88 Queen's Gate, S.W.7 *
BAILEY'S, Gloucester Road, S.W.7 **
BUCKINGHAM, 94 Cromwell Road, S.W.7 *
GORE, 189 Queen's Gate, S.W.7 *
MONTANA, 67 Gloucester Road, S.W.7 **
NORFOLK, 2 Harrington Road, S.W.7 *
REMBRANDT, Thurloe Place, S.W.7 **

There are many more smallish hotels in this range (but many of them unlicensed) in this area, about the Museums and the Air Terminal, and spreading west to Earl's Court. Another big concentration of small, reasonably-priced hotels is to be found in the Bayswater area on the north of Hyde Park, from Paddington westwards. The Royal Lancaster, Lancaster Gate, W.2, is definitely luxury class.

City

GREAT EASTERN, Liverpool Street Station, E.C.2 * * *
TOWER HOTEL, St. Katherine's Way, E.I. * * *

For Commonwealth visitors, the Royal Overseas League has comfortable and moderately priced rooms for members at Overseas House, Park Place, St. James's Street, (493 5051); apply for membership terms. The English-speaking Union, Dartmouth House, 37 Charles Street, Mayfair, W.1, also has accommodation for its members from the Commonwealth and the U.S.A. The central Y.M.C.A. is in Endell Street, W.C.2 and the Y.W.C.A. is in Great Russell Street, W.C.1, and the Youth Hostels Association has hostels in Holland Park, Kensington, W.8; 84 Highgate West Hill, Highgate, N.6; and 38 Bolton Gardens, Earl's Court, S.W.5.

Eating and Drinking

Eating and drinking in London, despite old-fashioned rumours to the contrary that still persist, can be all right. Of food and drink one can at least and at last with confidence assert that it is a matter of taste—*de gustibus*—and London in its immensity caters for all tastes. What the average Londoner likes is faithfully reflected in hundreds of inexpensive restaurants, especially perhaps in the many branches of the Jolyon restaurants, of the A.B.C., and of Quality Inn; a more specialised interest is catered for by the establishments that deal almost exclusively in what Egon Ronay calls 'things-with-chips,' the fry-up—the Golden Egg chain in the West End is a good example. The great English failing in some of the fry-up and barbecue places is poor ventilation; on entering, sniff, and if the density is high, back out or your clothes will remember (particularly if they are of wool) for weeks afterwards. Fish-and-chips shops, of the traditional wrap-it-up-in-newspaper and eat-it-as-you-walk variety, have yielded from the majority of the areas covered by this book, but are to be found on the fringes, and especially in the East End (and jellied eels, winkles, and other Cockney specialities). The old chop-houses have also mostly gone, and the modern substitute is the steak-house, sometimes rather American in styling; the Angus Steak-House chain, the London Steak-Houses, the Peter Evans Eating Houses. In most of the above you will probably be able to get, without too much fuss, a bottle of the traditional lubricant, a branded sauce. 'If Harold has a fault it is that he will drown everything with H.P. sauce'—reported to have been said by Mrs. Wilson of Harold Wilson (not by Lady Dorothy of Harold Macmillan). For lunches, many London pubs provide simple straightforward and sometimes very good dishes; sandwich bars will be found throughout—not to be judged by decor but by the look of the sandwiches. Snacks, and sometimes more ambitious dishes, will be found also in coffee-bars.

For the connoisseur of food and wine, for the tuned palate in expectancy of the subtle ranges of all kinds of European and Oriental cooking, London can supply most answers, generally of course more expensively than in the range indicated above. Indeed if you wish to eat expensively, you can do so at almost as great a cost as anywhere in the world, but it is also true that, for example, you can get the best French wines in many top-class London restaurants better and cheaper than in France. Standards in individual establishments can change most abruptly, and the only really reliable guide is the advice of a resident, practising and well-to-do (at least highly-expense-accounted) gourmet. The British Travel and Holidays Association's list of *Hotels and Restaurants in Great Britain* is fairly comprehensive. For a selective, critical account, Egon Ronay's Guide to *1,000 Eating Places in Great Britain* (which will continue, I hope, to be published annually) is invaluable; this grades restaurants according to quality of food, luxury, and service, and allows itself enough space to be able to indicate clearly the character, specialities and price-range of each place. The criticism for all except the very pure against it is that some of its exclusions seem over-rigorous—should a friend recommend some little place in Soho that is not in Egon Ronay, do not not go there simply for that reason. Egon Ronay has also a very useful section on London pubs, on which subject A. Reeve-Jones's *London Pubs* is helpful. Christopher Driver's *Good Food Guide* is also excellent.

The traditional English habit of afternoon tea seems on the wane; while this book has been in progress Gunter's has finally vanished completely from Mayfair, and with it has gone part of a civilisation, and a tinkle in the drawing-down of London winter dusks has been almost silenced. However there is always Jolyons and the A.B.C. and the coffee-bars (though actual tea in them is sometimes almost European in horror), and at most department stores gossip flies among the tea-cups from about four. The following are in the old-tea time tradition still: Barbellion, 70 New Bond Street; Ceylon Tea Centre, 22 Lower Regent Street; branches of Fullers, and others. It is inadvisable to leave London without having taken tea in the Palm Court of the Ritz, but almost all hotels provide it still with some ceremony.

The difficult subject of tips. Some London establishments add a percentage charge for service. The average rate in practice is between 10 or 15 new pence in the pound. In addition, since 1973, Value Added Tax (VAT), is payable on meals and accommodation, as well as on many other services and manufactured goods, at a rate of 10%. VAT may either be included in the listed price, or it may be added at the time of payment.

Callers outside the London area should remember to dial 01 and then the number.

Forty-three West-End Restaurants

AU JARDIN DES GOURMETS, 5 Greek Street, Soho, W.1. *First-class French; expensive* 437 1816

BERTORELLI, 19 Charlotte Street, Soho W.1. *Inexpensive* 636 4174

BIANCHI'S, 21a Frith Street, W. 1. *Italian* 437 8504

BOULESTIN, 25 Southampton Street (Covent Garden), W.C.2. *First-class French; expensive* 836 7061

CAFÉ ROYAL GRILL, 68 Regent Street (Piccadilly Circus), W.1. *Edwardian decor* 930 2473

CANTON, 11 Newport Street, Soho, W.C.2. *Chinese; inexpensive* 437 6220

CAPRICE, Arlington Street, St. James's, S.W.1 *Under new Management* 493 3183

CLARIDGE'S CAUSERIE, Brook Street, W. 1. *Smorgesbord, good for lunch* 629 8860

CONNAUGHT HOTEL, Carlos Place, W.1. *First-class, expensive* 499 7070

DUKES, 55–59 Duke Street, W.1. *Inexpensive* 499 5000

ÉCU DE FRANCE, 111 Jermyn Street, S.W.1. *French* 930 2837

EMPRESS, 15 Berkeley Street, W.1. *French, first-class, expensive* 629 6126

L'ÉPICURE, 28 Frith Street, W.1. *Expensive* 437 2829

ÉTOILE, 30 Charlotte Street, Soho, W.1. *French, first-class, expensive* 636 7189

GAY HUSSAR, 2 Greek Street, Soho, W.1. *Hungarian and French: expensive* 437 0973

GENNARO'S, 44 Dean Street, W.1. *Italian* 437 3950

GROSVENOR HOUSE (Burghley Room), Park Lane, W.1. *Expensive* 499 6363

HOSTARIA ROMANA, 70 Dean Street, Soho, W.1. *Italian, excellent and not expensive* 734 2869

HUNTING LODGE, 18 Lower Regent Street, S.W.1. *English, expensive* 930 4222

INIGO JONES, 14 Garrick Street, W.C.2. *Expensive; exotic decor* 836 6456

KETTNER'S, Romilly Street, W.1. *Long established; expensive; Edwardian decor* 437 3437

LEE HO FOOK, 15 Gerrard Street, W.1. *Chinese.* 734 9578

MANZI'S HOUSE OF HAMBURGER, Leicester Square, W.C.2. *Actually fish-specialists; inexpensive* 437 4864

MARQUIS, 121a Mount Street, Mayfair, W.1. 499 1256

MARTINEZ, 25 Swallow Street, W.1   734 5066

MAY FAIR HOTEL (Châteaubriand), Berkeley Street, W.1. *French; expensive*   629 7777

MIRABELLE, 56 Curzon Street, Mayfair, W.1. *French, first-class, expensive*   499 1940

MON PLAISIR, 21 Monmouth Street (off Cambridge Circus), W.C.2. *French; inexpensive*   836 7243

RULES, 35 Maiden Lane, W.C.2. *Edwardian decor*   836 5314

SAVOY (HOTEL) GRILL, Strand, W.C.2. *A top European restaurant; expensive*   836 4343

SHEEKEY'S, 29–31 St. Martin's Court, off St. Martin's Lane. *Fish; not expensive*   836 4118

SIMPSON'S-IN-THE-STRAND, 100 Strand, W.C.2. *Classic home of the English roast*   836 9112

TIBERIO, 22 Queen Street, Mayfair, W.1. *Italian, first-class; expensive*   629 3561

TRADER VICS, Hilton Hotel, Park Lane, W.1. *Polynesian and Chinese; expensive*   493 7586

TRATTORIA DEI PESCATORI, 57 Charlotte Street, W.1. *Fish; expensive*   580 3289

VEERASWAMY'S, 99–101 Regent Street, W.1. *Indian, splendid decor*   734 1401

VINE, 3 Piccadilly Place (by the Piccadilly Hotel), W.1. *English* 734 5789

WASHINGTON HOTEL RESTAURANT, Curzon Street, Mayfair, W.1   499 6911

WHEELER'S OYSTERS, 19 Old Compton Street, Soho, W.1. *Especially fish. Wheeler's also have a restaurant at 12a Duke of York Street, Jermyn Street* (930 2460)   437 7661

WHITE TOWER, 1 Percy Street, W.1. *Greek, first-class, expensive* 636 8141

WILTON'S, 27 Bury Street, St. James's, S.W.1. *Very English, very expensive, mostly fish*   930 8391

*Twenty-four Restaurants in Belgravia, Knightsbridge
and Kensington*

ARK RESTAURANT, 122 Palace Gardens Terrace, W.8. *Small;
inexpensive* 229 4024

AU PÈRE DE NICO, 10 Lincoln Street, S.W.3   584 1833

BRITISH AIRWAYS TERMINAL, Buckingham Palace Road,
S.W.1.
Modern decor, English cooking; inexpensive 834 2323

BROMPTON GRILL, 243 Brompton Road, S.W.3. *French; inexpensive* 589 8005

BUMBLES, 16 Buckingham Palace Road, S.W.1. *Inexpensive*
828 2903

CARAFE, 15 Lowndes Street, S.W.1   235 2525

CONTENTED SOLE, 19 Exhibition Road, South Kensington,
S.W.7. *Fish; inexpensive* 584 8359

DE VERE HOTEL, 1 De Vere Gardens, Knightsbridge, W.8
584 0051

HYDE PARK HOTEL, Knightsbridge, S.W.1   235 2000

KENSINGTON PALACE HOTEL, De Vere Gardens, W.8   937 8121

LA FONTANA, 101 Pimlico Road, S.W.1. *Italian, cheap* 730
6630

LA POULE AU POT, 231 Ebury Street, S.W.1. *French provincial,
cheap* 730 7763

LA TOQUE BLANCHE, Abingdon Road, W.8. *French; fairly
expensive* 937 5832

LE COQ HARDI, 353 Kensington High Street, W.8. *French*
603 6951

LEITH'S, 92 Kensington Park Road, W.11   229 4483

LONDON STEAK HOUSE, 130 Kensington High Street, W.8
937 7500

MARYNKA, 232–4 Brompton Road, Knightsbridge, S.W.3.
Austrian 589 6753

NORMANDIE, 163 Knightsbridge, S.W.1   589 1400

NORWAY FOOD CENTRE, 166 Brompton Road, S.W.1. *Inexpensive* 584 6062

OVERTON'S, 14 Victoria Buildings, S.W.1 *Fish, fine old-
fashioned decor. Overton's also own the former Hatchett's,
67a Piccadilly* (493-1804)   834 3774

PARKES, 4 Beauchamp Place, Knightsbridge, S.W.3. *Minute,
but first-class, and expensive* 589 1390

PONTEVECCHIO, 256 Old Brompton Road, S.W.5. *Italian* 373 9082

RIB ROOM (Carlton Tower Hotel), Cadogan Place, S.W.1. *Roast beef* 235 5411

SHANGRI LA, 233 Brompton Road, Knightsbridge, S.W.3. *Chinese; inexpensive* 589 3658

Ten Restaurants in Chelsea

ASTERIX, 329 King's Road, S.W.3 *Crêpes. Cheap* 352 3891

AU BON ACCEUIL, 27 Elystan Street, S.W.3. *Inexpensive French food* 589 3718

CHANTERELLE, 119 Old Brompton Road, S.W.7 373 5522

DON LUIGI, 33c King's Road, Chelsea, S.W.3. *Italian, not expensive* 730 3023

LA FRINGALE, 4 Hollywood Road, S.W.10. *Inexpensive 'Victorian' bistro* 351 1011

LE CAROSSE, 19–21 Elystan Street, S.W.3. *Expensive* 584 5248

LE FRANÇAIS, 259 Fulham Road, S.W.3. *Expensive; excellent French food* 352 4748

NINETEEN, 19 Mossop Street, S.W.3. *Inexpensive; Chelsea atmosphere* 589 4971

STAR OF INDIA, 154 Old Brompton Road, S.W.5. *Excellent Indian; not expensive* 373 2901

'235', 235 King's Road, Chelsea, S.W.3. *Plain but cheap* 352 2350

Seven Restaurants in Marylebone, Bayswater and north

AU BOIS ST. JEAN, 122 St. John's Wood High Street, N.W.8. *Expensive French food* 586 1022

BARQUE AND BITE, 15 Prince Albert Road, N.W.1. *Inexpensive; on a moored barge on Regent's Canal* 485 8137

BOULEVARD, 56 Wigmore Street, W.1. *Viennese-style cafe-restaurant* 935 9803

CARRIER'S, 2 Camden Passage, N.1. *Expensive; run by Robert Carrier* 226 5353

FROOPS, 17 Princess Road, N.W.1. *Inexpensive homely food* 722 9663

GENEVIEVE, 13–14 Thayer Street, Marylebone, W.1. *Expensive* 935 5023

WHITE'S HOTEL, Lancaster Gate, Bayswater, W.2. *Not expensive* 262 2711

Some City Restaurants (including Fleet Street)

BARON OF BEEF, Gutter Lane, off Gresham Street, City, E.C.2. *Best English, expensive* 606 6961

BLOOM'S, 90 Whitechapel High Street, E.1. *Really East End. Jewish (closed Saturdays)* 247 6001

CHARTERHOUSE RESTAURANT, 33–35 Charterhouse Square, E.C.1. *Steaks* 606 7616

COTILLION ROOM, Bucklersbury House, Cannon Street. *Solid City affluent luncheoning* 248 4735

ESSEX, Dunster House, Mark Lane, City, E.C.3. *Expensive* 623 8581

FORUM, Bush House, Aldwych, W.C.2 *Italian; lunch only* 405 1927

GREAT EASTERN HOTEL, Liverpool Street, E.C.2 283 4363

LE POULBOT, 45 Cheapside, E.C.2. *Lunch only; Mlinaric designed basement restaurant* 236 4379

MERMAID THEATRE, Puddle Dock (Blackfriars Bridge), E.C.4. *Especially for lunch; not expensive* 248 2835

SIR CHRISTOPHER WREN, Paternoster Square, E.C.4. *Lunch only; inexpensive chophouse* 248 1708

SWEETINGS, Albert Buildings, 39 Queen Victoria Street, E.C.4. *Lunch only; inexpensive plain English 'pub' food* 248 3062

N.B. Almost all the above are closed on Saturdays and Sundays; the Great Eastern is one of the few places in the City where the visitor can be assured of food day in, day out.

Late Night Dancing and Cabaret

HILTON ROOF RESTAURANT, Park Lane, W.1. *No cabaret*
493 8000
HIPPODROME THEATRE RESTAURANT (Talk of the Town, by
Leicester Square Station), W.C.2   734 5051
LATIN QUARTER, 13–17 Wardour Street, W.1   437 6001
QUAGLINO, 16 Bury Street, S.W.1   930 6767
SAVOY HOTEL, Strand, W.C.2   836 4343
STORK ROOM, 99 Regent Street, W.1   734 3686

CLUBS: *N.B. Non-members should always telephone in advance
to check on membership formalities.*

Night Clubs

ANNABEL'S, 44 Berkeley Square, W.1   629 3558
ASTOR CLUB, Fitzmaurice Place, W.1   499 3181
CHURCHILL'S CLUB, 160 New Bond Street, W.1   493 2626
EMBASSY CLUB, 6 Old Bond Street, W.1   493 5275
EVE CLUB, 189 Regent Street, W.1   734 0557
GARGOYLE CLUB, 69 Dean Street, W.1.   437 6455
PLAYBOY CLUB, 45 Park Lane, W.1   629 6666
SADDLE ROOM CLUB, 1a Hamilton Mews, Park Lane, W.1
499 4994
21 CLUB, Chesterfield Gardens, W.1   499 3233

Gambling Clubs

CLERMONT CLUB, 44 Berkeley Square, W.1   499 6522
PALM BEACH CLUB, 31 Berkeley Street, W.1   493 6585
VICTORIA SPORTING CLUB, 150 Edgware Road, W.2   262 2467

Pubs

A list aimed to give no more than a cross-section of the main varieties of London pubs; in many of them the food is far from negligible.

ANGEL, 21 Rotherhithe Street, S.E.16
East end south bank river pub; good dining-room

ANTELOPE, 22 Eaton Terrace, S.W.1
Smart Belgravia pub; good dining-room

W. COATES, 109 Old Broad Street, City, E.C.2
Typical City wine bar (weekdays 11–3 only)

COCK TAVERN, 22 Fleet Street, E.C.4
Under the sign that Dickens knew; good food

CROWN, 43 Charing Cross Road, W.C.2
Good modern-type West End pub, with musack, grill counter and good cheap restaurant

DEVEREUX, 20 Devereux Court, W.C.2
G. K. Chesterton's favourite; full of prosperous lawyers; excellent food

THE DOVE, 19 Upper Mall, Hammersmith, W.6
Riverside pub; good cold counter

EL VINO, 47 Fleet Street, E.C.4
Famous among journalists and lawyers

FLASK TAVERN, 77 Highgate West Hill, N.6
Village pub, especially for fine summer usage

GEORGE AND VULTURE, George Yard, off Lombard Street, E.C.3
Dickens associations and a tourist's 'must'

GEORGE INN, 77 Borough High Street, Southwark, S.E.1
With the last remaining seventeenth-century gallery in London

GRAPES, 121 Borough High Street, E.1

GRENADIER, Wilton Row, S.W.1
Classic Belgravian Mews pub

HENEKEY'S, 22–23 High Holborn, W.C.1
Wine-bar with mulled wine, reading-stand, etc.

HOG IN THE POUND, South Molton Street, W.1
Good specimen of new pub design

HORSE AND GROOM, 17 Kinnerton Street, S.W.1
Minute Belgravian-Knightsbridgian mews local

KING'S ARMS, 190 Fulham Road, S.W.10
Good cross-section of Chelsea clientele

KING'S HEAD AND EIGHT BELLS, 50 Cheyne Walk, S.W.3
Chelsea; excellent on a warm summer's night
LAMB, Lambs Conduit Street, W.C.1
Victorian, Bloomsbury clientele
LAMB AND FLAG, 33 Rose Street, W.C.2
Traditional and unspoiled
MAYFLOWER, 117 Rotherhithe Street, S.E.16
Riverside; the Mayflower left from the steps alongside
MUSEUM TAVERN, 49 Great Russell Street, W.C.1
Old-fashioned, cosy; the pub for the British Museum; cheap simple lunches
NAG'S HEAD, 53 Kinnerton Street, S.W.1
Even smaller than the Horse and Groom nearby
NELL GWYNNE TAVERN, 2 Bull Inn Court, W.C.2
Strand or Fleet Street alley-type pub
OLD WINE SHADES, 6 Martin Lane, Cannon Street, E.C.4
A sight; much as in 1663
PROSPECT OF WHITBY, 57 Wapping Wall, London Docks, E.1
Most famous of the river pubs, somewhat consolidated for tourist trade, but worth the trade
RED HOUSE, 94–100 Bishopsgate, E.C.2
Copious City eating and drinking house
RED LION, Lombard Court, off Lombard Street, E.C.4
ST. STEPHEN'S TAVERN, 10 Bridge Street, S.W.1
Good dining-room; has an extension of the Parliamentary division bell from the House of Commons the other side of the street
SALISBURY, 90 St. Martin's Lane, W.C.2
Classic of the London Victorian pub in theatre-land
SAMUEL WHITBREAD, Leicester Square, W.C.2
An interesting transposition of the pub into modern idiom; good first-floor restaurant
SHEPHERD'S TAVERN, 50 Hertford Street, W.1
Smart Mayfair version of the pub
SHERLOCK HOLMES, 10 Northumberland Street, W.C.2
With relics and tableaux of Sherlock Holmes
SIX BELLS, 197 King's Road, S.W.3
Capacious Chelsea pub, with garden, jazz club on first floor
SPANIARD'S INN, North End Way, N.W.3
Former highwaymen's pub over Hampstead Heath
WINDSOR CASTLE, 114 Campden Hill Road, W.8
Smart Kensington pub

WATERMAN'S ARMS, 1 Glengarnock Avenue, E.14
One of the finest East End pubs, best on Saturday nights
YE OLDE CHESHIRE CHEESE, 145 Fleet Street, E.C.4
Legendarily associated with Dr. Johnson, and highly picturesque; good English food
YE OLDE MITRE TAVERN, Ely Court, Ely Place, E.C.1
In the Ely sanctuary; cherry tree by the bar said to have been planted in 1546
YORK MINSTER, 49 Dean Street, W.1
Soho pub with a French accent

Shopping

BANKS are freely and thickly scattered in the City and West End and most of them change foreign currency or travellers' cheques (as also the bigger hotels). Banking hours are normally Monday to Friday, 9.30–3.30; all banks are closed on Bank Holidays, Saturdays and Sundays.

SHOPPING HOURS in the City and West End generally until 5.30, though the larger stores mostly stay open one day a week until about 7 p.m. Many are open on Saturdays until 5 p.m. but it is advisable to check with any special shop you may have in mind on a Saturday by telephone beforehand, as the five-day week is spreading fast.

SHOPPING GUIDES: for those in search of the best in contemporary manufacture by British firms, the **Design Centre** (Council of Industrial Design), Haymarket, near Piccadilly Circus, is invaluable. This does not sell, but shows a changing selection of contemporary furniture, fabrics, porcelain, glass, silverware, lamps, carpets, kitchen equipment, typewriters, radio, etc. The display is supplemented by an extensive card index; thus if you need, for example, an arm-chair, you can see photographs of scores of them and find out where your choice is available and its price. Of printed guides the most useful are *Shopping in London* (from the British Travel and Holiday Association, 4 St. James's Street, S.W.1); Denys Parsons' *What's Where in London* and Nicholson's *London Guide*.

Department Stores

ARMY AND NAVY, 105 Victoria Street, S.W.1
BARKER'S, Kensington High Street, W.8
BOURNE AND HOLLINGSWORTH, 116–28 Oxford Street, W.1
CIVIL SERVICE, 425 Strand, W.C.2
FORTNUM & MASON, Piccadilly, W.1
HARROD'S, 87–135 Brompton Road, S.W.1 (*closes at 5*)
HEAL & SON, 196 Tottenham Court Road, W.1
PETER JONES, Sloane Square, S.W.1
SELFRIDGE'S, 398–429 Oxford Street, W.1
DEBENHAM & FREEBODY, 27–37 Wigmore Street, W.1
DICKINS & JONES, 224–44 Regent Street, W.1

D. H. EVANS, 308–22 Oxford Street, W.1
JOHN LEWIS, 242–306 Oxford Street, W.1
LIBERTY'S, 210–20 Regent Street, W.1
HARVEY NICHOLS, Knightsbridge, S.W.1
ROBINSON & CLEAVER, 156–68 Regent Street, W.1
PETER ROBINSON, 65–72 Strand, W.C.2 and Oxford Street and
    Regent Street, W.1
SWAN & EDGAR, 49–63 Regent Street, W.1 (Piccadilly Circus)

Dress shops—prices medium, expensive and cheap

BROWNS, 27 South Molton Street, W.1
BUS STOP, 3 Kensington Church Street, W.8
C. & A., Oxford Street, and many others in the Oxford Street,
    Regent Street, and Knightsbridge areas
CHANELLE, 23 Brompton Road, S.W.3, and other branches
FENWICK LTD., 63 New Bond Street, W.1
JAEGER, 204 Regent Street, W.1, and other branches
MARYON, 39 Brompton Road, S.W.3, and other branches
MISS SELFRIDGE, 75 Brompton Road, S.W.3, and other
    branches
RICHARD SHOPS, 180 Regent Street, W.1, and other branches
WALLIS, 49 Oxford Street, W.1, and other branches

Expensive couturiers

HARDY AMIES, 14 Savile Row, W.1
JOHN CAVANAGH, 26 Curzon Street, W.1
NORMAN HARTNELL, 26 Bruton Street, W.1
LACHASSE, 4 Farm Street, W.1
MATTLI, 3 Carlos Place, W.1
MICHAEL, 2 Carlos Place, W.1

Shoes—simply walk down Oxford Street (see p. 79)

CHARLES JOURDAN, 47 Brompton Road, S.W.3
DOLCIS, 350 Oxford Street, W.1, and other branches
ELLIOTT, 76 New Bond Street, W.1, and other branches
GAMBA, 55 Beauchamp Place, S.W.3, and many others
LILLEY & SKINNER, 358 Oxford Street, W.1, and other branches

RUSSELL & BROMLEY, 24 New Bond Street, W.1
RAYNE, 15 Old Bond Street, W.1
SAXONE, 297 Oxford Street, W.1, and other branches
THE LONDON SHOE COMPANY, 30 Old Bond Street, W.1 and
other branches

Hats—in Fortnum & Mason's, Harvey Nichols, etc.

JOHN BOYD, 25 Lowndes Street, S.W.1
LIBERTY'S, 210–20 Regent Street, W.1
RUDOLF, 40 Davies Street, W.1
SIMONE MIRMAN, 9 Chesham Place, S.W.1

Gloves

GLOVE SHOP, 138 New Bond Street, W.1
GLOVE CORPORATION, 192 Broadhurst Gardens, N.W.6

Jewellery—especially Bond Street

ARMOUR WINSTON, 43 Burlington Arcade, W.1
BOUCHERON, 180 New Bond Street, W.1
CAMEO CORNER, 26 Museum Street, W.C.1 (*exotics*)
CARTIER, 175 New Bond Street, W.1
CHAUMET, 178 New Bond Street, W.1
COLLINGWOOD, 46 Conduit Street, W.1
FIOR, 28 New Bond Street, W.1 (*costume jewellery*)
GARRARD, 112 Regent Street, W.1
HUNT & ROSKELL, 25 Old Bond Street, W.1
MAPPIN & WEBB, 172 Regent Street, W.1
PARIS HOUSE, 41 South Molton Street, W.1 (*costume jewellery*)
RICHARD OGDEN, 28 Burlington Arcade, W.1
TESSIER, 26 New Bond Street, W.1
WARTSKI, 11 Grafton Street, W.1 (*Fabergé specialist*)

Hairdressers

CARITA, 44 Sloane Street, S.W.1
DOROTHY GRAY, 45 Conduit Street, W.1
JOHN OF KNIGHTSBRIDGE, 1 Thurloe Place, S.W.7
LEONARD, 6 Upper Grosvenor Street, W.1

OLOFSON HAUTE COIFFURE, 176 Brompton Road, S.W.3
RENE, 66 South Audley Street, S.W.1
VIDAL SASSOON, 171 New Bond Street, W.1, Grosvenor House,
Park Lane, W.1. For men, 44 Sloane Street, S.W.1

Hand-knitteds—Fortnum & Mason

ADRIENNE, 93b Marylebone High Street, W.1
TRACY, 71 New Bond Street, W.1
WOMEN'S HOME INDUSTRIES, 11 Halkin Street, S.W.1
and the Burlington Arcade

Furriers

CALMAN LINKS, 149 Brompton Road, S.W.3
S. LONDON, 39 Dover Street, W.1

Materials

ALLANS, 56 Duke Street, W.1
BILL, 93 New Bond Street, W.1 (*tweeds, suitings, cashmere sweaters, etc.*)
HIGHLIGHTS, 25 Beauchamp Place, S.W.3 (*tweeds, etc.*)
HUNT & WINTERBOTHAM, 4 Old Bond Street, W.1
JACQMAR, 76 Mortimer Street, W.1
SCOTCH HOUSE, 2 Brompton Road, S.W.1 (*Tartans, kilts*)
WHITE, 245 Regent Street, W.1 (*worsted, cashmere, etc.*)

For men

Clothes off-the-peg at Department Stores, Jaeger's, Harrod's, etc.

AQUASCUTUM, 100 Regent Street, W.1
AUSTIN REED, 103 Regent Street, W.1
BURBERRY'S, 18 Haymarket, S.W.1
SIMPSON'S, Piccadilly, W.1
and many others

Savile Row tailors

ADENEY & BOUTROY, 5 Cork Street, W.1
ANDERSON & SHEPPARD, 30 Savile Row, W.1
BENSON, PERRY & WHITLEY, 9 Cork Street, W.1

BLADES, 8 Burlington Gardens, W.1 (specialists in modern-cut suits)

CARR, SON & WOOR, 9 Savile Row, W.1

DAVIES & SON, 19 Hanover Street, W.1

EADE PECKOVER, 35 Sackville Street, W.1

ERIC SQUIRES, 19 Clifford Street, W.1

HAWES & CURTIS, 43 Dover Street, W.1

HENRY POOLE, 10 Cork Street, W.1

HOGG SONS & J. B. JOHNSTONE LTD, 35 Sackville Street, W.1

HUNTSMAN, 11 Savile Row, W.1

JAMES & JAMES, 11 Old Burlington Street, W.1

J. B. JOHNSTONE, 35 Sackville Street, W.1

JOCE, 4 Clifford Street, W.1

JOHN MORGAN, 11 St George's Street, W.1

JONES, CHALK AND DAWSON, 6 Sackville Street, W.1

KILGOUR, FRENCH & STANBURY, 33a Dover Street, W.1

PEACOCK, 18 Conduit Street, W.1

POPE & BRADLEY, 35 Sackville Street, W.1

SANDON & CO., 7 Savile Row, W.1

STOVEL & MASON, 32 Old Burlington Street, W.1

SULLIVAN WILLIAMS, 18 Conduit Street, W.1

WEALESON & LEGATE, 8a Sackville Street, W.1

A suit will cost upwards of £100, and three weeks should be allowed for the making at least (Chamberlain & Jones, 39 Aldwych, W.C.2, will make suits to measure at shorter notice). Suits to measure are also made by the off-the-peg establishments listed above very satisfactorily.

For sports clothes, Lillywhite's, Piccadilly Circus, W.1. For academic and legal gowns and robes, Ede & Ravenscroft, 93 Chancery Lane, W.C.2 (for sale or hire—also, in the event of elevation, peers' robes). For hire of formal clothes for evening wear, etc., the legendary suppliers are Moss Bros., 20 King Street, Covent Garden, W.C.2.

Men's Shoes—the following for handmades

LOBB, 26 St. James's Street, S.W.1

MAXWELL, 9 Dover Street, W.1

TRICKER, 67 Jermyn Street, S.W.1

Men's Hats

HERBERT JOHNSON, 38 New Bond Street, W.1
LOCK'S, 6 St. James's Street, S.W.1
And in St. James's, as also other male accessories of dress—
handmade shirts; toilet waters (Floris, 89 Jermyn Street); ties,
etc.

Umbrellas

SMITH, 53 New Oxford Street, W.1—*also sword-sticks, ceremonial maces, horsewhips, etc.*
SWAINE, ADENEY, BRIGG, 185 Piccadilly, W.1

Pipes

DUNHILL, 30 Duke Street, W.1
INDERWICK, 45 Carnaby Street, W.1

For Children

HARRODS, 87–135 Brompton Road, S.W.1
MOTHERCARE, Oxford Street, W.1
POLLYANNA, 660 Fulham Road, W.1
ROWE, 120 New Bond Street, W.1
THE DOLLS HOUSE, 4a Symons Street, S.W.3
THE WHITE HOUSE, 51 New Bond Street, W.1

Toys

JAMES GALT & CO. LTD., 30 Great Marlborough Street, W.1
HAMLEY'S, 200 Regent Street, W.1
PAUL & MARJORIE ABBATT, 74 Wigmore Street, W.1
POLLOCK'S TOY MUSEUM, 1 Scala Street, W.1

Boutiques, leather goods, china, glass, novelties etc.

GENERAL TRADING COMPANY, 144 Sloane Street, S.W.1
JOHN SIDDELEY, 4 Harriet Street, S.W.1
PRESENTS OF SLOANE STREET, 129 Sloane Street, W.1
SAVITA, 30 Lowndes Street, S.W.1 (Indian)

Antiques

For antiques of all kinds London is one of the major world centres. Watch the auction rooms at Christies and Sotheby's. For the dealers in all varieties, the main beats are: Bond Street and adjacent roads; Wigmore Street (especially St. Christopher's Place); St. James's (western area between St. James's Street and St. James's Square—in fact, around Christies); the streets south of the British Museum, between it and New Oxford Street; Brompton Road and South Kensington; King's Road Chelsea and the Fulham Road. Also the Portobello Road markets on Saturdays and the Camden Passage one in Islington; and Kensington Church Street, W.8.

Books

HATCHARDS, 187 Piccadilly, W.1
FOYLES, 119 Charing Cross Road, W.C.2 (and others in this road)
DILLON'S UNIVERSITY BOOKSHOP, 1 Malet Street, W.C.1
HEYWOOD HILL, 10 Curzon Street, W.1
TRUSLOVE AND HANSON, 6b Sloane Street, S.W.1
HARRODS, 87–135 Brompton Road, S.W.1
ARMY AND NAVY STORES, 105 Victoria Street, S.W.1
SELFRIDGES, 398–429 Oxford Street, W.1
HIGH HILL, 6 Hampstead High Street, N.W.3
Branches of W. H. SMITH throughout London
HACHETTE, 4 Regent Place, W.1

There are also many excellent specialist bookshops. The National Book League, 7 Albemarle Street (493 3501), are glad to answer queries.

Florists

ANGELA SAUNDERS, London Hilton, Park Lane, W.1
CONSTANCE SPRY, 64 South Audley Street, W.1, and other branches
FELTON AND SONS, 220 Brompton Road, S.W.3, and other branches.

MOYSES STEVENS, Landsdowne House, Berkeley Square, W.1, and 146 Victoria Street, S.W.1

PULBROOK AND GOULD, 181 Sloane Street, S.W.1

Miscellaneous

All branches of MARKS AND SPENCER for good cheap clothes, especially underwear and nightwear

CORDOBA SUEDEWEAR, 134 New Bond Street, W.1, and 53 Beauchamp Place, S.W.3 (suedewear)

GIVANS IRISH LINEN STORES, 207 King's Road

GORDON LOWE, Sloane Street, S.W.1 (sportswear and sports equipment)

GUCCI, 172 New Bond Street, W.1 (leather goods)

HABITAT, 158 Tottenham Court Road, W.1 and 206 King's Road, S.W.3 (modern furniture, china, kitchenware, etc.)

HEAL & SON, 196 Tottenham Court Road, W.1 (best modern furniture store)

JACKSONS OF PICCADILLY, 171 Piccadilly, W.1 (grocers)

Museums

BRITISH MUSEUM, Great Russell Street, W.C.1	(Tottenham Court Road Station, Northern Line or Central Line; Holborn Station, Piccadilly or Central Line)	10–5; *Sun.* 2.30 6 *See chapter 15*
BRITISH MUSEUM (Museum of Man) Burlington Gardens, W.1	(Green Park Station, Piccadilly or Victoria Line)	*Ethnological collections in new display*

Arts

BUCKINGHAM PALACE, QUEEN'S GALLERY, Buckingham Palace Road, S.W.1	(St. James's Park Station, Circle and District Lines)	*Tues.–Sat. 11–5; Sun. 2–5 A selection from the Royal Collection, changed from time to time. See p. 150*
DULWICH GALLERY, College Road, Dulwich	(Main Line, Southern Region, from Victoria to Dulwich; from London Bridge to North Dulwich)	*Tues.–Sat. 10–4, 5 or 6; Sun. (summer only) 2–5 or 6 Old Master Paintings in a building by Soane. See p. 312*

FOUNDLING HOSPITAL, 40 Brunswick Square, W.C.1	(Russell Square Station, Piccadilly Line)	*Mon. and Fri. only, 10–12; 2–4 English eighteenth-century paintings. See p. 319*
NATIONAL GALLERY, Trafalgar Square, W.C.2	(Trafalgar Square Station, Bakerloo Line; or Strand Station, Northern Line)	*10–6; Sun. 2–6 Old Master paintings, Giotto to Cézanne. See chapter 6*
PERCIVAL DAVID FOUNDATION OF CHINESE ART, 53 Gordon Square, W.C.1	(Euston Square Station, Circle or Metropolitan Lines)	*Mon. 2–5; Tues.– Fri. 10.30–5; Sat. 10.30–1*
COURTAULD INSTITUTE GALLERIES, Woburn Square, W.C.1	(Euston Square Station, Circle Line; or Goodge Street, Northern Line; or Russell Square, Piccadilly Line)	*10–5; Sun. 2–5 Old Masters, Impressionist and Post-Impressionist paintings. See p. 223*
TATE GALLERY, Millbank, S.W.1	(No. 88 bus from Oxford Street, Haymarket, Trafalgar Square or Whitehall)	*10–6; Sun. 2–6 Paintings, British School; Twentieth-century Foreign Schools; modern British and Foreign Sculpture. See p. 153*
VICTORIA AND ALBERT MUSEUM, South Kensington, S.W.7	(South Kensington Station, District, Circle, or Piccadilly Lines)	*10–6; Sun. 2.30– 6 Fine and applied arts of almost all schools. See Chapter 12*

WALLACE COLLECTION, Manchester Square, W.1	(Bond Street Station, Central Line; Baker Street Station, Bakerloo and District Lines)	*10–5; Sun. 2–5 Old Master Paintings, particularly French; furniture, china, armour, etc. See p. 241*

The fine and applied arts are also copiously represented in many of the National and Local Historical Museums, in which, while quality is not the crucial factor, there are of course many masterpieces; also in some of the Houses of Great Men (especially the Soane and Wellington Museums), and in the Palaces and Historical Buildings—for which see below.

Historical Museums

BETHNAL GREEN MUSEUM, Cambridge Heath Road, E.2	(Bethnal Green Station, Central Line)	*10–6; Sun. 2.30–6 A branch of the Victoria and Albert Museum; special East-End collections, also paintings, applied arts, costume and dolls' houses. See p. 408*
DONALD COLLECTION MUSICAL INSTRUMENTS, Royal College of Music, Prince Consort Road, S.W.7	(Buses, 9, 46, 52, 73 to Albert Hall)	*Term time only, Mon.–Fri. 10–5 Also portraits of musicians. See p. 188*

GEFFRYE MUSEUM, Kingsland Road, Shoreditch, E.2	(To Liverpool Street Station, Metropolitan, Circle, District and Central Lines; thence by bus, Nos. 22, 35, 47 or 149 north up Bishopsgate to Kingsland Road, Pearson Street request stop)	*Tues.–Sat. 10–5; Sun. 2–5 Period rooms, furniture, etc., in the charming old Ironmongers' Almshouses (about 1715)*
GUILDHALL MUSEUM	Closed 1974. To be consolidated with the new Museum of London, London Wall	*Mon.–Sat. 10–5 City of London archaeology and history. See p. 396*
IMPERIAL WAR MUSEUM, Lambeth Road, S.E.1	(Lambeth North Station, Bakerloo Line, or Elephant and Castle Station, Northern Line)	*10–6; Sun. 2–6 Illustration and record principally of the two world wars, 1914–18 and 1939–45. See p. 407*
JEWISH MUSEUM, Woburn House, Upper Woburn Place, W.C.1	(Buses Nos. 68, 77, 188 and 196 to Upper Woburn Place)	*Mon.–Thurs. 2.30–5; Fri. and Sun. 10.30–12.45 Antiquities illustrating Jewish domestic and public worship. See p. 222*
LONDON MUSEUM	Closed 1975. To be consolidated with the old Guildhall Museum in the new Museum of London, London Wall	

MUSEUM OF LEATHERCRAFT,	To be consolidated with the new Museum of London, 1976	
NATIONAL ARMY MUSEUM, Royal Hospital Road, Chelsea, S.W.3	Sloane Square Station, Circle and District Line	*10–5.30; Sun 2–5.30*
NATIONAL MARITIME MUSEUM, Romney Road, Greenwich, S.E.10	(Main Line Southern Region from Charing Cross, Waterloo, London Bridge, or Cannon Street to Maze Hill Station; thence five minutes on foot; or by boat in summer from Westminster Pier)	*10–6; Sun. 2.30–6* *The Maritime history of Great Britain. See p. 264*
NATIONAL PORTRAIT GALLERY, St. Martin's Place, W.C.2	(As for Trafalgar Square; Trafalgar Square Station, Bakerloo Line; Leicester Square Station, Northern and Piccadilly Lines)	*10–5; Sat. 10–6; Sun. 2–6* *Portraits in all media of famous British men and women of the past. See p. 99*
PUBLIC RECORD OFFICE, MUSEUM, Chancery Lane, W.C.2	(Chancery Lane Station, Central Line)	*Mon.–Fri. 1–4* *Historical documents. See p. 308*
ROYAL GEOGRAPHICAL SOCIETY, 1 Kensington Gore, S.W.7	(Buses 9, 46, 52 or 73 from Piccadilly or Hyde Park Corner to Albert Hall)	*(ring to see if open)* *Relics of famous explorers, and exhibitions. See also British Museum*

Science and Industry

COMMONWEALTH INSTITUTE, Holland Park, Kensington High Street, W.8	(Buses 9 or 73 from Hyde Park Corner; Kensington High Street Station, Circle Line)	*10–5.30; Sun. 2.30–6 Commercial and industrial resources of the Commonwealth. See p. 416*
GEOLOGICAL MUSEUM (as for the Victoria and Albert Museum)		*10–6; Sun. 2.30–6 See p. 191*
HORNIMAN MUSEUM, London Road, Forest Hill, S.E.23	(Main Line Southern Region from London Bridge to Forest Hill)	*10.30–6 (except Tues.) Sun. 2–6 Man and his environment; ethnographical, and zoological collections. Also a large collection of musical instruments*
NATURAL HISTORY MUSEUM, Cromwell Road, South Kensington	(As for the Victoria and Albert Museum)	*10–6; Sun. 2.30–6 Officially known as the British Museum (Natural History); animals and plants, minerals and rocks. See p. 191*

ROYAL COLLEGE OF SURGEONS, Lincoln's Inn Fields, W.C.2	(Holborn Station, Piccadilly and Central Lines)	*By previous arrangement only (the Secretary) The collection of anatomical and pathological specimens founded by John Hunter, also some good paintings. See p. 311*
INDUSTRIAL HEALTH AND SAFETY CENTRE, Horseferry Road, S.W.1	(Bus 88 from Oxford Street, Piccadilly Circus or Whitehall to Marsham Street)	*Mon.–Fri. 10–5 Health and safety in industry; up-to-date and sometimes rather macabre*
SCIENCE MUSEUM, Exhibition Road, South Kensington, S.W.7	(As for the Victoria and Albert Museum)	*10–6; Sun. 2.30–6 See p. 189*
WELLCOME HISTORICAL MEDICAL MUSEUM, Wellcome Building, Euston Road, N.W.1	(Euston Square Station, Metropolitan and Circle Lines; Euston Station, Northern Line)	*Mon.–Sat. 10–5 History of medicine and allied sciences*

Houses of Great Men

CARLYLE'S HOUSE, 24 Cheyne Row, Chelsea, S.W.3		*10–1 and 2–6 or dusk (except Tues.); Sun. from 2 See p. 208*

DICKENS HOUSE, 48 Doughty Street, W.C.1		*Weekdays 10–5* *See p. 318*
HOGARTH'S HOUSE, Hogarth Lane, Chiswick, W.4	(71 bus)	*11–6; Sun. 2–6* *(Winter 11–5, closed Tues.)* *See p. 269*
DR. JOHNSON'S HOUSE, 17 Gough Square, Fleet Street, E.C.4		*Weekdays 10.30–5; Oct.– April to 4.30* *See p. 291*
KEATS HOUSE, Wentworth Place, Keats Grove, Hampstead, N.W.3		*Weekdays 10–6* *See p. 413*
LEIGHTON HOUSE ART GALLERY AND MUSEUM, 12 Holland Park Road, W.14 (off Kensington High Street)		*Weekdays 11–5* *See p. 417*
WILLIAM MORRIS GALLERY, Water House, Lloyd Park, Forest Road, Walthamstow, E.17	(Bus 38, or local buses from Manor House Station, Piccadilly Line)	*Weekdays usually 10–5; first Sunday each month 10–12, 2–5*
SIR JOHN SOANE'S MUSEUM, 13 Lincoln's Inn Fields, W.C.2		*Tues.–Sat. only 10–5; closed in August; lecture tours Sat. 2.30* *See p. 312*

WELLINGTON MUSEUM, Apsley House, Piccadilly, W.1 (at Hyde Park Corner)	*10–6; Sun. 2.30– 6* *See p. 37*

WESLEY'S HOUSE, 47 City Road, E.C.1	*Weekdays 10–1; 2–4* *See p. 419*

Houses, or sites of houses, once occupied by famous people are in many cases marked with commemorative plaques put up by the G.L.C. or the City of London; this does not mean however, that the houses are open for inspection (the house where Lenin stayed, 16 Percy Circus, W.C.1, is covered by a protective clause by which the G.L.C. agreed, when the plaque was put up, to make good any damage caused by demonstrators).

Some Palaces and other Historical Buildings

BANQUETING HOUSE, Whitehall *Till 1963 the home of the Royal United Service Museum, now dispersed; the classic example of Inigo Jones's architecture, with ceiling by Rubens.*	*Weekdays 10–5; Sun. 2–5.* *See p. 108*

CHARTERHOUSE, Charterhouse Square, E.C.1	*By arrangement* *See p. 391*

FENTON HOUSE, The Grove, Hampstead, N.W.3	*Weekdays (except Tues.) 10–5 or dusk; Sun. from 2–5 or dusk* *See p. 415*

GUNNERSBURY PARK MUSEUM, Gunnersbury Park, Acton, W.3	(Acton Town Station, District and Piccadilly Lines)	*April–Sept., Mon.–Fri. 2–5; Sat. and Sun. 2–6. Winter hours under review. Formerly the Rothschilds' house, Regency, with park, Rothschild relics and local history*
HAM HOUSE, Petersham, nr. Richmond, Surrey		*March to Oct., Tues. to Sun., 2–6; Nov. to Feb., Tues. to Sun. 12–4 Seventeenth-century house with remarkable original décor and pictures See p. 272*
HAMPTON COURT PALACE, Hampton Court, Middlesex		*Nov. to Feb. 9.30–4, Sun. 2–4; March, April and Oct. to 5; May to Sept. to 6 See p. 272*
IVEAGH BEQUEST, Ken Wood, Hampstead Heath, N.W.3	(Bus 210 from Archway; Golders Green Station, Northern Line)	*Weekdays 10–5; Sun. 2–5; open until 7 April– Sept. Adam décor, with great collection of paintings. Seè p. 415*

KENSINGTON PALACE Broad Walk Kensington Gardens		*State Rooms.* *Check for Times*
LAMBETH PALACE		*By arrangement* *See p. 405*
LANCASTER HOUSE, Stable Yard, St. James's Palace, S.W.1		*Usually Easter to* *mid-Dec., Sat.,* *Sun. and Bank* *Holidays 2–6* *See p. 67*
MARLBOROUGH HOUSE, Pall Mall, S.W.1		*Easter to late* *Oct., conducted* *tours at 12.30, 3* *and 4.30, Mon.–* *Fri.; Sat. and* *Sun. 2–6* *(Tours include* *the Queen's* *Chapel)* *See p. 65*
OSTERLEY PARK, Isleworth, Middlesex	(Green Line bus, 704 or 705; Osterley Station, Piccadilly Line)	*Tues.–Sun., 2–6* *(March to Oct.);* *12–4 (Nov. to* *Feb.)* *House first built* *for Sir Thomas* *Gresham, 1577;* *rebuilt by Robert* *Adam for Child* *the banker, 1761;* *complete Adam* *décor*
SYON HOUSE	(Main Line from Waterloo to Syon Lane station; bus 37)	*Opening times* *variable* *(telephone* *567 2353)* *Adam house;* *seat of Duke of* *Northumberland.* *See p. 271*

TOWER OF LONDON, Tower Hill, E.C.3		*March–Oct. 9.30–5; Sun. 2–5; Nov.–Feb. 9.30– 4; Sun. 2–5 See Chapter 1*
WALTHAMSTOW MUSEUM, Vestry House, Walthamstow, E.17	(Main Line from Liverpool Street Station to Hoe Street Station. Buses 35, 38)	*Weekdays 10–12, 1–5 Early eighteenth- century workhouse, local relics and historical objects*

Temporary Exhibitions

The Victoria and Albert Museum, the Tate Gallery, the Imperial War Museum, the Guildhall Art Gallery, all stage frequent temporary exhibitions; the Arts Council also uses its own Hayward Gallery (South Bank). The Whitechapel Art Gallery (Whitechapel High Street, E.1; Aldgate East Station, District Line; closed Mondays) has staged a number of re-markable exhibitions of contemporary art in recent years. The Iveagh Bequest, Ken Wood (see above) also stages an exhibi-tion in the summer months; look out also for shows at the South London Art Gallery, Peckham Road, S.E.5, and at major art dealers in the West End (for full lists, see *The Arts Review*, fortnightly). The Institute of Contemporary Arts (Nash House, the Mall) is usually at least a jump ahead of the field in avant-garde art, and often not apparently in the same race as the Royal Academy (*see p. 42*), whose traditional annual exhibition is in the summer months—in the winter it stages very important loan exhibitions usually of Old Masters. Other traditional group shows, Royal Societies of British Artists, of Portrait Painters, Painters in Water-colours, etc., the London Group, the New English Art Club, etc., also usually hold annual shows (see the Press). August and Septem-ber are generally dim months for exhibitions, particularly at the dealers, and the auction rooms, Christies and Sotheby's, which at normal times offer a perpetually changing exhibition with the whiff of a gamble thrown in, are closed.

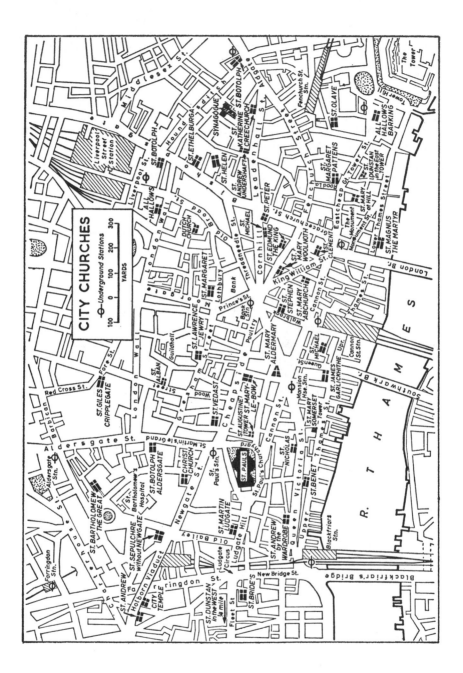

CITY CHURCHES

Underground Stations

YARDS
100 0 100 200 300

City Churches

In 1971, a fairly fundamental rethinking of the functions of many City churches was advocated. This may affect the availability of some.

ALL HALLOWS BARKING, Eastcheap
Mon.–Sat. 7.30–6 *Sun.* 10.30–12; 1–5.30
ALL HALLOWS, London Wall *Mon.–Fri.* 10–5.30
ST. ANDREW, Holborn Viaduct *Mon.–Fri.* 8–5
ST. ANDREW BY THE WARDROBE, Wardrobe Terrace
Mon.–Fri. 1–2 *Sun.* 9.15 a.m.–1 p.m.
ST. ANDREW UNDERSHAFT, Leadenhall Street
Mon.–Fri. 11–3 *Sun.* 10–1
ST. BARTHOLOMEW THE GREAT, West Smithfield
Daily 7.45 a.m. to dusk
ST. BENET, Upper Thames Street
Mon.–Fri. 12 noon–3
ST. BOTOLPH, Aldersgate *Mon.–Fri.* 10–5
ST. BOTOLPH (Aldgate), Duke's Place
Mon.–Fri. 8–6 *Sun.* 9.30 a.m.–12 noon
ST. BOTOLPH, Bishopsgate
Mon.–Fri. 8–6 *Sat.; Sun.* 8–1
ST. BRIDE, Fleet Street
Mon.–Sat. 9–5.30 *Sun.* 10.15–7.30
CITY TEMPLE, Holborn Viaduct *Daily* 8–6.30
ST. CLEMENT EASTCHEAP, Clements Lane
Mon.–Fri. 8.15–5.30
ST. DUNSTAN-IN-THE-WEST, Fleet Street
Mon.–Fri. 7.30–5. *Sat.* 7.30–1
ST. EDMUND THE KING, Lombard Street
Mon.–Fri. 8.30–6 *Sun.* 10 a.m.–12 noon
ST. ETHELBURGA, Bishopsgate *Mon.–Fri.* 8–5
ST. GILES CRIPPLEGATE, Aldersgate Street
Mon.–Fri. 12–2.15 *Sun.* 12–2.15
ST. HELENS, Great St. Helens
Mon.–Fri. 9.30–5 *Sun.* 9.30–1
ST. JAMES GARLICKHITHE, Upper Thames Street
Mon.–Fri. 10.30–2 *Sun.* 9.45 a.m.–10.30 a.m.
ST. KATHERINE CREECHURCH, Leadenhall Street
Mon.–Fri. 9.30–5

ST. LAWRENCE JEWRY, Gresham Street
Mon.–Fri. 8–6   *Sat.* 8–5   *Sun.* 2 p.m.–5 p.m. (except Dec., Jan. and Feb.)

ST. MAGNUS THE MARTYR, Upper Thames Street
Tues.–Fri. 10.45–4   *Sat.* 12 noon–4   *Sun.* 10.30–12.30

ST. MARGARET LOTHBURY, Princes Street
Mon.–Fri. 8–5   *Sat.–Sun.* 10–5

ST. MARGARET PATTENS, Rood Lane
Mon.–Fri. 9.30–4.45

ST. MARTIN LUDGATE, Ludgate Hill   *Mon.–Fri.* 10–4

ST. MARY ABCHURCH, Abchurch Lane   *Mon.–Fri.* 10–4

ST. MARY ALDERMARY, Watling Street
Mon.–Fri. 8–5

ST. MARY-AT-HILL, Lovat Lane
Mon.–Fri. 10.30–2.30   *Sun.* Service 10.15 a.m.

ST. MARY-LE-BOW, Cheapside
Mon.–Sat. 2

ST. MARY WOOLNOTH, King William Street
Mon.–Sat. 8–5.30   *Sun.* 10.30 a.m.–8 p.m.

ST. MICHAEL, Cornhill
Mon.–Fri. 8.30–5.30   *Sun.* 10–1.30

ST. NICHOLAS COLE ABBEY, Queen Victoria Street
Mon.–Fri. 10–4 (except during August)

ST. OLAVE, Hart Street
Mon.–Fri. 9–3   *Sat.* 2.30–5   *Sun.* Services: 11 a.m. and 6 p.m.

ST. PETER-UPON-CORNHILL
Mon.–Fri. 8.30–5   *Sun.* 9.30 until after Matins

ST. SEPULCHRE WITHOUT NEWGATE, Holborn Viaduct
Mon.–Fri. 8–4   *Sat.* 8–1   *Sun.* Service 9.15 a.m. Open until 12.30 p.m.

ST. STEPHEN WALBROOK
Daily 8 a.m.–10 p.m.

SYNAGOGUE, Heneage Lane
Mon.–Fri. 10.30–1   *Sat.* Service 8.30 a.m.–11.30 a.m. *Sun.* 10–1

ST. VEDAST, Foster Lane
Mon.–Fri. 10–6   *Sun.* Service 11 a.m.

Art Dealers

There are well over a hundred art dealers in the West End, and most of them are to be found in St. James's and especially Mayfair, known in this context as the Bond Street axis, though there seems to be as so often in London some movement of the trade to the west. The following are merely some of the more interesting ones. Details of almost all current shows can be found in *The Arts Review* (fortnightly).

AGNEW, 43 Old Bond Street, W.1   *Old Masters; English School; water-colours and drawings*

APPLEBY, 10 Ryder Street, St. James's, S.W.1   *All schools*

ARCADE, 28 Old Bond Street, W.1   *Mannerist and baroque; also sculpture*

BERNARD, 21 Ryder Street, S.W.1   *English paintings eighteenth and nineteenth centuries*

BROD, Economist Building, St. James's S.W.1   *Dutch seventeenth century*

COLNAGHI, 14 Old Bond Street, W.1   *Old Masters; paintings, drawings and prints*

CRADDOCK AND BARNARD, 32 Museum Street, W.C.1   *Prints*

CRANE KALMAN, 178 Brompton Road, S.W.3   *Twentieth century*

B. CROWTHER, Syon Lodge, Isleworth   *Statuary*

T. CROWTHER, 282 North End Road, S.W.6   *Statuary*

DRIAN, 5–6 Porchester Place, W.2   *Modern*

DUITS, 104 Wigmore Street, W.1   *Dutch and Flemish*

EDITIONS ALECTO, Kelso Place   *Modern English lithographs and prints*

FINE ART SOCIETY, 148 New Bond Street, W.1   *English water-colours and nineteenth-century paintings*

GIMPEL FILS, 30 Davies Street, W.1   *Modern*

HAZLITT, GOODEN AND FOX, 38 Bury Street, S.W.1   *English School*

KASMIN, 8 Gloucester Gate, N.W.1   *Modern avant-garde*

KNOEDLER, 34 St. James's Street, S.W.1   *Old Masters*

LEGER, 13 Old Bond Street, W.1   *Old Masters and water-colours*

LEGGATT, 30 St. James's Street, S.W.1   *English school*

LEICESTER, 22a Cork Street, W.1   *Modern*

LISSON GALLERY, 68 Bell Street, N.W.1   *Modern avant-garde*

LOWNDES LODGE, Cadogan Place, S.W.1   *English school*

LUMLEY CAZALET, 24 Davies Street, W.1   *Modern prints and watercolours*

MAAS, 15a Clifford Street, W.1   *English nineteenth century*

MARLBOROUGH FINE ART, 39 Old Bond Street, W.1, and 6 Albemarle Street, W.1

MARLBOROUGH GRAPHICS, 6 Albemarle Street, W.1   *The post-war tycoons of London, dealing in contemporary art, they have cornered most of the most famous names in English art under contract*

NEW ART CENTRE, 41 Sloane Street, S.W.1   *Modern*

OBELISK, 15 Crawford Street, W.1   *Modern (ancient sculpture)*

PARKER, 2 Albemarle Street, W.1   *Old prints*

PICCADILLY, 16a Cork Street, W.1   *Modern*

REDFERN, 20 Cork Street, W.1   *Modern*

REID, 23 Cork Street, W.1   *Modern*

ROLAND, BROWSE & DELBANCO, 19 Cork Street, W.1   *Modern (usually strong in Sickert)*

SPEELMAN, 175 Piccadilly, W.1   *Old Masters*

TOOTH, 31 Bruton Street, W.1   *Modern*

WADDINGTON, 25 Cork Street, W.1   *Modern, especially English abstract*

WILDENSTEIN, 147 New Bond Street, W.1   *Old Masters*

Theatres, Cinemas, Variety, Opera, Music

Most of the London theatres are concentrated between Piccadilly to the west and Aldwych, to the east. For current performances and times, see the Press, or the *London Theatre Guide* (to be found free in most big hotels and ticket agencies). Performances usually begin between 7.30 and 8.30; most theatres have matinees twice a week (almost always one on Saturday). Most West End cinemas run continuous performances from about lunchtime until about 11 p.m., but seats for important or long films are sometimes bookable in advance. Some cinemas run late-night performances, starting about 11 p.m. (usually on Saturday); for current programmes and times, see the Press. The home of opera and ballet is Covent Garden Theatre (always book as far possible in advance), or

Sadlers Wells at the Coliseum. Major concerts are usually held at the Royal Festival Hall on the South Bank, or at the Royal Albert Hall; the classic site for chamber recitals is the Wigmore Hall, which seems to have survived threat of closure; chamber music is also played at the Festival Hall; Queen Elizabeth Hall and Purcell Room (S. Bank), etc. The City churches are also loud with music at some lunch-times; the Victoria and Albert Museum stages excellent concerts in the rare site of the Raphael Cartoon Gallery, and the most romantic of the summer open-air series are those by the lake at Ken Wood. Music-hall proper has vanished from the London scene; it gave way to Variety, of which the classic homes are the Palladium Theatre and the Victoria Palace (the Lyceum Theatre, where Henry Irving won some of his greatest triumphs, has subsided into a Bingo palace). The Windmill, also (off Shaftesbury Avenue by Piccadilly Circus) has lost its 'we-never-closed' mixture of variety and near-naked girls and is now a cinema. For the programmes at Strip-Tease clubs, mostly in Soho and booming for the last ten years, see the advertisements in *What's On*. Jazz clubs also boom, their reputation and indeed their existences very ephemeral; they are mainly in Soho and the Oxford Street area—for addresses and current performers, see the *Melody Maker* or *Jazz News* (both weekly).

The traditional home of Shakespeare performance, the Old Vic, was made over in 1963 to the new National Theatre Company, and, since the opening of the new National Theatre, has been occupied by the Young Vic. The Aldwych Theatre, Aldwych, has been appropriated, one hopes more than temporarily, by the Royal Shakespeare Company from Stratford, and also keeps various Shakespeare and other productions in its repertory.

Of theatres rather outside the orbit, the Royal Court, Sloane Square, became famous again (for it was there that so many Shaw plays were first staged) with the production of John Osborne's *Look Back in Anger* in 1956, and is associated with many of the leading younger playwrights—Wesker, Arden, Jellicoe and Bond. The Mermaid, by Blackfriars Bridge, is a gallant and so far successful attempt to reintroduce living theatre to the City of London, and has a very attractive restaurant. But the most glamorous extension of London theatrical life is into Glyndebourne, in Sussex, some fifty miles clear of London, where the most sophisticated opera is staged in a little theatre in a lovely park. The wraith-like characters in full evening dress that you may have sighted at Victoria Station at three o'clock of a summer's afternoon are going to Glyndebourne (information and tickets from Glyndebourne Festival Opera, London office, 23 Baker Street, W.1; 935 0571).

Markets, Annual Exhibitions and other Events

The main wholesale markets are mentioned in the text— Billingsgate for fish, Borough and Covent Garden for fruit and vegetables and flowers, Smithfield for meat. Art exhibitions are mentioned under the section 'Museums and Galleries' above.

Many of the street markets are worth looking at—there are more than a hundred of them in London ranging from a few rather decrepit stalls to whole streets chock-a-block with business. The following are some of the most rewarding.

East End: Petticoat Lane (Middlesex Street) trades in immense variety of goods on Sundays (mornings), but is to be redeveloped.

Club Row (Sclater Street), also Sundays, has pets of all kinds.

Columbia Road for potted plants on Sundays.

Petticoat Lane sports a few antiques among the motley, but the established street market for these is now the Portobello Road at Notting Hill—Saturdays for the full market. But there is also now a flourishing Saturday antiques market at Camden Passage, Upper Street, Islington. Books are worth searching in the Farringdon Road market (between Charterhouse Street and Clerkenwell Road, in the City).

Of other weekday markets, some of the best are the Cut, Waterloo Road, S.E.1; Mile End Waste, Whitechapel, E.1; Leather Lane, Holborn, E.C.1; Berwick Street, Soho; Lambeth Walk, Lambeth.

Some Annual Events

SCHOOLBOYS' OWN EXHIBITION, Olympia   *January*
NATIONAL STAMP EXHIBITION, Central Hall, Westminster
    January

CRUFT'S DOG SHOW, Olympia *February*
DAILY MAIL IDEAL HOME, Olympia *March*
OXFORD AND CAMBRIDGE BOAT RACE, Putney to Mortlake
March–April
ROYAL CHELSEA FLOWER SHOW, Chelsea Hospital *May*
RICHMOND ROYAL HORSE SHOW, Richmond *May–June*
ROYAL MILITARY TOURNAMENT, Earl's Court *June*
TROOPING THE COLOUR, Horse Guards' Parade *June*
ANTIQUE DEALERS' FAIR, Grosvenor House *June*
ALL-ENGLAND LAWN TENNIS, Wimbledon *June*
ROYAL INTERNATIONAL HORSE SHOW, White City *July*
HENRY WOOD PROMENADE CONCERTS, Albert Hall *July–September*
HORSE OF THE YEAR SHOW, Harringay *September*
INTERNATIONAL MOTOR SHOW, Olympia *October*
LORD MAYOR'S SHOW, Mansion House to Law Courts
November
STATE OPENING OF PARLIAMENT, Buckingham Palace to Houses
of Parliament *November*
SERVICE OF REMEMBRANCE, Cenotaph, Whitehall *November*
SMITHFIELD SHOW, Earl's Court *December*

Some Books on London

About a book a week seems to appear on some aspect of
London or other. The best bibliography, up to 1939, is the
printed catalogue of the Members' Library of the G.L.C.; for
the City, see Raymond Smith, *Bibliography of the City of
London* (National Book League, 1951). The Survey of London,
started in 1900, is still progressing on its long assessment of
London almost building by building, and the Royal Commis-
sion on Ancient Monuments has published five volumes on
London: *Westminster Abbey* (1924); *West London* (1925);
Roman London (1928); *The City* (1929); *East London* (1930).
The invaluable historical dictionary, arranged alphabetically
under streets and buildings, is still H. B. Wheatley, *London,
Past and Present* (3 vols., 1891).

Some classics

JOHN STOW, *The Survey of London* (1598; best modern edition by C. L. Kingsford, 2 vols.; there is also a one-volume Everyman edition)

E. V. LUCAS, *A Wanderer in London* (1906, and still very readable)

JAMES BONE, *The London Perambulator* (1925)

S. E. RASMUSSEN, *London: the Unique City* (1934; Pelican Books, 1960)

J. SUMMERSON, *Georgian London* (1945; Pelican Books, 1962)

T. F. REDDAWAY, *The Rebuilding of London after the Great Fire* (1951)

M. D. GEORGE, *London Life in the Eighteenth Century* (1925)

O. SITWELL, *The People's Album of London Statues* (1928)

V. S. PRITCHETT, *London Perceived* (1962; the most perceptive and brilliant, and beautifully produced and illustrated, general essay on London to appear since the war)

Some special guides

NICHOLSON'S *London Guide* (constantly revised), excellent mini-directory that really does fit into the breast-pocket

F. R. BANKS, *The Penguin Guide to London* (4th edition, 1968); stuffed admirably with facts

D. PARSONS, *What's Where in London*, constantly revised; invaluable encyclopedic guide to shopping and services, even the most abstruse and exotic

S. LAMBERT, *New Architecture of London* (British Travel and Holidays Association; a guide to contemporary building in London since 1930)

N. PEVSNER, *London I; the Cities of London and Westminster* (2nd edition, Pelican Books, 1962)

London II; except the Cities of London and Westminster (Pelican Books, 1952; 2nd edition, 1970). In the Buildings of England Series. Invaluable, stimulating, often almost building-by-building architectural guide. There is no substitute for Pevsner.

E. AND W. YOUNG, *Old London Churches* (1956)

G. COBB, *The Old Churches of London* (1948); primarily for the City (the same author's *London City Churches: A Brief Guide* (1962) is a handy pocket-size and includes a recognition diagram for Wren-spire-spotters)

G. FLETCHER, *The London Nobody Knows* (1962) and subsequent books; for the detail and texture particularly of Victorian London.

N. BRAYBROOKE, *London Green* (1959); for the Parks.

P. FERRIS, *The City* (1960; Pelican Books, 1962)

E. DE MARÉ, *London's Riverside* (1958)

W. GAUNT, *Chelsea* (1954)

W. GAUNT, *Kensington* (1958)

J. POPE-HENNESSY, *The Houses of Parliament* (1945)

L. E. TANNER, *History and Treasures of Westminster Abbey* (1953)

W. R. MATTHEWS and W. M. ATKINS, *A History of St. Paul's Cathedral* (1957)

R. MANDER and J. MITCHENSON, *The Theatres of London* (1961)

Some recent general accounts include

C. MACINNES, *London, City of any Dream* (1962; his novels also offer sharp reflection of contemporary life in London)

I. BROWN, *Winter in London* (1951); *A Book of London* (1961)

W. GAUNT, *London* (1961)

E. CARTER, *The Future of London* (Pelican Books, 1962)

R. CHURCH, *London, Flower of Cities All* (1966)

IAN NAIRN, *Nairn's London* (Penguin Books, 1966)

LEN DEIGHTON, *London Dossier* (Penguin Books, 1967)

B. JAMES, *London on a pound a day*

H. DAVIES, *The New London Spy* (1966)

J. HAYES, *London—A Pictorial History* (1969)

Index

❧

The Index is in two sections: *a* persons (including their statues and memorials); *b* places, streets, buildings and subjects. Entries relating to shops and business firms, however, appear in Index *b*. Churches, pubs, restaurants and theatres are grouped together (in their own alphabetical order) under those respective general headings in Index *b*. The names of art dealers, books and their authors, clubs, exhibitions, hotels, pubs, restaurants, shops and stores, appearing in the Appendix, are not included in the Index, as they will be easily and immediately traced by reference to the sections dealing with them; they are, however, indexed when they are also mentioned in the body of the book. Page numbers in italics show the place where the subject of the entry is most fully dealt with.

a Index of Persons

b Index of Places and Subjects